Aldeburgh Studies in Music
General Editor: Paul Banks

Volume 4

Britten and the Far East

Tea ceremony in Japan, 14 February 1956

Britten and the Far East

ASIAN INFLUENCES IN
THE MUSIC OF BENJAMIN BRITTEN

Mervyn Cooke

THE BOYDELL PRESS

THE BRITTEN–PEARS LIBRARY

First published 1998 by The Boydell Press, Woodbridge
in conjunction with
The Britten–Pears Library, Aldeburgh

ISBN 0 85115 579 0

Aldeburgh Studies in Music
ISSN 0969–3548

The Boydell Press is an imprint of Boydell & Brewer Ltd
PO Box 9, Woodbridge, Suffolk IP12 3DF, UK
and of Boydell & Brewer Inc.
PO Box 41026, Rochester, NY 14604–4126, USA

A catalogue record for this book is available
from the British Library

Library of Congress Cataloging-in-Publication Data
Cooke, Mervyn.
  Britten and the Far East : Asian influences in the music of
Benjamin Britten / Mervyn Cooke.
      p. cm. – (Aldeburgh studies in music, ISSN 0969–3548 ; v. 4)
  Includes bibliographical references (p. ****) and index.
  ISBN 0–85115–579–0 (alk. paper)
  1. Britten, Benjamin, 1913–1976 – Criticism and interpretation.
  2. Britten, Benjamin, 1913–1976 – Knowledge – Orient.   3. Music –
England – Oriental influences.   I. Title.   II. Series.
  ML410.B853C74   1998
  780'.92–dc21   97–32608

This publication is printed on acid-free paper

Printed in Great Britain by
St Edmundsbury Press Ltd, Bury St Edmunds, Suffolk

For Donald Mitchell

Contents

Illustrations

Tables

Musical Examples on Compact Disc

1–5 arr. Colin McPhee, *Balinese Ceremonial Music* (11:14)

     1 'Pemoengkah' (2:41)
     2 'Gambangan' (2.35)
     3 'Taboeh teloe' (2:38)
     4 'Rebong' (unpublished) (2:56)
     5 'Lagu delem' (unpublished) (1:24)

Performed by Colin McPhee and Benjamin Britten (two pianos)
From 78rpm discs (Schirmer 513/14), recorded in New York in 1941

6–8 Gamelan music from Bali (13:47)

     6 'Kapi radja' ('Monkey King') (3:00)
     7 'Tamililingan' ('Bumblebees') (10:47)

Performed by the gamelan gong *kebyar* from Peliatan village, Ubud
From Britten's copy of *Music from Bali*, Argo RG1 (undated: *c.*1952)
Courtesy of the Decca Record Company Limited

     8 'Tabuh teluh' (7:07)

Performed by an unidentified gamelan from Ubud
Recorded for Britten on 23 January 1956 at the studios of Radio Indonesia, Denpasar, Bali

9–12 Japanese music

     9–11 Nō play *Sumidagawa* (extracts) (12:29)

From Britten's tape recording, made in Tokyo at his request after 19 February 1956

     12 Gagaku piece 'Etenraku' (9:35)

From *Japon: Gagaku*, Ocora 559018 HM65 (recorded 1979)
Courtesy of Radio France

13 Indian music

     13 'Raag Yaman' (19:00)

Performed by Pannalal Ghosh
From Britten's copy of *Pannalal Ghosh*, EALP 1252 (undated)
Courtesy of The Gramophone Company of India Limited

Acknowledgements

This study began life as a Ph.D. dissertation entitled 'Oriental Influences in the Music of Benjamin Britten' (University of Cambridge, 1989) and my first debt of thanks is therefore due to Dr Robin Holloway, who supervised the project from inception to completion, and whose interest and encouragement were a constant inspiration. Dr Donald Mitchell tirelessly shared his enthusiasm for and detailed knowledge of the topic with me throughout my research. His interest in the subject area is so intense and longstanding that this is a book he might himself have written if his many other activities had allowed him breathing space: it is entirely fitting that his name stands at its head. The late Sir Peter Pears gave generously of his time and was able to fill several gaps in our knowledge of Britten's experiences in the Far East during the course of discussions, and I was greatly aided by the efficiency of the staff of the Britten–Pears Library at Aldeburgh (Rosamund Strode, the late Paul Wilson and Dr Philip Reed), who answered many queries during my visits to the Archive. To Dr Reed I owe a particular debt of thanks for allowing me to see an early draft of his edition of Pears's travel diaries, which helped establish numerous details in Chapters 3 and 5. The current Librarian, Professor Paul Banks (General Editor of the Aldeburgh Studies in Music series), read the entire manuscript of this book on more than one occasion and I am greatly indebted to him for his helpful comments and advice. I am also grateful to Ian Rumbold for his painstaking sub-editing of the text, to Michael Durnin for his setting of the music examples, to Jill Burrows for the finesse of her typesetting and to Judith LeGrove for her meticulous checking of source materials and proof-reading.

A number of ethnomusicologists freely shared their specialized knowledge with me. Dr Neil Sorrell (University of York) and Dr Annette Sanger (formerly of The Queen's University, Belfast) both advised me on matters relating to Indonesian gamelan music, while Dr David Hughes (School of Oriental and African Studies, University of London) and Dr Laurence Picken (Jesus College, Cambridge) were kind enough to perform the same task with my Japanese material.

Financial assistance for the project from King's College Cambridge, Fitzwilliam College Cambridge and the University of Nottingham's Department of Music is gratefully acknowledged. I should like to thank both the British Academy and the Britten Estate for substantial grants which made possible my research trip to Thailand, Bali and Japan in the summer of 1986.

In Japan I was greatly helped by the following individuals and institutions: Mrs Yoko Ito (National Academy, Tokyo), Professor Kazuo Fukushima (Research Archives for Japanese Music, Ueno Gakuen College, Tokyo), Mr Hiroshi Kurosawa, Miss Nutuba (British Council, Kyoto), Otsuki Nōgaku Kaikan (Osaka), Satake Shōten (Kyoto) and Dr Hiroharu Sono (Music Department of the Imperial Household Agency, Tokyo). In Indonesia I was lucky enough to be guided by the Balinese dancer I Gst. Kt. Rai Sukiartha MC who showed me many facets of Balinese society I would not otherwise have experienced. I am also grateful to Mrs Bernard IJzerdraat in Java for her assistance in correspondence.

In England, America and Australia I am indebted to the following for help on various matters: Dr Peter Alexander, Stephen Allen, Professor James Blades, Henry Boys, Professor Philip Brett, David Burnett (Special Collection, Durham University Library), John Coast, David Corkhill (English Chamber Orchestra), Dr Jenny Doctor (Britten–Pears Library), Francesca Franchi (Archive Office, Royal Opera House), Professor Peter Hill (University of Sheffield), Clifford Hindley, Dr Roy Howat, Yukiko Kishinami, Jason James, Dr Carol Oja (Brooklyn College, New York), the late Mrs Myfanwy Piper, G. Schirmer Inc., Malcolm Smith (Boosey & Hawkes), the late Virgil Thomson, Jenny Vogel, the late Patrick Wilkinson, Jenny Wilson and Rié Yanagisawa. To my wife Mimi, unofficial dedicatee of all I do, I extend warmest thanks for her unstinting love and support throughout the project.

All extracts from Benjamin Britten's manuscript sketches and quotations from his letters, and quotations from the travel diaries of Sir Peter Pears, are copyright the Trustees of the Britten–Pears Foundation and may not be further reproduced without written permission from the Trustees. The photographs of Britten in Japan were kindly made available by Hiroshi Kurosawa. Quotations from Prince Ludwig of Hesse's travel diary *Ausflug Ost* (Darmstadt, 1956) are made by kind permission of HRH the late Princess Margaret of Hesse and the Rhine; all translations from the original German are by the author. The quotations from William Plomer's libretto drafts and letters to Britten are included by permission of Sir Rupert Hart-Davis. Extracts from Britten's letters to Roger Duncan appear by kind permission of Mr Duncan. I am especially grateful to Northeastern University Press for permission to re-use in Chapter 1 material from my contribution to Jonathan Bellman's symposium *The Exotic in Western Music* (Boston, 1998). Music examples from Britten's works composed before 1964 are reproduced by permission of Boosey & Hawkes (Music Publishers) Ltd. All music examples from Britten's works published after 1964, and the production drawings for the Church Parables, are copyright Faber Music Ltd, London, and are reproduced by kind permission of the publishers. The extract from Colin McPhee's *Balinese Ceremonial Music* is reproduced by permission of G. Schirmer Inc. and that from Poulenc's Concerto for Two Pianos by permission of Editions Salabert.

Glossary of Indonesian and Japanese Terms

Indonesian and Balinese

Note: Modern spellings are used throughout, with the older Dutch-influenced equivalents given in parentheses where appropriate. Instrument names are given in roman type.

ageng	large; of deep pitch
angklung	tuned rattle made from bamboo
angsel	break in musical rhythm and dance movement common in *kebyar* style (q.v.)
arja	popular music-theatre
baris	male ceremonial warrior dance
barong	mythical creature of good fortune
bungbung	see *joged bungbung*
calung	see jublag
cengceng	pair of small cymbals
djoged	see *joged*
djoged bungbung	see *joged bungbung*
gambang	sacred bamboo xylophone usually reserved for cremation rites
gamelan gong *gedé*	large ensemble (25–40 players) composed of metallophones and gongs; used for traditional temple ceremonies
gamelan gong *kebyar*	modified form of gamelan gong *gedé*; see *kebyar*
gamelan *pejogedan*	xylophone ensemble accompanying *joged* dance (q.v.)
gamelan *semar pegulingan*	'gamelan of the God of Love'; obsolescent ensemble revived by McPhee in the 1930s
gangsa	metallophone with keys hanging over resonators (played with one mallet)
gangsa *gantung*	modified gender (q.v.) found in gamelan gong *kebyar*
gangsa *jongkok*	rare form of gangsa (q.v.) in which keys rest on a wooden sounding-trough
gedé	large; of deep pitch

gender	metallophone with keys resting over tubular resonators (played with two mallets)
genggong	Jew's harp
giying	common form of gender (q.v.) found in the gamelan gong *kebyar*
gong *ageng*	the two largest vertical gongs in the gamelan gong *gedé* and gamelan gong *kebyar*
jegogan	largest form of gender (q.v.)
joged (= *djoged*)	female enticement dance involving audience participation
joged bungbung (= *djoged b.*)	fertility dance featuring *bungbung* (bamboo poles used for rice pounding)
jublag	second largest form of gender (q.v.); synonymous with calung
kacapi (= *katjapi*)	zither
kantilan	'figuration'; smallest type of gender (q.v.)
kebyar	'explosion'; twentieth-century gamelan music notable for vitality and virtuosity; also a dance for a solo boy performer
kecak (= *ketjak*)	male monkey dance
kempli	small horizontal gong keeping time at secondary level of punctuation
kempur	smallest of three vertical gongs in the gamelan gong *gedé* and gamelan gong *kebyar*
kendang	double-headed drum; two usually found in the gamelan gong *gedé* and gamelan gong *kebyar*
keras	evil (or unrefined, uncouth) character
ketjak	see *kecak*
kotekan	four-part figurations performed by reong (q.v.)
kris	'dagger'; sacred male dagger dance
lagu	melody
lanang	'male' (high pitch)
legong	dance for three pre-adolescent girls
manis	gentle character
ngaben	cremation ceremony
ngibing	male dancer in the *joged* (q.v.)
odalan	semi-annual temple festival
patet (= *pathet*)	'mode' (Java)
patutan	generic term for Balinese gamelan tuning systems
pelog (Java)	heptatonic tuning system related to Balinese *saih pitu* (q.v.)
pemungkah (= *pemoengkah*)	preludial music to the *wayang kulit* (q.v.)

pokok	'stem'; melodic cell forming basis for composition, similar to Javanese *balungan* ('skeleton')
rebab	two-stringed fiddle, held vertically and played with bow
rejang (= *redjang*)	female processional dance used as a purification ritual
reong	set of twelve gong-chimes mounted horizontally and played by four performers
reongan	the interlocking accompanimental figuration of the reong (q.v.)
rincik	small cymbals
rindik	xylophone found in the gamelan *pejogedan* (q.v.)
saih gender wayang	anhemitonic tuning system employed in the *wayang kulit* (q.v.); related to Javanese *slendro*
saih pitu	'row of seven'; heptatonic tuning system including various pentatonic combinations; related to Javanese *pelog*
sangyang dedari (= *sanghyang d.*)	female trance dance
seka	village music club
selisir gong	common five-note form of *saih pitu* (q.v.)
slendro (Java)	anhemitonic pentatonic tuning system related to Balinese *saih gender wayang* (q.v.)
suling	popular bamboo flute
tabuh (= *taboeh*)	'stroke'; mallet; composition
trompong	solo instrument consisting of ten horizontally mounted gong-chimes
wadon	'female' (low pitch)
wayang kulit	shadow-play performed with leather puppets on a translucent screen

Japanese

aitake	'complementary bamboos'; the harmonic vocabulary of the shō (q.v.)
ashirai	music accompanying the action of the *shite* (q.v.)
ato-za	rear stage in Nō, reserved for the *hayashi* (q.v.) and *kōken* (q.v.)

bi	a chord in the *aitake* (q.v.)
biwa	four-stringed lute, played with wooden plectrum
bō	a chord in the *aitake* (q.v.)
Bugaku	danced form of Tōgaku (q.v.) and Komagaku (q.v.)
Bunraku	puppet theatre
butai	the Nō stage
chōshi	according to context, variously 'note', 'mode' or 'tuning'; collective term for the Gagaku modes; also the name of a canonic prelude in Bugaku
chū	middle axial pitch in *yowa-gin* (q.v.)
daishō-mono	category of Nō play without taiko (q.v.), e.g. *Sumidagawa*
dan	structural unit
de-goto	exit music in Nō
dōgu	Nō props
embai	portamento embellishment technique of the hichiriki (q.v.)
fue	flute (generic term)
fukai	'deep well'; the mask worn by the *shite* (q.v.) in *Sumidagawa*
Gagaku	collective term for five different genres of traditional court music
gakusō	correct name for the Gagaku koto (q.v.)
ge	low axial pitch in *yowa-gin* (q.v.); a chord in the *aitake* (q.v.)
gyō	a chord in the *aitake* (q.v.)
hakobi	movement of a Nō actor ('carriage')
hanamichi	apron stage-aisle ('flower way') in Kabuki
hashi-gakari	bridge leading to the Nō stage from the *kagami no ma* (q.v.)
hataraki-goto	descriptive instrumental music in Nō
hayashi	the Nō orchestra
hayashi-kata	the Nō musicians
hayashi-goto	sections of instrumental music in Nō
hennon	the two exchange notes in each Gagaku *chōshi* (q.v.)
hi	a chord in the *aitake* (q.v.)
hichiriki	double-reed instrument employed in Gagaku
hinoki	cypress wood from which the Nō stage is manufactured
hon-butai	the main Nō acting area
ichi	a chord in the *aitake* (q.v.)
iri-goto	generic term for entrance music in Nō
issei	type of entrance music in Nō
ji-utai	the Nō chorus
jō	high axial pitch in *yowa-gin* (q.v.)
jo–ha–kyū	tripartite structure conditioning formal units in Nō and Gagaku
jū	a chord in the *aitake* (q.v.)
Kabuki	traditional popular theatre
kagami-ita	stage pine tree in Nō (lit. 'mirror panel')

kagami no ma	off-stage mirror room in Nō
kake-buki	strict imitation in Bugaku canonic prelude *chōshi*
kakeri	a dance used in war-like or mad scenes in Nō
kakko	twin-headed barrel-drum in Gagaku
kamae	the stance of a Nō actor
Kangen	Gagaku instrumental music
kata	acting; gesture; step
kata-shiori	gesture for weeping in Nō in which one hand is raised to the eye
katarai	accelerating rhythm performed by the kakko (q.v.)
katari	narration
katari-goto	spoken prose in Nō
kiri	concluding piece in Nō
kirido-guchi	sliding door in Nō used by the *ji-utai* (q.v.)
ko-dōgu	personal props (i.e. held by actor) in Nō
kokata	child actor in Nō
kōken	Nō attendant responsible for stage properties
Komagaku	the 'Right' school of Gagaku, evolved principally from music imported from Korea
koto	thirteen-stringed zither played with three ivory plectra
kotoba	intoned speech in Nō
kotsu	a chord in the *aitake* (q.v.)
ko-tsuzumi	the Nō shoulder-drum
kū	a chord in the *aitake* (q.v.)
kudoki	'lament' (Nō)
Kunaicho-Gakubu	Music Department of the Imperial Household Agency (Tokyo)
Kyōgen	comic interludes in Nōgaku (q.v.)
kyōjo-mono	madwoman plays (Nō), e.g. *Sumidagawa*
machi-utai	'waiting song' (Nō)
mai	dance
mai-goto	instrumental dance music in Nō
michi-yuki	travel song (Nō)
mondō	interrogation of *waki* (q.v.) by *shite* (q.v.), or vice versa
monogurui-mono	lunatic plays (Nō), e.g. *Sumidagawa*
mororai	rhythm of regular repeated strokes performed by the kakko (q.v.)
moro-shiori	gesture for weeping in Nō in which both hands are raised to the eyes
nagashi	accelerating rhythm performed by the kakko (q.v.) in Gagaku
nanori	'name-saying' (Nō)

nanori-bue	'name-saying flute'; entrance music in Nō
netori	prelude in Tōgaku and Komagaku
Nippon Gakujutsu Shinkokai	Japanese Classics Translation Committee
Nippon Hoso Kyokai	Japanese broadcasting authority
Nōgaku	'accomplished entertainment'; generic term for Nō and Kyōgen
nōgaku-dō	the Nō theatre (building)
nōkan	bamboo flute with seven fingerholes employed in Nō
nōmen	the Nō masks
ogamu	gesture of worship in Nō, both arms raised horizontally with the fingertips brought together
oi-buki	close stretto in Bugaku canonic prelude *chōshi*
omote o kiru	a quick movement of the mask from side to side to express anger (Nō)
omote o kumorasu	a movement of the mask downwards to express sorrow (Nō)
omote o terasu	a movement of the mask upwards to express joy (Nō)
omote o tsukau	a slow movement of the mask from side to side to express profundity (Nō)
osae	descending vocal portamento in Nō
otsu	a chord in the *aitake* (q.v.)
ō-tsuzumi	the Nō hip-drum
ritsu	one of two scale-types into which the *chōshi* fall
ryō	one of two scale-types into which the *chōshi* fall
ryokan	traditional Japanese inn
ryōō	type of mask worn by a Bugaku dancer
ryūteki	the Gagaku bamboo flute
sayū	abstract movements from side to side in Nō
shakubyōshi	the Gagaku clapperboard, i.e. whip
shamisen	three-stringed banjo played with plectrum
shidai	'next in order'; entrance music in Nō
shijima-goto	'silent pieces' (Nō)
shinobue	popular bamboo flute
shiori	the raising of hands to eyes in Nō to depict weeping (cf. *kata-shiori* and *moro-shiori*)
shirabe	'tuning up'; an off-stage instrumental prelude in Nō; the tuning chords on the ko-tsuzumi (q.v.)

shirasu	the pebble moat separating stage from auditorium in Nō
shite	principal actor in Nō
shite-tsure	assistant principal actor in Nō
shō	the Gagaku mouth organ
shōdan	structural subdivision in a Nō play
shōko (= shōgo)	the Gagaku gong
shōzoku	Nō costumes
taiko	stick-drum, mounted horizontally
taiko-mono	Nō play accompanied by full four-man *hayashi* (q.v.)
takai-jū	a chord in the *aitake* (q.v.); alternative form of *jū*
Tōgaku	the 'Left' school of Gagaku, evolved from music imported from T'ang Dynasty China
tōyō-dōgu	multi-purpose props in Nō
tsuki-zerifu	'arrival lines' in Nō
tsukuri-mono	stage props in Nō
tsunagi-goto	linking instrumental music in Nō
utai	Nō chant
utai-goto	chanted verse in Nō
waki	secondary actor in Nō
waki-tsure	assistant secondary actor in Nō
waki-za	side-stage in Nō, reserved for *ji-utai* (q.v.)
yowa-gin	'weak' melodic mode in Nō
yubigawa	parchment or leather thimbles worn by the player of the ō-tsuzumi (q.v.)

Explanatory Note

The following convention is used when referring to rehearsal figures in musical scores:

fig. $^{4}86$ represents four bars before fig. 86
fig. 19^{10} represents ten bars after fig. 19

1

Making Tonic and Dominant
Seem like Ghosts

In November 1955 Benjamin Britten and Peter Pears left England on a five-month concert tour which took them to Austria, Yugoslavia, Turkey, Singapore, Indonesia, Hong Kong, Japan, Thailand and Sri Lanka. When he was not engaged in recital work or giving broadcasts locally, Britten found many opportunities to pursue the strong interest in oriental music he had originally gained during the Second World War as a result of his close friendship with the Canadian composer and ethnomusicologist Colin McPhee.

The fortnight Britten spent in Bali in January 1956 was kept completely free from engagements, and was intended to be a holiday from the punishing recital schedule. Whilst relaxing on the idyllic island, he found time to make a remarkably thorough study of the local gamelan music, visiting temples, dances and the shadow-play, and immersing himself in many different genres of Balinese music. On his return to England, the composer directly incorporated Balinese material into the score of the ballet *The Prince of the Pagodas*, completed later in 1956 – his first work to make use of specific oriental borrowings (although not the first to demonstrate his latent interest in the music of the Far East). From 1957 onwards, Britten's music exhibits an increasing debt to the gamelan which culminates in his final opera, *Death in Venice* (1973), where Balinese elements are fully synthesized into the composer's personal idiom.

The twelve days Britten spent in Japan in February 1956 after his stay in Bali provided him with a very different artistic and cultural experience. With scant previous knowledge of the Nō theatre, and apparently none at all of Gagaku (instrumental court music), his experience of these two performing arts led to an involvement so intense that their aesthetic and musical characteristics exerted a strong influence on the subsequent course of his own operatic development. The impact of Nō led directly to the composition of the first Church Parable, *Curlew River* (completed in 1964 after an eight-year gestation), a work which embodies an unconventional dramatic aesthetic created from a combination of elements borrowed from the Japanese theatre and from the mediaeval English mystery play. In its musical idiom, *Curlew River* is also heavily indebted to Gagaku techniques. The two later Church

1

Parables – *The Burning Fiery Furnace* (1966) and *The Prodigal Son* (1968) – demonstrate the extent to which Britten absorbed specifically Japanese features into a highly novel musico-dramatic style.

The present study has two aims. First, it provides a detailed discussion of the source material used by Britten in the reconstruction or reinterpretation of specific oriental techniques in certain works where the influence of Asian music is both precisely definable and unequivocable. Secondly, an attempt is made to isolate those characteristics of the composer's style which may be related to his interest in oriental music on a more general level. This broader stylistic investigation is of fundamental importance for two reasons. It reveals in a number of striking instances that Britten's interest in oriental music surfaced in works where one might least expect to encounter it (e.g. *Paul Bunyan*, *Peter Grimes* and *Death in Venice*). More significantly, it also highlights a number of technical preoccupations which can offer a possible explanation for Britten's interest in Balinese and Japanese musical procedures. In some cases the extent to which the appearance of a particular musical technique may be attributed to a process of 'influence' is clearly open to question. (One is reminded of Jaap Kunst's laconic remark that the final phrase of the Javanese theme 'Plenchung wetah' is virtually identical to a cello melody in the finale of Beethoven's String Quartet in F major, Op. 135.)[1] But, as explained in detail in Chapter 2, Britten's early compositional style was undeniably well suited to the admixture of more explicitly oriental material, and the success of his combination of Eastern and Western elements was undoubtedly made possible by a degree of inherent stylistic affinity. Whether or not the appearance elsewhere in Britten's music of certain 'oriental' characteristics is merely coincidental or the result of conscious borrowing is therefore relatively unimportant: the fact that such correspondences exist at all is noteworthy, and they occur with sufficient frequency to warrant closer investigation. The precise nature of the personal significance with which Britten appears to have invested his oriental borrowings is a subject still open to debate: as one commentator has recently asserted, the close connection between the phenomena of orientalism and homo-eroticism is clearly of relevance (see pp. 248–9).

Although Britten's achievements in the field of cross-cultural artistic fertilization are among the most impressive to date, he was by no means the first composer to have responded creatively to the stimulus offered by Far Eastern music. Several earlier musicians had been captivated by the sonorities and textural procedures of Indonesian gamelan music, but few had shown much interest in the traditional music of Japan. A major reason for the predominance of the gamelan amongst Eastern influences on Western music must be the existence of a number of close parallels between gamelan

---

[1] Jaap Kunst, *Music in Java*, 2 vols., trans. Emile van Loo (The Hague: Martinus Nijhoff, 1949; 3rd edn, 1973), I, 326.

techniques and Western compositional methods. For the most part, gamelan music is cast in a regular quadruple metre, and the lively syncopated style of some repertories (notably in Bali) is surprisingly close to certain Western styles.[2] The pitches employed by the gamelan, although not standardized and not corresponding directly to the Western tempered scale, may nevertheless be represented fairly successfully by Western equivalents. Western tuned percussion instruments (including the piano) can capture something of the resonant qualities of the gamelan sound without the need for authentic Indonesian instruments. With Japanese music, however, the situation is much more daunting. The tonal system of Nō music, for example, entirely defies transcription into Western notation; not surprisingly, Britten's debt to Nō is far greater in terms of its dramatic aesthetic than in terms of musical specifics. On the other hand, Britten was the first Western composer to borrow specific musical ideas from Gagaku, which may be transcribed into Western notation with some success, but even here he showed far greater flexibility in his handling of the source material than in his initially 'authentic' reconstructions of gamelan models in *The Prince of the Pagodas*. For these reasons, the story of cross-cultural musical borrowings in the years leading up to Britten's emerging interest in Far Eastern music during World War II was largely (though not exclusively) the history of Western composers' involvement with the Indonesian gamelan.

An interest in generalized musical exoticism, in which the Middle and Far East were evoked by atmospheric suggestion rather than by detailed musical correspondences, began to make itself felt in France during the later nineteenth century. Saint-Saëns used pentatonic melodies in his one-act opéra comique *La princesse jaune* (1872) and commented in a letter written seven years later:

> Tonality, which is the basis of modern harmony, is in a state of crisis. The major and minor scales no longer have exclusive rights . . . The ancient modes are making a comeback, to be hotly pursued by the scales of the East in all their tremendous variety. All this will strengthen melody in her present exhausted state . . . Harmony too is bound to change and we shall see developments in rhythm, which has so far hardly been exploited. From all this will spring a new art.[3]

In 1877 Saint-Saëns based various melodies in his *Samson et Dalila* on the Arab hijāz mode with its 'exotic' augmented second between second and third

---

[2] Indonesian rhythmic patterns are conceived with the fourth of each quadruple group as the principal beat. Westerners are likely to perceive these fourth beats as downbeats rather than upbeats, and as a result many transcriptions of gamelan pieces are notated with nominal barlines placed one beat too soon. The syncopated style of much Balinese music was brought home to Colin McPhee when living on Bali in the 1930s: after playing to local musicians recordings of various Western genres, he discovered that they responded most positively to jazz.

[3] Quoted in Roger Nichols, *Debussy* (Oxford: Oxford University Press, 1972), 7.

scale degrees.[4] The growing canon of French orientalist stage works, initiated as far back as 1844 by Félicien David's *Le désert* and later including Gounod's *La reine de Saba* (1862), Bizet's *Les pêcheurs de perles* (1863) and Massenet's *Le roi de Lahore* (1877), culminated in Delibes's *Lakmé* (1883) – the last curtly dismissed by Debussy as 'sham, imitative Oriental *bric-à-brac*'.[5]

The *fons et origo* of all derivations from the Indonesian gamelan in the music of Western composers is undoubtedly the highly original synthesis of occidental and oriental procedures attained by Claude Debussy. The famous Exposition Universelle held in Paris in 1889 featured a variety of Middle and Far Eastern ethnic musics which were heard by Western composers with far-reaching consequences. It was on this occasion, for example, that Rimsky-Korsakov encountered folk instruments from Algeria which provided the stimulus for his own octatonic panpipes in the opera *Mlada* (1892) and thereby laid the foundations for one of the most significant new tonal concepts of the early twentieth century, later to be adopted by Debussy, Stravinsky, Bartók, Ravel, Messiaen and many others. Debussy's attention was drawn to performances on the Champ de Mars by a gamelan from Cirebon in north-west Java, which played in accompaniment to authentic Javanese dancing.[6] The gamelan in question had been presented to the Paris Conservatoire in 1887 by van Vleuten, the Minister for the Interior of the Dutch East Indies; in 1933 it was installed at the Musée de l'Homme.[7] According to Richard Mueller,[8] in addition to Javanese dance music Debussy also heard the gamelan angklung, consisting of a group of tuned bamboo rattles, and is likely to have known transcriptions prepared from both genres by Julien Tiersot and Louis Bénédictus (the latter's revived in performance at the 1900 Exposition).[9] Debussy's first recorded reaction to hearing the gamelan is to be found in a letter to Pierre Louÿs written on 22 January 1895 in which he asks, 'Do you not remember the Javanese music, able to express every shade of meaning, even unmentionable shades, and which make our tonic and dominant seem like ghosts?'[10] In an article written in 1913, Debussy briefly alluded to one of the most characteristic features of the texture of gamelan music:

---

[4] See Ralph P. Locke, 'Constructing the Oriental "Other": Saint-Saëns's *Samson et Dalila'*, *Cambridge Opera Journal*, 3 (1991), 266–8.

[5] Debussy's remark was made in the course of a conversation with Ernest Guiraud recorded by Maurice Emmanuel: see Edward Lockspeiser, *Debussy: His Life and Mind* (Cambridge: Cambridge University Press, 1962; 2nd edn, 1966; repr. with corrections, 1978), I, 208.

[6] Photographs of dances witnessed by Debussy are reproduced in Anik Devriès, 'Les musiques d'Extrême-Orient à l'Exposition Universelle de 1889', *Cahiers Debussy*, new series, 1 (1977), 25–37.

[7] Neil Sorrell, *A Guide to the Gamelan* (London: Faber and Faber, 1990), 2.

[8] Richard Mueller, 'Javanese Influence on Debussy's *Fantaisie* and Beyond', *19th Century Music*, 10 (1986–7), 158.

[9] Julien Tiersot, *Musiques pittoresques: Promenades musicales à l'Exposition de 1889* (Paris: Fischbacher, 1889), and Louis Bénédictus, *Les musiques bizarres à l'Exposition* (Paris, 1889).

[10] Debussy's remark that Javanese music makes 'our tonic and dominant seem like ghosts' is misattributed to Britten by Robin Holloway in his discussion of the Church Parables:

Javanese music is based on a type of counterpoint by comparison with which that of Palestrina is child's play. And if we listen without European prejudice to the charm of their percussion, we must confess that our percussion is like primitive noises at a country fair.[11]

Elsewhere in the essay, Debussy alludes to Chinese theatrical performances he saw during the 1889 festival; the same Exposition led the composer to a greater awareness of the Japanese art that he later came to favour. Debussy's final flirtation with an authentic gamelan occurred in 1914, when he considered composing a ballet set in Taiwan which was to have utilized a Malaysian ensemble.[12]

No convincing argument has yet been advanced to support the view that Debussy borrowed specific musical techniques from the Javanese music he heard in 1889, *pace* Mueller's attempts to show that the *Fantaisie* for piano and orchestra composed in the same year derives its melodic material from a Javanese piece entitled 'Wani-Wani'.[13] The most important observation to be made about the impact of the gamelan on Debussy's style is that the experience intensified techniques already latent in his music which stood well apart from the conventional and soon to be outmoded procedures that had dominated central European tonal music for the previous 200 years. In this respect, Debussy's reaction to the gamelan stimulus is in essence identical with Britten's. Both composers had shown themselves to be exploring novel compositional techniques prior to their contact with Indonesian music, and the gamelan acted as a catalyst by throwing up fortuitous musical parallels which focused their attention on more radical aspects of their own style. As Neil Sorrell has persuasively concluded:

The key word is *influence*, with its suggestion of bringing about a change of course. With Debussy a much more fruitful word would be *confirmation*. It seems far more plausible that what he heard in 1889 confirmed what he had, at least subconsciously, always felt about music, and this experience went far deeper than a desire to imitate something new and exotic.[14]

see 'The Church Parables II: Limits and Renewals', in Christopher Palmer (ed.), *The Britten Companion* (London: Faber and Faber, 1984), 216.

[11] Quoted in Lockspeiser, *Debussy*, I, 115. It should be noted that Lockspeiser's comments on the gamelan appearances at the 1889 and 1900 Expositions are not entirely reliable: he reports that the ensemble attending the 1900 festivities was 'apparently the Solo gamelan from Bali'. Solo (synonymous with Surakarta) is, of course, in Java.

[12] See Robert Orledge, *Debussy in the Theatre* (Cambridge: Cambridge University Press, 1982), 190.

[13] Mueller, 'Javanese Influence', 162–73. See also Roy Howat's criticism of Mueller's specific claim in his article 'Debussy and the Orient' in Andrew Gerstle and Anthony Milner (eds.), *Recovering the Orient: Artists, Scholars, Appropriations* (London: Harwood Academic Publishers, 1995), 48, note 10. For further discussion of the Javanese influence on Debussy, see Jürgen Arndt, *Der Einfluß der javanischen Gamelan-Musik auf Kompositionen von Claude Debussy* (Frankfurt: Lang, 1993).

[14] Sorrell, *A Guide to the Gamelan*, 3.

Donald Mitchell has said of Britten's gamelan encounter that 'the experience of Bali was not so much the moment of ignition . . . but rather the living confirmation of what Britten had in mind'.[15] The only difference in Britten's case arises from his conscious use of specific Balinese material as part of this process of compositional 'reinforcement'.

Part of Debussy's rebellion against the hegemony of nineteenth-century Austro-German music resided in his cultivation of so-called 'non-functional' harmony which rejected conventional concepts of dissonance, consonance and resolution. He frequently adopted scales which lay outside the orthodox tonal system, including the ancient church modes and synthetic formulations such as the octatonic and acoustic scales (cf. Saint-Saëns's prophetic remark quoted above). Two of the most striking scales are the whole-tone and pentatonic varieties, both of which have at various times been likened to gamelan tuning systems. The *slendro* tuning in which the Javanese ensemble heard at the 1889 Exposition was constructed theoretically employs equidistant steps within the octave; but there are five such steps, not six (as in the whole-tone scale), and in practice the five tones of *slendro* tend to gravitate towards the distinctive pattern familiar to everyone as the black notes of the Western keyboard (see Ex. 1.1).[16] This anhemitonic pentatonic scale was well known to Debussy long before his contact with the gamelan, and its early use in his music may have derived from sources as diverse as Russian music (the scale appears regularly in works by his two idols, Borodin and Musorgsky), Liszt (whose *Sposalizio* of 1858 contains pentatonic figurations imitated by Debussy at the same pitches and in the same triplet rhythm in his First Arabesque of 1888), and numerous European folk-song traditions.

Ex. 1.1

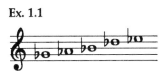

In only one work of Debussy's does the pentatonic scale occur prominently in a specifically oriental context (unless one subscribes to the common speculation that the pentatonic opening of *La mer* was intended to symbolize the sun's rising in the east!). This is the piano piece *Pagodes*, published in 1903 as the first of the three *Estampes* and probably inspired by Debussy's second experience of a Javanese gamelan at the Exposition

[15] Donald Mitchell, 'An Afterword on Britten's *Pagodas*: The Balinese Sources', *Tempo*, 152 (1985), 9, note 4.
[16] In 1946 Kodály composed a set of *Children's Dances* which put the euphonious properties of black-note pentatonicism to educational use, an idea also developed by Carl Orff in his method of class improvisation invoiving Western metallophones organized into a 'gamelan'.

Ex. 1.2

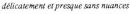
délicatement et presque sans nuances

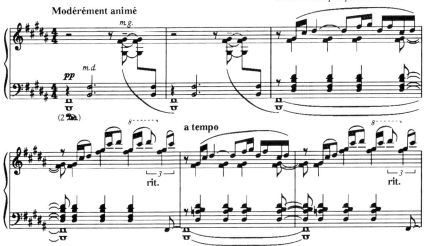

Universelle in 1900. Even here, one notes, the title does not conjure up a specific image of Indonesia (where pagodas are not to be found), but the confluence of pentatonicism and stratified polyphony is sufficiently striking to render a gamelan stimulus plausible. At the outset, Debussy forms an anhemitonic pentatonic scale from the pitches B, C♯, D♯, F♯ and G♯ (see Ex. 1.2), and this formulation provides the tonal material for much of the piece. What is most significant (and usually overlooked) about this celebrated opening, however, is the way in which Debussy anchors his pentatonic scale firmly to the B major triad contained within its five pitches, and even goes so far as to include a B major key signature with its redundant A♯. This constitutes a notably early fusion of Eastern and Western tonal procedures, and reflects Debussy's inevitably Westernized perception of the gamelan's pentatonic tuning. Later in the piece, however, he abandons triadic support and allows the pentatonicism to revolve freely without a Western tonal focus (e.g. bars 11–14), although this approach rapidly yields to another more synthetic treatment in which a pentatonic melodic fragment is harmonized chromatically (bars 15–18).

Of wider-reaching significance in *Pagodes* is the development of a stratified contrapuntal texture built up from superimposed ostinato patterns. Although seen here only in embryonic form, in later orchestral works Debussy developed such 'layered' textures to a high degree of sophistication. In both piano and orchestral writing, these textures share with the gamelan a direct relationship between tessitura and rapidity of figuration. The slowest-moving element in a gamelan piece is the scheme of 'colotomic' (i.e. dissecting) punctuation provided by the deepest gongs and loosely represented in Ex. 1.2

by the repetitions of the lowest B/F♯ dyad.[17] Above this rock-like support are superimposed various melodic and accompanimental ostinato figurations which, in gamelan music, tend to move more quickly the higher the range of the instrument. Ex. 1.2 demonstrates three such rhythmic layers in a simplified scheme, but later examples (such as at fig. 17 in *Ibéria*, the second of the orchestral *Images* of 1906–12) superimpose numerous layers of ostinati in far more ambitious textures based on the same principle of stratification.[18] As with his tonal language, Debussy's preference for these stratified textures represents a further revolt against the traditional contrapuntal and melody-plus-accompaniment textures of much nineteenth-century music.

Although Debussy never resorted to using ensembles of tuned percussion to suggest gamelan sonorities, as did later composers, his music is infused with echoes of the gamelan sound. This is most noticeable in his piano writing, especially where the texture involves bass notes prolonged by the sustaining pedal for considerable periods of time beneath more active figurations. As E. J. Dent observed in 1916, drawing attention to a fundamental discovery associated with the pedal's acoustical function that underlies much twentieth-century piano music,

> It is in fact the right-hand pedal which gives the pianoforte an advantage possessed by no other instrument to any appreciable extent ... For the principal value of the pedal is not merely to sustain sounds when the finger is for some reason obliged to release the key, but to reinforce sounds by allowing other strings to vibrate in sympathy with them.[19]

It seems likely that Debussy's extraordinary exploitation of this phenomenon of sympathetic vibration in his piano music was partly inspired by the gamelan's uniquely resonant tone. As early as 1937, E. Robert Schmitz perceptively noted that

> Debussy regarded the piano as the Balinese musicians regard their gamelan orchestras. He was interested not so much in the single tone that was obviously heard when a note was struck, as in the patterns of resonance which that tone sets up around itself. Many of his pieces are built entirely on this acoustical sense of the piano.[20]

Connected with the desire to create a resonant 'wash' of sound which reinforced the essentially static nature of much of Debussy's non-functional

[17] According to Léon Pillaut's article 'Le gamelan javanais' in the 3 July 1887 issue of *Le ménestrel*, the two lowest punctuating gongs in the Conservatoire's gamelan were tuned to pitches approximating to F♯ and B.

[18] For further examples, see Howat, 'Debussy and the Orient', 54–6.

[19] Edward J. Dent, 'The Pianoforte and its Influence on Modern Music', *Musical Quarterly*, 2 (1916), 271–94.

[20] Quoted in Roger Nichols (ed.), *Debussy Remembered* (London: Faber and Faber, 1992), 171.

harmony was his self-confessed need (as recorded by Marguerite Long) to make the piano appear as if it were an instrument *sans marteaux* (i.e. without hammers). In the finest examples of gamelan music the players miraculously manage to create mellifluous effects, even in virtuoso passagework, in spite of the need to strike every single note with a hand-held mallet.

Later French composers subscribed to Debussy's interest in the piano's sympathetic resonance. Ravel recommended that his 1902 piano piece *Jeux d'eau* be played with copious use of the sustaining pedal to emphasize 'the hazy impression of vibrations in the air', while Messiaen's early *Préludes* for piano (1929) first experimented with what the composer termed 'added resonance'. Not content to achieve acoustical effects by the use of the sustaining pedal alone, Messiaen went so far as to include deliberately 'wrong' notes (played more softly than the prevailing musical material) which function as an illusory extension of the natural sympathetic vibrations set up by the release of the pedal. Significantly, both Ravel and Messiaen shared Debussy's interest in the gamelan; Messiaen, too, was later to respond creatively to Japanese court music at around the time Britten was absorbing elements from the same genre in the novel musical idiom of *Curlew River*.

Ravel displayed an interest in orientalism in his early song-cycle *Shéhérazade* (1903), and went on to choose the piano as his preferred medium for capturing the gamelan sonority. In *La vallée des cloches* from *Miroirs*, written in 1905 close on the heels of Debussy's *Pagodes*, the subtle exploitation of the piano's sympathetic resonances and gently undulating pentatonic ostinato patterns marked 'très doux et sans accentuation' recall Debussy's example. (Although no explicitly oriental interpretation is suggested by the title of the piece, Ravel dedicated it to Maurice Delage, who later became well known for his musical orientalisms.) Particularly prophetic of later composers' gamelan-derived techniques is Ravel's use of low sustained dissonant notes which disrupt the prevailing pentatonicism and equally suggest the bells of the title or the colotomic punctuation of the gamelan's largest gongs.

The piano was again used by Ravel to suggest gamelan sonorities in the original duet version of the suite *Ma mère l'oye* (1908–10). The third movement is entitled 'Laideronette, impératrice des pagodes' after the fairy-tale *Serpentin vert* by Madame D'Aulnoy (d. 1705), the source Cranko and Britten were later to use for the plot of *The Prince of the Pagodas*. Orchestrating *Ma mère l'oye* as a ballet in 1911, Ravel went one stage further than Debussy by employing a carefully selected percussion group to capture the sonorities of a Far Eastern percussion ensemble more vividly. The combination of xylophone, glocken-spiel and celeste, variously supported by cymbal, harp and string pizzicato figurations, so uncannily suggests a gamelan orchestra in 'Laideronette' that it may be supposed that Ravel was also acquainted with the sound of the Conservatoire's gamelan. Equally 'authentic' is the use of colotomic tam-tam punctuation in the central section (figs. 8–14) where the celeste is required to play in its unorthodox low register in what again seems to be an attempt to capture a characteristic gamelan sonority. Even if these parallels with Indonesian models were unintentional, Ravel's generalized orientalism embraces compositional techniques already familiar from Debussy's example, principally anhemitonic pentatonicism and ostinato patterns organized in layers according to principles of rhythmic stratification (e.g. fig. 14). Ravel's pentatonic pitches are those found conveniently on the black notes of the piano (perhaps suggesting he wrote the piece at the keyboard), and in both pitch content and scoring the movement provided a model for Stravinsky's parodistic 'Marche chinoise' in Act II of *Le rossignol* (1913), yet another member of the operatic fairy-tale tradition. Ravel briefly returned to chinoiserie in *L'enfant et les sortilèges* (1925), where pentatonicism characterizes the Chinese cup and forms an incongruous element in the 'Five o'clock' foxtrot she dances in company with a matching black Wedgwood teapot.

The influence of Ravel on Britten has long remained a neglected topic of inquiry, in spite of obvious superficial correspondences such as the multiple string glissandi used to depict swaying trees in both *L'enfant et les sortilèges* and Britten's *A Midsummer Night's Dream* (1960). Ravel's 'Laideronette' undoubtedly exhibits a number of parallels with Britten's later gamelan derivations, not least in its original piano-duet instrumentation which recurs prominently in the orchestration of the 'gamelan' sections in *The Prince of the Pagodas*. Britten was a keen duet-player and probably first encountered *Ma mère l'oye* in its original version. The choice of a piano-duet sonority in *Pagodas* is also linked to two-piano works by McPhee and Poulenc which both directly incorporate Balinese material. Ravel's pentatonicism, like Debussy's before it, produces ubiquitous major-second clashes which are also to be found throughout *Pagodas*, the similarity being especially prominent where tuned percussion instruments are involved. The pentatonic cluster chords hammered out by the full orchestra in the last three bars of 'Laideronette' may have been in Britten's mind as he composed the similar effects in *Pagodas*; the same may hold true for Ravel's use of colotomic gong punctuation. Lastly, and by no means insignificantly, Ravel explicitly thought of *Ma mère l'oye* as embodying 'the poetry of childhood',[21] subtitling the suite 'Cinq pièces enfantines'. With Britten's oriental borrowings, too, there is a strong sense of identification with the innocence of childhood, most potently to be seen in the choice of gamelan material to represent the children in *Death in Venice* but also prefigured in *The Turn of the Screw* and other works employing prominent tuned percussion.

Like Ravel, Bartók owed a considerable stylistic debt to Debussy in his early years and adopted anhemitonic pentatonicism around 1907. In his work, too, pentatonicism stems as much from European folk-music as from the Orient. But certain of Bartók's keyboard techniques are radical enough to parallel the work of more notoriously avant-garde composers. An offshoot of

[21] Maurice Ravel, 'Esquisse autobiographique', *Revue musicale* (December 1938), 21.

Bartók's interest in pentatonicism was the cultivation of opposing tone-clusters on black and white notes to create maximum harmonic tension. This cluster device is reputed to have been a conscious borrowing from Henry Cowell, whom Bartók met in London in 1923.[22] Significantly, Cowell was one of the earliest American composers to have shown an interest in the gamelan, and tone-clusters (already used by Ravel) were to figure prominently in the work of most later composers involved with Indonesian music. The only specific reference to Indonesia in the title of a work by Bartók, however, is the movement 'Island of Bali' from Volume IV of the *Mikrokosmos* (no. 109): here we find an allusion to the specific Balinese scale later to be used by Poulenc and Britten (see Ex. 1.3), but no attempt to capture the stratified textures of genuine gamelan music. In February 1942, two years after the publication of *Mikrokosmos*, Bartók and his wife performed McPhee's *Balinese Ceremonial Music* at Amherst College, Massachusetts.[23]

Ex. 1.3

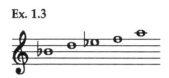

While the impact of Debussy's gamelan derivations was being felt in France, Mahler's exploration of musical techniques inspired by Chinese music in *Das Lied von der Erde* (1909) showed how pentatonicism and heterophony could be absorbed into a thoroughly Western idiom without incongruity. It was especially Mahler's treatment of heterophony, which may be defined as the simultaneous presentation of different variants of the same melody (a distinctively non-Western approach to musical texture to be found in different guises in considerably varied ethnic contexts), that may have provided a potent stylistic model for the young Britten. Britten's early passion for Mahler has been well documented, but the extent of Mahler's debt to Chinese culture was only revealed in full as recently as 1985, when Donald Mitchell published his exhaustive investigation of *Das Lied*.[24]

In the same year as Debussy's *Pagodes*, Puccini had produced his own contribution to the then flourishing fashion for operatic exoticism in the shape of *Madama Butterfly*. Like *Lakmé* and Meyerbeer's *L'Africaine* (1865), *Butterfly* is concerned with a perceived incompatibility between Eastern and Western

[22] Malcolm Gillies (ed.), *Bartók Remembered* (London: Faber and Faber, 1990), 118.
[23] Carol Oja, *Colin McPhee: Composer in Two Worlds* (Washington and London: Smithsonian Institution Press, 1990), 153, 179. Donald Mitchell has reminded me that the accelerating xylophone rhythm in the slow movement of Bartók's *Music for Strings, Percussion and Celeste* (1936) seems to derive from the Balinese gamelan, and that this work was greatly admired by Britten.
[24] Donald Mitchell, *Gustav Mahler, III: Songs and Symphonies of Life and Death* (London: Faber and Faber, 1985).

cultures. Set in contemporaneous Nagasaki, the opera was imbued with a degree of topicality: the relaxation of the formerly strict Japanese attitudes to the West had begun to take place under the Meiji Restoration (1866–8),[25] and temporary marriages of convenience between Japanese women and visiting American servicemen such as that uniting Butterfly and Pinkerton were relatively common. The basis for Puccini's libretto was Pierre Loti's novel *Madame Chrysanthème* (1887), which had already spawned an opera by Saint-Saëns's pupil André Messager in 1893.

Puccini's version is something of a disappointment in terms of its handling of the limited Japanese material at its composer's disposal. Mosco Carner identified seven Japanese themes in the score, all folk-songs and therefore cast in a generally lyrical melodic vein entirely suited to the composer's requirements.[26] What Carner describes as the opera's 'exotic aroma' is in fact far less pervasive than might have been expected, and Puccini's decision to open the work with a surprisingly intellectual fugal introduction is symptomatic of his lack of concern for establishing an oriental atmosphere at the outset. In spite of the use of genuine Japanese melodies, the harmonic language remains conventionally Western, with the occasional splash of superficially exotic colouring from glockenspiel or gong. There is little attempt to integrate Eastern and Western musical ingredients, and Carner's claim that the opera represents 'a perfect assimilation of features from Japanese music into [Puccini's] own style' is, to say the least, exaggerated.

An altogether more notable achievement is the same composer's *Turandot* (1920–24), set in Peking 'in legendary times' and forming part of the well-established tradition of stage works based on oriental fairy-tales. Gozzi's five-act play *Turandotte* (1765) was a typical product of its time, the eighteenth century having shown a marked predilection for exotic fables of its type. Gozzi's story had been promoted in Germany by Goethe and Schiller, the latter's 1801 German adaptation having been furnished with an overture and incidental music by Weber in 1809. Busoni wrote both incidental music (1905) and an operatic version (1917) of the tale.[27] Busoni's incidental score not

---

[25] The new policy welcoming Western ideas has, of course, achieved spectacular results in both industrial and artistic spheres. The Meiji Restoration promoted, amongst other things, an increased awareness of Western music, and a fascinating study could be written of the changing style of indigenous Japanese composers in the wake of this broadening of artistic horizons. Interestingly, the Japanese have come to develop a notable affection for Western works based on Japanese material. Thus *Madama Butterfly* has received one of its most notable stagings at the hands of a Japanese director, and Britten's *Curlew River* has been adopted by more than one Japanese company.

[26] Mosco Carner, *Puccini: A Critical Biography* (London: Duckworth, 1958; 2nd edn, 1974), 385–7.

[27] Further musical treatments of Gozzi's *Turandotte* include Gottfried von Einem's ballet *Prinzessin Turandot* (1944) and an incidental score by Ernst Toch. Prokofiev's opera *The Love for Three Oranges* (1921) was based on another Gozzi tale, while Britten's *The Prince of the Pagodas* was itself a continuation of the same fairy-tale tradition, its plot deriving in part from an eighteenth-century fairy-tale by Madame D'Aulnoy which had also been the source for Ravel's 'Laideronnette, impératrice des pagodes' (see above).

surprisingly utilizes ostinato techniques and pentatonicism for 'generalized orientalism',[28] in addition to the borrowing of Arabian, Persian, Turkish, Indian and Chinese melodies from A. W. Ambros's *Geschichte der Musik* (1880); the operatic version includes a 'gamelan-like figure'[29] based on anhemitonic pentatonic ostinato patterns above a dissonant bass.

By the 1920s Puccini's compositional idiom had notably advanced under the combined influences of Debussy, Ravel, Stravinsky and even Bartók. His harmonic vocabulary had widened to embrace modality and bitonality, thereby allowing him to integrate the strongly pentatonic Chinese melodies on which many of the opera's themes are based far more successfully than had been the case with the more conservative tonal language of *Madama Butterfly*.[30] The music gravitates towards flat keys such as G♭ major in many pentatonically orientated passages, presumably reflecting Puccini's habit of composing at the piano and alighting on the 'black-note' anhemitonic scale. In spite of a higher degree of integration between Chinese melody and modal accompaniment, however, Puccini still reveals himself to be capable of supporting a pentatonic melody with conventional harmonies that serve to disguise its exotic nature (see, for example, Liù's aria 'Signore, ascolta!', Act I, fig. 42 – one of the G♭ major passages). Apart from Puccini's new harmonic sophistication, his increased reliance on ostinato figurations (deriving from the influence of Debussy and Stravinsky) is again fortuitous in helping to set up pseudo-oriental textures which do not sound out of place: a particularly fine example, in which both pentatonicism and heterophony are used to effect, occurs at fig. 9 in Act III where the debt to his French impressionist forebears is self-evident.

Lastly, *Turandot* exhibits an orchestrational virtuosity unparalleled elsewhere in the composer's output, much of the instrumental colour calculated to achieve Carner's 'exotic aroma'. Most importantly, the percussion section is significantly expanded to include a set of tuned Chinese gongs, two xylophones of different registers, two gongs of different pitches, glockenspiel and celeste. The tuned percussion instruments are occasionally heard in ensemble (e.g. Act III, fig. 10) and are a prototype of the 'nuclear gamelan' which will later be seen to figure prominently in works by McPhee, Messiaen, Britten and others.[31]

[28] Antony Beaumont, *Busoni the Composer* (London: Faber and Faber, 1985), 85.

[29] *Ibid.*, 242–3.

[30] Carner (*Puccini*, 468–70) identifies eight such themes, two of which the composer apparently heard on a friend's Chinese musical box. See also William Ashbrook and Harold Powers, *Puccini's Turandot: The End of the Great Tradition* (Princeton: Princeton University Press, 1991), 94–5.

[31] Britten's antipathy towards Puccini is well known, which might suggest Puccini as an unlikely influence on his style. According to the Earl of Harewood, Britten declared that Puccini's operas were 'dreadful' (to which his interlocutor, Shostakovich, replied: 'No, Ben, you are wrong. He wrote marvellous operas, but dreadful music'): see George [Earl of] Harewood, *The Tongs and the Bones* (London: Weidenfeld and Nicholson, 1981), 133. But it is worth recalling that Britten was equally uncharitable about Stravinsky

In England, the trend towards exoticism in stage works found an early and famous manifestation in Sullivan's *The Mikado* (1885), followed by Sidney Jones's operetta *The Geisha* (1896). In 1913, Clarence Raybould produced an operatic version of the Nō play *Sumidagawa* on which Britten would base his *Curlew River* nearly 50 years later. Gustav Holst, for whose music Britten retained strong sympathies, was steeped in Sanskrit literature, and this provided the inspiration for his four groups of *Choral Hymns from the Rig Veda* (1908–12) and the chamber opera *Sāvitri* (1908), a notably early precedent for the economical music-theatre resources later cultivated in Britten's Church Parables.[32] More notable in terms of specific technical procedures are the 'oriental suite' *Beni Mora* (1910), based on themes collected by Holst during a holiday in Algeria, and the *Japanese Suite* (1915), both for orchestra. The latter was written for the Japanese dancer Michio Ito, who supplied most of the melodic material, and represents a notable attempt to integrate Japanese modality with the composer's characteristically European harmonic language. Scales corresponding to those employed by Puccini in *Madama Butterfly* appear in predominantly dark orchestral colourings suggesting Holst viewed his oriental material with a sense of mysticism typical of his artistic outlook in general. The most 'authentic' sonority appears in the flute solo accompanied by pseudo-koto ostinato patterns on the harp in the 'Dance under the Cherry Tree' (flute and harp were to be treated with similar deference to Japanese models in Britten's Church Parables), and in the final 'Dance of the Wolves', where Holst's ostinato treatment acquires an almost Stravinskian intensity. The least interesting section of the score is the 'Dance of the Marionette', the only movement not to take a Japanese theme as its basis, with the result that Holst reverts to a less inspiring version of the fragmented scherzo style used to better effect in 'Mercury' from *The Planets* (on which he was working at the time of composition).

Although gamelan instruments were known in the UK during the nineteenth century and their tuning systems studied here as early as 1885,[33] the

(undoubtedly a potent influence on him), and that Debussy was less than complimentary about Wagner. *Turandot* was well known to Peter Pears, at least, since he recorded the role of the Emperor under Zubin Mehta with Joan Sutherland and Luciano Pavarotti in 1973; he had also been well known as Rodolfo in *La Bohème*, a part he first sang in 1944. *Madama Butterfly* had formed part of the same 1945 Sadler's Wells season as saw the first production of *Peter Grimes*. Julian Herbage wrote of the latter in a BBC memorandum that 'the style throughout was extremely eclectic – one of Ellen's arias had come almost straight out of "Madam Butterfly"' (quoted in Donald Mitchell and Philip Reed, eds., *Letters from a Life: The Selected Letters and Diaries of Benjamin Britten*, 2 vols., London: Faber and Faber, 1991, II, 655). Desmond Shawe-Taylor noted in his review of the first performance of *Grimes* that Britten's handling of 'the big choral scenes' recalled *Turandot* (see Philip Brett, ed., *Benjamin Britten: Peter Grimes*, Cambridge Opera Handbooks, Cambridge: Cambridge University Press, 1983, 157).

32 *Sāvitri*, with Pears as Satyavān, was mounted at the 1956 Aldeburgh Festival shortly after Britten's return from his Far Eastern tour; it was revived at Aldeburgh in 1974.

33 A. J. Ellis, 'On the Musical Scales of Various Nations', *Journal of the Society of Arts*, 33 (1885), 485–527.

first instance of a specific allusion to the gamelan in the work of an English composer appears to date from the 1930s, shortly before Britten's first involvement with Indonesian music. The work in question is Tippett's Piano Sonata no. 1 (1936–8), which contains in the fifth variation of its first movement a fleeting allusion to the same Balinese tuning system as that imitated by Poulenc (see below). Tippett had been lent a recorded anthology of ethnic musics by Aubrey Russ, and in borrowing material from a gramophone record he anticipated the later work of Grainger and Britten. It was not until 1978, however, that Tippett found the opportunity to visit Indonesia for himself, on which occasion the experience of live gamelan performances left its mark on the Triple Concerto.[34] It was at this time (1979) that a gamelan first made an appearance at the BBC Promenade Concerts.

The most explicit borrowing from gamelan music in France after Debussy occurs in the Concerto for Two Pianos by Poulenc, composed in 1932 in the wake of an appearance by a Balinese gamelan at the Exposition Coloniale in Paris during the previous year. The gamelan in question was the gamelan gong *kebyar* 'Gunung Sari' from the village of Peliatan, later made famous by its Western tours under John Coast and as the source for some of Britten's Balinese borrowings. Commissioned by Princess Edmond de Polignac, Poulenc's concerto was given its first performance at the Venice festival of the ISCM on 5 September 1932; the soloists were the composer and Jacques Février, with the orchestra of La Scala, Milan, directed by Désiré Defauw. Poulenc commented to Paul Collaer one month after the première that 'it did in fact stun everyone at the Festival . . . You will see for yourself what an enormous step forward it is from my previous work and that I am really entering my great period.'[35] The concerto was well known to Britten, who performed it with Poulenc at a 'Saturday Book' concert at the Royal Albert Hall on 6 January 1945; the London Philharmonic Orchestra was conducted by Basil Cameron, and the programme included Britten's *Sinfonia da Requiem* in a prophetic mating of works with Balinese and Japanese connections. By this time Britten had already become acquainted with Balinese music through McPhee's two-piano transcriptions (see below, Chapter 2), and he can hardly have failed to be aware of Poulenc's gamelan borrowings. In 1955 Poulenc and Britten again performed the work, this time at the Royal Festival Hall, and the timing of this occasion – coming as it does in the midst of Britten's work on *The Prince of the Pagodas* – is undoubtedly significant.

Poulenc described his Concerto for Two Pianos as 'blithely bravura',[36] and the Balinese material it contains is of no greater significance than the composer's habitually haphazard allusions elsewhere in the score to the

[34] Michael Tippett, *Those Twentieth-Century Blues: An Autobiography* (London: Hutchinson, 1991), 258–9.
[35] Letter dated 1 October 1932; see Sidney Buckland (ed.), *Francis Poulenc: Selected Correspondence, 1915–1963* (London: Gollancz, 1991), 97.
[36] *Ibid.*, 236.

idioms of composers as diverse as Mozart, Tchaikovsky, Prokofiev and Stravinsky. (In a posthumous appreciation of Poulenc published in the 1964 Aldeburgh Festival Programme Book, Britten and Pears wrote: 'He was not ashamed to admire and to borrow.') As is often the case in Poulenc's music, no attempt is made to synthesize this veritable pot-pourri of stylistic mannerisms; and the explicit reference to Balinese procedures may therefore be considered as less satisfying artistically than Debussy's subtle and no doubt largely subconscious manipulation of Javanese textures and scales. Nevertheless, Poulenc's modest handling of Balinese pentatonicism demonstrates a reinterpretation of gamelan scales from a Western viewpoint analogous to that already seen in Debussy's *Pagodes*. His contribution to the field of cross-cultural borrowing is also significant for its use of the other principal pentatonic scale to which gamelans are tuned, which was ignored by Debussy in his exclusive reliance on the anhemitonic variety.[37] The concerto contains five sections based on this scale, the pitches of which presumably correspond to those heard by Poulenc at the Exposition: interestingly, these are identical to the pitches selected by Britten for the majority of his gamelan-inspired effects in *The Prince of the Pagodas* (see Ex. 1.3). Britten borrowed these pitches from recordings made by the gamelan from Peliatan,[38] and the coincidence is unlikely to have escaped him.

Poulenc's 'gamelan' passages are brief, and principally serve to usher in or round off each of the concerto's three movements. The work commences with a flurry of semiquavers based on the pitches of Ex. 1.3, which are then abandoned apart from a fleeting reappearance in the right-hand dyads of the first piano part at fig. 14. Tonally, the opening gesture is significant: the scale is presented in the context of the tonic key D minor (asserted by the two initial chords), and it is therefore inevitably interpreted as part of a Phrygian mode based on D. The most extended passage to use Balinese material occurs at fig. 25 and forms the coda to the first movement. Poulenc here sets up oscillating semiquaver figurations based on ostinato patterns derived from Ex. 1.3 in an atmospheric texture to be played 'mystérieux et clair tout à la fois', and then presents a simple melody above it (see Ex. 1.4). The 'gamelan' texture at this point is authentic enough, but the rhythm of the melody is decidedly Western and the theme itself contains one pitch (C) alien to the pentatonicism prevailing in its accompaniment. The melody thus makes explicit the B♭ major tonality which Poulenc perceived to be implied by the Balinese scale, a procedure recalling Debussy's extraction of a B major triad from his penta-tonic scale in Ex. 1.2. At fig. 27 Poulenc introduces another additional pitch (G) in the cellos, thereby effecting a further reinterpretation of the scale as part of the Aeolian mode on G. Also notable at this point is the reiteration of the melody from Ex. 1.4 on solo cello harmonics, an ethereal sonority used

---

[37] The system in question here (*pelog*) is in fact heptatonic in theory, but often pentatonic in practice.

[38] Preserved at the Britten–Pears Library, Aldeburgh (hereafter *GB-ALb*), 3-9401051–9401060.

Ex. 1.4

independently by both McPhee and Britten to capture the evanescent sound of the Balinese flute (suling). At fig. 26, however, the music had lapsed into an indulgently lush harmonic progression more redolent of Rachmaninov than Indonesia, and sitting uncomfortably at odds with its musical surroundings. Brief reminiscences of the Balinese scale and its associated ostinato-based textures occur at the end of the slow movement (final six bars) and at the conclusion of the work as a whole (fig. 68).

Poulenc went on to make a further brief allusion to the gamelan in his opera *Les mamelles de Tirésias* (1944), a work also well known to Britten, who mounted its English première at the Aldeburgh Festival on 13 June 1958. Poulenc had originally been engaged to perform a two-piano reduction of the orchestral score with Britten, but in the event the French composer's pathological fear of sea travel forced him to cancel and Britten performed the orchestral parts with Viola Tunnard. Pears took the role of the Husband, and the production (which Poulenc later hailed as 'absolute perfection')[39] was

---

[39] Francis Poulenc, 'Hommage à Benjamin Britten', in Anthony Gishford (ed.), *A Tribute to Benjamin Britten on his Fiftieth Birthday* (London: Faber and Faber, 1963), 13.

directed by John Cranko, who had choreographed the première staging of *The Prince of the Pagodas* in the previous year. The fleeting allusion to Bali occurs at the end of the Prologue, where Poulenc again reworks the semiquaver figurations found in the two-piano concerto using pitches identical to those in Ex. 1.3.

While McPhee was transcribing gamelan music for two pianos in Bali, another composer – also to be connected with Britten in later years – was notating Balinese and Javanese music from gramophone recordings. In 1932–3 Percy Grainger transcribed (with the assistance of Norman Voelcker) a recording of 'Sekar gadung' for an ensemble of Western tuned percussion and voices, with piccolos representing the Indonesian flute (suling).[40] In July 1935, Grainger went on (with the collaboration of James Scott-Power) to draw up a full score of a Balinese piece entitled 'Berong pengètjèt' for gamelan angklung. Both transcriptions were based on Parlophone 78rpm discs recorded in 1928, that of the Balinese piece (Odéon 0-1936a, reissued as MO 105) forming the twelfth record in the company's pioneering set 'Music of the Orient'.[41] Coincidentally, Britten owned a copy of the same disc, although there is no evidence to suggest that he was aware of Grainger's transcription and he did not meet the Australian composer until 1958, after the completion of *The Prince of the Pagodas*.[42] Grainger's interest in ethno-musicology originated many years before this transcription, however. When studying the piano in Frankfurt during the late 1890s he asked his teacher 'If I should win [the Mendelssohn Prize], would they let me study Chinese music with the money?' The reply duly came: 'No, they don't give prizes to idiots.'[43] His involvement with Western composers' borrowings from the gamelan dates from 1905, when he gave the first British performance of Debussy's *Pagodes* at the Bechstein Hall, London.

In 1912 Grainger broke daring new compositional ground in his *Random Round*, which explored the phenomenon of stratified polyphony in the context of an aleatory musical structure many years ahead of its time. Each subsection of the work is initiated by a stroke on a Javanese gong and then built up from between ten and twenty melodic variants; choice of variant and

40 See Teresa Balough, *A Complete Catalogue of the Works of Percy Grainger* (Nedlands: Department of Music, University of Western Australia, 1975), 91.

41 Grainger's transcription was edited by Christopher Palmer, who prepared a complete set of performing parts. A copy of Palmer's (unpublished) edition is preserved in the personal collection of Donald Mitchell.

42 See John Bird, *Percy Grainger* (London: Faber and Faber, 1976), 248. Britten and Pears wrote a prefatory note to Bird's biography praising Grainger's 'masterly folksong arrangements with their acutely beautiful feeling for sound', some of which they recorded for Decca in 1968 (reissued on CD, London 425 159-2, in 1989). In a conversation with Pears, John Morris and Grainger's widow Ella broadcast by the BBC on 15 June 1966, Britten drew attention to the impact of Grainger's work on his own folk-song settings.

43 Teresa Balough, *A Musical Genius from Australia* (Nedlands: Department of Music, University of Western Australia, 1982), 78.

tempo are left to the performers' discretion. The motivation underlying Grainger's experiment was the desire to unite performers in spontaneous communal music-making, and he commented after a performance of *Random Round* in London in 1914 that

> several of [the fifteen musicians] taking part quickly developed the power of merging themselves into the artistic whole . . . I look forward to some day presenting to English and American audiences a performance of this blend of modern harmonic tendencies with experiences drawn from the improvised polyphony of primitive music.[44]

In 1934, shortly before embarking on his Balinese transcription, Grainger published a series of twelve lectures under the collective title *A Commonsense View of All Music* which set out his philosophy 'to approach all the world's available music with an open mind'. The eleventh lecture was entitled 'Tuneful Percussion' (Grainger's idiosyncratic adaptation of the more conventional expression 'tuned percussion'), which he deemed to include 'Bali bell-orchestras' and 'Javanese gong-orchestras'. Once more he returned to the cross-cultural significance of Debussy's *Pagodes*:

> Of late years the bell-makers of Europe and America have adapted many Asiatic and other exotic tuneful percussion instruments to our European pitch and scale requirements, with the result that we are able to decipher Oriental music from gramophone records and perform them on these Europeanized Oriental instruments whenever we want to. I have tried the experiment of orchestrating Debussy's 'Pagodas' (the piano piece he wrote after studying the Javanese gong-orchestras at a Paris exhibition around 1888 [*sic*]) for a complete tuneful percussion group – thus, as it were, turning back to its Oriental beginnings the Asiatic music he transcribed for a Western instrument (the piano). In so doing I am merely giving it back to the sound-type from which it originally emerged.[45]

The lecture was illustrated by a performance of the Debussy piece in its original solo-piano guise, followed by Grainger's adaptation for harmonium, celeste, dulcitone, three pianos (twelve hands), xylophone, 'metal marimba' and 'wooden marimba' (each played by three percussionists), bells and glockenspiel; the manuscript of the arrangement is dated 1918.[46] Interestingly, Grainger also played on this occasion Ravel's *La vallée des cloches*, which Grainger went on to arrange for 'tuneful percussion' in 1944. The lecture

---

[44] Quoted in Wilfrid Mellers, *Percy Grainger* (Oxford: Oxford University Press, 1992), 142.

[45] The full texts of all twelve lectures are to be found in John Blacking, *'A Commonsense View of All Music': Reflections on Percy Grainger's Contribution to Ethnomusicology and Music Education* (Cambridge: Cambridge University Press, 1987), Appendix A.

[46] Balough, *A Complete Catalogue*, 234.

culminated in a performance of Grainger's own *Eastern Intermezzo* for twenty percussionists.

Britten was to encounter Indonesian music for the first time in the USA during the early 1940s, and it is surely significant that his fruitful meeting with Colin McPhee should have neatly coincided with a general rise in American composers' level of awareness of Far Eastern music. Henry Eichheim had composed a *Javanese Sketch* as early as 1918, and when he subsequently visited Java with Stokowski in 1928 he immediately afterwards embarked on an orchestral work entitled *Java* (1929) which recalls Debussy in its attempt to prolong ostinato patterns in layered textures.[47] Four years later a companion piece, *Bali*, was to follow. Writing to his mentor Henry Cowell in early 1935, McPhee dismissed Eichheim's tone-poems as 'dished-up impressionism'.[48]

Cowell (who was at one time Grainger's secretary) had been intrigued by ethnic musics since childhood and became involved in an ethnomusicology lecture course ('Music of the World's Peoples') at the New School for Social Research in New York in the 1920s. Also at this time he discovered the celebrated 1928 gramophone records of Balinese music and listened to them with McPhee. In an article written in 1933, Cowell declared that the growing tendency on the part of Western composers to borrow material from ethnic musics arose from a

> drive for vitality and simplicity. It is not an attempt to imitate primitive music, but rather to draw on those materials common to the music of all the peoples of the world, to build a new music particularly relating to our own century.[49]

Cowell's unorthodox piano writing (see below) was not the only manner in which his works betrayed his interest in Eastern musics. In 1946 he broke significant new ground in writing a solo piece entitled *The Universal Flute* for the Japanese shakuhachi, initiating a trend in the composition of Western music for authentic Japanese instruments which was to blossom in the 1970s.[50] Further innovations with a Japanese connection were made in 1962 when Cowell wrote a concerto for koto.

---

[47] Mueller, 'Javanese Influence', 177–8.

[48] Oja, *Colin McPhee*, 93.

[49] Cowell, 'Towards Neo-Primitivism', *Modern Music*, 10 (1933), 150–51.

[50] See the extensive catalogue of American compositions for shakuhachi in Kondō Jō and Joaquim Bernítez (eds.), *Contemporary Music Review*, 8/2: *Flute and Shakuhachi* (Yverdon: Harwood Academic Publishers, 1994). A fine example of contemporary writing for Japanese flute (in this case, the shinobue) is to be found in the haunting score to Akira Kurosawa's film *Ran* (which treats the plot of Shakespeare's *King Lear* in a Samurai setting), composed by Toru Takemitsu in 1985. In this score, Takemitsu also incorporates music for the drums of the Nō ensemble. Such allusions to traditional Japanese music in Takemitsu's work tend to be found in his incidental scores rather than concert works, his early stylistic development having been formulated more under the aegis of the Western avant-garde.

Cowell is best remembered, however, for his systematic exploitation of unconventional timbral effects in writing for the piano – some of which were related to his fascination with the gamelan. Tone-clusters (for which Cowell devised a special notation) are first encountered in his piano music at around the same time as Ives was trying them out in his *Concord Sonata* (1911), and a ferocious *ffff* opposition of white- and black-note clusters appears in *Antimony* (1917). To meet the increasing desire for more eccentric sonorities, the phenomenon of the 'prepared piano' emerged in the late 1930s. This blanket term describes the use of various gadgets to modify the normal piano timbre, some of Cowell's innovations requiring the strings to be stopped manually or to be struck by using hand-held mallets or plectra. John Cage was influenced by Cowell both in the sphere of ethnomusicology (Cage heard some of Cowell's 'Music of the World's Peoples' lectures in New York) and in radical piano techniques. Cage began by modifying the internal glissando played on Cowell's 'string piano' by using a gong beater and metal rod to strike the strings in *First Construction in Metal* (1939), and went on to introduce the 'prepared piano' in *Bacchanale* (1940). The latter may have been directly influenced by the sonorities and ostinato patterns of Balinese gamelan music, to which Cowell's lectures had introduced him. Cage's timbral experimentation was not necessarily allied to avant-garde musical material, however, and a work for the dull gong-like sonorities of the 'prepared piano' such as *Amores* (1943) is heavily dependent on simple modality and ostinato figurations reflecting Cage's post-Debussian interest in the gamelan. A series of works for percussion ensemble demonstrated Cage's fondness for the gamelan more overtly, especially in the stratified ostinato patterns and syncopations of *First Construction in Metal* and *Double Music* (1941). *Second Construction* (1940) includes a glockenspiel melody alluding to Balinese scales and punctuated by gong strokes. In 1946 Cage wrote an article entitled 'The East in the West' for *Modern Music*,[51] but his oriental interests were soon to be diverted into the less musically specific realm of Zen and I-Ching philosophy.

At around the same time as Cage was introducing his 'prepared piano', his fellow American Lou Harrison (who had studied with Cowell in San Francisco in 1934–5) created a metallic piano sonority by the simple ploy of sticking drawing pins into the felt covering of the hammers. Harrison collaborated with Cage in some of his percussion-ensemble projects of the 1940s, notably *Double Music*, which had utilized four percussionists and numbered three Japanese temple gongs and six Chinese gongs among its instruments. In 1949 Harrison read McPhee's article 'The Five-Tone Gamelan Music of Bali' in *Musical Quarterly*[52] and was sufficiently impressed by it to go to the trouble of writing out all McPhee's musical examples.[53] In April 1961 Harrison joined McPhee in

---

[51]   *Modern Music*, 23 (1945–6), 111–15.
[52]   *Musical Quarterly*, 35 (1949), 250–81.
[53]   Oja, *Colin McPhee*, 166.

attending a conference entitled 'East–West Music Encounter' in Tokyo; other members of the American delegation were Cowell, Elliott Carter, Virgil Thomson and the noted scholar of Javanese music, Mantle Hood. In 1963 Harrison's cross-cultural interests assumed an educational dimension when he composed his *Pacifika Rondo* for a youth orchestra consisting of both Western and oriental instruments. More recent works have included a Double Concerto for violin, cello and Javanese gamelan (1981), and together with William Colvig he has explored the construction of Western 'gamelans' tuned in just intonation and manufactured from thinwall electrical conduit and metal furniture. Neither of these last two ventures would have been possible without the extraordinary flowering of ethnomusicology in American universities and the attendant proliferation of genuine gamelans in music departments up and down the country, all ultimately stemming from McPhee's work at UCLA in the 1950s.

If Debussy's emulation of oriental musical exotica had been symptomatic of a rebellion against the tenets of nineteenth-century Austro-German music, then the so-called minimalist movement which emerged in the 1970s was equally a rebellion against the complexity and pretentiousness of much produced by the 1960s avant-garde. Minimalist composers saw in the gamelan and other ethnic musics a rhythmic and textural clarity allied to an almost hypnotic repetitiveness and absorbed these features into a new idiom which injected a breath of fresh air into contemporary music. Steve Reich studied the drumming of Ghana during the 1970s and became involved in research on the Balinese gamelan, writing in 1973 that 'non-Western music is presently the single most important source of new ideas for Western composers and musicians'.[54] These words echoed a prediction of Cowell's made some 25 years before: 'It seems to me certain that future progress in creative music for composers of the Western world must inevitably go towards the exploration and integration of elements drawn from more than one of the world's cultures.'[55] By the 1980s, borrowings from – and more generalized emulations of – oriental music had become something of a commonplace. An entire disc devoted to gamelan-inspired pieces by young Canadian composers has recently been released,[56] one blending twelve-note writing with stratified counterpoint, another subscribing to a post-Cageian interest in 'ancient Chinese philosophical thought through a Canadian perspective', and another blending elements as varied as Elvis Presley and Stravinsky in a work designed to be performed on a genuine gamelan from Sunda (West Java). That this extraordinary collection should have originated in Canada is a timely reminder of the seminal importance of that earlier Canadian composer, Colin McPhee, who in many ways made it all possible.

[54] Steve Reich, 'Postscript to a Brief Study of Balinese and African Music, 1973', in *Writings about Music* (New York: New York University Press, 1974), 38.

[55] Henry Cowell, 'Current Chronicle', *Musical Quarterly*, 34 (1948), 412. Cowell's remarks were prompted by his admiration for McPhee's *Tabuh-tabuhan* (see pp. 28–9).

[56] *Ô Bali: Colin McPhee and his Legacy* (MVCD 1057, 1993). Composers represented are Jose Evangelista, Mark Duggan, Jon Siddall and Andrew Timar.

2

Britten and Colin McPhee

Britten's precocious compositional talents revealed from an early age an unusually wide range of musical tastes. From the influences of French Impressionism and the Second Viennese School evident in the *Quatre chansons françaises* (written in the summer of 1928 at the age of fourteen) to the emulations of Mahler, Stravinsky, Schoenberg, Shostakovich and Prokofiev to be seen in works dating from his time at the Royal College of Music as a composition scholar (1930–33), the range of influences absorbed into Britten's early style was phenomenally broad. During his working apprenticeship as a composer for the GPO Film Unit (1936–8), and as the creator of incidental music for stage projects mounted by the Group Theatre and Left Theatre in the same period, Britten's ability to assimilate any musical idiom required of him grew still more pronounced. His stylistic boundaries broadened to the extent of absorbing jazz elements, either reproduced in straight pastiche (as in his music to a West End production of J. B. Priestley's *Johnson over Jordan* in 1939) or more subtly disguised (as in his brilliantly inventive score to the Auden– Isherwood collaboration *The Ascent of F6* in 1937).

Such astonishing facility was not destined to endear Britten to his critics, all the more so because he had resolutely rejected the idiom of earlier establishment composers such as Vaughan Williams in absorbing almost exclusively Continental influences. The impressive *Variations on a Theme of Frank Bridge* (1937), perhaps the finest outcome of the young composer's eclecticism, were hailed merely for their 'virtuosity', 'brilliant ingenuity' and 'strikingly original effects'.[1] Britten's Piano Concerto, dating from the following year, provoked this response from the same distinguished reviewer:

> This is not a stylish work. Mr Britten's cleverness, of which he has frequently been told, has got the better of him and led him into all sorts of errors, the worst of which are errors of taste. How did he come to write the tune of the last movement? Now and then real music crops up . . . but on the whole Mr Britten is exploiting a brilliant facility that ought to be kept in subservience.[2]

[1]   William McNaught, 'String Orchestras', *Musical Times*, 78 (1937), 990.
[2]   William McNaught, 'The Promenade Concerts', *Musical Times*, 79 (1938), 702–3.

It was to be several years before the critical tide began to turn in the composer's favour.

Britten's eclectic tastes during the 1930s were sufficiently enterprising to embrace an incipient interest in non-Western music. Between 1933 and 1940 he encountered for the first time the three musical cultures with which he was to identify more closely in later years: those of Indonesia, Japan and India. His first recorded experience of ethnic music in live performance came on 6 May 1933, when he confessed in his personal diary to having been greatly impressed by a concert of Indian music and dancing he attended at the Ambassador Theatre:

> I go to Amb. Th. at 8.45 – ticket paid for by Miss Fass[3] – to see Uday Shan-kar & his Hindu dancers (inc. Simkie & Robindra – quite young) and musicians (inc. Vishnu Dan – marvellous drummer & Timir Bawan). I haven't seen anything for ages which has thrilled me more. Marvellously intellectual & perfectly wrought dancing. Finest I have yet seen. Music, full of variety, rhythmically & tonally. One perfect creation of Shan-kar – an ecstatic dance. Tandawa Nrittya was a longer ballet with a very exciting fight.[4]

It was not until 32 years later, however, that Britten first made a specific musical sketch from Indian music, and his only direct borrowing from an Indian piece came as late as 1968 in *The Prodigal Son*.

A similarly delayed reaction is to be seen in Britten's experience of the Japanese theatre, which again he encountered for the first time during the 1930s but was not to assimilate artistically until after his seminal trip to the Far East in 1956. In 1938 Ronald Duncan (the future librettist of *The Rape of Lucretia*) founded the *Townsman*, to which the poet Ezra Pound contributed several articles on musical criticism. Noel Stock recounts a fascinating anecdote concerning a meeting between Pound and Duncan in London during 1938 which shows that Britten became involved in a rather eccentric attempt to reconstruct the atmosphere of a Japanese Nō play:

> [Pound] wanted badly to see a Noh play performed in a theatre and to this end Ronald Duncan persuaded Ashley Dukes to lend them the Mercury Theatre.[5] Benjamin Britten produced a musician who could play gongs and another of Duncan's friends, Henry Boys,[6] suggested a female dancer by the name of Suria Magito. One afternoon, with Duncan as audience, Pound recited one of his own Noh translations while the girl danced.[7]

---

3 Marjorie Fass (1884–1968), an amateur painter and musician closely connected with Britten's private composition teacher, Frank Bridge.
4 Quoted in Donald Mitchell, 'What Do We Know about Britten Now?', in Palmer (ed.), *The Britten Companion*, 40, note 23.
5 The principal haunt of the Group Theatre, where the first production of *The Ascent of F6* had been staged on 26 February 1937.
6 Henry Boys (b. 1910) was to be the dedicatee of Britten's Violin Concerto in 1939.
7 Noel Stock, *The Life of Ezra Pound* (London: Routledge and Kegan Paul, 1970), 356.

This bizarre staging was scarcely authentic, since neither female dancers nor gongs figure in the genuine Nō theatre. In 1916 Pound had published translations of fifteen Nō plays, but Britten did not obtain a copy of Pound's edition until 1953 when his thoughts turned more positively towards the Japanese theatrical arts.[8]

Only in the sphere of Indonesian music did Britten's early experiences bear almost immediate fruit, and then almost by accident. In May 1939 the composer set sail for North America in company with the tenor Peter Pears, spending a few weeks in Canada before moving south to settle in New York. After attending a performance of the *Variations on a Theme of Frank Bridge* given by the New York Philharmonic on 21 August, Britten and Pears became guests at the Long Island home of Dr William Mayer and his wife Elizabeth. These German émigrés, he a psychiatrist and she a noted patroness of the arts, provided a secure family environment in which Britten could meet many of the notable artistic personalities then active in New York City. The Mayers' visitors' book records a visit by the Canadian composer and ethno-musicologist Colin McPhee on 7 September 1939, and it may be assumed that he was a frequent guest thereafter since Dr Mayer took an active and helpful interest in the severe personal problems which constantly plagued him.[9] During the course of the next three years (Britten signed out of the same visitors' book on 16 March 1942), Britten and McPhee performed the latter's transcriptions of Balinese music for two pianos (see below) and recorded them in New York in 1941 for Schirmer (78rpm set, 513/4; tracks 1–5 on the CD accompanying this book).[10] Apart from their work on McPhee's transcriptions, the two men also performed two-piano music by other composers.[11] In February and March 1942, McPhee prepared a two-piano version of Britten's *Bridge Variations* for use as a ballet entitled *Jinx*, staged at the National Theatre by Eugene Loring's Dance Players.[12] McPhee's enthusiasm for Britten's work at this time led him to contemplate writing a survey of his output for publication in the journal *Modern Music*.

McPhee's compositions have suffered a long posthumous neglect, and at

---

[8] Britten's copy of Ezra Pound, *The Translations of Ezra Pound* (London: Faber and Faber, 1953), is preserved in *GB-ALb* 1-9500762.

[9] The Britten–Pears Library holds a collection of letters from McPhee to Dr and Mrs Mayer (acquired by Donald Mitchell from their daughter Beata) which provide a frank and sometimes harrowing insight into McPhee's clinical depression.

[10] Britten's copy of the original recordings is preserved in *GB-ALb* 3-9401034–9401038. The recordings were issued on CD in 1995 (Pearl GEMM CD 9177), transferred from a copy of the 78s in the International Piano Archives at the University of Maryland; the production team appears not to have been aware of the existence of Britten's set.

[11] A facsimile of the programme to one of their duo concerts at the Southwold Town Choral Society on 13 May 1941, which included music by Arensky and Handel, is reproduced in Mitchell and Reed (eds.), *Letters from a Life*, II, 927.

[12] See Donald Mitchell, '*Jinx*', in David Drew (ed.), *The Decca Book of Ballet* (London: Muller, 1958), 414–16. The manuscript of McPhee's arrangement is preserved at *GB-ALb*, 2-9700604.

the time of writing his music is only just beginning to achieve a modest degree of recognition, having been overshadowed by his enterprising achievements as a self-taught ethnomusicologist. Born in Montreal in 1900,[13] McPhee spent his adolescence in Toronto, beginning his musical studies at the Hamborg Conservatory where his fellow students included the English accompanist Gerald Moore. By the age of fourteen his early attempts at composition had already received press notices, and he went on to pursue more advanced studies in composition and piano at the Peabody Conservatory, Baltimore, where he graduated in 1921. Returning to Canada, McPhee began to establish a reputation as a composer, performing his own Piano Concerto with the Toronto Symphony Orchestra in 1923. A brief period of study in Paris in 1924 encouraged him, like many other American composers at the time, to adopt a neoclassical style; but his awareness of more adventurous musical idioms expanded during a subsequent apprenticeship with Varèse in New York in 1926.

In 1931 McPhee visited Bali for the first time, staying for six months in the region around Kedaton. He had already come to know something of the exciting nature of Balinese gamelan music by listening to gramophone recordings in the company of Henry Cowell (who had been active in promoting McPhee's work in New York). McPhee later recalled:

The records had been made in Bali, and the clear, metallic sounds of the music were like the stirring of a thousand bells, delicate, confused, with a sensuous charm, a mystery that was quite overpowering. I begged to keep the records for a few days, and as I played them over and over I became more and more enchanted with the sound . . . How was it possible, in this late day, for such a music to have been able to survive?[14]

It seems likely that, shortly before his departure for Indonesia, he saw the Balinese gamelan then appearing at the Paris Exposition Coloniale which was soon to influence Poulenc's Concerto for Two Pianos. This event, staged in the Dutch Pavilion, was important as the first appearance of a Balinese gamelan in the West, and the ensemble included two of the musicians from the village of Peliatan who were soon to become McPhee's friends.[15] Once on the island, his involvement with Balinese culture became so intense that (after a further three months in Paris) he returned to Indonesia in the following year, building his own house at Sayan and moving in permanently in 1933.

McPhee rapidly became established as the leading Western authority on Balinese music and in 1934 and 1935 he worked with the local composer

---

[13] Confusion surrounds the exact date of McPhee's birth, with some sources recording 1901 instead of 1900. According to Carol Oja (*Colin McPhee*, 289, note 2), McPhee was born on 15 March 1900 but began using the date 1901 after 1924 for no apparent reason.

[14] Colin McPhee, *A House in Bali* (New York: The John Day Company, 1946; repr. New York: Oxford University Press, 1987), 10.

[15] Oja, *Colin McPhee*, 65; 302, note 1.

I Wayan Lotring on the modern *kebyar* style in a special hut constructed on the beach at Kuta. Among his more notable achievements was his successful attempt to encourage the Balinese to resurrect archaic ensembles such as the gamelan *semar pegulingan* which were in danger of becoming obsolete. McPhee left Bali in December 1935 but, after two years back in the Americas, he returned for a final visit in 1936 and stayed until Christmas 1938. McPhee's time on the island is vividly chronicled in his book *A House in Bali*, and his personal effects included valuable home-movie footage of local performances.

After World War II, McPhee was appointed composer-in-residence at the Huntington Hartford Foundation in Los Angeles, and in 1960 he took up the post of lecturer in composition and Indonesian music at the University of California at Los Angeles. Ill health and lack of financial support combined to thwart his plans to revisit Bali in 1962. His unsurpassed knowledge of Balinese music as it had existed in the 1930s was distilled into the encyclo-paedic *Music in Bali*, begun in 1941 with the practical and moral support of Cowell and aided by a grant from the Guggenheim Foundation in 1942. The task of writing the book proved to be daunting, however, and on 21 July that year McPhee wrote to Britten (by that time back in the UK) to describe the Guggenheim grant as 'a drop in a bucket that leaks like a sieve'.[16] The book was not completed until shortly before McPhee's death in 1964; it was published posthumously in 1966.[17] (Britten does not appear to have obtained a copy, having long since lost contact with McPhee's work.) *Music in Bali* has remained the standard work on the subject, and is even used as a textbook at the Balinese Conservatory of the Performing Arts (Konservatorium Kerawitan, colloquially contracted to 'Kokar') in Denpasar, the island's capital city. This singular situation is an eloquent rebuff to those of today's ethnomusicologists who scorn McPhee's pioneering work in their discipline as 'amateurish'.

The contribution to ethnomusicology made by this brilliant but undisciplined mind might have been yet more significant had McPhee not bungled an early opportunity to return to Bali in September 1938 to make a systematic series of audio recordings. As we have seen, lack of funding in later years prevented his subsequent return, and his monumental book does not therefore contain any account of important post-war developments in Balinese music. There is little doubt that McPhee's idyllic years on the island in the 1930s were prolonged as a deliberate escape from his many personal problems and career insecurity. Although greatly assisted by moral and financial support from his anthropologist wife Jane Belo, whose faith in him had made the entire Balinese venture possible, McPhee's homosexual liaisons with Balinese youths placed an excessive strain on their relationship, which

[16] Mitchell and Reed (eds.), *Letters from a Life*, II, 1101.
[17] Colin McPhee, *Music in Bali: A Study in Form and Instrumental Organization in Balinese Orchestral Music* (New Haven: Yale University Press, 1966; repr. New York: The Da Capo Press, 1976).

she terminated in 1938 shortly before McPhee left Bali for the final time. Indeed, a possible reason for McPhee's departure in December 1938 was the fact that Walter Spies, the German artist responsible for the promotion of a new style of Balinese painting in Ubud, had just been imprisoned by the Dutch authorities as part of a ruthless witch-hunt against homosexuals. McPhee's later years in the USA were blighted by continuing financial insecurity (he lived for a time in a notorious New York slum) and alcoholism, to which he finally succumbed in 1964, dying of cirrhosis of the liver. The Balinese experience had been a spiritual oasis in an otherwise bleak life. As he himself commented, 'I stand for all things which might have been done – a rich blend of nostalgia and futility.'

McPhee's lack of instant success as a composer in the 1930s was typical of the creative and material struggles suffered by many emergent young American composers in those years. He destroyed many of his early works, and when he arrived in Bali he ceased composing altogether. It was the creative stimulus provided by the gamelan that inspired him to resume composition in 1935. Several of his works after this date were heavily influenced by Balinese musical procedures, although this was not to every critic's taste: Virgil Thomson, the noted US composer, told me in conversation shortly before his death that he considered McPhee to have been a fine composer 'before he got screwed up and went all Balinese'. Although McPhee's *Octette* had shown a tentative interest in Balinese scales as early as 1931, it was not until the toccata for two pianos and orchestra entitled *Tabuh-tabuhan* (1936) that McPhee showed the lengths to which he was prepared to go in the field of cross-cultural compositional borrowing.[18] The vigorous outer movements of *Tabuh-tabuhan*, which is undoubtedly McPhee's master-piece, skilfully combine elements borrowed not only from the gamelan but also from jazz and Latin American popular music, which formed two of McPhee's other great interests. The central 'Nocturne' is a setting of a tranquil melody for the Balinese flute (suling) called 'Lagu ardja'. Some of McPhee's orchestration is remarkably close to the procedures later adopted by Britten in *The Prince of the Pagodas*; so close, in fact, that it comes as something of a surprise to discover that Britten probably never heard McPhee's piece. As Britten and McPhee spent a good deal of time working on two pianos together it is, however, not inconceivable that McPhee showed Britten the score of his work for two pianos and orchestra.

McPhee described his approach to the work's instrumentation in a preface to the full score:

---

[18] The phrase 'tabuh-tabuhan' has a variety of meanings in Bali, being the name of a mallet or stick and (by extension) a generic term for percussion instruments, compositions, metrical structures or drum rhythms: see McPhee, *Music in Bali*, 25. Later McPhee works to be influenced by gamelan procedures include the Symphony no. 2 (1957) and Nocturne for Chamber Orchestra (1958).

To transfer the intricate chime-like polyphonic figurations of the gamelan keyed instruments and gong-chimes, I have used a 'nuclear gamelan' composed of two pianos, celesta, xylophone, marimba and glockenspiel. These form the core of the orchestra. The various sounds produced by hand-beaten drums are produced by pizzicato cellos and basses, low harp and staccato piano tones. I have included two Balinese gongs of special pitch, and Balinese cymbals, to which are added further gong tones simulated by pianos, horns, etc.

The choice of prominent piano sonorities to capture the gamelan sound makes McPhee's derivations part of the tradition of keyboard gamelan borrowings extending back to Debussy and Poulenc. As McPhee later commented in a 1958 radio broadcast, 'the clear, incisive tones of the gamelan seemed to find a natural echo in the tones of the piano'.[19]

Not surprisingly, therefore, the bulk of McPhee's transcriptions of gamelan pieces were conceived for one or more pianos. The most important as far as his connection with Britten is concerned are the two-piano transcriptions, three of which were published by Schirmer in 1940 under the title *Balinese Ceremonial Music*. McPhee described the genesis of these transcriptions as follows:

For the past months [in Bali during 1934] I had been engaged in writing arrangements for two pianos of some of the music I had got from Lunyuh, Lèbah and even the children. I had already given a little concert and performed a number of these with Walter [Spies], who played the piano very well, on board one of the ships from Java. There had been a 'Bali Conference', a visit of Dutch archaeologists, officials and Javanese princes to the island, and two pianos had been sent especially for the event. I was now asked to repeat it in the little harmony club at Den Pasar, and this time I invited the Regents and a few musicians to come and hear what their music sounded like when arranged in this way. They were quite delighted. They had not believed it possible. The percussive sound of the pianos was at times surprisingly close to the sound of the gamelan, and they wondered how only two musicians were able to play all the different parts, the melody, the flowers, the basic tones, the gongs. Only the drums were missing! When it was over the Regent of Tabanan made a quite charming little speech of compliments in which he lamented only that the tuning of the piano did not always match.[20]

Before the Schirmer edition appeared, McPhee had performed the first two of the published transcriptions from manuscript in concerts held in New York and Mexico City in 1936. The third transcription was made during his final

---

[19] Quoted in Oja, *Colin McPhee*, 208.
[20] McPhee, *A House in Bali*, 203–4.

stay in Bali in 1938. As well as being known to Britten, the transcriptions were performed in New York in February 1942 by Bartók and his wife.

The recordings made by Britten and McPhee in 1941 contain five pieces for two pianos: the three movements of the *Balinese Ceremonial Music* ('Pemoengkah', 'Gambangan' and 'Taboeh teloe') together with two additional unpublished numbers ('Rebong' and 'Lagu delem'). It appears that Schirmer originally planned to bring out a second set of two-piano transcriptions, but this projected volume never materialized in spite of being advertised in McPhee's *A House in Bali* in 1946.[21] Britten owned a copy of the three published pieces,[22] but does not appear to have retained a score of the two unpublished numbers. In addition to the five two-piano works, the recordings were issued with two Balinese pieces arranged by McPhee for flute and piano (including the melody 'Lagu ardja' reworked by him in *Tabuh-tabuhan*), performed by the flautist Georges Barrère. These had originated as melodies for unaccompanied suling to which McPhee had added his own piano accompaniments in Balinese style. The three 10-inch discs retailed for $2.50, and were reviewed in the *New York Times* on 15 June 1941. Ross Parmenter's article described the issues as 'enchanting music . . . excellently recorded', and praised the 'unobtrusive background' McPhee provided for the flautist's playing. He wrote:

> Artists, writers, tourists and photographers without number have returned from Bali with tales of its beauty, its civilization, and the charm of its people, but probably none has come back with more convincing proof than Colin McPhee, who has brought back, not passages of lyrical prose or mere visual representations, but the island's music.

In 1946, stimulated by the widespread success of the transcriptions, McPhee re-arranged 'Pemoengkah' and 'Gambangan' for chamber ensemble along with three Javanese pieces.

Britten was still involved with McPhee's transcriptions after his return to the UK in 1942: on 29 March 1944 he and Clifford Curzon gave them their first English performance at the Wigmore Hall, London. The programme notes for this concert were provided by Britten himself and were taken directly from the introductory notes written by McPhee for inclusion in the published scores.[23] Britten's copy of the transcriptions is inscribed from McPhee with the words: 'To Ben – hoping he will find something in this music, after all. Colin April 1940.'[24] This intriguing remark implies that Britten had not yet been convinced that Balinese music ought to interest him, and is all the more surprising in view of the undeniable influence McPhee's transcriptions

---

[21] *Ibid.*, 214.
[22] *GB-ALb* 2-9202908–9202910.
[23] See Donald Mitchell and John Evans, *Benjamin Britten: Pictures from a Life, 1913–76* (London: Faber and Faber, 1978), Plate 174.
[24] *Ibid.*, Plate 176.

appear to have had on Britten's subsequent output. Britten's awareness of Bali was rekindled in November 1943 when Pears presented him with a set of 'Bali pictures' over which the composer was 'quite crazy'.[25] By this time, however, McPhee had fallen from Britten's favour by publishing a review of the latter's *Seven Sonnets of Michelangelo* in which he described them as 'pompous show-pieces, pastiches that hold little interest . . . I am always amazed at the apparently great urge in Britten, a man of real musical gifts, to turn out one more genre piece.'[26] On 19 July 1944 Britten wrote to Elizabeth Mayer to say: 'Colin's outburst in Modern Music made me sad, but I think of him with as much affection as ever.'[27] By this time, McPhee was lodging at the same Brooklyn Heights address where Britten and Pears had rented rooms in September 1940.

Since McPhee's two-piano arrangements presented Britten with his sole experience of gamelan techniques before his renewed interest in Balinese music during the mid-1950s, it is important to examine their contents in some detail. The five transcriptions provide a comprehensive introduction to the principal styles of Balinese music, clearly illustrating the two Balinese tuning systems. 'Pemoengkah', 'Rebong' and 'Lagu delem' employ *saih gender wayang* (equivalent to Ex. 1.1), while 'Gambangan' and 'Taboeh teloe' are both in the pentatonic variant (*selisir gong*) of the heptatonic system (*saih pitu*) corresponding to Ex. 1.3. In the case of the three published items, McPhee gives the relevant scale in his introductory notes: Britten would therefore have been aware of their nature from the outset.

'Pemoengkah' (CD track 1) consists of the opening music to the *wayang kulit*, originally transcribed by McPhee in 1934. The *wayang kulit* (literally meaning 'leather puppet') is the celebrated Indonesian shadow-play in which the silhouettes of intricate two-dimensional leather puppets are cast on to a translucent screen, the long nocturnal performances accompanied by music for a quartet of metallophones (gender).[28] Donald Mitchell first pointed out the similarity between the lively, syncopated style of McPhee's transcription and a passage from *Death in Venice*,[29] and Britten's knowledge of the *wayang kulit* is confirmed by two sketches he subsequently made in Bali of a scale representing the *saih gender wayang* tuning system used principally in this genre, one of which is labelled 'Pemungkah' – the more modern spelling of the Indonesian word for 'prelude'. Britten was to hear the quartet of gender which provides the music for the shadow-play on 24 January 1956 (his last day on the island) and after his return to England he made transcriptions from the commercial recording (Parlophone MO 105) of a piece entitled

---

25 Letter from Britten to Pears, 24 November 1943: see Mitchell and Reed (eds.), *Letters from a Life*, II, 1168.
26 McPhee, 'Scores and Records', *Modern Music*, 21 (1943–4), 48–9.
27 Mitchell and Reed (eds.), *Letters from a Life*, II, 1212.
28 In Java the *wayang kulit* is accompanied by a much larger gamelan ensemble.
29 Mitchell, 'What Do We Know about Britten Now?', 43.

'gender wayang selendero' – 'selendero' here being an alternative spelling of *slendro* (the Javanese equivalent of *saih gender wayang*).[30] In addition, 'Pemungkah' forms one of the tracks on his reel-to-reel tape recording of Indonesian music (see below, Chapter 3).

McPhee's transcription of 'Gambangan' (CD track 2) also dates from 1934 and consists of music for cremation rites (*ngaben*). Britten heard the gamelan gambang himself in Bali during 1956 (several of his sketches are labelled 'cremation') and also noted down the distinctive gambang theme which he subsequently incorporated directly into *The Prince of the Pagodas* (see below, Chapter 4). McPhee's two-piano arrangement was made from a version of the 'Gambangan' scored for the full ceremonial gamelan gong *gedé*, with the melody played by the family of metallophones known as gangsa and typical interlocking accompanimental figurations provided by the reong (twelve gong-chimes strung horizontally in a wooden rack, played by four musicians). McPhee's introductory note illustrates the fashion in which the reong patterns interlock, and Britten's own interest in this technique is attested by the sketches he later made in Bali. The solo introductory passage, originally for trompong (an instrument similar to the reong but consisting of ten gong-chimes played by a single performer), displays a syncopated style strongly recalled by certain vibraphone passages in *The Prince of the Pagodas* and *Death in Venice*, and the colotomic gong punctuation was to influence many later Britten works.

The third piece of the *Balinese Ceremonial Music*, 'Taboeh teloe' (CD track 3),[31] had the furthest-reaching influence on Britten's style. It provides a particularly clear example of the *selisir* scale, and McPhee transposed the music up a semitone so that the scale centres on B♭, coincidentally the pitch at which the 'gamelan' passages of *The Prince of the Pagodas* and some in *Death in Venice* operate. These had also been the pitches used by Poulenc in borrowing material from the Peliatan gamelan in his Concerto for Two Pianos (see above, Exx. 1.3–4). The most important feature of McPhee's arrangement is the representation of the three colotomic gong strokes by three chords which are harshly dissonant with the prevailing pentatonicism. In his introductory remarks, McPhee comments: 'The fact that these three notes [*sic*] often sound dissonant with the melody must be ignored, for the gongs aim not to harmonize but to *punctuate* the melody. They should always be played comparatively softly.' In Britten's copy of the transcriptions this passage has been emphasized by a marginal pencil stroke; a representative extract showing the use of these punctuating chords is given in Figure 1, a facsimile taken from Britten's performing copy that bears his pencilled reminder to

---

[30] The sketches Britten made from live performances in Bali and from recordings after he returned home are discussed in more detail on pp. 75–85 below.

[31] The title was defined by McPhee (*Music in Bali*, 107) as a short group of compositions, any one of which may be played as a prelude to a complete programme of gamelan pieces.

Figure 1. Colin McPhee, *Balinese Ceremonial Music*,
showing Britten's pencil annotations

Ex. 2.1

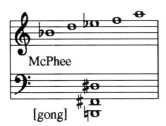

McPhee

[gong]

Britten

play the chords 'comparatively softly'. McPhee's representation of this characteristic sonority proved to be a significant influence on Britten's style. David Matthews first pointed out the striking similarity between McPhee's transcription and the 'Sunday Morning' interlude from *Peter Grimes*.[32] The parallel is even more striking than Matthews suggests, and Ex. 2.1 demonstrates the close tonal correspondence between the two works. Britten appears to have transposed the *selisir* scale down by a semitone and used this as the basis for the layered ostinati of the upper parts of the orchestral texture, which clearly owe much to his post-Debussian awareness of stratified gamelan polyphony. The punctuating triad (scored by Britten for bell, gong, harp, bassoons, tuba and double-basses) is also transposed down a semitone in order to preserve the characteristically dissonant effect. It seems unlikely to be coincidental that this derivation should occur in a work written while Britten was studying the *Balinese Ceremonial Music* with Clifford Curzon.

Many further examples of this 'punctuation' procedure will be encountered in the following pages, but an instance which may be cited here occurs in *Canadian Carnival*, a work Britten composed shortly after meeting McPhee in 1939. In a remarkable passage scored for six violin parts in a double canon (figs. 18–22), the music is punctuated by triads on harp and brass in much the same fashion as the B♭ major 'bell' triad in the example from *Peter Grimes*. Both the motivically intricate upper parts (which give an impression of suspended tonality) and the prominent punctuation strongly recall Balinese procedures, yet the jaunty compound rhythm – metrically quite alien to Balinese music – suggests even at this early stage a degree of stylistic synthesis prophetic of later developments.

McPhee's two-piano arrangements evidently had a significant effect on Britten's own style and it may safely be assumed that he retained some knowledge of their contents up to the time of his own visit to Bali in 1956. This is evident from the close connection between the sketches Britten made on the island and the material originally transcribed by McPhee. Whether or not

---

[32] David Matthews, 'Act II Scene 1: An Examination of the Music', in Brett (ed.), *Benjamin Britten: Peter Grimes*, 122. Matthews credits this insight to Bayan Northcott.

Britten's memory of the Balinese techniques introduced to him by McPhee was conscious or subconscious is clearly a matter for debate. Nevertheless, the following discussion attempts to isolate those features of works composed by Britten up to the time of his Far Eastern trip which correspond to Balinese procedures. In certain cases the direct influence of McPhee's *Balinese Ceremonial Music* is unmistakable; in others, the general approach illustrates the inherent similarity between many of Britten's methods and Balinese techniques. As argued in Chapter 1, this is an important consideration which both accounts for Britten's later revived interest in gamelan music and explains the ease of stylistic synthesis he was subsequently able to achieve.

Britten's works from the period 1939–56 contain many tonal configurations identical to the two principal Balinese scales illustrated in Exx. 1.1 and 1.3. The occurrence of *selisir* (Ex. 1.3), whether coincidental or as the result of the

Ex. 2.2

Ex. 2.3

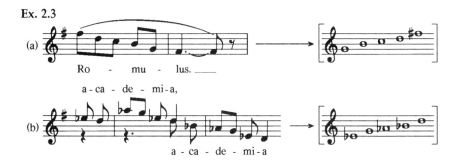

specific influence of McPhee's transcriptions, is especially notable since it was later to appear much more obviously in the 'gamelan' passages of *The Prince of the Pagodas* and *Death in Venice*. Naturally enough, the most striking examples of Britten's use of this scale before 1956 date from the period when he was most closely in contact with McPhee's transcriptions. A curious passage from *Les illuminations* (1939) accompanies the words 'les rauques musiques' with a very close canon on pizzicato strings, the melodic shape clearly derived from the unmistakable intervallic contours of *selisir* (see Ex. 2.2). Britten's use of the most distinctive Balinese scale in this almost sarcastic context may perhaps reflect his initial dislike for McPhee's arrangements, as suggested by the transcriber's inscription on Britten's copy. The intervallic pattern of Ex. 2.2, in which seconds and thirds alternate, was to become a common hallmark of Britten's style and may be compared with two passages from the later *Cantata academica*, written in 1959 – some three years after the visit to Bali (see Ex. 2.3). *Peter Grimes* (1945) contains several notable examples of melodic shapes directly recalling the intervallic contours of *selisir*, perhaps arising from the fact that the opera was composed while Britten was working on McPhee's transcriptions with Curzon. In addition to the ostinato figurations in the 'Sunday Morning' interlude, both the off-stage 'Benedicite' in Act II scene 1 (fig. 12) and Ellen's subsequent version of the same melody (fig. 15[8]) are formed from the scale. Several of the idiosyncratic chords in Britten's harmonic vocabulary at this time correspond to verticalized forms of *selisir*: examples may be drawn from *The Rape of Lucretia* (1946) and *A Charm of Lullabies* (1947) as shown in Exx. 2.4a–b. In addition, Britten frequently employs the chord given in Ex. 2.4c in contexts describing fear or anxiety (notable instances may be found in the 'Dies irae' of the *Sinfonia da Requiem*, in *A Midsummer Night's Dream* and indeed in almost every other major dramatic work) and this configuration is also contained within the intervallic pattern of *selisir*.

It is to some extent irrelevant whether these examples are the result of conscious or subconscious thought processes, or indeed merely coincidental. In view of Britten's later adoption of specific Balinese material it is far more important to isolate the ways in which Britten's tonal procedures display an

Ex. 2.4

(a) *The Rape of Lucretia*

(b) *A Charm of Lullabies*

(c)

inherent similarity to *selisir*. The tuning system contains several intervallic features which might imply to the Westerner certain characteristics of Western tonality and modality that Britten had already extensively exploited before his contact with McPhee. These properties are illustrated in Ex. 2.5. If the scale stresses F as its 'tonic',[33] the Lydian mode is strongly suggested; and

Ex. 2.5

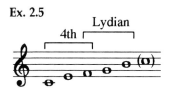

[33] In McPhee's discussion of Balinese tuning systems (*Music in Bali*, 39), the author states that any one of the five notes may become a 'tonic' by virtue of its frequent reiteration.

if C is stressed, there is a secondary emphasis on F as 'subdominant'. Both interpretations correspond to features of Britten's tonality throughout his output: he always retained a fondness for the Lydian mode and frequently stresses the subdominant of a key, sometimes sounding it simultaneously with the mediant to produce a chord directly recalling the vertical configurations which occur in gamelan compositions based on *selisir*. A fine example of the latter device is to be heard at the close of 'The Morning Star' in the *Spring Symphony* (1949), in which the tubular bells predominate in an audible reference to gamelan sonorities.

Ex. 2.6

Si co - me nel - la pen - na e nell' in - chio - stro E l'al - to e'l

We have seen that Britten was familiar with the other principal Balinese tuning system (*saih gender wayang*) from McPhee's transcriptions of 'Pemoengkah', 'Rebong' and 'Lagu delem'. Anhemitonic pentatonic scales occur in Britten's work long before his friendship with McPhee, and examples are to be found as early as the *Sinfonietta* of 1932 (opening horn theme) and *Our Hunting Fathers* (1936). They are, however, encountered with increasing frequency in the years following his contact with the Canadian: Ex. 2.6 is taken from the first of the *Seven Sonnets of Michelangelo* (1940), whilst certain passages in the *Scottish Ballad* (1941) remind us that pentatonicism is as much the property of folk-music nearer home as of the Far East.[34] The use of two pianos in the latter example, however, suggests the tangential influence of the *Balinese Ceremonial Music*, and it is significant that the later 'gamelan' effects in *The Prince of the Pagodas* were also to include a prominent part for piano duet. As we have found to be the case with *selisir*, *saih gender wayang* can produce many pentatonic chords which are a feature of Britten's harmonic vocabulary from a relatively early stage. In the *Michelangelo Sonnet* cited above, a chord of this type constitutes the principal harmony, and similar instances occur in Sonnetto XXXII.

Britten's early interest in pentatonic configurations may also be related to the strong influence on his style of the music of Mahler and Berg. Mahler was, of course, himself influenced by oriental cultures and deliberately used pentatonic scales to create exotic musical effects. Especially notable in the present

---

[34] As Roy Howat has pointed out ('Debussy and the Orient', 48, note 10), this is equally true of Debussy, whose fondness for pentatonic folk-songs (including Scottish examples) similarly parallels his interest in Javanese pentatonicism.

context is his use of an unresolved added-sixth chord at the conclusion of *Das Lied von der Erde* (1909), which was directly emulated by Berg in the closing bars of his Violin Concerto – the posthumous première of which Britten attended in Barcelona on 19 April 1936. Chords of this type are a direct product of anhemitonic pentatonicism. Britten's use of them in the third movement of the *Sinfonia da Requiem* of 1940 (fig. 42) recalls the work of both Austrian composers, both in terms of sonority and in the structural importance assigned to the chords themselves. Furthermore, Donald Mitchell has explored Mahler's use of heterophonic procedures in *Das Lied*, which may well have stimulated Britten's interest in similar polyphonic techniques to be found in the Balinese gamelan.

Ex. 2.7

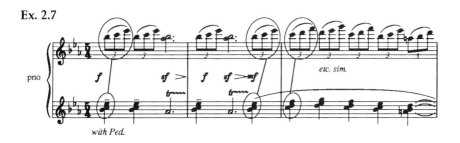

We could considerably extend the list of examples of pentatonicism in early Britten without much further profit, but one occurrence is worthy of isolation. The pentatonic opening of 'Proud Songsters' from *Winter Words* (1953) demonstrates an important equality between melody and harmony which is subsequently exploited throughout the piece (see Ex. 2.7). In much of Britten's music, both melody and harmony are different manifestations of an identical pitch content, and we will see in Chapter 6 how this harmonic device reaches its culmination in the sparse textures of the Church Parables. In these three works, composed under the direct influence of Japanese Gagaku techniques, the harmony is mostly an aggregation of successive melodic notes, sustained and thus sounding simultaneously. Two much earlier but no less striking examples of this procedure may be cited: the first, from *The Rape of Lucretia* (1946), occurs in the brawl in Act I scene 1, where each vocal taunt is sustained to create the harmony which underpins the subsequent section (fig. 17), while the second is the first appearance of the dodecaphonic theme in *The Turn of the Screw* (1954), where every melodic note is sustained to form a twelve-note chord.

Britten's strong interest in the vertical conflation of linear material explains his notable fondness for the harp, an instrument in which the melodic and harmonic dimensions are always delimited by the same restrictive scale. The

Ex. 2.8

relationship between this basic characteristic of Britten's style and his interest in gamelan music is fairly obvious: the quintessentially melodic conception of the Balinese repertory ensures that any 'harmonic' element is a by-product of, and directly related to, the melody. With *saih gender wayang* the combination of several melodic strands will always sound euphonious to the Westerner, but the semitones in the *selisir* scale create colourful 'dissonances' which are reproduced whenever Britten uses it himself. It should be stressed, however, that the absence of a real harmonic dimension in gamelan music makes the Western concept of dissonance meaningless to the Balinese. In all the various chord structures Britten later derived directly from *selisir* and *saih gender wayang*, the interval of a second is prominent. A list of Britten's use of this interval (in both major and minor forms) as a harmonic feature would be almost endless,[35] and there can be little doubt that the composer would have been predictably attracted by the frequent occurrence of what he would have interpreted as tone and semitone clashes in Balinese music. In playing McPhee's two-piano transcriptions, of course, Britten would certainly have been struck by the ubiquitous appearance of major and minor seconds and the transcriptions would have provided a clear illustration of a musical characteristic already inherent in Britten's compositional practice.

Britten's first significant use of heterophonic techniques which may be related to those of the Balinese gamelan occurs during the Prologue to *Paul Bunyan* (see Ex. 2.8), written in 1940 when the composer was in close contact with McPhee. Mitchell writes that

in the brief, chiefly orchestral passage that heralds the unusual phenomenon of the moon turning blue (Figures 11–12), we discover that . . . Britten's ear and imagination had seized on something in the McPhee transcriptions and put it to bold, if brief, use. The passage represents, albeit in very simple though effective form, the pure heterophonic principle with which Britten had become familiar through his acquaintance with McPhee and with McPhee's pioneering work as transcriber . . . The importation of an exotic technique into *Paul Bunyan* (which otherwise had more to do with Broadway than Bali) would be inexplicable were it not for the model that *Balinese Ceremonial Music* provided. It is true, of course, that something alien and unexpected was musically required in order to match the exceptional dramatic moment (a blue moon) and Britten was stimulated to seek out a kind of music that was equally outside everyday expectation. However, that it took the shape it did was entirely due to the meeting in New York with McPhee.[36]

---

[35] Many examples are cited in Donald Mitchell, 'Catching on to the Technique in Pagoda-land', *Tempo*, 146 (1983), 13–24, repr. in Palmer (ed.), *The Britten Companion*, 208–10; subsequent citations of this article also refer to the reprint.

[36] 'What Do We Know about Britten Now?', 41.

There can be no doubt that the polyphonic stratification of this passage, in which rhythmic activity increases as the register rises, was influenced by Balinese music. Britten's heterophony employs various augmentations and diminutions of a basic melodic cell (labelled x in Ex. 2.8), moving in minims at the lowest level, and clearly inspired by the *pokok* ('stem', i.e. nuclear theme) in gamelan music. The triplet figurations, E minor tonality and motivic rigour are not part of the Balinese style, but the surface debt to the gamelan is unmistakable. The use of this 'exotic' technique to depict a super-natural event is itself significant, since many of Britten's later applications of Balinese material were to fulfil precisely the same musico-dramatic function.

Ex. 2.9

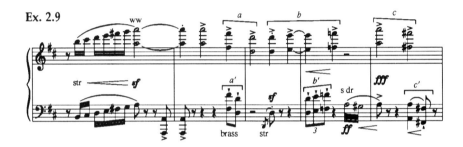

In spite of Mitchell's description of Ex. 2.8 as Britten's 'first heterophonic exercise',[37] there is evidence to suggest that Britten was interested in similar heterophonic techniques long before he met McPhee. One of the most striking examples appears in *Our Hunting Fathers* (1936). In the extract given in Ex. 2.9, motivic cells are subject to simultaneous diminution and augmentation in a fashion analogous to the more extended procedure shown in the *Bunyan* example. More importantly, in both cases this technique constitutes a deliberate blurring through displacement of what is, in effect, a single melodic line. It is in this respect that Britten's heterophonic procedures most closely resemble those of Balinese music. If the treatment of the individual melodic cells labelled $a-c$ in Ex. 2.9 is further examined, however, we may see that Britten is merely extending his strong interest in close canonic imitation. This contrapuntal preoccupation surfaces as early as the *Sinfonietta* of 1932. If we look again at Ex. 2.2 above, we find that Britten employs very close stretto at the unison and octave in the passage from *Les illuminations* derived from *selisir*. This implies, especially in the light of the essentially imitative construction of Ex. 2.9, that Britten himself saw some connection between canon and heterophony. As we shall see in Chapter 6, the robing music in the Church Parables (widely considered to be the most conspicuous examples of

---

[37] *Ibid.*

Plate 1. Britten and Colin McPhee in New York, *c.*1940

Plate 2. Britten's tour party in Balinese costume, 20 January 1956

a heterophony specifically influenced by oriental music in Britten's entire output) is also constructed from stretto imitation and the simultaneous rhythmic diminution of melodic cells.

In all these cases, it was clearly the effect of 'blurring' a single melodic line which was uppermost in Britten's mind. Both in this and in the evident concern for polyphonic stratification of the kind exemplified by the Balinese gamelan, Britten's heterophony in this early period may indeed have been influenced by McPhee's transcriptions. As we have seen, the type of heterophony he was to develop after 1939 exploited contrapuntal preoccupations already evident in his style well before his contact with McPhee. We shall also see that his experience of Japanese Gagaku and shamisen songs in 1956 provided him with a closer model for the 'blurring' of a single melodic line.

Between 1941 and 1955 Britten's use of the heterophonic techniques outlined above significantly increased. *A Ceremony of Carols* (1942) provides two examples of the simple non-alignment of two parts carrying the same melody (in 'That yongë child' and the final eight bars of 'Interlude'; the intervallic contours of the second passage strongly suggest the continuing influence of *selisir*). Works composed in 1945 yield a larger amount of heterophonic or canonic writing, with passages in *The Holy Sonnets of John Donne* (no. 3) and the Second String Quartet (second movement, fig. A) demonstrating the displacement of a single line to produce the frequent tone and semitone clashes we have already shown to be part of Britten's perception of gamelan music. In *Peter Grimes* the fluid canonic entries of the strings in Peter's famous aria 'Now the Great Bear and Pleiades' (Act I, fig. 76) and the ostinati in the 'Sunday Morning' interlude can both be interpreted in similar terms. The subsequent development of ensemble recitatives in *Albert Herring* (1947) saw an important rhythmic liberation which allowed several imitative parts to be presented in free metrical displacement, thus strikingly foreshadowing the Japanese-inspired rhythmic procedures of the Church Parables. The *Spring Symphony* (1949) contains a passage of heterophony in which the prominent octave doublings recall Balinese melodic techniques (see Ex. 2.10). *Billy Budd* (1951) utilizes heterophonic symbolism in the drumhead court-martial scene, where the deliberations of the three officers are all variants of one melodic line which represents the only possible outcome of the situation (Act II, figs. 89–93). Finally, *The Turn of the Screw* continues to

Ex. 2.10

Ex. 2.11

demonstrate Britten's proclivity for canonic techniques and also contains more adventurous heterophonic displacements of the kind illustrated in Ex. 2.11.

It will be evident that Britten had developed his own brand of heterophony to a considerable extent by the time of his visit to Bali in 1956, and explored a number of varied musical and musico-dramatic applications of the technique which leave the gamelan model far behind. Nevertheless, as Mitchell asserts, there can be little doubt that the knowledge of Balinese music he had originally gained through his friendship with McPhee provided the stimulus which encouraged him to develop this aspect of his compositional style.

As we have already pointed out, the construction of gamelan music is fundamentally linear, with various decorated forms of the basic melody or *pokok* superimposed; harmonic considerations are therefore of secondary, if not entirely negligible, importance. It has often been noted that Britten employs similar priorities in the Church Parables, where restrictive modalities allow for a paradoxical freedom in superimposing rhythmically independent lines. Once again, this compositional feature is not merely a direct importation from oriental music as a result of the world tour of 1955–6 but a characteristic already discernible many years earlier. To some extent its development is connected with the search for a versatile recitative idiom in Britten's operatic output, and certainly its first significant appearance is at the end of Act I of *Peter Grimes* where the characters' concluding remarks are set in a tempo quite independent of the quaver ostinati prolonged by the strings (which represent the storm outside). The idea is more fully and flexibly developed in *Albert Herring*, and by the time of *The Turn of the Screw* this device has become sufficiently widespread to give the strong impression of what might usefully be termed 'polyphonic stratification' – a label we have already applied to gamelan music and to the distinctive layered textures Debussy first derived from it. Such stratification also occurs within a fixed metrical framework in a manner correspondingly more reminiscent of the gamelan style: the opening movement of the *Spring Symphony*, for example, culminates in the simultaneous presentation of the passages for percussion, strings, woodwind and brass which were heard independently earlier in the movement. The entire section is punctuated by gong strokes, a feature emphasizing the similarity to Balinese structural methods. A similar procedure is adopted for the final scene of Act I in *The Turn of the Screw*, where all the melodic strands are superimposed as the twelve-note 'screw' theme is recapitulated by the horn (fig. 87). In this instance the resonant gong punctuation, here symbolizing the presence of the ghost of Miss Jessel, is all the more important in view of the complete absence of harmonic progression: the music revolves a static pitch collection in the manner of much of the composer's later 'gamelan' effects, and the gong acts as a necessary sonorous anchor to the texture.

Britten's fondness for the sonority of broad gong strokes will be evident from the preceding section, and other illustrations of his use of this instrument as a form of punctuation in the gamelan fashion may be found as early as the *Scottish Ballad* of 1941 (bars 65–76 and 124–30) and *The Young Person's Guide to the Orchestra* (1945), where the harp variation looks directly ahead to the music for the King of the East in Act I of *The Prince of the Pagodas*. The gong is an important instrument in *Peter Grimes*, punctuating the central section of the 'Storm' interlude (Act I, fig. 58) and adding resonance to the McPhee-inspired bitonal bell strokes in 'Sunday Morning'. The orchestration of *The Turn of the Screw* is an especially rich example of Britten's general fondness for tuned and metallic percussion even prior to his Balinese trip. Variation VII (which portrays nightfall) is scored for horn, harp and celeste with prominent gong punctuation in a texture curiously reminiscent of gamelan music. Although there is no specific thematic or tonal connection with Balinese music in this instance, the shimmering effect in performance is uncannily close to the indistinct sound of a gamelan heard at night from some distance away. The effect is all the more surprising since it occurs before Britten's own visit to Bali in 1956, but it is fascinating to note that Britten's travelling-companion Prince Ludwig made a point of referring to this aural phenomenon during their Balinese trip ('there is a gurgling and growling from the distance – the gamelan is rehearsing').[38] It is quite possible, of course, that Britten might have heard some of McPhee's tape recordings of live gamelan music in addition to playing his two-piano transcriptions, and some of Britten's gramophone records of gamelan music may have been in the composer's possession before 1954. The symbolic importance of the celeste and gong sonorities in the *Screw* (which represent throughout the opera the fatal allure the two ghosts hold over the children) is also significant in the light of later musico-dramatic developments, and we have already seen that Britten employed consciously 'exotic' devices for dramatic effect as early as *Paul Bunyan*.

[38] Prince Ludwig of Hesse and the Rhine, *Ausflug Ost* (Darmstadt: privately printed, 1956), 49. For further discussion of this source, see below, Chapter 3. Britten's fondness for tuned percussion is examined in Christopher Palmer, 'Britten's Venice Orchestra', in Donald Mitchell (ed.), *Benjamin Britten: Death in Venice*, Cambridge Opera Handbooks (Cambridge: Cambridge University Press, 1987), 130–32.

It is not surprising to discover that the last work Britten composed before leaving the UK for the Far East in November 1955 is particularly important in terms of the technical features outlined above. The exact date of the little-known *Hymn to St Peter* is therefore of some interest and it is ironic that this should be one of the very few Britten manuscripts not to have been dated by the composer. It was first performed on 20 November 1955 at St Peter Mancroft, Norwich, as part of the church's quincentenary celebrations. The only evidence assisting in a more exact date for the work's composition is a letter dated 2 March 1955 from BBC Birmingham to the composer, which asks if the anthem will be ready in time for a BBC Midland Singers concert to be given at St Peter Mancroft on 26 June. This performance presumably never materialized and we can be relatively certain that Britten was occupied with the work in the late spring or early summer of that year, and that for some reason its completion was delayed – perhaps because of the difficulties work on *The Prince of the Pagodas* was causing him at the time.

Ex. 2.12

A notable feature of the plainsong 'Tu es Petrus' (Alleluia and Verse of the Common of Holy Popes) on which the piece is based is the pentatonic passage first heard in the organ's announcement of the first two phrases of the chant at the beginning of the anthem (marked with a bracket in Ex. 2.12). As with the plainsongs Britten later selected as his melodic raw material for the three Church Parables, this pentatonic flavour affects much of the work. The chant's second phrase is heard throughout the subsequent choral section as an ostinato in the pedals (marked with brackets in Ex. 2.13). This is repeated eleven times, its five-and-a-half beat rhythmic profile setting up a subtle

Ex. 2.13

metrical scheme as it constantly changes its relationship to the steadily progressing crotchets of the voices. The concept of polyphonic stratification is obvious (here with the most active part in the lowest register in contrast to the norm), and both the pentatonic emphasis and the repetitive motivic structure may be directly related to gamelan techniques. Above this bass ostinato, the first phrase of the vocal line is derived from the Alleluia of the chant and is itself pentatonic; it is sufficiently similar to the ground-bass pattern to produce a heterophonic effect when the two are combined. The only non-pentatonic note in the entire treble melody of this first section is the accented E♭ at 'They shall remember Thy name', a part of the text requiring deliberate emphasis. After a rather dry middle section and subsequent reprise, the final note (G) in the coda is sustained throughout the pentatonic ascending phrase on the organ which closes the work, and it is left unresolved as the added sixth to a B♭ major chord. This chord again recalls the influence of Mahler and Berg,[39] and Britten emphasizes the fluidity of the pentatonic scale from which it is derived by inconclusively retaining F as the root in the pedals.

There can be no doubt that, by the time of his own visit to the Far East in 1956, Britten's style was in a number of significant respects well suited for the importation of more specific Balinese material that was to take place in *The Prince of the Pagodas*. It has been seen that scales equivalent to *selisir* and *saih gender wayang* occur in Britten's music throughout the period *c.*1939–55. The appearance of *selisir*, with its distinctive intervallic contours, probably reflects the direct influence of McPhee's *Balinese Ceremonial Music*. In contrast, we have seen how anhemitonic pentatonicism was already a feature of Britten's style well before his contact with the transcriptions. His interest in the possibilities offered by heterophony and polyphonic stratification is similarly divisible into two categories: extended examples clearly inspired by Balinese music, and frequent cases which illustrate the composer's general fascination with related contrapuntal techniques. In addition, we have seen how Britten favoured schemes of colotomic gong punctuation and the sonorities of tuned percussion instruments which were almost certainly inspired by the limited knowledge of the gamelan he had gained from McPhee. In some cases, it is clearly impossible to decide whether these correspondences with gamelan techniques are coincidental or the result of conscious borrowing, but their very frequency convincingly demonstrates a notable degree of inherent affinity with the overtly Balinese procedures that were to emerge in Britten's music after 1956.

---

[39] Britten's chord is identical in its pitch content to the famous example which closes Berg's Violin Concerto (see above).

3

Bali

When Britten and Pears set off for Harwich on Monday, 31 October 1955, driven by their assistant Jeremy Cullum, they were faced with a five-month itinerary comprising a punishing schedule of recitals, orchestral concerts, broadcasts and official functions scattered across half the globe. The tour had been in the planning stages for many months, with Pears writing to Britten from the Ansbach Festival on 30 July 1955 to say:

> Peg & Lu [Hesse][1] are of course very much here . . . We have of course discussed the world tour a lot (Peg's brother David [Geddes][2] & wife have been here till today) & everyone advises us not to cross the Pacific, v. expensive and tiring – Much better they say to come back same way or over the top. In any case I suggest we agree to cut the Pacific & Mexico etc, & either come back the way we came more or less, or stay longer everywhere & then dash back over the old North Pole.

The route finally adopted did indeed avoid traversing the Pacific, the party returning home westwards from Japan (which marked the limit of their travels east). Their movements may be reconstructed in some detail, since Britten wrote many substantial letters home during the tour and Pears kept an informative but somewhat erratic diary during its latter stages.[3] From January 1956 these accounts are augmented by Prince Ludwig's travel diary, which relates their movements in the Far East and in the Indian subcontinent on the journey home.[4]

---

[1] Prince Ludwig of Hesse and the Rhine (1908–68) and his Scots wife Margaret ('Peg') Geddes were both generous patrons of the Aldeburgh Festival. Under the pseudonym Ludwig Landgraf, the prince provided the German translations of Britten's *The Turn of the Screw, Noye's Fludde, Nocturne, War Requiem, Curlew River* and *The Burning Fiery Furnace*. Britten was later to complete *Death in Venice* at the Hesses' home, Schloss Wolfsgarten.

[2] David Geddes was a director of Jardine Matheson, Hong Kong, and was to provide hospitality for Britten's tour party during their time in the colony in February 1956.

[3] See Philip Reed (ed.), *The Travel Diaries of Peter Pears, 1936–1978*, Aldeburgh Studies in Music, 2 (Woodbridge: The Boydell Press, 1995) – a mine of invaluable information on details relating to Britten's world tour, especially his exhausting concert and broadcasting schedule.

[4] Prince Ludwig of Hesse, *Ausflug Ost.* This invaluable document runs to more than 160 pages and the bulk has remained untranslated apart from four brief extracts included in Prince Ludwig of Hesse, 'Ausflug Ost, 1956', in Gishford (ed.), *A Tribute to Benjamin Britten*, 56–66. All translations included here are by the present author, and appear by kind permission of HRH the late Princess Margaret of Hesse and the Rhine.

Lastly, both Britten's and Pears's pocket engagement diaries provide a full record of their travelling arrangements and details of their many public appearances.[5]

Crossing on the day boat to The Hook, where they met their agent Peter Diamand, Britten and Pears drove on to Amsterdam in good time for their first concert on 1 November. They remained in Holland for a few days in order to rehearse for forthcoming recitals and visit friends, including the British ambassador, Sir Paul Mason, who supplied them with contact addresses which were to prove useful when they arrived in the Far East. On 4 November they travelled by train to Düsseldorf for a stay of three days, giving a concert in the city and another at the Stadthalle, Wuppertal. Moving on to Stuttgart for a recital on 8 November, they then travelled into Switzerland and performed at Geneva (10 November) and Zürich (11 November). In Switzerland Britten was characteristically struck down with a stomach bug, a complaint which was to dog him throughout the remainder of the tour and which was not to be improved by his later, somewhat reluctant, contact with oriental cuisines. On 12 November they flew to Vienna and were received at the airport in the manner of international celebrities, finding the city in the throes of celebrating the opening of the rebuilt opera house. Pears performed Britten's *Winter Words* on the day after their arrival, and three days later Britten conducted an orchestral concert including his *Serenade*, *Sinfonietta* and own arrangement of Purcell's Chacony in G minor. By way of relaxation, they were taken to a 'dreary' performance of Wagner's *Die Meistersinger* conducted by Fritz Reiner in the newly refurbished Opera.

After a visit to Salzburg to give a concert in the Mozarteum (17 November), the next country on the itinerary was Yugoslavia where they arrived on 20 November. Two concerts were given, one at Ljubljana on 21 November, the other in Maribor a day later (this coming as a surprise to Britten and Pears, who had not been informed of it in their schedule). At Zagreb they attended *Peter Grimes* in Serbo-Croat on 23 November, having been unable to arrive in the city in time to see it as a forty-second birthday present for Britten the day before. On 29 November, Britten and Pears met President Tito in the Serbian capital Belgrade after attending a performance by the local university choir.

'We really are in the East now . . . We see Asia close across the Bosphorus opposite the Hotel!', wrote Britten excitedly to Anthony Gishford from the Istanbul Hilton on 2 December. They had arrived in Turkey three days before and were due to stay for ten days, during which time Britten found a spare moment to dash off (for James Blades) his *Timpani Piece for Jimmy*, sending the manuscript directly to Imogen Holst back in the UK. Britten later described his reaction to the musical climate they encountered in Turkey:

5 *GB-ALb* [uncatalogued].

What was also exciting about Turkey, was the keeness [sic] of the young people about music – <u>our</u> Western music, that is. They have themselves their own Turkish music, Oriental stuff, which honestly I think pretty poor & boring (nothing like Indian music), & one of the things Attatürk did was to encourage, along with all things Western, European music. So you have a great split – the older people liking their own monodic stuff, & the younger craving for our stuff, & sometimes doing it well. I met one very good composer, Cemal Reşid,[6] whom I'm trying to get published in England . . .[7]

Britten's ability to discriminate sharply between ethnic musics is not surprising from a composer who was subsequently able to demonstrate such an extraordinarily perceptive grasp of the essential techniques of Balinese and Japanese music after only limited exposure to them.

Britten and Pears gave two recitals in Turkey, one at Ankara on 6 December (unlikely highlights of their stay in the city were a local rehearsal of *Let's Make an Opera* and a performance of Verdi's *Un ballo in maschera*) and the second back in Istanbul on 11 December, the day of their evening departure for Karachi via Beirut. On 13 December they travelled to Bombay and were in Delhi six days later, Britten complaining that he found it difficult to make the sudden adjustment from the snows of eastern Europe to the intense heat of the Indian subcontinent.[8] Apart from single concerts in Bombay (15 December) and Delhi (a radio broadcast on 21 December), which included *Winter Words* and songs by Haydn and Schubert, Britten and Pears found the opportunity to relax for the first time on the tour. On 18 December they made an excursion to the Poona and Khale Caves, and four days later were bowled over by hearing Indian music in live performance. Britten wrote to Mary Potter:

Yesterday we had our first <u>real</u> taste of Indian music, & it was tremendously fascinating. We had the luck to hear one of the best living performers (composer too), & he played in a small room to us alone – which is as it should be, not in concerts. Like everything they do it seemed much more relaxed & spontaneous than what we do, & the

---

6   Cemal Reşit Rey (1904–85), who wrote under the name Djémac Réchid. He held appointments as Professor of Piano at the Istanbul Conservatory and Director of Music to Ankara Radio. Britten probably met him at a morning concert of modern Turkish music held in an Istanbul cinema on 4 December.

7   Letter to Roger Duncan, written from Bombay on 19 December 1955. Britten had promised to write a series of diary letters to Roger, son of Ronald Duncan and then a boy of twelve, and he remained true to his word. Roger, who was Britten's godson, had spent part of the previous August with him at Aldeburgh, as Britten reveals in a letter to Basil Coleman dated 25 September 1955: 'I had little Roger here for a fortnight – which was enchanting. He is a dear child, & a most sweet & gay companion. He stayed a few days with us in Chester Gate last week, seeing the operas before he went back to school. His is not an easy home life, as you know, & I think it's a relief to him to have an avuncular refuge!' For further information on Britten's young correspondent, see Humphrey Carpenter, *Benjamin Britten: A Biography* (London: Faber and Faber, 1992), 336–8.

8   Letter to Mary Potter, 23 December 1955.

reactions of the other musicians sitting around was really orgiastic. Wonderful sounds, intellectually complicated & controlled. By jove, the clever Indian is a brilliant creature – one feels like a bit of Yorkshire Pudd. in comparison.[9]

The performer in question was none other than the famous sitarist Ravi Shankar (b. 1920), who played to Britten and Pears in a studio of All India Radio. By this time Pears had begun his travel diary, in which he comments:

Ravi Shankar, a wonderful virtuoso, played his own Indian music to us at the Radio station & we attended a Broadcast. Brilliant, fascinating, stimulating, wonderfully played – first on a full orchestra of about 20 musicians, then solo on a sort of zither [sitar]. Starting solo (with a plucked drone background from 2 instruments always) & then joined halfway through by a man playing two drums; unbelievable skill & invention.[10]

We know Britten to have been fascinated by Indian music as early as the 1930s, and he was to enthuse about it further during the return leg of the world tour.

After meeting Prime Minister Nehru, Britten and Pears spent the Christmas period at Agra, close to the Taj Mahal ('a superb building, wonderfully beautiful – made of white marble with inlays – & with a superb dome floating (or apparently – in the moonlight) above it').[11] They returned to Delhi on Boxing Day to stay with a friend of Pears's who was active in the petroleum business, and then flew to Calcutta on the following morning in a Douglas Skymaster with an eccentric ventilation system which, according to the account in Pears's diary, 'swung wildly from icy breeziness which made one cower under a rug, to blasts of heat which set one gasping. Arrived shattered.'[12] In Calcutta, they gave a concert on 28 December and made a half-hour broadcast for the local studio of All India Radio on New Year's Day 1956. They also saw a performance by Martha Graham's ballet company, Pears noting in his travel diary that it constituted 'basically pretentious and sentimental American folksiness'.[13] They left a New Year's party early, 'but not before Ben had been cornered by Martha Graham and asked for a Ballett [sic] about Heloise & Abelard, to be made as a Coloured Film!'[14]

---

[9] *Ibid.*
[10] Reed (ed.), *The Travel Diaries of Peter Pears*, 30.
[11] Letter from Britten to Roger Duncan, 23 December 1955.
[12] Reed (ed.), *The Travel Diaries of Peter Pears*, 32–3.
[13] *Ibid.*, 33.
[14] *Ibid.*, 35. This project was destined never to reach fruition. With the (as yet unfinished) score of *The Prince of the Pagodas* lying on his desk back in Aldeburgh, Britten must have seemed fair game for an approach with a view to his producing a further ballet score. See also Mitchell and Reed (eds.), *Letters from a Life*, II, 1205, for Britten's interest in the story of Abelard and Héloïse.

While Britten and Pears were in Calcutta, Prince Ludwig and Peg Hesse had flown from Frankfurt to India, spending eight days independently in the country before flying further east for their rendezvous with Britten and Pears in Singapore. They had been in the Lion City since 2 January, performing Schumann's *Dichterliebe* on the 4th. On 6 January, the day the Hesses joined them, a second recital included Schubert's *Die schöne Müllerin*. After the concert the augmented tour party repaired to the performers' hotel for a Chinese dinner. Pears, who always relished exotic cuisine,[15] described the meal in his diary:

> I had been bold and had ordered fascinating things like fried prawns, & some sort of old meat in rice, but Ben thinking of his tummy had ordered safe sounding things which turned out to be identical dishes i.e. Chicken Soup with beans, beans with noodles, & chicken chop suey or something, all quite uneatable with chopsticks. After an hour we went to bed, Ben exhausted with frustration and still hungry . . .[16]

Britten commented:

> I couldn't get the stuff to my mouth, and after an hour I gave up, still hungry, & quite exhausted. The only people who enjoyed it were the waiters, who laughed themselves silly.
> Actually since then we've had other Chinese food, much nicer – shark's fin soup, & bird's nest soup too . . . one eats the oddest things in these parts of the world, but often they are very nice, if you can forget what it is you are actually eating.[17]

On the day following their performance of the *Müllerin* cycle, Britten and Pears left Singapore with the Hesses and flew to Java (see Figure 2) for the first week of their visit to Indonesia. They landed in Jakarta at 5.50 p.m. on 7 January, having broken their flight at Palembang in Sumatra, and were greeted with horrendous traffic jams. The party were due to stay with friends from the British Council, and their concert in the Indonesian capital took place on the evening of their arrival. Pears paused to record in his diary the arrangements governing their activities in Indonesia:

> Our patrons in Indonesia are 'the Union of Art-circles' (KunstKring Bond), a Dutch organisation consisting of 30 centres in Indonesia, a membership which pays a little subscription, the whole thing heavily sub-sidised by Holland [. . .] they are arranging all travel, accomodation [*sic*],

---

15 Both Pears's 1955–6 travel diary and his later privately published journal *Armenian Holiday* (Colchester: Benham and Company, 1965) attest the verve with which he sampled local fare, which is often described in inordinate detail. This was in marked contrast to Britten, who always favoured old-fashioned English recipes and was never happier than when devouring a pot of clotted cream or a suet pudding.

16 Reed (ed.), *The Travel Diaries of Peter Pears*, 36.

17 Letter from Britten to Roger Duncan, written from Bali on 18 January 1956.

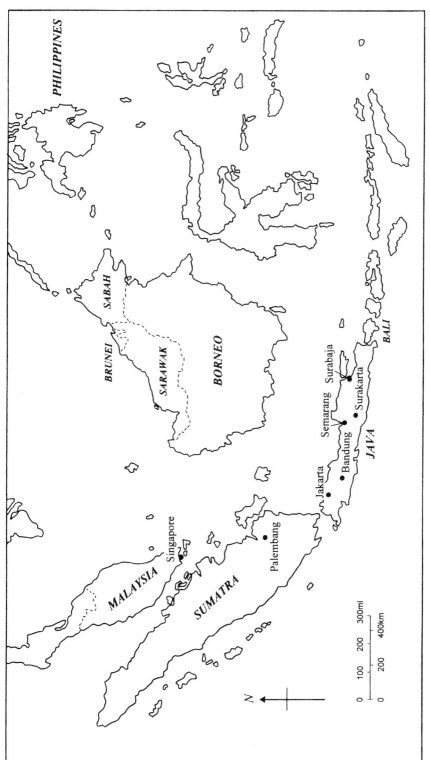

Figure 2. Map of South-East Asia

etc for BB., PP., & the Hessens, and have provided us with a mentor, guide, & musical-lexicon in Bernhard van Ijzerdraat,[18] of whom also more later. The KunstKring asked us in the first place to do 30 concerts in Insia; that meant at least 2 months here. We said NO but we might do 5 or 6. They said 'Yes'.

We have met our Secretary, Treasurer, etc and all seem agreeable.

. . . First concert in Djakarta[19] [8 January] in long narrow hall: awkward for singing: Dutch officials being very Dutch and stiff in interval and after concert: my voice hates the tropics: very wet and hot: more weak whisky and water after concert: 'Kidneys must be flushed frequently in tropics.'[20]

Pears went on to record details of their flight in an 'old Dakota' to Bandung on 8 January, where

Ijzerdraat put on some very sweet music for us, a bamboo flute and a sort of zither played by two teachers, gentle, charming, skilful, civilised; also witnessed class of tots (5–9) being coached in dance – much finger-, wrist-, arm-movement, slow, control-needing. Concert in school hall holding 1000; pleasant; a number of Indonesians in audience . . .[21]

Britten was later to receive a tape recording of this 'very sweet music' from Bandung, which constituted his first experience of Indonesian music in live performance. Prince Ludwig provides a more detailed description of the occasion:

Siesta. Then Mr Ijserdraat (who is escorting us for the whole tour of Indonesia) takes us to a schoolhouse situated behind our hotel . . . All the rooms inside are full of little girls learning to dance to the sound of a small orchestra consisting chiefly of percussion. They swing their bodies and move hands which are bent backwards, gliding and standing still. The youngest group is about five years of age. They all wear, over European children's clothes, batik sarongs with waistbands from which sashes hang down at both ends . . . A zither- and flute-player come into the adjoining room. The zither [kacapi] is very large, shaped like a ship, with many metal strings stretched over it. The bamboo flute [suling] has six fingerholes[22] . . . The zither begins, a sound like groping around. The flute follows suit. I cannot comprehend the whole effect,

---

[18] The correct spelling is IJzerdraat, with two initial capital letters. Not surprisingly, the name appears in Britten's, Pears's and Prince Ludwig's writings in a variety of different forms. Regrettably, Bernard IJzerdraat died on 25 January 1986, approximately two months before the author was able to trace his address; his widow (Mrs Suryabrata) still lives in Jakarta.

[19] Pears uses the old, Dutch-influenced spelling.

[20] Reed (ed.), *The Travel Diaries of Peter Pears*, 40–41.

[21] *Ibid.*, 41–2.

[22] This description is curious, since the Javanese suling traditionally has only four or five fingerholes. See Sorrell, *A Guide to the Gamelan*, 42.

hearing only the waterlike tone of the flute and the sound of the zither changing direction, seemingly independent of each other. Then a song, where they both come together in a strident melody. The pieces die away slowly and without a final emphasis. Ben and Peter distinguish between the tune (which stays firm) and the decoration which the performer adds himself. My aural ability and musical knowledge fail me for such an appreciation. The players are happy when Ben sings out to them the scale on which it is based. They laugh.[23]

Britten's perception of the Javanese scale is, of course, highly significant in the light of the sketches he was subsequently to make in Bali and his own specific use of the equivalent Balinese scales.

Throughout *Ausflug Ost*, Prince Ludwig is frank about his own lack of musical knowledge and most of the accounts of musical experiences in the diary are understandably of a non-technical nature. We have seen, however, that Britten availed himself of specialized instruction. Bernard 'Penny' IJzerdraat undoubtedly proved to be a highly informative guide, as is shown by Britten's accurate use of Balinese technical terms throughout the sketches he made during the visit to Indonesia. Britten later wrote to Imogen Holst: 'We are lucky in being taken around everywhere by an intelligent Dutch musicologist, married to a Balinese, who knows all musicians – so we go to rehearsals, find out about and visit cremations, trance dances, shadow plays – a bewildering richness.'[24] IJzerdraat was director of the gamelan 'Babar Layar' at the Royal Tropical Institute in Amsterdam, and was an expert on rhythmic patterns in gamelan music; he had contributed a transcription of West Javanese angklung music to Jaap Kunst's monumental study of Javanese music in 1949.[25] John Coast recalls that Mr IJzerdraat actually played for a time in the Peliatan gamelan – an extremely rare privilege for a Westerner.[26] As we shall see, this corroborates the suggestion made below that Britten is likely to have visited Peliatan during his time on the island.

Soon after their Bandung concert, the party arrived at the airport hoping to fly to Surabaya, but in the event were taken only as far as Semarang.[27] In the event, the diversion to Semarang proved to be of considerable interest to Britten, since the town is an important centre of gong manufacture in South-East Asia and he was thus provided with the opportunity to see gamelan instruments being made. Knowing Britten's fondness for gongs and tuned percussion, there can be little doubt that he would have found this experience

---

[23] Prince Ludwig of Hesse, *Ausflug Ost*, 30–31.
[24] Letter from Britten to Imogen Holst, written from Ubud (Bali) on 17 January 1956.
[25] Kunst, *Music in Java*, 362.
[26] Personal communication.
[27] Here the exact chronology of the tour becomes confused, with Pears noting in his diary 'We left Bandung on Tuesday 9th' (tacitly corrected to 'Tuesday 10th' in Reed (ed.), *The Travel Diaries of Peter Pears*, 42), but Prince Ludwig (*Ausflug Ost*, 34–6) recording the journey as taking place on 10 January. The latter date is more reliable, as Britten's pocket-diary entry for 10 January reads '(Samarung [sic] in transit)'.

fascinating, particularly as it also provided his first introduction to authentic gamelan instruments. Prince Ludwig describes the visit to the gong factory on 11 January in some detail:

[We go] to a famous gong factory, in an alley off the main road. In the backhouse there [have been] blacksmiths for a thousand years. Hellish heat. Pitch-black – only two charcoal fires glowing at the bottom, which are growing red-hot in the air stream coming from bellows operated by the men who stand close by. Nearby there sits another blacksmith who turns the rough shape of a large gong in the fire with a long stick. Then, as the speed of the bellows increases with a groaning noise, the man who is near him turns it out in a frenzy of activity. There is a renewed cry, and a third man seizes the gong from the fire with pincers and [drops it] onto a soft mud area on the floor: the three remaining workers rhythmically and purposefully hit with large hammers what look like blunt pimples in the middle of the circle to produce the swelling central boss characteristic of Javanese gongs. Charcoal, dust and sparks fly. A shout – the gong flies back into the fire to be heated once more. In the clearing at the front, Ijserdraat brings us a metallophone: rectangular bronze keys with cylindrical resonators underneath. It is played with the hand[28] and small mallets – a sweet, flautato sound. A wider frame supports small, spherical gongs like kettles with the typical boss on top, the opening turned underneath.[29] This produces a bright bell sound. Then there is yet another large, genuine xylophone made from Borneo ironwood, the best in Java . . . This has a sweet, resonant and water-clear flautato tone.[30]

Since we know that IJzerdraat was proficient in gamelan performance, it seems highly likely that he would have given the party a practical demonstration of performing techniques at the factory. Britten's enthusiasm for the instruments is revealed somewhat later by an undated postcard sporting a picture of typical gongs sent to James Blades from Indonesia with the following message: 'I've heard Gongs of all shapes, sizes and metals here – producing fantastic notes – you'd be very interested. I hope to bring back some tapes of the music here – fantastic stuff.' It was to Blades that Britten would later turn for specialized advice on the exact choice of Western percussion instruments to represent gamelan sonorities in *The Prince of the Pagodas*.

The tour party's travel arrangements started to grow chaotic, with only two Garuda tickets available to fly Britten and Pears on to Surabaya after their visit to the gong factory: the Hesses and IJzerdraat were forced to make the journey by train.[31] Britten and Pears gave a concert in Surabaya on 11 January,

---

[28] A reference to the method of damping the keys, not the means of striking them. The description refers to the gender.

[29] The Javanese kenong or bonang, broadly equivalent to the Balinese reong.

[30] Prince Ludwig of Hesse, *Ausflug Ost*, 34–5.

[31] Again, Pears's diary is confused in dating this journey: he records it as taking place on

rejoined forces with the Hesses and then flew on to Bali the next day. Pears lamented the airline's meagre hospitality:

> The G.I.A. (Garuda Indonesian Airways) provided us with lunch consisting of: 1 piece of cold breaded fish, 1 potato croquette, 2 creamy cakes, 4 biscuits and 1 cup of chocolate milk. In spite of this, we arrived at Bali none the worse!!
> BALI! BALI! BALI![32]

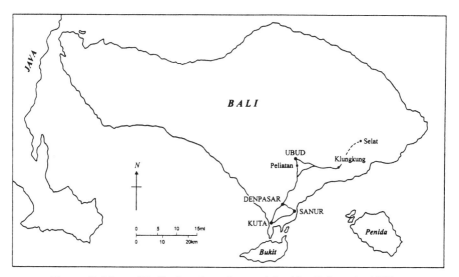

Figure 3. Map of Bali, showing places visited by Britten in 1956

The volcanic island of Bali (Figure 3) is one of the smallest in the Indonesian archipelago, with an area of just 5,620 square kilometres. It lies immediately to the east of Java, eight degrees south of the equator, and is separated from the larger island by a shallow strait less than three kilometres wide (see Figure 2). Bali is dramatically divided into northern and southern districts by its spectacular central mountain range which includes several peaks above 2,000 metres in height, among them the island's 'mother' volcano (Gunung Agung), which was 3,140 metres high before the disastrous eruption which killed thousands in 1963. The southern part of the island is a wide, gently sloping area notable for its extravagantly fertile soil and

10 January (tacitly corrected to 11 January in Reed, ed., *The Travel Diaries of Peter Pears*, 42), whereas Prince Ludwig (*Ausflug Ost*, 34–6) more plausibly gives 11 January. It was Pears's habit to write up his diary entries in batches after an interval of several days, during which time his memory became unreliable.

[32] Reed (ed.), *The Travel Diaries of Peter Pears*, 43.

correspondingly abundant rice crop. The lush tropical scenery in this area first began to attract foreign visitors in the 1920s, and by 1930 as many as 100 visitors per month were arriving for a few days of idyllic escapism. When Britten came to Bali in 1956, tourism had just begun to take its hold on the beautiful beaches at Sanur and Kuta, and the bathing hut rented by Prince Ludwig at Sanur was typical of the early tourist bungalows. Since that time, the beaches have become unrecognizable and it is now necessary to travel considerable distances inland to experience unspoilt Balinese culture.

Britten's visit was confined to the south of the island, the foothills of Gunung Agung and Gunung Batur marking the limit of his excursions north-wards.[33] Most of his artistic experiences seem to have occurred during the few days he spent in the central village of Ubud. This attractively peaceful colony of Balinese painters and craftsmen has to this day remained largely unspoilt in spite of a significant increase in visitors. It is still possible to hear a local gamelan most evenings and to recapture the impression of cultural richness which captivated Britten in 1956. On the threshold of Ubud is the much smaller village of Peliatan (sometimes spelt Pliatan), noted for its famous gamelan which had toured the Western world with the entrepreneur John Coast in 1952.[34] As we shall see in Chapter 4, this particular gamelan was unwittingly to play a significant role in the creation of the music Britten wrote for *The Prince of the Pagodas* after his return to England.

In Balinese society, music and dance are inextricably linked: both have their origins in religious devotion and still preserve a strong spiritual basis, although with the development of the independent *kebyar* school of composition (see below) and the dramatic rise in tourism some of this significance has been lost in more recent years. It is, however, still possible in every large village to see the gamelan playing throughout the night to celebrate a temple festival. During his time on the island, Britten saw a representative (and, one suspects, systematically planned) selection of Balinese dances, from genuine temple devotions to the extracts performed for the benefit of visitors, and heard a wide range of musical styles. This thoroughness allowed him to achieve a good working knowledge of gamelan techniques.

The gamelan traditions of Java and Bali originated in central Java but are now stylistically quite distinct. The Javanese gamelan is characterized by soft, legato playing and a tendency towards slow and stately tempi with little dynamic contrast. Balinese gamelan music is generally more vigorous and rhythmical, its bright percussive sound deriving from the hard hammers employed by the performers. Today, Bali has the greater profusion of styles with the existence of over twenty different types of ensemble. Although Britten visited both islands during his tour of Indonesia in 1956, he was

---

[33] For Pears's evocative description of the island, see *ibid.*, 43–7.

[34] Their extraordinary story is recounted in John Coast's memoirs *Dancing out of Bali* (London: Faber and Faber, 1954).

clearly influenced more by Balinese music than by the Javanese gamelan; this observation is confirmed by the fact that all the sketches he took down from gamelan performances originated in Bali and only one of his gramophone recordings of gamelan music contains Javanese pieces. In addition, his contact with McPhee had introduced him only to the Balinese style.

The various types of Balinese gamelan orchestra are composed primarily of idiophones, a category of instruments which includes metallophones, gong-chimes, gongs and cymbals. Almost all the metallophones currently in use (generic term 'gangsa') have bronze keys which hang over resonating tubes made from bamboo. A notable exception is the (now rare) gangsa *jongkok* in which the keys lie in direct contact with a wooden sounding-trough. Many types of gangsa are played with a single mallet, but the category known as gender (normally of two-octave range) employs two mallets. Both types of instrument are made in different sizes and are organized in pairs tuned slightly imperfectly in order to produce acoustical beats which result in a highly resonant effect. The gong-chimes are strung on a horizontal rack, in sets either of twelve played by a group of four men (reong) or of ten played by a soloist (trompong). Two large gongs (gong *ageng*) are hung vertically from frames, the male instrument (gong *lanang*) pitched higher than the female (gong *wadon*). The kempur is a smaller vertical gong of secondary importance, and the kempli is a gong held horizontally and used for time-keeping (somewhat in the fashion of a Western metronome). Two types of small cymbals (cengceng and rincik) add brilliance to the upper register. In addition to the idiophones, the category of membranophones is represented by two double-headed drums (kendang, one *lanang* and one *wadon*) which lead the ensemble and create a variety of rhythmic patterns. A popular bamboo flute of simple construction (suling) is encountered in various ensembles of widely differing constitutions.

All the instruments listed above are to be found in the gamelan gong *gedé*, which was originally a court ensemble of some 40 instruments but is now very rare and mostly survives in much smaller village versions of around 25 performers. It was the most important ensemble during McPhee's period of research in Bali during the 1930s, but is now becoming obsolete. Its modern counterpart is the gamelan gong *kebyar*, which also generally consists of some 25 instruments. The new style of composition which it embodies is notable for its often spectacular virtuosity, coupled with a wide range of dynamic contrast and rhythmic vitality (the word *kebyar* literally means 'explosion'). The genre evolved in the early twentieth century and is unique in being the only type of gamelan music to involve the creative composition of a new performing repertory. Apart from a number of older ritual pieces for the gong *gedé*, it is also the only genre to exist as instrumental music conceived independently from an element of dance or theatre. Since this style of Balinese music was to exert a decisive influence on Britten, it will be useful briefly to examine its characteristics here.

The gamelan gong *kebyar* is a modified version of the gamelan gong *gedé* in which the trompong is often discarded, although we shall later discover that Britten was well versed in the trompong idiom. The principal melodic instrument is the gangsa *gantung*, an adaptation of the gender played with one hand in the gangsa fashion. The reong achieves a new prominence with its four-part interlocking figurations known as *kotekan*. The *kebyar* gamelan contains the same arrangement of gongs as the gamelan gong *gedé*, a number of larger gender (termed 'jegogan' and 'jublag') and also the small rincik cymbals.

In common with the gamelan gong *gedé*, *kebyar* music is intricately organized by a method of polyphonic stratification in which melodic and rhythmic activity increase towards the upper part of the gamelan's five-octave register. This is fundamentally similar to the texture of the Javanese gamelan by which Debussy had been so profoundly affected. At the lowest pitch level the vertical gongs provide a slowly moving scheme of regular punctuation, which may be termed the colotomic structure. The lowest members of the gender family (jegogan and jublag) present the melodic cell on which the piece is based (*pokok*) at a stately tempo, whilst the metallo-phones of higher pitch elaborate this motive with a variety of ornamental figurations. The figurations in *kebyar* music are on the whole more complex than those of the gong *gedé*, but the principle of polyphonic stratification is essentially the same. Textures are based on a complex and highly sophisti-cated form of heterophony, which usually takes the form of simultaneous paraphrasing and embellishment of the *pokok* in different figurations.

McPhee provides an evocative description of the effect this characteristic procedure had on him during the early days of his acquaintance with Balinese music:

> Already I began to have a feeling of form and elaborate architecture. Gradually, the music revealed itself as being composed, as it were, of different strata of sound. Over a slow and chantlike bass that hummed with curious penetration the melody moved in the middle register, fluid, free, appearing and vanishing in the incessant, shimmering arabesques that rang high in the treble as though beaten out on a thousand little anvils. Gongs of different sizes punctuated this stream of sound, divided and subdivided it into sections and inner sections, giving it metre and meaning. Through all this came the rapid and ever-changing beat of the drums, throbbing softly, or suddenly ringing out with sharp accents. They beat in perpetual cross-rhythm, negating the regular flow of the music, disturbing the balance, adding a tension and excitement which came to rest only with the cadence that marked the end of a section in the music.
>
> Tiny cymbals pointed up the rhythm of the drums, emphasized it with their delicate clash . . .[35]

---

[35] McPhee, *A House in Bali*, 40–41.

A later passage provides an intriguing insight which links the structure of a gamelan composition to the characteristics of Balinese dance:

> Thus music, I learned, had its 'stem' [the literal meaning of *pokok*], its primary tones (which it was possible to preserve in writing) from which the melody expanded and developed as a plant grows out of a seed. The glittering ornamental parts which gave the music its shimmer, its sensuous charm, its movement – these were the 'flower parts', the 'blossoms', the *kantilan*. (Like a dancer, Nyoman explained in parenthesis, whose body is the trunk, whose arms and head are melody, and whose hands form the flowers, which are the 'gilding' of the dance.)[36]

A particularly distinctive feature of the *kebyar* style, which we shall find Britten frequently emulating, is the simultaneous striking of four or five different notes by the reong players. These chords are not harmonies in the Western sense, and are mostly used for rhythmic emphasis and dramatic effect. At the beginning of a composition, the entire gamelan often joins in a single explosive chord – a stunning effect which gave the style its name.

Britten encountered at least two other smaller ensembles during his stay in Bali. One is the gamelan *pejogedan*, which accompanies the popular *joged* dance: this consists of several sizes of xylophone termed 'rindik', often doubled by the popular bamboo suling. The other is the quartet of gender which provides the intricately polyphonic music to the shadow-play (*wayang kulit*). As we shall see, this is significant as the most important example of the *saih gender wayang* tuning system.

Britten's tour party was to spend two weeks on Bali, leaving for Java once more on 25 January.[37] The Bali Hotel, which still stands on Jalan Veteran in the capital Denpasar, served as their permanent base for the fortnight, but they were to spend long periods away from the town, particularly at Prince Ludwig's bathing hut at the south-eastern resort of Sanur and in the district of Ubud to the north. The first night was spent at the Sanur bungalow, the luxuriant setting described by Pears in his diary:

> The annexe was close to the beach, separated from it by coconut palms: the beach itself is pale honey coloured, and composed entirely of minutely crushed shells, rather prickly for the feet, and you find all sorts & sizes of lovely shells. Bathing is possible here because of the reef 200 yds out on which the surf breaks gloriously white. This keeps all but the smallest sharks out but means that the water inside is very shallow, and swimming difficult . . . It is a mistake to think of Bali (anyway in January) as being perpetually sunny. There were nearly all the time clouds, beautiful swelling shapes . . .[38]

---

[36] *Ibid.*, 43–4.
[37] Not 2 February, as incorrectly given in Mitchell, 'An Afterword on Britten's *Pagodas*', 8.
[38] Reed (ed.), *The Travel Diaries of Peter Pears*, 44.

During their first evening IJzerdraat introduced them to the music of Java, Bali and Borneo by playing a number of tape recordings. The Sanur district housed many *seka* (traditional music clubs), and during the second evening here Britten witnessed an ensemble of jew's harps (genggong) at the neighbouring home of James Pandy, a local art-dealer whose gallery is now well known. Pears described the instruments as sounding

> rather like frogs, very small, & the pieces played are short and descriptive such as 'The dragonfly dipping over the waves' or 'The deer trying to climb the banana-tree' or just 'The Frogs'. It is real chamber music; there were eight players, sitting on the ground, earnest and intense; the dark was lit up by little wicks in oil. An adorable experience.[39]

After the evening meal they drove to a temple at Batuan to see the purification dance called *rejang*, a processional performed by young girls. This was but the first of many dances seen by Britten during his stay on the island (Pears commented that it was one of the least interesting, 'although strikingly intense because of its extreme slowness'),[40] and the aesthetic of Balinese dancing later had a significant effect on his own approach to the balletic medium.

Britten had already begun to compile a set of manuscript sketches from the music he heard on the island, recording this particular evening's activities under the headings 'Gangong (Jew's Harp)' and 'Redjang (Purification)'.[41] We know from Pears's journal that performances of a trance dance (*sangyang dedari*) and shadow-play (*wayang kulit*) were also seen during the course of the evening, and these also figure on the same sketch page. Pears commented:

> As Ben was announced as being engaged in making a study of Balinese music, and as we had our cicerone Bernard Eizerdraat, the best young Dutch authority on Indonesian music, we were all set for a course of intensive music listening.[42]

On the morning of 14 January the group travelled by car to the village of Klentang. The aim was to catch sight of a cremation ceremony, which promised to be spectacular since it was in honour of an eminent priest. But all did not go according to plan, as Pears relates:

> Unfortunately rain was about all the time and it came down in buckets before the cremation began and finally we left after two hours soaking. We therefore missed the actual ceremony but witnessed many

---

[39] *Ibid.*, 45.
[40] *Ibid.*
[41] Britten uses the old Dutch spellings of Balinese terms throughout the sketches; these have since been superseded and standardized.
[42] Reed (ed.), *The Travel Diaries of Peter Pears*, 45.

preparatory rites, & heard much music & saw the splendid many coloured bier which was to take the corpse on its journey. There were constant streams of splendid Balinese women carrying offerings on their heads, bananas on leaves, rice on leaves, & fruit etc.[43]

In spite of their disappointment at missing the cremation itself, Britten here saw for the first time a full gamelan in performance and proceeded to transcribe its music in addition to isolating its scale under the heading 'Gamelan Klentang (Cremation)'. Prince Ludwig recorded the scene in some detail:

Beneath the roof of the meeting place in front of the entrance to a complicated and highly ornate temple sits a gamelan (that is to say, an orchestra that has at least one gong and one drum). There are about twenty instruments: metallophones, gongs, drums. They play beautiful, complex music without looking at each other; they have the confidence of sleepwalkers and are smoking cigarettes. The gamelan gradually gets to its feet and moves off in a small procession round the area. An old priest mumbles nasally from a high bamboo stall in front of the temple. He plays skilfully with his fingers, spraying water from stalks of flowers and ringing a small handbell here and there.[44]

As we shall see in Chapter 7, Britten may well have had the gamelan's procession in mind when he instructed the instrumentalists to process around the church in *The Burning Fiery Furnace* and then resume their places beneath the image of the Babylonian god Merodak. The use of bells in Balinese religious ceremonies must also have appealed to a composer who had already revealed a liking for this type of instrument and was to employ them tellingly in later works (e.g. the handbells in *Noye's Fludde*, tubular bells in the *War Requiem* and the tolling of the chapel bell in *Curlew River*).

The same evening (14 January) was spent with Mr Pandy in relaxed entertainment at Sanur:

We take our seats behind a gamelan comprising many bamboo xylophones. Music strikes up and entices a girl, isolated from the others, out from behind a curtain. She then creates her own individual dance, the same thing happening with each girl in turn. The Djoged 'bung-bung' is free . . . Single girls ask men up to dance with them. Ijserdraat . . . can dance gracefully: he has elegant hands and is eminently musical. Some idiot has a try and is naturally clumsy and comical. I make my excuses, Ben declines.[45]

The *joged* is curious on account of its social rather than religious orientation,

---

[43] *Ibid.*, 46.
[44] Prince Ludwig of Hesse, *Ausflug Ost*, 43–4.
[45] *Ibid.*, 45.

and the idea that the onlookers can join in is a unique feature.[46] The bamboo xylophones which accompany it (rindik) are adaptations of gender and the ensemble is known as the gamelan *pejogedan*. Its music is similar to that of the *legong* since the solo dances performed by each girl are in *legong* style, but many repeated notes are employed to compensate for the comparatively poor resonance of the wooden instruments.[47] Although Britten made no musical sketches on this occasion (in spite of the inclusion of the words 'Djogèd (luring dance)' on one sketch page), it seems likely that the gamelan *pejogedan* was later to leave its mark on the style of certain passages in *Death in Venice*.

The following day (15 January) was devoted to an excursion into the foothills of Gunung Agung, Bali's great volcano. Stops were made at Klungkung, the eighteenth-century capital famous for its Kerta Gosa (Hall of Justice) and Bale Kambang (Floating Pavilion), and at the small village of Selat. Towards evening the party arrived in Ubud, where they were to spend the night. Britten must have been captivated by the environs of Ubud: even today the small town is a haven from the hectic tourism of Sanur and Kuta, and Ubud has remained one of the island's most important artistic centres. Since the time of Walter Spies's residency in the 1930s (contemporaneous with that of McPhee's), Ubud has been a community of painters: the distinctive brand of Balinese art cultivated there was in fact profoundly influenced by the Western style of Spies.[48] At the time of Britten's visit, Ubud was considerably more primitive than it is today (the electricity supply was connected as recently as 1975), but the area boasted several fine gamelans – one of which is the renowned Peliatan ensemble.

On his first evening in Ubud, Britten witnessed a *legong* in rehearsal and made several musical sketches from the gamelan which accompanied the dancing. This appears to have been a particularly exciting experience:

Already during the evening meal there is a gurgling and growling from the distance – the gamelan is rehearsing. We go then with pocket torches through the pitch-black, slippery night to a small hall with bamboo fencing as walls where, under the petrol lamp, the whole orchestra of about thirty to forty men squats on the ground and hammers away. In the small space it is sometimes frankly deafening. Then comes the skilled 'Legong'. There appear five child dancers, each exercising for about three-quarters of an hour in minute detail a pre-composed dance

46 Prince Ludwig uses the term *bungbung* incorrectly. The *joged bungbung* is a fertility dance in which bamboo poles (*bungbung*) are use to pound grains of rice. The choreographical styles of the *joged* and other Balinese dances are comprehensively described in Beryl de Zoete and Walter Spies, *Dance and Drama in Bali* (London: Faber and Faber, 1938; repr. Kuala Lumpur: Oxford University Press, 1973).
47 See McPhee, *Music in Bali*, 191–200. The author illustrates the feature of repeated notes by transcribing the melody 'Lagu chondong' in two versions, one for gender and the other played by rindik from the village of Sayan (p. 193).
48 See Miguel Covarrubias, *Island of Bali* (New York: Alfred A. Knopf, 1942; repr. KPI Ltd, 1986), 160–204.

Plate 3. Dancing lesson in Bali, 16 January 1956

Plate 4. Britten at Tenganan, Bali, January 1956

made up of graceful, decorative insect-like movements. At the end they are swimming in perspiration . . . Position on the ground: feet turned outwards, knees bent, shoulder-blades back, arms horizontal at the side, hands bent backwards, fluttering fingers.

These children, apparently dancing for ever, the swelling and yet again contracting rhythmic storm of the gamelan in the tiny hall, half the village hanging through the fence in the lamplight from outside – these things remain unforgettable.[49]

After breakfast the next day a small gamelan and three dancers arrived to be photographed (see Plate 3) before the party set off for lunch in Denpasar and an afternoon's relaxation on Kuta beach. They were back in Ubud the same evening and attended the rehearsal of a children's gamelan. Prince Ludwig comments: 'Here is another fairly large orchestra with boys of up to fourteen years old as musicians. The instruments sound somewhat tinny; the players are splendid.'[50] Britten was also enthusiastic about this group in a letter to Roger Duncan:

I must tell you all about Balinese music when I see you, and perhaps play you some (I am bringing some recordings back with me) but what would have amused you was one Gamelan (the Balinese orchestra) made up of about thirty instruments, gongs, drums, xylophones, glockenspiels of all shapes & sizes – all played by little boys less than 14 years old. Jolly good they were too, and enjoying it like fun![51]

It is possible that this incident provided the long-term stimulus for Britten's later adoption of the gamelan style as a representation of adolescent boys in *Death in Venice*.

After the evening meal Britten again visited the rehearsal hall where the *legong* dancers were training. Following their second night in Ubud, the next day (17 January) was spent strolling through the rice-fields and neighbouring villages. It was then that Britten undoubtedly passed through Peliatan, the small village just south of Ubud on the main road to Mas and Denpasar. As already mentioned, the Peliatan gamelan had toured the West under the guidance of John Coast in 1952[52] and made two long-playing records during live performances, both of which were in Britten's possession at the time of the composition of *The Prince of the Pagodas*. As noted above, Bernard IJzerdraat was himself actively involved with the Peliatan musicians and he is unlikely to have neglected to show Britten around this important 'suburb'

[49] Prince Ludwig of Hesse, *Ausflug Ost*, 49–50.
[50] *Ibid.*, 50–51.
[51] Written on 8 February whilst aboard his flight from Hong Kong to Tokyo.
[52] See Mitchell, 'An Afterword on Britten's *Pagodas*', for a discussion of the extraordinary connection – apparently unknown to Britten – between one of the pieces in their repertoire ('Kapi radja'; see below, Chapter 4) and *The Young Person's Guide to the Orchestra*.

of Ubud. One of Britten's sketches from Bali is labelled 'Penny's gamelan (near Ubud legong)' in a clear reference to IJzerdraat's affectionate nickname.

It was on this day (17 January) that Britten wrote a long and well-known letter to Imogen Holst:

> . . . everything is completely and deliciously casual in Indonesia – no trains, jolly few roads, & occasionally eccentric planes (as we discovered to our cost, trying to get round Java to do some concerts!) . . . But after a week of hectic concerts & dotty travelling in Java, we came on here – the island where musical sounds are as part of the atmosphere as the palm trees, the spicy smells, & the charming beautiful people. The music is <u>fantastically</u> rich – melodically, rhythmically, texture (such <u>orchestration</u>!!) & above all <u>formally</u>. It is a remarkable culture . . . At last I'm beginning to catch on to the technique, but it's about as complicated as Schönberg.
>
> The dancing would thrill you – usually done by minute & beautiful little girls, & of a length & elaborateness which is alarming, but also by wonderful elderly men with breath-taking grace & beauty; & little boys with unbelievable stillness & poise. The stories of Bali being spoiled are quite untrue – in Denpassar [*sic*] (the only town of any size) there are about 8 Americans, & 7 Dutch (& a Viennese danceband trio!!) – but it is quite amazing that it's <u>not</u> spoiled; because the art is so easy, & the people so charming – just too far away I suppose.

In the light of Hans Keller's perceptive remark that Britten's interest in the heterophonic techniques of oriental music should be related to his equally strong involvement with twelve-note procedures (see below, Chapter 9), Britten's mention of Schoenberg in this context is especially striking.

The last two days of the first week (18 and 19 January) were spent in the vicinity of Kuta as the guests of Çokorde Gde Agung. Britten describes the scene in a letter to Roger Duncan written on their first day at the Çokorde's palace, a document which also includes the composer's fullest description of gamelan instruments:

> I am writing this early in the morning. The sun is already up, & it is as warm as a lovely English mid-day. I am sitting outside Peter's and my room in the courtyard of a palace in this little Balinese village. The palace is owned by a prince who takes guests, specially selected (but paying too!); but it isn't a palace in the Buckingham ditto sense, since it's really a collection of innumerable thatched tents, nestling around a complicated & exotic-looking Hindu temple. Even at this hour there is a sound of a musical gong; in fact the air is always filled by the sound of native music – flutes, xylophones, metalophones [*sic*], and extra-ordinary booming gongs – just as it is filled by the oddest spicey smells, of flowers, of trees, & of cooking, as one's eye is filled by similar sights plus that of the really most beautiful people, of a lovely dark brown colour, sweet pathetic expressive faces, wearing strange clothes, sarongs

of vivid colours, & sometimes wearing nothing at all. Sorry, old boy, to write in this 'high-falutin'' way, but one is really knocked sideways by the newness of the experience of coming to this tiny island in the middle of Indonesia – about half-way between Singapore and Australia – where people live, & things grow, in a way one had never dreamed of.

. . . We spent [the first three] days in a very simple little hotel by the sea – bathing in the warm, <u>really</u> warm sea, inside the coral reef so there were no sharks. We went to see dancing in the evenings, mostly done by small girls, about 7–10 years old, the most incredibly complicated & long dances. The music accompanying them is so unlike any we know in Europe that it is difficult to describe. It's mostly played on metal xylophones (sometimes wooden, bamboo), of all sizes, with gongs of tremendous size, long thin drums [kendang], and occasionally a curious one string fiddle [rebab],[53] & instruments rather like our treble recorders [suling]. They have bands of 20–30, always men, sometimes including quite tiny boys. But although it is quite unlike our music, it is worked out technically and rhythmically so that one can scarcely follow it. It isn't '<u>primitive</u>' at all, & neither are the people. They have been living cut off from the Western world, and have a highly organised life of their own, a most intelligent and sympathetic life too . . .

In an undated postcard sent to Erwin and Sofie Stein at around this time, the composer described the gamelan as 'fantastic, most complicated & beautiful, & they are <u>everywhere</u>! . . . the air is always full of the sound of gongs, drums and metallophones!'

On 20 January the group posed for photographs in traditional Balinese costume (see Plate 2) and then visited a nearby village where they encountered the mythical *barong*, a creature of good fortune similar to the Chinese New Year's Lion and described by Britten as a 'lion-tiger-horse'.[54] Prince Ludwig narrates the scene:

On the ground to the left is the gamelan. Music: the Barong appears at the [temple] gate. Two men are inside a wild caricature of a lion . . . At the end there is a great combat between the Barong and an evil demon. The Barong disappears through the gate . . . It is over. Magnificent – a performance lasting about an hour and a half. The gamelan accompanies and augments what is happening . . . Ben, who is indeed the most sensitive amongst us, is strongly moved by the realistic mad rage of a beautiful warrior.[55]

On the next day the party made the hour-long journey to Ubud for the last time and saw what Prince Ludwig terms a 'Monster-legong' arranged by the

53 Britten's description is inaccurate, since the instrument in fact boasts two strings.
54 Letter to Roger Duncan, 8 February 1956.
55 Prince Ludwig of Hesse, *Ausflug Ost*, 60–61.

Çokorde. They saw the *baris* (solo male warrior dance) and *kris* (sacred dagger dance) in the district of Sanur on 22 January.

During the morning of 23 January an event took place which resulted in the provision of important source material for the Balinese sections Britten was shortly to include in *The Prince of the Pagodas*: the tape recording of gamelan pieces mentioned by Britten in the letters to James Blades and Roger Duncan cited above. The studio session is described by Prince Ludwig:

> In the morning to Denpasar where Penny [IJzerdraat] sets up tape recordings with the best gamelan from Ubud of pieces which particularly interest Ben. In the little studio hall it is like a turkish bath. After about two hours the instruments are at last disposed to everyone's satisfaction. Two pieces are played, each of about 26 minutes' duration. Our skulls boom at the fortissimo sections, but there is a great impression of fantastic discipline and of astonishing empathy in tone and rhythm. We are soaked in sweat and the performers, who are at work from nine to one, are in the same state. In the afternoon a further three pieces were given without me.[56]

The identity of the 'beste Gamelang aus Ubud' involved in this recording session remains a mystery: in many ways the Peliatan group would fit this description, but no one connected with the gamelan can recall the event.

A reel-to-reel tape recording preserved at the Britten–Pears Library, Aldeburgh, is clearly the result of the session described above. It is a Scotch-brand tape (¼" x 1800', 7½" per second) bearing the label 'B. IJzerdraat '56/Bali – Indonesia'.[57] The recording contains a wide variety of Asian musics, suggesting it was edited by IJzerdraat from various sources, including the tapes he played to the party on their first night in Sanur. Table 1 gives a brief description of the ten tracks it contains, based upon notes sent by IJzerdraat to Britten on 7 June 1956 after the composer had returned to England.

The covering letter IJzerdraat sent with the tape reads as follows:

Dear Ben,[58]
It was with the greatest pleasure that I received those four long-play records you sent me. You have no idea at all how much I appreciate this precious gift.

Your telegram reached me after a long tour I had to make. In the meantime the tapes are sent through the diplomatic mailbag.

During the past months we did not have any good taperecorders

---

[56] *Ibid.*, 65.
[57] *GB-ALb* 3-9401043–9401050.
[58] The familiar 'Ben' indicates the warm relationship between Britten and the Dutchman. In contrast, Kei-ichi Kurosawa wrote to Britten from Tokyo after the composer's visit to Japan with characteristically Japanese restraint, addressing him as 'Dear Benjamin Britten'.

Table 1. Britten's tape recording of Indonesian music

Track no.	Duration	Title	Tuning system	Description
1	0'50"	'Bale pulang'	*pelog*	West-Javanese suling with 4 kacapi
2	1'40"	'Dangdanggula kentar tjisaät'	*pelog*	west-Javanese song for female voice with kacapi (soloist: Nji Mimin)
3	9'40"	'Tabuh telu' (Introduction)	*saih pitu*	Gamelan gong from Ubud (28 musicians)
4	7'07"	'Tabuh telu'	*saih pitu*	Gamelan gong from Ubud (Parts I–II) (27 musicians in Part I, 17 in Part II); versions by Çokorde Mas entitled 'Suling bambu' and 'Gegenderan'
5	5'40"	'Merak ngilo'	*saih gender wayang*	quartet of gender from *wayang kulit* in Denpasar
6	2'35"	'Gegenderan'	*saih pitu*	10 suling from Mengwi village
7	1'05"	'Polo bunju'	*slendro*	2 kacapi and dancer from Samarinda (Borneo)
8	3'04"	'Pemungkah'	*saih gender wayang*	quartet of gender from *wayang kulit* in Denpasar
9	3'50"	'Prang garuda'	*saih pitu*	*legong* from Ubud (gamelan gong)
10	0'50"	'Angklung'	*pelog*	Javanese angklung, performed by beggar children from Jakarta

(except mine) in running condition. Not even Philips! This is the reason for the delay in copying the tapes, and I am truly sorry for this. Now I have finished them.

Enclosed you will find a list with all the titles. There are actually more than what we have arranged before, among which you will hear the 'katjapi' players, which we saw in Bandung before.

Well, Ben, I hope to hear from you again . . .[59]

The most important item on the tape proved to be the performance of 'Tabuh telu' (tracks 3–4) which, as we shall see in the following chapter, Britten

[59] Letter from Bernard IJzerdraat to Britten, 7 June 1956. For the Bandung 'katjapi' (kacapi) performance, see above.

incorporated more or less directly into the score of *The Prince of the Pagodas*. On the sketches he brought back from Bali, Britten notated this melody with its accompaniment in a ballpoint pen which is quite distinct from the pencil he habitually used in all the remaining sketches; this might well suggest that he took it down from the tape at a later date and not from a live performance in Bali.

It was on the day these recordings were made that Britten sent an optimistic telegram to Dame Ninette de Valois at Covent Garden: 'CONFIDENT BALLET READY FOR MIDSEPTEMBER LOVE BRITTEN' – a sure sign that he had at last found a new musical stimulus which would allow him to break out of the impasse which had afflicted his work on the score before leaving the UK. The same studio which formed the location for this seminal gamelan recording provided the composer with the opportunity to view a performance of the *wayang kulit* on the following day (24 January).

This proved to be his last musical experience on Bali. He left on 25 January for Surabaya, where the exhausting recital schedule was due to resume, taking with him a miniature *barong* and three metallophones.[60] The *barong* was presented to Britten by IJzerdraat at the airport, and had to be carried under Pears's arm 'like a Balinese Skye-terrier'.[61] Britten spent the next week in Java and was ill with a serious gall attack for the last three days which resulted in the cancellation of a second concert scheduled to take place at Nedan in Sumatra.[62] He had, however, experienced two further musical performances in Surakarta on 26 January, when he heard a Javanese gamelan and attended a popular folk-play with musical accompaniment:

> In a long empty hall like a stable we take our places on fibre mats and the stone floor. In front of us sits the orchestra, about 14 strong, with many instruments on the ground. Each participant had about three instruments before him or at his side . . . Metallophones, knee-fiddles [rebab], flutes [suling], gongs, etc., resembling those in Bali but more opulent and venerable . . . The music is beautiful and sweet-toned, heavy and slow in rhythm. I cannot follow their labyrinthine movements . . .
>
> Then at about 11pm to the theatre where a folk-play is being put on. A large room like a cinema, open on all sides, for about 600–800 spectators. Stage with a painted prospect . . . Three clowns with pale expressions provoke a storm of laughter. Regal maids and knaves talk with stiff gestures and monotones . . . from time to time breaking out into bleating song. The gamelan strikes up from time to time . . .[63]

---

[60] The *barong* may be seen on display at the Britten–Pears Library (5-9700554), but the whereabouts of the metallophones has never been traced.

[61] Prince Ludwig of Hesse, *Ausflug Ost*, 67.

[62] According to Philip Reed (*The Travel Diaries of Peter Pears*, 52), a further recital was given by Britten and Pears on 28 January at the residence of the Dutch High Commissioner in Jakarta.

[63] Prince Ludwig of Hesse, *Ausflug Ost*, 69–71.

The Princess of Hesse wrote home from Jakarta on 29 January:

> Wc stayed with kindest Dutch consul in Surabaya – concert programme a great success and then we moved on at 6am by train . . . We ended up in a smallest hotel belonging to the islamic political party – 5 beds in each room, tiny windows, no sheets, no towels and the sanitary arrangements were such you simply <u>couldn't</u> use them.
>
> A nightmare visit [–] our money ran out, we travelled 11 hours (800km) yesterday living on bananas and warm beer! The 'porters' are ganged boy thugs . . . We borrow money from the taxi man and arrived here (British Embassy) <u>exhausted</u> last night . . .
>
> In Surajakarta [sic] we saw Javanese dances and heard Javanese music – quite different from Bali. Very beautiful and less wild.

The party left Java for Singapore on 31 January on a Qantas Airways Super Constellation flight, having cancelled their trip to Sumatra for the Nedan concert; they flew on to Hong Kong on 2 February. Six days later they arrived in Tokyo, where a completely new aesthetic experience awaited Britten in the shape of the Nō theatre.

The sketches Britten took down from the various musical performances he witnessed during his brief stay in Bali are preserved on all four sides of a single intact bifolio of fourteen-stave manuscript paper (reproduced complete in Figures 4–7).[64] This folio should not be confused with an additional folio bearing dictations taken down at a later date from Britten's own gramophone recordings of gamelan music (Figures 8–9).[65] Each sketch is carefully labelled with the name of the relevant dance and often the place of origin. Three dances are listed but given no sketch: these are 'Redjang (Purification)', 'Sang Hang Dedari (Trance dance)' and 'Djogèd (luring dance)' (see Figure 5).

The majority of the remaining sketches consist of Balinese scales. Each Balinese gamelan is built to one of two tuning systems (*patutan*), but pitches vary considerably from one gamelan to the next. The theoretical principles involved are not entirely understood and are still the subject of research by Western ethnomusicologists (who characteristically take a greater interest in such matters than the Balinese themselves). Considerably more work has been carried out on the Javanese system than on its counterpart in Bali, and McPhee's account of the Balinese system is still the fullest in print.[66] Unfortunately, McPhee uses imprecise terminology and his discussion of Balinese theory has been criticized with some justification:

> McPhee apparently uses the terms 'scale' and 'tuning' interchangeably in a rather loose way. It seems to this reviewer that when referring to the

[64] GB-ALb 2-9700606.
[65] GB-ALb 2-9700605. See Mitchell, 'An Afterword on Britten's *Pagodas*', 8.
[66] McPhee, *Music in Bali*, Chapter 7.

Figure 4. Britten's gamelan sketches from Bali, fol. 1r

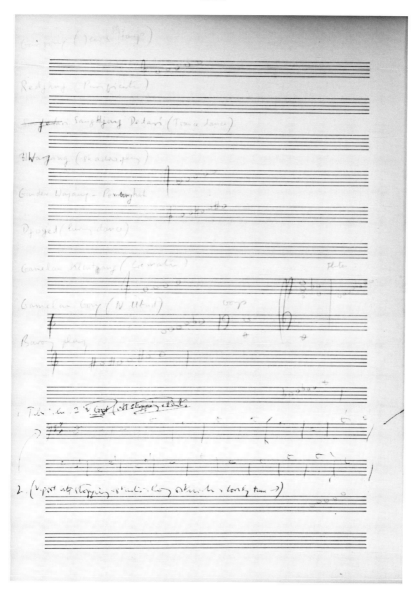

Figure 5. Britten's gamelan sketches from Bali, fol. 1v

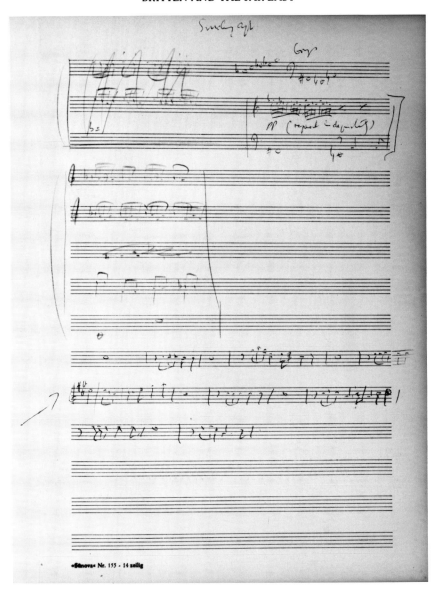

Figure 6. Britten's gamelan sketches from Bali, fol. 2r

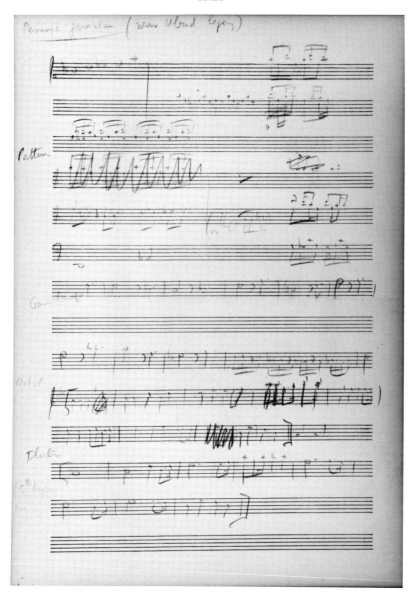

Figure 7. Britten's gamelan sketches from Bali, fol. 2v

Figure 8. Britten's transcriptions from 33rpm recordings

Figure 9. Britten's transcriptions from 78rpm recordings

sounds capable of being produced by an instrument . . . the term 'tuning' is appropriate. When referring to a set of pitches, chosen from the available pitches, and used as principal pitches for one or more compositions, the term 'mode' (implying a predetermined set of pitches with a specific pattern of intervals) might be used. For those pitches – principal, secondary, exchange tones, ornamenting tones, vocal tones, and so forth – used in any composition, placed arbitrarily in ascending or descending order, the term 'scale' could be employed . . .

Also, it is surprising that McPhee, being the musician that he was, has almost, if not completely, avoided the subject of mode in Balinese music. He does not enter into it in the chapter on scale systems and tuning, aside from a single use of the Balinese word *patutan* . . . which is probably allied to the Javanese word *patet*, usually translated as 'mode' . . . From my study with McPhee in 1961, it was my impression that strict modal theory and practice has disintegrated and become diffused in Balinese music . . . [McPhee] seemed curiously loath to discuss it, preferring to spend time on the more stimulating (to him) and perhaps characteristically 'Balinese' elements of the music, such as the figuration techniques . . . He makes such tantalizing statements as 'each of the five main tones of each scale can become the tonal centre or tonic – the tone on which the composition opens and closes. A composition may also shift its tonal centre at some time, starting on one tone and ending on another' (page 39), and then he drops the subject.[67]

This confusion is hardly clarified in Ruby Ornstein's more recent and concise account of Balinese theory, which contains equally tantalizing statements such as '*saih pitu* . . . incorporates numerous modal scales'.[68]

As far as Britten is concerned, however, the situation is comparatively simple. He appears to have had no knowledge of, and little interest in, the largely speculative principles behind the two Balinese tuning systems. Instead, he was easily able to distinguish between them aurally and was no doubt assisted in this by his recollections of the introductory notes to McPhee's *Balinese Ceremonial Music*. He clearly perceived them as 'scales' in a Western sense; indeed, he labelled them as such on a page headed 'Balinese scales' which he discarded from the composition sketch of *The Prince of the Pagodas*.[69]

---

[67] David Morton, reviewing McPhee, *Music in Bali*, in *Ethnomusicology*, 11 (1967), 412–15. It should be mentioned, however, that the general tone of Morton's review is complimentary, and he concludes: 'the book stands as a monumental contribution to our knowledge of one of the high art cultures of Asia, and a living proof of the ability of one Westerner, not just to become attracted to a music other than his own, and not just to feel it, get inside it, and understand it, but to explain it in such a way that other Westerners can understand it'.

[68] Ruby Ornstein, 'Indonesia III: Bali', in Stanley Sadie (ed.), *The New Grove Dictionary of Music and Musicians*, 20 vols. (London, 1980), XI, 186.

[69] *GB-ALb* 2-9700607.

Ex. 3.1

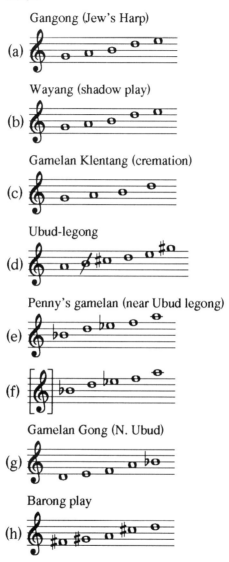

Gangong (Jew's Harp)

(a)

Wayang (shadow play)

(b)

Gamelan Klentang (cremation)

(c)

Ubud-legong

(d)

Penny's gamelan (near Ubud legong)

(e)

(f)

Gamelan Gong (N. Ubud)

(g)

Barong play

(h)

Ex. 3.1 is a transcript of some of the scales notated by Britten in the sketches he made in Bali. Exx. 3.1a–b illustrate *saih gender wayang*, notated under the headings 'Gangong (Jew's Harp)' and 'Wayang (shadow play)' (see Figure 5), using the pitches found most frequently in these sketches. As mentioned above, this is principally employed by the quartet of gender which accompanies the shadow-play (*wayang kulit*) and is related to Javanese *slendro* (cf. Ex. 1.1). It is effectively identical to the anhemitonic pentatonic scale frequently encountered in Britten's music. A rare but authentic four-note form of the scale appears under the heading 'Gamelan Klentang (cremation)' (see Ex. 3.1c and Figure 5) and is employed in the lengthy sketch of cremation music reproduced in Figure 4.

The other tuning system, *saih pitu* ('row of seven'), theoretically consists of seven notes and is related to Javanese *pelog*. In Balinese practice, however, five-note tunings derived from *saih pitu* are much more common. We shall be almost entirely concerned with the five-note pattern called *selisir gong*, notated with the pitches encountered most frequently in Britten's sketches (cf. Ex. 1.3) under the headings 'Ubud-legong' (see Ex. 3.1d and Figure 4) and 'Penny's gamelan (near Ubud legong)' (see Ex. 3.1e and Figure 7), and in isolation (see Ex. 3.1f and Figure 5). *Selisir* is now regarded as a system in its own right, and has become particularly associated with the gamelan gong *kebyar*.

A different scale which at first appears to fit into neither category is found twice in the sketches under the headings 'Gamelan Gong (N. Ubud)' and 'Barong play' (Exx. 3.1g–h and Figure 5). This is, in fact, also a *selisir* scale: the difference arises from the widely differing tunings found in different gamelans. As Ex. 3.2 shows, a simple re-ordering of the notes of the 'Barong play' scale reveals that Britten took it as the basis for Tadzio's music in *Death in Venice* (see below, Chapter 8).

Ex. 3.2

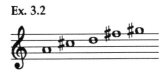

Apart from these simple jottings of Balinese scales, Britten notated several passages in more detail. Figure 4 contains figurations for the Klentang cremation music heard on 14 January and for the *legong* at Ubud; Figure 5 includes the ostinato for 'Tabuh telu' which underlies the melody reproduced at the bottom of Figure 6; and the sketches on Figures 6–7 represent an attempt to come to terms with interlocking *reongan* patterns. Most of the sketches may be related directly to the cultural incidents described in the source material on which the above account is based: the first four lines of Figure 5 originated on 13 January, the many references to the Ubud *legong* must date from either 15–17 or 21 January, 'Penny's gamelan' from 17 January, the *barong* play sketch from 20 January, and the *wayang kulit* scale either from 13 January or Britten's very last day on the island (25 January).

In the following chapters an attempt will be made to relate specific sketches from this intriguing manuscript to Britten's compositions in the period following his visit to Bali, and it will become evident that this *aide-mémoire* provided the composer with a highly useful stock of musical raw material.

* * *

As a postscript to this account of Britten's visit to Bali, the story may briefly be told of his intriguing attempt to compose a national anthem for Malaysia on the occasion of its independence in 1957, whereby his contacts with South-East Asia were renewed. Britten's contact with the country on his world tour was slight, being confined to a day-trip from Singapore to see a mainland rubber plantation in the first week of January 1956. Although short, their stay in Malaysia proved to be memorable due to the constant threat of attack from Chinese communist guerillas. Britten described the excursion as 'really hairraising . . . We were pretty scared, especially when our car got stuck for an hour in a thunderstorm.'[70]

The Malaysian Chief Minister wrote to Boosey & Hawkes on 19 June 1957 suggesting that perhaps Britten or Walton might be interested in the national-anthem commission, which was to include a 'slight oriental strain'. This invitation was followed up by a telegram dated 1 July in which a response was urgently requested. Britten took up the offer and completed his composition sketch for the new anthem on 10 July. On the same day, Britten wrote to his librettist William Plomer: 'I have been trying, the last 24 hours, to write a National Anthem for Malay, a curious, and I'm afraid rather unsuccessful job!' Plomer replied on 16 July: 'I wonder if the influences of your time in Asia show themselves in what you have been composing for the Malays.' The first version of the anthem was scored for military band by Norman Richardson and sent out to Malaysia.[71] On 25 July Britten received tape recordings of Malaysian folk-songs from the Chief Minister who suggested that it might be appropriate to incorporate one into the new piece.[72] Britten accordingly extended the central section of the work and dispatched the new version to Malaysia on 29 July. This manuscript was apparently returned to the UK on 18 September;[73] the work does not appear to have been performed although Britten duly received the agreed fee of 50 guineas, plus an ex-gratia payment of a further 50 guineas.

Britten's first version is reproduced in Figure 10. The anthem is an

[70] Letter from Britten to Imogen Holst, 17 January 1956. The State of Emergency prevailing in Malaysia was not lifted until 1960. See also Reed (ed.), *The Travel Diaries of Peter Pears*, 37–8, for Pears's dramatic description of the excursion.
[71] The history of the work is outlined in a collection of copies of letters and telegrams at GB-ALb, Works: Malaysian National Anthem.
[72] GB-ALb ibid.
[73] GB-ALb ibid.

Figure 10. Malaysian national anthem, sketch

Figure 11. Malaysian national anthem, sketch, extension to central section

unpretentious piece in ternary form in which the 'slight oriental strain' requested by the Malaysian authorities consists of a simple but appealing pentatonic melody harmonized entirely diatonically in the outer sections. The vigorous central section lapses into harmonies more typical of British ceremonial music, and was extended by Britten to accommodate one of the Malaysian folk-songs sent him by the Chief Minister (Figure 11). In a letter the composer wrote to Anthony Gishford on the day he received the tapes from the Chief Minister he claimed to be unhappy about the task, complaining about the uninspiring nature of the material he had been sent but taking a characteristic delight in observing that one of the recorded folk-songs used exactly the same pentatonic scale as his own original theme.

4

The Prince of the Pagodas

The genesis of *The Prince of the Pagodas* dates back to January 1954, three years before the ballet's first performance and two years before Britten's trip to Bali. The choreographer John Cranko had been introduced to Britten by John Piper in 1952, and had choreographed the première of *Gloriana* the following year. According to the second of two articles published by Cranko at the time of the première of *Pagodas*, work had already begun on a draft scenario for the projected three-act ballet and Piper had been consulted on the question of scenery well before Britten agreed to compose the music:

> The decor was under way, but what about the music? No composer available to me seemed to have the kind of imagination the ballet demanded. One evening I asked Britten if he had ideas about composers, little dreaming that he would become excited enough with Pagodas to undertake it himself.[1]

If this account is trustworthy (and it must be admitted that it seems highly unlikely for such a large-scale venture to have been planned without the composer in mind from the outset) then Cranko must have prepared his scenario well before the announcement of the forthcoming Britten–Cranko collaboration by the Sadler's Wells Ballet in January 1954. This deduction disproves the assumption made by John Percival in his biography of Cranko that the choreographer was first approached on the subject of the new ballet in February 1954.[2]

Britten first mentions the project in a letter delivered to Poulenc by Cranko and written on 14 July 1954:

> Ce qui porte cette lettre est un grand ami de moi, un jeune homme (il s'appele John Cranko), très très doné, vif et gai, que je suis sûr que vous aimerez assez que moi. Il fait les chorégraphie pour les ballets de Sadlers Wells, & a fait les choses vraiment remarquable. Je vais moi-même écrire un ballet (dans trois actes!) avec lui, dans le printemps prochain.

[1] John Cranko, 'Making a Ballet', *Sunday Times*, 13 and 20 January 1957.
[2] John Percival, *Theatre in my Blood: A Biography of John Cranko* (London: Franklin Watts, 1983), 102.

In the light of Poulenc's earlier Balinese borrowings in his Concerto for Two Pianos, it is fitting that Britten should have communicated his forthcoming oriental ballet to him in the first instance. On 3 September Britten informed David Webster (then General Administrator of the Royal Opera House):

I must confess I am rather alarmed at the prospect of my first ballet being given at Covent Garden, because I feel rather tentative. Also I am not quite sure whether the idea of this ballet is suitable for the large stage at the Garden. But I am seeing Cranko at Venice, and will discuss it with him and John Piper, and hope to see you when I return.

On an undated postcard from Venice, written about a fortnight later while the composer was in the Italian city to conduct the world première of *The Turn of the Screw*, he reported 'Talked abit with J. Cranko about Ballet.' On 28 December, Britten told Anthony Gishford at Boosey & Hawkes 'I'm getting interested in the ballet', and he had certainly begun work on the music in the spring of 1955 since he received a letter from Cranko dated 18 April which appears to make specific reference to the 'Variation of the King of the West' in Act I:

I loved what you had done, & feel one could practically coreograph [sic] it now it all falls so perfectly into place.
    But a new doubt fills me about the intellectual variation – I feel that perhaps it is not obvious enough to dance to . . . either rhythmically or melodically. It is quite possible to coreograph [sic] but I feel that its an intellectual piece of music & not an intellectual dance. Also its fugal shape is not obvious enough to amuse and gets in the way of the theatrical shape . . .
    Sorry to be a bore, but I hasten to say this before you start the adage and get it all involved in the waltz.

On 15 August, Britten wrote to Cranko to inform him that he could not meet the October deadline originally agreed, and the letter reveals that the composer had begun the music for Act II:

I am sorry to have to write this letter to you, but I hope you will understand. I got back here from the Continent [where he had been conducting *The Turn of the Screw* at the Holland Festival] at the end of July absolutely exhausted – not surprisingly because I have been at it for months, even years, without a break. With considerable effort, with only a short break, I made myself start on Act II of the ballet last week, but for the above reason and for a variety of others, work went very slowly. The other reasons were – the feeling that I had to have the bulk of the ballet finished by early September when you go off to America to rehearse it; the ghastly dateline for the full score to be ready by the time I go off for the world tour at the end of October; the tension with John P[iper] over the decor-battle (Flute versus Ballet); the (as far as I know) non-existence of a conductor [see below], in fact the non-existence of a date for the first night (about which I hear nothing but rumours, never a direct communication from Covent Garden, not even a twitter to say they are serious about the whole matter).

I have therefore come reluctantly to this conclusion: I cannot make myself ill with worry and over-work about anything so vague. I will continue to sketch the work in what time I have in these next two months. I hope, but cannot guarantee, to have the piano score completed before I leave. I will be back mid-March, and will if necessary complete the sketches and write the full score then.

The obvious solution seems to be the postponement for at least six months which will allow the work to be completed, the conductor engaged, and solve the problem of Piper having to do two major productions on top of each other.

The one thing that has never varied in spite of these vicissitudes has been my interest in the ballet itself, and I hope eventually to write the work worthy of you and the Company. That I fear may be your only crumb of consolation in the rather dreary matter.

Britten's hope to have the piano score ready before his departure for the five-month world tour was something of a rash statement: he had still not completed the piano score in April 1956, some eight months later, when he reported to Ernest Ansermet that he was still only 'in the middle of the second act'. Britten wrote to Webster at Covent Garden to say 'Here is a copy of a letter I've had to write to Johnny Cranko; it's a pity, but it had to be done. Shall I be hearing from you?' A new February deadline for completion of the score was scrapped, and the ballet was postponed until July 1956. Britten wrote again to Webster with increasing irritation on 1 October 1955, one month before his departure on the world tour, to say:

But if the main reason [for meeting] is to discuss the dates of the ballet surely that has been done already – Ninette [de Valois] came down to Aldeburgh to do this, and we threshed it all out thoroughly. As she will have told you in America the earliest I could possibly manage would be the last half of July, and that is only possible if you can somehow extend the season. She was going to let me know your reactions to this, but I have heard nothing. With my complete absence from England and work this winter you will realise that this is going to be a tight squeeze, and I do not see how I can guarantee completion by that date, try as I will . . . Why can we not postpone the work till the autumn without further ado?

Webster replied on 18 October, agreeing to abandon the July deadline.

It was, in the event, highly propitious that Britten should have had Act II of the ballet in his mind when he arrived in Bali, since it was into this act that he subsequently incorporated material borrowed from the gamelan music he encountered there. As we saw in the previous chapter, the composer telegraphed Ninette de Valois with renewed enthusiasm from Denpasar on

23 January 1956: significantly, this was the date of the important recording session in Bali which provided the musical raw material for Britten's continuation of the score.

After his return from the world tour, Britten met Cranko on 23 March and resumed discussions with Ninette de Valois at Covent Garden six days later. He once again began to find his workload too great, commenting in a letter to Ronald Duncan on 27 March that 'I've cancelled every concert for some time now in order to get on with the Ballet.' By April it seemed as if Ansermet was willing to undertake the responsibility of directing the work's first performance. Britten wrote to the Swiss conductor on 17 April:

> I was delighted to have a telephone call from David Webster this morning saying that there was a good chance of your being able to conduct my new ballet at Covent Garden this autumn. May I say how thrilled and honoured I shall be if you can really find time and inclination to do this. I have hopes that the music will interest you. As Webster most likely told you, it is a three act ballet, and I am doing my best to follow the conventional classical ballet forms – quite a task these days!
>
> I am afraid the full score will not be ready for a little time; I am busy with the piano sketch (in the middle of the second act) so that the rehearsals can start soon. If it would interest you to see a piano version of the first act we can send one to you almost immediately.
>
> I hope you and Madame Ansermet are well. As you may know, Peter Pears and I have just finished a fascinating tour of the Near and Far East up to and including Japan. The art we saw and heard baffles description. Have you ever, for instance, been to the Noh plays in Japan, some of the most wonderful drama I have ever seen?
>
> This comes with every good wish to you both, and in the greatest excitement that I may have the chance of working soon again with my favourite conductor.

Ansermet replied from Geneva (in English) on 27 April, his letter indicating that September had been scheduled for the initial performances of *Pagodas*:

> I thank you immensely for your kind letter and am very proud from your confidence and your appeal. I would be very glad to accept. A difficulty is that I have a concert here on Sept 28, with rehearsal on 27 Sept. I am trying to postpone both from, at least one day – more is impossible, and I am writing to Mr Webster in order to see if it can be arranged. Anyhow if you can send me the piano score of your ballet for a few days I would be glad to know it.

Britten passed the good news on to Webster himself in a letter dated 1 May:

> I have had an extremely sweet letter back from Ansermet who seems most keen to do the new ballet for us. The only snag seems to be dates in Geneva on 27th and 28th September, from which he is trying to

extricate himself. Does that mean that the first performance [initially scheduled for 19 September] has been shifted to a slightly later date? I must confess that even those few days would be a blessing, since although the work is progressing well, there is a colossal amount to write, and the date-line is beginning to keep me awake of nights. He says, by the way, that he would like to see a piano score of whatever is done. Could you please arrange for one of the copies of Act I to be sent to him?

On 11 May, however, Ansermet wrote again to Britten:

You know perhaps allready [sic] that I must renounce to conduct your ballet. I feel tired and I have so much to do this summer – namely with the opera of Frank Martin[3] – and till the middle of August, that, if I don't have some holiday and the necessary time for my cure at Montecatini, I will not be able to undertake my winter season. I am terribly sad as I was extremely interested in your work and I would have been proud and happy to make the baptism. My only hope is to conduct it later, as I have spoken with David Webster about a possibility of taking (later) a new activity with the Ballet.

. . . So, forgive me and believe to my deep regret: I am so sure that you are one of the two or three true composers of our time and that your ballet will be an important work.

Britten replied one week later:

Your letter was not entirely unexpected. When I knew what a tremendous amount of work you had before you as a conductor, not to mention the hours and energy needed for your new book,[4] I was quite frankly rather apprehensive about your finding time to do the first performance of the new ballet. I was terribly touched that you felt you wanted to do it so much that you initially agreed to it, but quite understand that on thinking it over you feel it would be too much. I only hope that when you come to Covent Garden later you will do some performances [these never materialized]. I must confess that I am very disappointed, not only because I have such trust in your great gifts as a conductor, but I was hoping for practical advice from you during the rehearsal periods since I am very conscious of being a newcomer in the ballet world, and there is no-one who could have been a better guide than yourself. However, I look forward to your hearing or conducting it later, and will hear your views then!

---

3   Martin's Shakespearean opera *Der Sturm* (*The Tempest*) received its first performance under Ansermet's baton at the Vienna Opera on 17 June 1956. See Jean-Claude Piguet and Jacques Burdet (eds.), *Ernest Ansermet–Frank Martin: Correspondance, 1934–68* (Neuchâtel: La Baconnière, 1976), 67–78.
4   Ernest Ansermet, *Les fondements de la musique dans la conscience humaine* (Neuchâtel: La Baconnière, 1961).

On 28 May 1956 Britten wrote to Webster to discuss other possible conductors for the première:

I had already had an extremely nice letter from Ansermet saying that he could not after all conduct the ballet, but saying that he had been in touch with you. As this was over a fortnight ago I am afraid I hoped that you had already spoken to [Rafael] Kubelik, who was you remember the next on our list. After him, as far as I can remember, came [Igor] Markevitch, [Paul] Sacher and [Rudolf] Schwartz, but I suppose at this late date it is going to be difficult to find anyone of this calibre who can fit in exactly with our dates.

May I add in parenthesis that any postponement of the first night would be a god-send to me, struggling to get the work finished in time – hence the brevity of this note!!

On 5 June Britten wrote to Gishford at Boosey's in more confident terms, but continued to lament the lack of organization which blighted the Covent Garden administration:

The ballet is pushing on steadily in spite of innumerable interruptions for rehearsals, concerts, festivals etc. The sketches are only a week or so off completion, and then there remains just the full score to be written(!) It is going to be a rush to get it done by the prescribed date, September 19th, but I think it will be possible. In the meantime, Covent Garden have not got a conductor to do it. Ansermet eventually refused, needing a holiday; Webster delayed telling me for a fortnight, and consequently delayed approaching the next person on the list i.e. Kubelik. The date is now getting alarmingly close for a first-class conductor to be able to rehearse and do a reasonable number of performances. I tell you this only to prepare you for the stand I am going to make, refusing to let the work be performed inadequately. Oh dear! will nothing ever make them wake up?

In the event, Britten was to conduct the new ballet himself.

At the end of July, Cranko travelled to Aldeburgh for extended discussions about the production.[5] On 26 July Britten wrote to Pears, who was in Germany participating in the Ansbach Festwoche:

There are quite alot of things to tell you, but not much time to write fully, because I'm slaving, slaving at the old ballet: trying at the moment to get the music of Act III written. We got Act I score off last week. Tony's suggestion to Webster of postponing had the usual Webster

---

[5]   Relations between Britten and Cranko may already have been growing strained at this point in their collaboration, since the choreographer had withdrawn at short notice from his engagement to produce Blow's *Venus and Adonis* and Holst's *Sāvitri* at the 1956 Aldeburgh Festival, having double-booked himself. For the final rupture between the two men, see below.

reaction (nothing at all). But I'm trying to get it done for Johnnie's sake. He is still here; lazing around & enjoying the complete rest, before plunging back into work next week.

Two days later the composer wrote again to Pears:

Here all goes to plan,[6] I've just finished the music of the ballet (Thank God!!!), & now I get down again to the score. There's a good old row developing between B[oosey] & H[awkes] & Covent Garden (Webster is the pink limit (a good term for him, don't you think?)), but no sign yet of postponement alas.

Webster finally issued a press release from Covent Garden on 9 August informing the public that the September première had been abandoned due to 'illness' on the part of the composer. According to the *News Chronicle* of that date, 'Mr Britten was said yesterday to be worn out after his recent world tour.' *The Times* added: 'The piano score, however, is ready, and this is to be used for some rehearsals.' Britten wrote to Ronald Duncan on 14 August to say 'The ballet will now be end of December I hear.'[7] By this time the composer had travelled to the Hesses' Swiss residence at Schloss Tarasp for a period of uninterrupted work on the full score, writing to Gishford from there on 18 August:

Imo[gen Holst] & I are now approaching the end of Act II,[8] working on the average I'd say about 4–5 hours a day. How we should [have] fared if we'd tried to finish the whole, I can't imagine & I think you will understand when you see the fragment of Act II posted 3 days ago to Erwin [Stein]!

The Prince of the Pagodas was finally performed on New Year's Day 1957, receiving 22 subsequent performances during the first run. It was revived at Covent Garden in 1958 (five performances), 1959 (three performances) and 1960 (three performances), but was then dropped from the repertory in spite of favourable receptions in New York (October 1957) and a triumphant production under Britten's baton at La Scala, Milan (May 1957) where *Il principe delle pagode* met with unanimous praise from the Italian press. Writing to the Pipers from Milan in April 1957, Cranko declared himself 'keen to remedy the defects in my part of the ballet' (the choreography of the première

---

6   Britten's pocket-diary (*GB-ALb*) notes that the music of Act III was required by 30 July. He had completed the sketch just two days before the deadline.

7   He added: 'hope Women's Journal weren't too cross!', referring to the magazine's unfulfilled request that he allow them to reproduce an extract from the ballet's manuscript composition sketch. Britten had told Duncan on 12 June: 'Certainly I can send them a page of the scribbles (sic!), if you'll tell me where and when – will they mind pencil?'

8   Britten wrote 'Act 2 score' in his pocket-diary (*GB-ALb*) on 13 August, presumably the date on which the orchestration of the act was begun.

had been widely criticized). In a later letter, also undated, he writes: 'I am much more pleased with my part, which I have very largely redone, and the whole thing is starting to flow as it never did before.' In a postscript scrawled at the bottom of a third letter, dated 16 April, he added: 'It is funny, after being so unsure about the ballet, I <u>care</u> so much about it now.' [9]

Back in November 1956 Britten had explored the possibility of securing additional productions of the ballet in Germany, writing to Gishford on the 27th:

> I've asked alot about the ballet situation, but probably Ernst [Roth] knows it as well as I do. Munich seems the best (but only if Carter is there, & his position seems uncertain). Düsseldorf is madly keen to do it, but they all say there is no company at all yet, & they'd more or less have to form one to do it properly. Frankfurt is a possibility, especially if they'd get someone like Kurt Jooss to produce it. Wuppertal has the best reputation, but is clearly too small. My preference honestly would be Munich (with Carter) or Frankfurt (with Jooss), but I've no idea whether they are interested, & Düsseldorf certainly is. P'raps Ernst can find out.

Of these projected German venues, only the Munich performance came to fruition (in March 1958). Cranko went on to stage the ballet at Stuttgart on 6 November 1960,[10] where it scored something of a success, the choreographer immediately being invited to take up the position of ballet director of the Württemberg State Theatres during the following January. By this stage, Cranko's relationship with Britten had completely foundered, principally through the choreographer's inefficiency when producing *A Midsummer Night's Dream* at the Aldeburgh Festival in June 1960, which Britten could not tolerate.[11] So bad had relations between the two men become that, when Cranko wished to revive his Stuttgart production of *Pagodas* in 1968, he felt unable to approach Britten to request alterations to the score.

The ballet's neglect after its initial performances was largely the result of antipathy on the part of the composer, who had developed an unfortunate aversion to a work which had (unusually) caused him considerable difficulties. Luckily, however, he recorded the score for Decca in February 1957 with the orchestra of the Royal Opera House;[12] unfortunately, he drastically reduced the score for this purpose by making over 40 cuts ranging from single bars to entire numbers. In their 1971–2 season, the Kirov Ballet mounted a new production of the score in Leningrad: surprisingly, Britten responded favourably to their request that he should modify several passages

---

[9] I am grateful to the late Mrs Myfanwy Piper for drawing my attention to these letters, which were in her personal collection, and for permission to quote from them.

[10] Percival, *Theatre in my Blood*, 130–32.

[11] See Carpenter, *Benjamin Britten*, 392–6.

[12] Decca Ace of Diamonds GOS-558-9, reissued on CD in 1989 (London 421 855-2).

of the music. British public interest in *Pagodas* notably revived following a concert performance of large sections from the score at the 1988 Aldeburgh Festival by the London Sinfonietta under Oliver Knussen, and the complete ballet returned to the Covent Garden stage in December 1989 after an absence of nearly 30 years.[13] Knussen went on to record the complete ballet for Virgin Classics in 1990, reinstating the four dances which Britten had completely excised in his 1957 Decca version.[14]

* * *

Cranko devised his own original story for *The Prince of the Pagodas* with the intention of creating a 'mythological fairy-tale' from diverse sources. The plot, which need not be given in full here,[15] contains elements of *King Lear, Beauty and the Beast* and certain fairy-tales of oriental origin. A detailed scenario in Cranko's hand is preserved at the Britten–Pears Library together with a list of approximate timings for the individual dances.[16] This scenario differs from the stage directions in the published full score and piano reduction in many respects,[17] but these alterations were evidently made at a comparatively late stage: Britten's composition sketch contains directions corresponding to this handwritten scenario which must therefore have been the document from which the composer worked.[18]

Cranko's original scenario shows that he was conversant with the fairy-tales of Madame D'Aulnoy (d. 1705): its title (*The Green Serpent*) betrays its origin in her *Serpentin vert* (Milan, 1782). The story concerns the plight of a certain Princess Laidronette,[19] exiled for ugliness from court, who encounters a sympathetic green serpent and is magically transported across the sea. Regaining consciousness in a gold-panelled chamber, she encounters 100 pagodas which attend on her as she is wooed by an invisible voice and consents to marry its owner. Eventually the Green Serpent is transformed into a handsome king and the two live happily ever after.[20] This tale forms the

[13] The choreography, which departed considerably from the original stage-directions and therefore made nonsense of some of Britten's musical conceptions, was by Kenneth MacMillan.

[14] Details of Britten's cuts are to be found in the present author's notes accompanying the Knussen recording (Virgin VCD 7 59578-2).

[15] See the synopses by Mitchell in 'Catching on to the Technique', 194–200, and by the present author in the booklet accompanying the Virgin recording (details in note 14 above).

[16] *GB-ALb* 2-9700608.

[17] This piano reduction is a rehearsal score prepared by Imogen Holst (who shared the dedication of the ballet with Ninette de Valois) in 1956 and, until the full score was issued by Boosey & Hawkes in 1989, was the only printed version available (for hire only).

[18] Britten's composition sketch is preserved in *GB-ALb* 2-9300894.

[19] Cf. Ravel's 'Laideronette, impératrice des pagodes' from *Ma mère l'oye* (see above, Chapter 1).

[20] Mme D'Aulnoy's tale may have had its own origins in oriental legend, in view of the emphasis placed not only on pagodas but, more importantly, on the whole idea of a

basic framework for the plot of *The Prince of the Pagodas*, in which a meek princess is borne from court to meet a green salamander (the change from 'serpent' was made in the full score at a late stage), who is later revealed to be the Prince of the Pagodas. In Cranko's draft the princess is called Gracieuse (presumably from another D'Aulnoy tale entitled *Gracieuse et Percinet*) and her evil sister is named Malina: both these names appear in Act I of Britten's composition sketch but by Act II they have been changed to their final form as Belle Rose and Belle Épine.

In all important respects Cranko's original scenario corresponds exactly to the final version. The list of timings for the individual dances is carefully thought out, and the duration for the three acts is established as 27½ minutes for Act I, 28½ minutes for Act II and 33 minutes for Act III.[21] Within this framework, Cranko generally works in units of three or four minutes and this comprehensive list must have provided a useful stimulus to Britten, who had served his apprenticeship in the film industry during the 1930s. Cranko himself draws this parallel when he remarks that they worked out 'a sort of "shooting script" for the whole ballet, almost as if we were planning a silent film'.[22]

Britten's ballet score contains all the compositional features we have already discerned in his earlier works. Polyphonic stratification occurs in the Prelude (a late addition written well after the Balinese trip), where the Prince-as-Salamander theme is superimposed in a variety of rhythmic patterns (see Ex. 4.1). It is also found in the rhythmic counterpoint characterizing the King of the South (Act I, fig. 29), in the simultaneous combination of the music for the stars and clouds (Act II, fig. 13) and, most strikingly of all, in the massive crescendo between figs. 19 and 23 in Act III, where all the themes associated with the Prince are combined as the lights come up on the Pagoda Palace. Familiar pentatonicism colours much of the ballet's music since it is employed for the motif representing the Emperor (see Ex. 4.2) and in the ubiquitous trumpet fanfares (see Ex. 4.3). The pattern of Ex. 4.3 is carefully contrived in an interlocking figuration which suggests a parallel with the subtle procedures of the Balinese *reongan*. In addition to these motivic examples, independent themes such as that in Act III, scene 2, at fig. 63

metamorphosis of the kind described here. In *A House in Bali* (p. 170) McPhee recounts a tale of 'Green Frog' once related to him by Sampih, the boy dancer he had adopted into his household. This story also concerns a dejected and humiliated princess who is brought to life three times by the magical frog, which is then transformed into a 'youth of royal appearance'. Once more the couple are married and live happily ever after. There is an obvious similarity to the story of *The Prince of the Pagodas*, not only in terms of the handsome prince's metamorphosis but also on account of the prominent role played in the ballet by the four green frogs who escort Belle Rose on her enchanted trip to Pagodaland. See also Mitchell, 'Catching on to the Technique', 205–6, note 20.

21 These durations are all much shorter than the final proportions, which amount to a total of 125 minutes of music.

22 Cranko, 'Making a Ballet', *Sunday Times*, 20 January 1957.

Ex. 4.1

Ex. 4.2

Ex. 4.3

Ex. 4.4

(see Ex. 4.4) are pentatonically constructed. Donald Mitchell has listed the numerous occurrences of cluster-chords in the ballet,[23] and the interval of a second is again predominant; as we saw in Chapter 1, Debussy's adoption of Javanese-inspired pentatonicism had frequently led to his use of clashing major seconds. Much of Britten's instrumentation recalls features we have isolated from the early works, particularly the use of gong, cymbal and bells as types of 'punctuation' and the prominent use of drums (e.g. the 'native drums' accompanying the King of the South).

By far the most interesting aspect of Britten's score, however, is the direct appropriation of Balinese musical material and the emulation of gamelan sonorities within the confines of the Western orchestra. These 'gamelan' passages symbolize the attraction the Prince holds over Belle Rose in his guise as Salamander and as ruler of the exotic Pagodaland, an important parallel with the symbolic use of tuned percussion in *The Turn of the Screw* discussed in Chapter 2. The Balinese material is therefore concentrated into the second half of Act II. The 'gamelan' sonority first appears at fig. 69, when Belle Rose bumps into the pagodas, and the section up to fig. 74 depicts the movements of the various pagodas surrounding her. The second 'gamelan' passage occurs at fig. 75, a much quieter section illustrative of the mystical Salamander. When the Prince assumes his human form the gamelan music disappears, returning at fig. 86 to close the act when the Prince suddenly reverts to his Salamander shape as Belle Rose pursues him. This distinctive music reappears only once, in the long orchestral crescendo for the Pagoda Palace in Act III mentioned above.

The source material employed by Britten in the reconstruction of gamelan sonorities in these remarkable passages consists of the sketches he brought back from Bali, four gramophone recordings of gamelan music which may have been in his possession before his visit to the island in 1956 and the reel-to-reel tape recording of miscellaneous Indonesian music made under the guidance of Bernard IJzerdraat. Two of the gramophone records were 78s (MO 104 and MO 105) which contain music from Java and Bali, and two were long-playing discs (Argo RG1 and RG2) containing Balinese *kebyar* music performed by the Peliatan group during their tour of the West in

---

[23] In 'Catching on to the Technique', 209.

1952.[24] Britten filled both sides of a half-folio of eighteen-stave manuscript paper with sketches taken down from four of the recorded pieces (Figures 8–9). Two are taken from the 78 disc of Balinese music and appear not to have been used in the ballet (Figure 9). The remaining sketches (Figure 8) are derived from the Peliatan recordings of 'Kapi radja' and 'Tamililingan' (CD tracks 6–7) and these proved to be the most important musical inspiration for Britten's own gamelan passages. The manuscript paper used for these sketches corresponds exactly to the type employed by the composer in the composition sketch of *The Prince of the Pagodas* and it is therefore highly likely that they date from the actual time of composition. The curious chords sketched at the bottom of Figure 8 bear no relation to gamelan music: they may represent an early harmonic plan for the 'Pas de deux' in *Pagodas* (Act III fig. 60), since the first two chords of the bottom system are similar to those used at figs. 60 and 61.

The sketches from Bali yielded a comparatively small amount of specific material: they provided Britten with a reminder of the gambang theme which he included in the ballet at fig. 73 in Act II. Exx. 4.5a–c show respectively the

Ex. 4.5

---

[24]   See Mitchell, 'An Afterword on Britten's *Pagodas*', 9, note 4. The 78rpm discs are currently uncatalogued; the LPs are *GB-ALb* 3-9401051–9401060.

Ex. 4.6

theme as it occurs in the 'Gambangan' of McPhee's *Balinese Ceremonial Music* (where it curiously lacks the distinctive syncopations), Britten's own sketch from Peliatan (see Figure 7) and the form in which the theme finally appeared in *Pagodas*. As we have seen, the Salamander theme was probably notated on the Balinese sketches from the tape recording Britten had made for him in Bali. It is labelled 'Tabu talu' by the composer and forms the second part of the original gamelan composition (track 4 on the tape recording; CD track 8). Ex. 4.6 gives three versions of the theme: the first (4.6a) is a transcription from the tape recording by the present author, the second (4.6b) a transcription of Britten's ballpoint sketch (see Figure 6) and the third (4.6c) as it appears in Act II of *Pagodas*, where Britten recaptured the original accompanying figures with the aid of the Peliatan recording of 'Tamililingan' (CD track 7). In addition to these two specific thematic derivations, Britten's gamelan sketches must have provided him with useful reminders of the two Balinese tuning systems and characteristic instrumentation. On a separate sheet of manuscript paper, again from the same batch used for the ballet's composition sketch, Britten compiled a convenient checklist headed 'Balinese scales'.

A notable precedent for the adaptation of gamelan sonorities to the limited resources of a Western percussion section is McPhee's *Tabuh-tabuhan*; we shall see below that Britten's orchestration in *The Prince of the Pagodas* reflects an approach strikingly similar to McPhee's, and is even more skilful in avoiding the necessity for any specialized Balinese instruments. Also in Britten's mind at the time must have been Poulenc's Concerto for Two Pianos, which he performed alongside its composer on 16 January 1955 at the Royal Festival Hall with the Royal Liverpool Philharmonic Orchestra under John Pritchard. Poulenc had written to Britten in the previous December:

> I will be arriving in London on 13 January for our rehearsals. We will play from the music, which will be easier for my convalescing memory. You are doing the second piano part, aren't you? I am so much looking forward to this concert. It will be my return to the platform!! Agreed for Aldeburgh '56.[25]
>
> I embrace you as well as Peter.[26]

Poulenc and Britten had performed the Concerto for Two Pianos for the first time at the Royal Albert Hall in 1945 (an occasion which Poulenc recalled 'with emotion'[27] and which Britten described as 'chic'),[28] and the timing of its 1955 London revival is surely significant. As noted in Chapter 1, the *selisir* scale appears in Poulenc's Concerto at the same pitch level used by Britten in *Pagodas* when following the tuning of his recordings by the Peliatan gamelan.

Britten's composition sketch is not explicit concerning the instrumentation of those passages in the score which reconstruct gamelan sonorities. A note at the foot of the title-page of Act I reads:

Balinese
Vibraphone (without fans), Chung (ancient cymbals)
(glock sticks).

The introduction of the gamelan sonority in Act II at fig. 69 is twice marked

---

[25] Poulenc had been engaged to perform his *Aubade: Concerto chorégraphique* at the Aldeburgh Festival.

[26] Sidney Buckland (ed.), *Francis Poulenc: Selected Correspondence 1915–1963* (London: Gollancz, 1991), 228.

[27] See Poulenc, 'Hommage à Benjamin Britten'.

[28] Letter from Britten to Poulenc, 8 November 1954, reproduced in the programme book to the October Britten Festival held at Aldeburgh in 1994 ('Britten and the French Connection'), 10.

'Gamelin' (sic),[29] the passage at fig. 71 carries the indication 'dry' with only 'xylo soft sticks' as an indication of the scoring, and the long section commencing at fig. 72 is marked only with the words 'vibr' and 'gong'. Fig. 78 is preceded by the simple note '(Gamelin stops)' and fig. [4]86 carries the indication 'Gamelin to end'. The entrance of the percussion at fig. 19[10] in Act III is again merely labelled '(Gamelin)'.

The orchestration revealed in the full score, however, demonstrates an intuitive grasp of the structure and instrumentation of gamelan music and an astonishing ear for percussion sonorities. The material for the section between figs. 69 and 74 is derived from the Peliatan recording of 'Kapi radja' (CD track 6) and labelled on Britten's sketches 'xyl. ~~Gongs~~ Metal. Soft high gongs. Cymbals' (see Figure 8). Britten allocates each type of instrument from the gamelan gong *kebyar* to a specific Western instrument with unerring precision. James Blades recalls that Britten seemed fully versed in the various components of the gamelan and needed little advice.[30] It seems that Blades merely suggested the use of jazz tom-toms (then a relatively uncommon orchestral instrument) as a substitute for the Balinese kendang and the vibraphone without motor (cf. Britten's note quoted above) as trompong or jublag, its musical function changing according to context.

Britten's systematic approach is best illustrated by the passage at fig. 72 (see Ex. 4.7). For the colotomic gong strokes Britten employs a conventional orchestral gong doubled with a sustained double-bass note of definite pitch. The distinctive timbre of the kempli is suggested by a repeated staccato C$\sharp$ on a 'piccolo timpano' (played with hard sticks) and harp *près de la table*. The gangsa *gantung* are replaced by rapid figurations on xylophone and two piccolos (a single line dovetailed between two instruments), while the vibraphone and celeste provide the slower ostinato of the jegogan and jublag. A small pair of clashed cymbals serves as the cengceng (presumably the 'Chung' of Britten's manuscript note)[31] and throughout the passage a piano duet doubles most of the individual lines, lending added resonance to the broad gong strokes in the lower register and increasing the brightness of the gangsa *gantung* figurations. The use of the piano's distinctive timbre in this context undoubtedly signifies the renewed influence of the McPhee and Poulenc precedents. As already mentioned, three tom-toms serve as kendang, and at several points (e.g. the first- and second-time bars before fig. 73 and fig. [2]74) the vibraphone solo recalls the melodic function of the trompong. At fig. 69 the vibraphone player is instructed to employ hard rubber beaters, a

---

[29] This curious spelling was also employed by Imogen Holst on the envelope containing the sketches from Bali.

[30] Personal communication. Blades also suggested to Britten the possibility of using genuine African drums to accompany the dancing of the King of the South in Act I (cf. fig. 31, which calls for unspecified 'native drums').

[31] In Indonesia, 'cengceng' is pronounced 'chengcheng' (which was the older spelling of the same word), clearly illustrating its endearingly onomatopoeic derivation.

Ex. 4.7

sonority clearly in Britten's mind from the outset when he jotted down '(glock sticks)' on the title page of Act I quoted above.

The section from figs. 69 to 74 is based on *selisir* centring on B♭, which Britten took down directly from the Peliatan recording of 'Kapi radja' at that pitch (see Figure 8), and had already noted down twice at the same pitch in Bali. The explosive chord with which the gamelan ensemble enters at fig. 69 is highly typical of the *kebyar* style, and Britten's sketch (marked 'Begin' on

Figure 8) reveals its origin from the opening passage of 'Kapi radja'. The lively glockenspiel solo at fig. 69⁴⁻⁵ exactly captures the rhythmic style of a solo gangsa. The two kendang are introduced at fig. 70 in dialogue with the cengceng in a passage not literally transcribed from 'Kapi radja' but clearly inspired by it. Here it is intriguing to note that Britten represents the sound of the two drums with three different pitches. The two drummers in the gamelan employ a vast range of drumming techniques, including stopped and open tones played with various parts of the hand or occasionally with hard sticks. Britten appears to have heard the effect of the kendang at three predominant levels, and in McPhee's authoritative book *Music in Bali* (which was not known to Britten) the author transcribes a kendang passage on no less than eight distinct levels (four *lanang* and four *wadon*), but then demonstrates how the overall effect is appreciated on only three.[32] It will be recalled that Britten's

Ex. 4.8

[32] McPhee, *Music in Bali*, 174.

fascination with the complexity of oriental drumming had been explicitly acknowledged on two separate occasions when he heard Indian drummers in action.

From fig. 71 the piano, celeste and xylophone present a much simplified version of a *reongan* cadenza which occurs shortly after the opening of 'Kapi radja' (see Ex. 4.8). Britten's tempo is much slower than that on the recording and he omits the characteristic metrical irregularities to produce a much more reflective and less frenetic effect. The vibraphone solo at fig. ⁴72 is reminiscent of another short cadenza from 'Kapi radja'. The notes in the left hand of the piano reduction at this point are outlined by cello pizzicato, piano duet (*secondo*) and tom-toms, and sustained by clarinets in a deft piece of scoring which subtly suggests the resonance of the jegogan. The use of cello pizzicato in this context strongly recalls McPhee's procedures in *Tabuh-tabuhan*.

These concentrated, self-contained incidents all reflect the actions of the individual pagodas on stage and are combined with independent music for a solo violin which has represented the tentative Belle Rose since fig. 68. At fig. 72 the violin is dispensed with, presumably because Belle Rose is now completely captivated (for a similar moment of symbolism in *Death in Venice*, see below, pp. 241–2). The music then launches into a brilliant and extended free reconstruction of one of the toccata-like sections from 'Kapi radja'. Although each element (the gong punctuation, kempli C♯, crotchet *pokok* ostinato and demisemiquaver figurations) is taken from the Peliatan recording, Britten's version makes no attempt to reproduce the exact notes of the original piece, and this is suggested by the vagueness of the sketch marked 'This for beginning of Pagodas scene' (Figure 8). The prominent cengceng parts are omitted and the forceful outbursts in bars 7 and 8 are again modelled on the recording in only a general sense. At fig. 73 Britten incorporates the gambang melody he had brought back from Bali, where he had notated it at the same pitch (see Ex. 4.5b above). The scoring of this theme for glockenspiel, celeste, harp harmonics, piano and solo violin uncannily suggests the combination of suling and gangsa: Britten was also to return to this sonority in *Death in Venice*. This is the first instance in the ballet of Britten's combining two Balinese elements of diverse origin in a synthesis which perfectly reflects the procedures and style of authentic gamelan music.

At fig. 74 the trumpet fanfares which began the entire work are modified to reflect the intervallic contours of *selisir*, and the music is now transposed down a semitone. The 'gamelan' then enters with a tutti chord at the new pitch level in a gradual, unmeasured accelerando. We have seen that such chords are a strong characteristic of the *kebyar* style: the accelerating rhythm is also typical, and Britten would have heard it with particular clarity towards the end of the *legong* on the second side of the Peliatan record (RG1) and in the *wayang kulit* piece 'Merak ngilo' on the reel-to-reel tape recording (track 5). At this stage he had not yet developed the special notation for this accelerating pattern which was to become a prominent feature of many works composed in the 1960s and 1970s.

The transposition of *selisir* at this point not only relieves the potential monotony for the Western ear: it also allows Britten to incorporate the Prince-as-Salamander theme at fig. 75[5] at the same pitch level at which he had encountered it in Bali and on IJzerdraat's tape recording (see Ex. 4.6 above). The hypnotically revolving accompanimental figure is similar to that on the recording of 'Tamililingan' (CD track 7), a dance created for the Peliatan troupe by the same Sampih who had been adopted into the McPhee household many years before. Britten's sketch (Figure 8) reproduces this figuration at its original pitch level (i.e. *selisir* centring on Bb, identical to that in 'Kapi radja') and this also had to be transposed down a semitone to correspond to the pitch of the Salamander theme. Once more double-bass, gong and low piano provide the gong punctuation, but the two kendang are now represented by tom-toms doubled by cello pizzicato, a procedure again recalling McPhee's in *Tabuh-tabuhan*. The accompaniment is allocated to two flutes, xylophone, vibraphone, celeste (left hand) and piano, while the theme is announced by glockenspiel, celeste (right hand), piano and cello solo (artificial harmonics). At fig. 76 Britten suddenly quickens the tempo, a characteristic device employed both in the performance of 'Tabuh telu' on the tape and in 'Tamililingan' (cf. Figure 8, where the composer has indicated 'accel. subits'). This effective synthesis of two separate Balinese elements corresponds to Britten's use of the gambang theme described above.

Britten relaxes the stringently applied *selisir* scale at fig. [4]77 to effect a transition to the entry of the full orchestra in an emphatic C major. The theme announced by the trumpet at this point represents the Prince-as-Human, and the contrast between the thoroughly Western key of C major and the preceding *selisir* is an obvious musical comment on the dramatic situation. Nevertheless, the interjected clusters from the 'gamelan' remind the listener of the duality in the Prince's character and, following a tender 'Pas de deux' between Belle Rose and the Prince during which the percussion is silent, the 'gamelan' makes a forceful re-entrance just before fig. 86, when Belle Rose tears the bandage away from her eyes in an attempt to see her partner. As she hunts for him, the syncopated figure in the strings is derived from *selisir* in its transposition on A; the demisemiquavers from 'Kapi radja' then return, now as semiquavers in a *presto* tempo. At fig. 87 the Prince emerges, transformed once again as his Salamander theme makes a climactic return. Belle Rose flees, slowly followed by the beast, to the 'gamelan' music which had accompanied its first appearance, and the second act closes with brief reminiscences of two passages from 'Kapi radja' at the original Bb pitch level. With characteristically economical tonal symbolism, the gong strokes punctuating this closing section are modified by Britten so that the double-bass and piano provide a pedal C♮ instead of the C♯ of the earlier version: this pitch, which is the Prince's 'tonic', serves as a graphic reminder of his duality and provides

Ex. 4.9

The Salamander comes to her rescue.

an uncomfortably expectant tonal ambiguity with which to end Belle Rose's eventful stay in Pagodaland.

The Balinese music from Act II makes two reappearances in the final act. In many ways the first, although very brief, is the more significant, since *selisir* appears in a conventional orchestral context as a symbol for the Salamander's entry into the Emperor's court. The scale occurs twice at the pitch level associated with the Salamander (i.e. centring on A) in a succession of chords which only loosely recall the Salamander theme (see Ex. 4.9).[33] Nevertheless, it is clear that these chords are deliberately constructed from *selisir* for a specific symbolic purpose; and the use of such a derivation without an explicit 'gamelan' sonority looks directly ahead to the musico-dramatic application of Balinese material in *Death in Venice*.

An interesting feature of the collage of musical material associated with the Prince which begins at fig. 19 in Act III is the use for the first time in Britten's work of two gongs of different pitches to provide the ostinato which underlies the entire section. This unmistakably recalls the influence of the Balinese gong *wadon* and gong *lanang*, and the procedure will be encountered again in *Death in Venice*. *Selisir* (again centring on Bb) returns with the entry of the celeste at fig. ⁴20 (the point marked 'Gamelin' in the composition sketch) and the

---

[33] This passage was one of the many cuts made in the composer's recording of the ballet. See p. 98 and note 14 above.

various ideas from 'Kapi radja' return after fig. 20, namely the vibraphone (= trompong) solo, the xylophone (= reong) cadenza in triplets, the tutti chord and the demisemiquaver figurations. Throughout this passage it may be seen that Britten treats the Balinese elements more flexibly in order to facilitate their combination with the Prince's diatonic trumpet theme, which is heard simultaneously in the main orchestra in a variety of instrumental combinations. (The entire passage is, once more, a representation of the Prince's duality.) At fig. ^{3}22 the gambang theme (Ex. 4.5) returns in the percussion, its distinctive rhythmic profile retained in spite of the new triplet shape in which it is presented. The theme is now presented in *selisir* on A, a scale that had been re-established at the return of the demisemiquavers from 'Kapi radja' four bars earlier. Although it is relaxed as the climax is approached, individual melodic fragments in the tuned percussion are still derived from newly transposed *selisir* patterns. Such transpositions are, of course, totally alien to Balinese music and they provide a notable contrast to the authentically strict treatment of *selisir* in the Act II gamelan reconstructions. We shall see in Chapter 8 that Britten continued to use Balinese scales in an idiosyncratically free fashion in *Death in Venice*.

The initial impetus behind the reconstruction of gamelan music in Act II of the ballet was clearly the desire to create a musical medium which, by its very exoticism, would vividly portray the attraction held by Pagodaland and its Salamander-Prince over Belle Rose. Thus the two principal 'gamelan' sections of Act II analysed above make little attempt to go beyond what is in reality a highly skilful Balinese pastiche based on the specific materials which Britten had at his disposal. (The aesthetic implications of these 'reconstructions', and the changing critical reaction to them, are discussed in Chapter 9 below.) However, once this separate sound-world had been established, Britten's flair for dramatic symbolism must have appreciated the possibilities it offered for ironic metamorphosis. On a very simple level we have seen how the end of Act II (with its pedal C♮) and the collage of Act III portray the duality of the Prince's character by straightforward superimposition. Two much more significant examples of the transformation of Balinese material occur before fig. 87 in Act II, where Belle Rose pursues the Prince, and at the entry of the Salamander in Act III. Britten had already begun successfully to unite Western and Balinese elements in his score for *The Prince of the Pagodas*, and isolated incidents such as these were later to provide the model for the accomplished appropriation he ultimately achieved in *Death in Venice*.

5

Japan

> Bali was heaven, scenicly, musically, dancicly. It was a glorious holiday of 12 days too. Unfortunately the holiday was rudely dispelled by our return to Java, where <u>everything</u> went wrong, & I got ill & had to cancel a concert.

So wrote Britten to Imogen Holst on 8 February 1956 from Hong Kong, where in the midst of having to give four concerts in the space of five days the recent 'glorious holiday' must have seemed remote indeed.

After two days back in Singapore, the tour party had flown to Hong Kong via Bangkok on 2 February. Britten described the colony to Miss Holst as 'a sweet place, very interesting', and commented warmly on the hospitality extended to them by Peg Hesse's brother-in-law David Geddes, who lived with his Norwegian wife Pytt on Victoria Peak. On the day after their arrival Britten and Pears performed in the Empire Theatre, and on 6 February they gave a broadcast recital and interview for Hong Kong Radio. Between these two events, they made the standard excursion to Macao by pleasure-steamer on 4 February in order to give another recital in an eighteenth-century theatre, and repaired afterwards to one of the Portuguese colony's many casinos ('it did seem a silly sport . . . Pretty poor fun, we thought, and yet they go on 24 hours a day, and people flock to it').[1] Whilst in Hong Kong, they also paid a visit to the mainland New Territories on the Chinese border. Their final commitment before departure was a private performance of Schumann's *Dichterliebe* at the residence of an 'unpleasant finance manager'.[2]

On the afternoon of 8 February the group boarded a Boeing Stratocruiser for the six-hour flight to Tokyo's Haneda airport. For some time during the early stages of the world tour it had seemed likely that the projected visit to Japan might have to be cancelled owing to difficulty experienced in obtaining the necessary visas. On 1 December, Pears had written to his cousin Janet Stone from Istanbul to say 'We plot to go to Peking instead of Tokyo'; and as late as 23 December Britten declared 'We may after all <u>not</u> go to Japan; things have fallen through a bit & we may spend longer in Ceylon & come back to

---

[1] Letter from Britten to Roger Duncan, 8 February 1956. A photograph taken at the Macao concert is to be found in Mitchell and Evans, *Benjamin Britten: Pictures*, Plate 295.
[2] Prince Ludwig of Hesse, *Ausflug Ost*, 84.

the <u>real</u> South of India which we've not yet seen.'[3] But the visa situation was eventually resolved satisfactorily. Britten wrote to Roger Duncan on board the flight from Hong Kong to Tokyo:

> And so we go on to Japan. I must say I don't want to, awfully. I don't like what I know about the country or the people – I certainly don't like the way they look (the Yellow races look very strange & suspicious – whereas the Brown, the Indians, or Indonesians, look touching & sympathetic, & can be very beautiful) – and judging by the difficulty Peter & I had in getting our visas, they don't like me any more than I like them. We had to send cables to the agents, to the British Ambassador, & the Council in Japan, & our agents – costing nearly £50 (really!) – before we could get permission to come here! But I mustn't be silly, & must try to like them.

In a later letter to Roger Duncan, the composer resumed this theme:

> . . . in a way I was right. It is far the <u>strangest</u> country we have yet been to; like, in a way, going to a country which is inhabited by a very intelligent kind of insect. Very industrious, very clever, but very different from us, very odd. They have very good manners, they bow & scrape all the time: they have most beautiful small things, all their houses, their flowers, the things they eat & drink out of, are wonderfully pretty, but their <u>big</u> things, their cities, their way of thinking, and behaving, have all somehow got wrong . . .[4]

If these expressions of anti-Japanese sentiment on Britten's part seem rather surprising, coming as they do some eleven years after the end of World War II and the natural antipathy towards the Japanese which that conflict engendered in the West, it should be remembered that Britten's own artistic contacts with Japan up to this point had been less than satisfactory.[5] Although he was to remain disquieted by some aspects of his Japanese experience (see his remarks quoted below), Britten delivered a warm address broadcast on Japanese Radio as a New Year's message on 1 January 1958:

> It gives me great pleasure to send this New Year's greeting to the music-lovers of Japan. Although my acquaintance with Japan is very limited, the short time I have spent there remains very vividly in my mind . . . We were treated with great courtesy and friendship, and I was very impressed with the high standard of playing of the [NHK] orchestra,

---

[3] Letter to Mary Potter, written in Delhi. On 8 February Britten was able to confirm to Imogen Holst: 'We have revised our return schedule so as to include a holiday in Ceylon, & a visit to Southern India.'

[4] Letter written on the later flight from Hong Kong to Bangkok on 21 February 1956 and posted on 24 February.

[5] For an account of the unhappy fate of the *Sinfonia da Requiem* in Japan in 1940, see Mitchell and Reed (eds.), *Letters from a Life*, II, Letters 211 and 297–9.

and with the players' considerable understanding of my music . . .

And I should like to take this opportunity to thank those Japanese who were so courteous and helpful to us, helping us to appreciate the beauties and subtleties of their great country . . .[6]

On arrival at Haneda Airport, the four travelling-companions were greeted by Kei-ichi Kurosawa and his son Hiroshi (known to English friends as Peter) before transferring to the Hotel Imperial, where they were to be based for the duration of their stay. Britten reported to Roger Duncan:

We arrived late one evening in Tokyo, after a long flight from Hong Kong (but with tremendous fuss about getting visas – having had to spend nearly £50 on cables to get them – just pure fuss) – and were met by hundreds of cameras and reporters. Japan is photography mad – Peter & I had every movement photographed on our first few days there, getting out of cars, going up lifts, meeting people, talking to people, getting up, sitting down.[7]

Britten's visit to the country had been arranged under the auspices of the British Council and the Japanese broadcasting authority, NHK (Nippon Hoso Kyokai). Kei-ichi Kurosawa had active connections with both organizations and proved to be a helpful guide to the visitors on their travels in and around the capital. He had been educated at Trinity College, Cambridge, from 1925 to 1928 and was the heir to the highly successful typewriter company founded by his father Teijiro at the turn of the century. In 1929, shortly after his return to Japan from England, Mr Kurosawa founded the Tokyo Madrigal Singers and the Tokyo Polyphonic Orchestra. He remained a committed anglophile and was made an Honorary Member of the Order of the British Empire in 1976 for his services to Anglo-Japanese relations, especially for his promotion of British music in Japan.

Kei-ichi Kurosawa died in 1978, and his son Peter now heads the family firm and directs the Tokyo Madrigal Singers, a group he first sang with at the age of eight. Peter Kurosawa graduated from Tokyo's Keio University and studied mechanical engineering in the United States before becoming president of the Kurosawa Company. In 1956 he acted as the driver when his father accompanied Britten and Pears on their activities in Japan, and he remembers much important information concerning their visit. I am greatly indebted to Mr Kurosawa for his untiring assistance in correspondence and for supplying a significant collection of photographs relating to Britten's stay in Tokyo. During my stay in Japan in 1986, his generosity allowed me to retrace Britten's footsteps in detail; the following account draws heavily on his own reminiscences of the events concerned.

---

6   The complete text of the address, which was recorded at Bush House, London, on 3 December 1957, is reproduced in the programme book to the 44th Aldeburgh Festival (1991), 18–19.
7   Letter written on 21 February (cf. note 4 above).

On Britten's first full day in Tokyo (9 February 1956), a morning press conference was followed by a lunch party with Bill MacAlpine (Deputy Director of the British Council) and Vere Redman, both experts on matters Japanese. In the afternoon Britten and Pears were occupied with a rehearsal for their first NHK concert, to be broadcast live that same evening on both radio and television from the NHK annexe auditorium at 7.30 p.m.[8] The event was reviewed in the *Asahi Shimbun* on 11 February:

Pears's voice may not have been excellent but was polished and beautiful in tone. The sweet melody of *The Salley Gardens*, characteristic of the Irish folk-songs, sounded even sweeter with his clear voice.

Britten's *Seven Sonnets of Michelangelo*, accompanied by the composer himself, was most interesting. They are songs about love and employ complex harmonies peculiar to Britten, but their controlled Italianness made them familiar and accessible, and the singer and the accompanist perfectly complemented each other.

The British folk-songs (*The Miller of Dee*, *Oliver Cromwell*, etc.) were all arranged by Britten. The long-lived and widely sung folk-songs have become works of art – using the modern compositional method but not trying to make them eccentric or difficult. There is much to be learnt from them. Their music bore the sophisticated elegance of the English gentlemen, just like their appearances.[9]

Peg Hesse noted in a letter written the next day:

Yesterday Ben and Peter were televised – we went along to watch them being made up and then in front of 3000 <u>invited</u> guests we enormously enjoyed their concert. Programmes hand printed on sort of velvet flock paper! All this sounds very dry, but we 4 laugh and fool so much and so many funny things happen we are a sort of travelling circus!

A busy social schedule started on 10 February when Britten visited the British ambassador, Sir Esler Denning, and played Bach and Mozart on two pianos with him.

The following day proved to be one of the most significant of the entire world tour. After lunch with Professor Klaus Pringsheim, the brother-in-law of Thomas Mann, the group attended a performance of the Nō theatre. It was William Plomer, soon to become the librettist of *Curlew River*, who had recommended that Britten should make the most of the opportunity to immerse himself in the Japanese dramatic arts. Plomer later recalled:

---

[8] A photograph of the occasion appears in Christopher Headington, *Peter Pears: A Biography* (London: Faber and Faber, 1992), Plate 9. A copy of the NHK broadcast is preserved on videotape at the Britten–Pears Library (VC0244). Britten recalled in his 1958 New Year's message to Japan that this event 'in fact was our first recital for television anywhere in the world'.

[9] I am grateful to Yukiko Kishinami for supplying this translation.

In 1955 Britten was planning a journey to the Far East. Knowing that I had lived in Japan when young, he asked if there was anything he should particularly see or do while there. I strongly recommended the Japanese theatre in its various forms, Kabuki, Bunraku and Nō – particularly the Nō. I remember describing a Nō play and imitating some of the gestures used by the actors.[10]

Britten's respect for Plomer's human and literary qualities is evident throughout their well-preserved correspondence (intact from 1948 until Plomer's death in 1973),[11] and it seems that Plomer's role in shaping Britten's interest in Japanese culture was analogous to McPhee's in the sphere of Balinese music.

Like McPhee, Plomer had extensive first-hand knowledge of his particular Far Eastern domain. He had first visited Japan in September 1926, at the age of 22. His reaction to what he saw was precisely the same as McPhee's was to be when he first set foot on Bali: after only a fortnight, Plomer was so captivated by the country that he felt he had to stay there permanently. Largely due to the influence of Edmund Blunden, he soon found himself teaching English in Tokyo. Plomer lived in Japan for nearly three years and was greatly helped by a factotum whose name, ironically enough, was Sumida.[12] In his autobiography Plomer describes the profound effect of the various Japanese dramatic arts he first witnessed at this time:

> We also went to the theatre . . . The three main kinds – the Nō, the Kabuki, and the Bunraku – depended for their effects upon tradition, stylisation, and the great accomplishment of actors who came of acting lineage and seemed to have hereditary poise . . . The Kabuki used to be called the 'popular' theatre; its appeal was the most direct. In the Bunraku, or puppet theatre, . . . the dolls were manipulated by visible men . . . And what was the Nō play? To this the European brought that total ignorance which, in its way, made him specially impressionable. One didn't understand the archaic language, the completely strange chanting; one knew nothing of the symbolism, and the briefly outlined plot was so steeped in the mysteries of antiquity, of a remote and venerable culture, of esoteric Buddhism, that one had to rely on little but the evidence of one's senses to perceive the great beauty and refinement and agelessness of a wholly non-popular tradition and convention, which, in present-day jargon, would perhaps be sneered at as 'élitist'.[13]

---

10 *Edinburgh Festival Programme Book* (1968), 28.
11 Housed in the Special Collection at Durham University Library. Plomer had received an honorary doctorate from the university and bequeathed his personal library to it on his death. The correspondence between Britten and Plomer relating to the Church Parables is examined in detail in Chapter 6.
12 The Sumida River, from which the Nō play *Sumidagawa* takes its name, runs through the Kantō Plain and enters the sea in Tokyo Bay. The noun *sumida* literally means 'corner of the ricefield'.
13 William Plomer, *Double Lives: An Autobiography* (London: Jonathan Cape, 1942; repr. as *The Autobiography of William Plomer*, 1975), 201–2.

Plomer's remark is perfectly illustrated by Britten's own reactions to *Sumidagawa*. Prince Ludwig's description of the performance concentrates on its verbal unintelligibility:

> Overall, the whole effect is strangely comical to us. But it turns out that, although the recitation of the text is entirely nonsensical up to the last syllable, it is nevertheless a humanly moving art form. This is especially true of the piece called 'Sumida River'.[14]

We shall also see that Britten's initial reaction to the genre was one of humour rather than profundity. Thus Britten, too, clearly 'had to rely on little but the evidence of [his] senses to perceive the great beauty and refinement and agelessness of a wholly non-popular tradition and convention'.

Britten's interest in Nō theatre in fact extended further back than Plomer's directive in 1955: we saw in Chapter 2 how he became involved in Ezra Pound's eccentric attempt to stage a Nō play in English translation in 1938. The connection with Pound was to resurface in the 1950s. In 1952, Ronald Duncan had been passed over as potential librettist for *Gloriana*, Plomer assuming the task.[15] Duncan recalled Britten's preparations for the Coronation opera:

> [Britten] said that there were two snags; firstly he was already committed to writing an opera for children, and William Plomer was already writing the libretto [*Tyco the Vegan*]. It was, I recall, based on the theme of a journey to the moon, and Britten had talked to me about its structure because he thought my association with Ezra Pound gave me some knowledge of the Japanese Noh plays, which Pound had translated and which Britten had found fascinating . . . He told George [Earl of Harewood] that if Plomer, as he thought likely, would refuse to be diverted from his Noh libretto, then he would like me to write the words of the Gala libretto . . . But I, myself, heard nothing of these exciting plans. Like Ben I would, of course, have dropped anything to contribute. But Ben was influenced to exclude me.[16]

If Duncan's memory is to be trusted, it seems that Britten was interested in the structure of Nō plays as early as 1952. The description of *Tyco the Vegan* as a 'Noh libretto' is puzzling, however, and it may be that Duncan has confused the origins of the space-travel opera with the genesis of *Curlew River*.

In 1916 Pound had published translations, based on the fragmentary notes of Professor Ernest Fenollosa, of some fifteen Nō plays.[17] These were reissued

---

[14] Prince Ludwig of Hesse, *Ausflug Ost*, 90.

[15] See Paul Banks (ed.), *Britten's Gloriana: Essays and Sources*, Aldeburgh Studies in Music, 1 (Woodbridge: The Boydell Press, 1993), 18–19.

[16] Ronald Duncan, *Working with Britten* (Welcombe: The Rebel Press, 1981), 112–13.

[17] In two volumes: *Certain Noble Plays of Japan* (Dublin: Dundrum Cuala Press, 1916) and *'Noh' or Accomplishment: A Study of the Classical Stage of Japan* (London: Macmillan, 1916). The latter title refers to the literal meaning of the word *nō*.

as part of *The Translations of Ezra Pound* by Faber and Faber in 1953, and Britten obtained a copy of the first printing. This confirms Duncan's observation that Britten was interested in Nō at around the time of *Gloriana*. Pound's translations are characterized by a respectful objectivity and linguistic plainness, and the accompanying introduction and commentary would have provided Britten with a helpful introduction to the principles of Nō drama. As was to be the case with his latent interest in Balinese music, however, Britten's fascination with Nō had to wait several years before finally surfacing and bearing artistic fruit.

Peter Kurosawa recalls that the live performance of *Sumidagawa* seen by Britten on 11 February 1956 took place in the Suidōbashi Nō Theatre before it was rebuilt, and that the play *Sumidagawa* was given by the Umetani Group of the Kanze School with Takehisa Umewaka as the protagonist (*shite*).[18] Since it was from this one event that the entire conception of Britten's Church Parables sprang, Prince Ludwig's detailed description of the occasion in *Ausflug Ost* is of particular interest and deserves quotation at some length:

> ... we come to an art school. Inside is a roofed stage to the right of a rectangular auditorium with tiered seating.
>
> The audience sits to the front and left of the stage, which is of constant height throughout, with a bridge furnished with a rail and small trees leading to a door in the rear left-hand corner of the auditorium. There hangs a curtained entrance through which the players come onto the bridge with an exciting jerking of the curtain. The stage area has in its rear right-hand corner a little door through which the chorus enters and exits. There are no decorations. In front, to the right, the stage is enlarged by an extension-like balcony on which the chorus of about twelve men dressed in black squat on the ground. Two drummers sit, somewhat higher, in the middle of the stage. Now and again they play drums bound with a network of lateral and diagonal strings with short, pounding strokes. In addition, they chant with a curiously strained and strangled tone ... The chorus recites in this fashion, but often sings properly on an urgent monotone ...
>
> The players move with slow steps, lifting up their white-socked feet and putting them down carefully in front of them. They wear clothes which are obviously very old but generally opulent in shape and colour. Overall, the whole effect is strangely comical to us. But it turns out that, although the recitation of the text is entirely nonsensical up to the last syllable, it is nevertheless a humanly moving art form. This is especially true of the piece called 'Sumida River'. There is a ferryman on the river; a traveller arrives, drawing attention to a woman. This mad mother is looking for her lost child and turns up on the river bank by the ferryman, who makes a point of refusing to take her with him.

18 Hiroshi Kurosawa, 'Benjamin Britten and *Sumidagawa*', in programme book to the Tokyo Chamber Opera Theatre production of *Curlew River* (July 1982). I am indebted to Jason James for supplying me with a translation of the article.

Finally, he conducts the traveller and mother across, and relates on the river a long tale about a child whom a thief kidnapped and who died of exhaustion on the other side of the river. The mother weeps, and then finds the grave of her child on the other river bank. She mourns. The mother is played by a large man in woman's clothes with a little wooden female mask. Props are used in the presentation of events: a bamboo frond represents madness, a staff for the ferryman, a little gong to represent sorrow. As soon as it is redundant, an attendant takes the prop off. The mother's grief, a high, swelling *Sprechstimme*, the gesturing of the hand to the weeping eyes, the little stroke on the small gong, . . . the mourning at the grave, the curiously strained and expressive voices, the sudden stamping with a white foot . . . At the end, the impression of the piece is moving and profound. It has greatly affected Ben.[19]

Britten himself confirmed that his initial reaction to the Nō convention had been one of humour rather than aesthetic profundity in a letter to Roger Duncan (quoted below). Something of this humour is reflected in an amusing photograph taken by the Kurosawas which shows Pears indulging in mimicry of Nō drumming techniques with the aid of a wastepaper basket.[20] Nō vocal chanting sounds uncannily like the comic character Eccles created by Spike Milligan in the 1950s radio hit *The Goon Show*: possibly this irreverent identification appealed to Britten's almost schoolboyish sense of fun.

That Britten's imagination was eventually captured by *Sumidagawa* is revealed by his desire to see the entire play once again before leaving Tokyo. This second visit to the Nō theatre took place on 19 February, when the group was augmented by the company of Reginald Close, the head of the British Council.[21] Prince Ludwig was himself not quite so enthusiastic about this occasion: 'We see another performance of the piece called Sunigawa [*sic*] River at Ben's particular wish. It is magical once again, although in my opinion the time from noon to 2pm is not ideal for dramatic profundity.'[22] Britten subsequently acquired a reel-to-reel tape recording of this production of *Sumidagawa* for his own use (CD track 9). The tape (which is preserved at Aldeburgh) is entitled 'Sumi-Kawa',[23] and its origin is recounted by Close:

As we were leaving the theatre, Peter put a wad of notes into my hand, begging me to get them a record of the *Sumidagawa* music. I got the Noh company to make a recording, and Lady Gascoigne, who was then on a brief visit to Tokyo, took it back to London and delivered it personally to Ben and Peter, who were then living in Chester Gate, Regent's Park.[24]

[19] Prince Ludwig of Hesse, *Ausflug Ost*, 89–90.
[20] Reproduced in Reed (ed.), *The Travel Diaries of Peter Pears*, Plate 11.
[21] For quotations from Close's unpublished memoirs relating to Britten's time in Japan, see *ibid.*, 56–7 and 64.
[22] Prince Ludwig of Hesse, *Ausflug Ost*, 110.
[23] GB-ALb 3-9401064.
[24] See Reed (ed.), *The Travel Diaries of Peter Pears*, 64. As Dr Reed notes, the recording

Britten expressed his feelings about Japanese theatre in a letter to Roger Duncan:

> One thing that I unreservedly loved in Japan was the theatre. They have two principal kinds – the Noh, & the Kabuki. The Noh is very severe & classical – very traditional, without any scenery to speak of, or lighting, and there are very few characters – one main one [*shite*], who wears a mask, & two or three supporting ones [*waki* and *waki-tsure*] & usually a very small boy too [*kokata*]. There is a chorus [*ji-utai*] that sits at the side, chanting, & a kind of orchestra of 2 drums (who also moan in the oddest way) & a flute, that squat in the centre of the stage, almost in the middle of the action. At first it all seemed too silly, and we giggled alot. But soon we began to catch on abit, & at the end it was very exciting. It's funny that if you are a good enough actor just one movement suggests lots of things, & in the Noh, there are <u>very</u> few movements (& those are all written down in the text books, & are never changed). There was one called 'Sumida River' which we saw twice. The other theatre, Kabuki, is the great popular one – with dancing, music, tremendous stage effects (a revolving stage) & wonderful lighting . . . It made Covent Garden or Drury Lane seem rather dull from that point of view. It was madly exciting.
>
> There is so much to tell you about Japan that would take ages – it is a most interesting place, & we had wonderful experiences. And yet, when we left, I wasn't sure I wanted ever to go back (in spite of the Theatres, the Temples etc.), because I felt rather uncomfortable there, as if, inspite of their exquisite manners & lovely things, one didn't quite know what they were thinking, nor quite trust them. But I expect I'm wrong.[25]

In his 1958 broadcast message to Japan, Britten commented:

> I shall never forget the impact made on me by the Japanese theatre – the tremendous Kabuki, but above all the profound Nō plays. I count the last among the greatest theatrical experiences of my life. Of course it was strange to start with, the language and the especially curious kind of chanting used; but we were fortunate in having excellent literal translations to follow from, and we soon became accustomed to the haunting sounds. The deep solemnity and *self*lessness of the acting, the perfect shaping of the drama (like a great Greek tragedy) coupled with the strength and universality of the stories are something which every Western artist can learn from.

The three days from 12 to 14 February were spent on an extended visit to

contains the entire play, not just the music: it would doubtless have been contrary to the Nō aesthetic to have extracted the musical components from the work as edited highlights since so much in Nō depends for its effect on a progressive cumulation of dramatic intensity.

25 See note 4 above (p. 113). For a fuller explication of the Japanese terminology, see below.

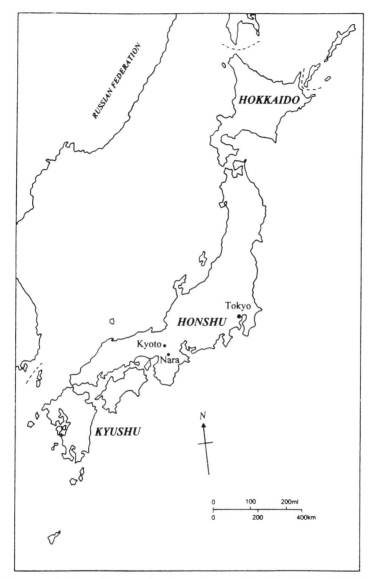

Figure 12. Map of Japan, showing places visited by Britten in 1956

the ancient Japanese cities of Kyoto and Nara (see Figure 12). Britten described the journey:

It was about 8 hours in the train, a lovely journey, sometime along the sea (rather like south Cornwall), & for 3 hours we went round Fuji-Jama, the great volcano, that appears in so many Japanese pictures – a tremendously tall, cone shaped, beautiful mountain. The Japanese Islands are volcanic, & Tokyo especially has earthquakes quite frequently (it was practically destroyed about 1923, & so houses are built quite small). We had two while we were there, a very funny feeling – like being in a lift.

While we were in Kyoto, we stayed in a Japanese Hotel [*ryokan*], and that really takes some describing – I don't know if I can do it here![26] It is entirely made of wood (except that the walls are made of paper!); there aren't any chairs, you squat on the floor, & my goodness, how stiff you get!! There aren't any beds; they put down quilts on the floor. The baths are quite different from ours, small & deep, & filled with boiling water. You wash before you get in, because everyone uses the same water, & there aren't locks on the doors (which anyhow are just sliding screens), so people can easily come in & out – no one minds! But all these things, like the food, & the green tea (which they can sometimes take 2 hours to make, while you squat around on your heels, saying polite nothings, but getting slowly relaxed), you get used to [it] gradually . . . it somehow fits with these curious little people, & their curious landscape, with its temples, and hills, and odd twisted trees, and gardens made of stones. We saw some wonderful things, temples, and museums, old palaces, one gigantic Buddha (made in 700 A.D. [at Nara]), so big that once a man hid for 3 days in its eye, and one can climb into its nostrils.[27]

In Kyoto the party was looked after by Osamu Fuwa (the local Director of Tourism) and his secretary Miss Yuasa. 13 February was devoted to sightseeing, the group visiting the Imperial and Nijo Palaces in the snow, and then calling in at a textile museum (described by Pears as 'ghastly') before moving on to the Detached Villa at Katsua.

The following morning they were driven to Nara, described by Peg Hesse as

A most lovely old town, with huge Buddha statues, old bronze bells and

---

[26] The inn was described in detail by Peg Hesse in a diary letter to Wolfsgarten dated 23 February: 'At the entrance to the inn, which was hidden away in a plain little street lined with wooden walls of other houses, all the maids in kimonos greeted us with deep bows – kneeling on the ground and touching the floor with their heads. We all took off our shoes at the door and feeling over life size and rather "British" we flapped along the polished floors to our rooms. All doors (and most of the walls are doors) slide and people pop in and out at any corner of the room and you never feel alone, you can't lock anything . . .

'At night our beds replaced the red lacquer table – quilts to lie on [*futon*] and quilts to cover you. We were all rather cold and a bit overcome till we were given saki (hot rice wine) in great quantities. Our gentle maids never left our sides and tried to read in our eyes our next wish. Ben (who is the most conservative of the lot) looked worried and like a wet depressed dog: he could find nowhere for his long legs and was cold and worried by the kimono [more correctly a *yukata*] he was made to wear! . . . Never can I describe how we four laughed at this inn. We nearly became hysterical and Ben, Lu and Peter were so funny and looked so odd my sides ached from laughing . . .'

[27] Letter to Roger Duncan posted on 24 February (see note 4 above).

shrines filled with images which have stood there since 600AD. We fed the famous holy deer and took part in the most impressive, complicated and full of deep meaning ceremony – the Tea ceremony – it takes (or took us) about two hours and at the end one has drunk three mouthfuls of very bitter and strong and excellent green tea.[28]

A second tea ceremony took place on the next day, this time in Kyoto, but in the more intimate surroundings of the Kumagei family home. We learn from Pears's travel diary and Peg Hesse's correspondence that the evening was enlivened by an impromptu performance by Pears of an aria from Puccini's *Tosca*, the singing of rounds, and a rendering of Brahms by Britten and Pears. As was the case many times during their fortnight in Japan, the party was disturbed by the constant presence of the Japanese press wielding tape recorders and cameras.

In Kyoto they met the English poet D. J. Enright at a geisha evening, an event recorded by Enright in his autobiography:

[We had] some visitors who gave as good as they took, like Benjamin Britten and Peter Pears, at a magnificent dinner which the Broadcasting Corporation of Japan gave for them at the Tsuraya, a notable Kyoto teahouse. The most highly-regarded samisen [*sic*] players and singers were brought in to entertain the guests. As they performed, Britten scribbled down the musical notation while Pears (an even greater feat, I should think) swiftly made his own transliteration of the words. Then Britten borrowed a samisen and plucked at it while Pears sang – the result being an uncanny playback. The effect on the geisha, a race who tend to be excessively conscious of their inimitability, their cultural uniqueness, and aggravatingly assured of the pitiable inability to understand their art inherent in all foreigners, was almost alarming. They paled beneath their whitewash. A more violent people would have seen to it that their guests' throats were cut the moment they left those sacred halls. This was one of the few indubitable triumphs for British art or artists which I noticed in Japan – and probably the most striking.[29]

The shamisen referred to by Enright is a three-stringed banjo played with a plectrum, the traditional accompanying instrument for geisha singing; unfortunately, Britten's jottings from this extraordinary evening have not survived. The composer was by this stage becoming familiar with the musical idiom, having already heard a geisha performance on the evening of 11 February in Tokyo. The heterophonic style of shamisen songs was later to exert an influence on the contrapuntal procedures of the Church Parables.

---

[28] Letter to Wolfsgarten, 23 February 1956. The tea ceremony in Nara is almost certainly that recorded in Mitchell and Evans, *Benjamin Britten: Pictures*, Plate 293, where the caption gives Kyoto as the location. This photograph is reproduced as the frontispiece to the present volume.

[29] D. J. Enright, *Memoirs of a Mendicant Professor* (London: Chatto and Windus, 1969), 45.

Oddly, Britten does not mention in his letters home the most significant event of his three-day excursion to Kyoto. Peter Kurosawa recalls that he took the composer to Tōzaburō Satake's 'Japanese Old Musical Instrument Company' in Kyoto, where he obtained his own shō, an instrument with which he had become particularly fascinated.[30] Mr Kurosawa took a striking photograph of Pears posing outside the Satake store in the *ryōō* mask employed in Bugaku dances. The Satake store still exists, and was visited by the present author in September 1986: it houses an impressive collection of Gagaku instruments.

Returning to Tokyo, both Britten and Pears joined the ranks of the Tokyo Madrigal Singers at a rehearsal conducted by Kei-ichi Kurosawa in the British Council Library on 16 February, Prince Ludwig commenting that Mr Kurosawa was 'overjoyed that Ben and Peter sing with them'.[31] Peter Kurosawa, who sang in the choir on the same occasion (and still conducts the group at the time of writing), recalls that Pears requested a special performance of John Wilbye's 'Sweet honey-sucking bees', and several photographs record the event.[32] The rehearsal was followed by dinner at the British Embassy and some post-prandial music-making. On the next day the party attended a performance of the popular Kabuki theatre and was overwhelmed by its vitality and excitement, Pears claiming to have been 'knocked sideways'.[33]

Next came the second visit to the Music Department of the Imperial Household Agency (Kunaicho-Gakubu), which Peter Kurosawa hosted on 18 February.[34] Here Britten heard again the haunting sonorities of the Gagaku orchestra which were to leave their mark on the musical textures of the Church Parables far more than proved to be the case with the music of Nō, which seems comparatively bland to the uninitiated Westerner. In Prince Ludwig's words:

> In the morning we go to a performance of the Imperial Court orchestra which has been specially organised for Ben to hear. Dignified old gentlemen in blue suits, like generals in mufti, play two long pieces for us on unknown and strange instruments. Bronze age serenades probably sounded like that. One realises that this music follows some pattern, though I for one cannot discern it. European 'music lovers' like myself are always on the look out for something they have heard before. Hence that hankering for 'expression' and romantic gusto. We cannot penetrate this kind of music, though there is some attraction in its hidden pattern or form.

[30] The fact that Britten was looking for a shō at this early stage suggests that the first of the two visits to the Gagaku which Mr Kurosawa recalls must have taken place before 12 February. The first visit is not mentioned by Prince Ludwig in *Ausflug Ost*. Britten's shō is preserved in *GB-ALb* 5-9600001.

[31] Prince Ludwig of Hesse, *Ausflug Ost*, 105.

[32] See Reed (ed.), *The Travel Diaries of Peter Pears*, Plate 13.

[33] Personal communication. See also below, pp. 197–8.

[34] See note 30 above.

It is disconcerting to see the dignified musicians take up penny whistles [ryūteki] to let off sudden shrieks, or others beating boat-shaped harps [gakusō, the Gagaku equivalent of the koto] without much sound. I feel not educated or musical enough to judge this ancient art.

The concert takes place at the theatre buildings in the gardens of the Imperial Palace.[35]

An authority on Gagaku, Hiroshige Sono, acted as an informative guide on the visit, and he and his son Hiroharu both comment on Britten's fascination with the genre. As a result of his interest in Gagaku, Britten obtained two Columbia long-playing recordings (BL 28–9) made by the Music Department of the Imperial Household which now form part of the composer's collection of ethnic recordings.[36] At some point during his stay in Japan he also acquired a volume of printed transcriptions from the Gagaku repertory.[37]

In the evening of 18 February Britten gave his second broadcast concert for NHK, the programme including the Japanese première of the *Sinfonia da Requiem* which had originally been rejected by the imperial authorities at the time of its commission in 1940 to celebrate the 2,600th anniversary of the foundation of the Mikado's dynasty by Jimmu Tenno in 660 BC.[38] Britten left Tokyo in the night of 19/20 February only a few hours after witnessing the second performance of the Nō play which was to transform his conception of opera throughout the following twenty years. Peter Kurosawa's photographs taken at Haneda Airport on the day of departure show the cheerful composer clutching his treasured shō under his arm and bidding farewell to Kei-ichi Kurosawa, Bill MacAlpine and Reginald Close (see Plate 6). He had been in Japan for only twelve days, an even shorter period than the busy fortnight he had spent in Bali, but his time had once more been put to good use and the experience was to haunt him for the rest of his life and lead to impressive artistic results.

After a short stopover in Hong Kong, Britten flew on to Bangkok where he witnessed a display of Thai dancing on 21 February which Prince Ludwig describes as 'distantly recalling Bali'.[39] Britten described the distinctive architectural style of Thai temples as similar to 'tremendously highly coloured cream cakes'.[40] On 23 February Britten and Pears gave a recital to celebrate the centenary of the Anglican cathedral in Singapore, whither they had returned the previous evening. They had met the archdeacon, Robin Woods, during their first stay on Singapore: Britten wrote 'Concert for Robin

---

[35] This English translation was one of the extracts from *Ausflug Ost* prepared by Prince Ludwig himself for inclusion in Gishford (ed.), *A Tribute*, 61–2.
[36] *GB-ALb* 3-9401031–9401032 and 3-9401041–9401042.
[37] Sukehiro Shiba, *Gagaku: Japanese Classical Court Music*, I (Tokyo: Ryugin-Sha, 1955). *GB-ALb* 2-9700615.
[38] See note 5 above, p. 113.
[39] Prince Ludwig of Hesse, *Ausflug Ost*, 114.
[40] Letter to Roger Duncan posted on 24 February (see note 4 above).

Woods' in his engagement diary for 1 February, but then deleted the entry. Woods was a former schoolfriend of Britten's, and a cousin of Pears's. In his travel diary, Pears described him and his cathedral as follows:

> He is a man of considerable charm and enormous energy who has built up a large and enthusiastic congregation (may one call a congregation enthusiastic?) in his vast parish. He has the major advantage of a large and really splendid Victorian Gothic cathedral (c. 1850) built by some civil engineer (from a book of plans by Pugin, I should think). Standing in a green grassy close and shining brightly all over with white paint, it makes a typically-English but v. successful contribution to the Singapore sky-line.[41]

St Andrew's Cathedral is still situated on Coleman Street, and has changed little since Pears described it in 1956.

The four travelling-companions then flew to Sri Lanka on 24 February for the final leg of their world tour. At the end of the month they heard local musicians in the ancient town of Kandy and made a tape recording of the performance, which survives at the Britten–Pears Library in a box marked 'Singalese drumming (Kandy)'.[42] Britten was on this occasion especially struck by what he termed 'magnificent drumming'.[43] Britten and Pears performed in Colombo on 4 March then flew on to Madras four days later. On 9 March they heard more local Indian performers, Britten describing their playing as 'outstanding music (again with very complicated and fine drumming)'.[44] A broadcast concert was given from the British Council in Madras on 11 March, and this completed their recital schedule for the tour. On the same day they had lunch with the French ethnomusicologist Alain Daniélou (an 'odd man', according to Pears's diary);[45] while at work on *The Prodigal Son* in 1968 (a score which borrows Indian musical material, as revealed in Chapter 7 below), Britten was to purchase Daniélou's book on Indian music.[46] All that now remained at the end of five months abroad were a few free days in Bombay, their arrival in the city delayed by the airline which Prince Ludwig punningly renamed 'British Overdue Airways'.[47] The party flew to Frankfurt on 16 March, where (after a night at Schloss Wolfsgarten) Britten and Pears bade farewell to the Hesses and returned to Suffolk by sea.

Britten summed up their experiences in almost half a year of unrelenting travelling to Roger Duncan in a letter written from Madras on 11 March:

---

[41] Reed (ed.), *The Travel Diaries of Peter Pears*, 38–9. The engagement diary is at *GB-ALb* (uncatalogued).

[42] *GB-ALb* 3-9500154; see *ibid*., 67.

[43] Letter to Roger Duncan, 11 March 1956.

[44] *Ibid*.

[45] Reed (ed.), *The Travel Diaries of Peter Pears*, 71.

[46] Alain Daniélou, *The Rāgā-s of Northern Indian Music* (London: The Cresset Press, Barrie and Rockliff, 1968); *GB-ALb* 1-9501237.

[47] Prince Ludwig of Hesse, *Ausflug Ost*, 161.

Plate 5. Britten playing the shō, Tokyo, February 1956

Plate 6. Britten (with shō) and Kei-ichi Kurosawa at Haneda Airport, Tokyo,
19 February 1956

It's been quite an experience I must say, tiring, but well worth while. We've flown (not counting boats & trains) about 25,000 miles, visited 16 countries, packed & unpacked just on 100 times, given nearly 40 concerts, heard nine quite different kinds of musical traditions, seen countless different arts, talked to Turks, Indians of all sorts, Chinese, Indonesians, Malayans, Siamese, Japanese – not counting the many kinds of Europeans. And feel much richer for it. I hope these letters have given you some little idea of it all – but I'm not a good letter-writer I'm afraid, and I'm sure alot of it has been rather boring. One thing I am keen on is that you should yourself go & see these places for yourself. Being told about it isn't enough, one must go & look, & when you are young enough too, to be influenced by these wonderful people, living full and rich lives, quite different from our own.

On 27 March, Britten wrote to Humphrey Searle and declared: 'Japanese music is the oddest I've ever heard, but very impressive, & beautiful.'

Back in England, Britten received on 31 March 1956 a warm letter from Kei-ichi Kurosawa enclosing an article on the shō specially written for him by Leo Traynor and wittily entitled 'A Young Britten's Guide to the Shō'.[48] The article was accompanied by a set of miniature photographs taken by Kurosawa to illustrate the hand positions used to hold the instrument. Kurosawa's covering letter expresses his pleasure at Britten's interest:

I wonder how you are getting on with this mysterious instrument. We shall be pleased to write further to you on the subject when you come across any particular difficulties.

Under the separate cover I am also sending you a back number of 'Journal of the Society for Reserch [sic] in Asiatic Music' in which you will find a diagram showing the position of various notes in Traynor's article on the 'Shō'.

Plate 5 shows Britten receiving a lesson in shō technique from Kei-ichi Kurosawa (who holds a copy of Traynor's article in his hand) during his stay in Tokyo.

On 26 July Britten sent his Dolmetsch treble recorder to the Kurosawas as a gesture of gratitude for their hospitality.[49] The instrument is inscribed with the initials 'BB' and is still a treasured possession in the Kurosawa household.

---

[48] The typescript of the article is preserved in *GB-ALb* 4-9700692.
[49] The dated posting certificate survives at the Britten–Pears Library (4-9700692).

6

From Nō to Church Parable: the Evolution of *Curlew River*, 1956–64

I The Nō Theatre

During his stay in Japan, Britten experienced three distinct genres of the traditional Japanese performing arts. The most ancient of these was Gagaku, the ceremonial ensemble music derived from the Bugaku dances of the imperial court and of the most important Shinto shrines and Buddhist temples, which he witnessed in Tokyo on 18 February 1956. Britten also paid visits to the Kabuki theatre (17 February) and twice attended the Nō theatre (on 11 and 19 February), but appears not to have seen Bunraku (puppet theatre). The latter incorporates vocal music with shamisen accompaniment; the composer heard similar music performed by geisha women, and this undoubtedly affected his development of heterophonic techniques in the musical idiom of *Curlew River*. In our study of the dramatic and musical style of the three Church Parables it will be necessary to examine features not only of the traditional Japanese performing arts, but also of the English mediaeval mystery play which contributed greatly to the aesthetic quality of Britten's novel dramatic medium.

Since the Nō theatre is in many ways the element most alien to a Western audience, and certainly the most significant influence in the shaping of the Church Parable trilogy, it will prove helpful to describe the characteristics of Nō in some detail before attempting any analysis of Britten's appropriation of them. The Nō theatre was a mediaeval development, founded in and constantly refined throughout the Muromachi period (1336–1568). Nō (which literally means 'ability', 'effect' or 'entertainment') was formalized from early folk entertainments such as Dengaku and Sarugaku by three successive generations of one acting family: Kan'ami Kiyotsugu (1333–84) and his son Zeami Motokiyo (1363–1443) and grandson Jūrō Motomasa (1395–1431)[1] who became head of the school in 1422 and wrote the play *Sumidagawa* on which *Curlew River* is based. Some 200 Nō plays survive from this period and very few have been added to the repertory since. In addition, Zeami left several

---

[1]   The published score of *Curlew River* correctly gives the date of his death as 1431. Britten deleted the inaccurate date (1459) on his copy of the English translation of *Sumidagawa* and wrote '1431 – according to Waley'.

treatises concerned with the study and performance of Nō.[2] From the time of Kan'ami and Zeami, the Nō theatre evolved specifically to suit the tastes of the aristocratic warrior class (Samurai) which forbade the uninhibited expression of emotions: this consideration was clearly crucial to the formulation of an art characterized by extreme stylization and restraint.

Nō is a symbiosis of vocal music (*utai*), instrumental music (*hayashi*), acting by gesture (*kata*), dance (*mai*), costume (*shōzoku*) and the rather less tangible aesthetic effects of the architectural and temporal dimensions in which it is performed. At the centre of the genre's success is an important paradox: by

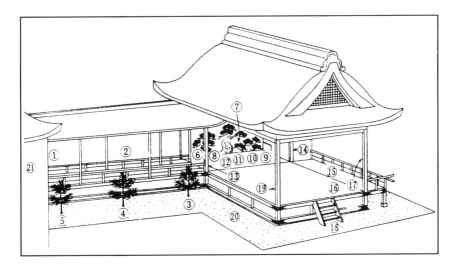

1 *Age-maku* (lift-curtain)
2 *Hashi-gakari* (bridge-like extension)
3 *Ichi-no-matsu* (first pine)
4 *Ni-no-matsu* (second pine)
5 *San-no-matsu* (third pine)
6 *Kōken-bashira* (stage assistant's seat)
7 *Kagami-ita* (sounding board)
8 *Ato-za* (upstage area behind the main stage)
9 *Fue-za* (flautist's seat)
10 *Ko-tsuzumi-za* (shoulder drummer's seat)
11 *Ō-tsuzumi-za* (hip drummer's seat)

12 *Taiko-za* (stick drummer's seat)
13 *Shite-bashira* (principal actor's pillar)
14 *Fue-bashira* (flautist's pillar)
15 *Jiutai-za* (chorus seating area)
16 *Waki-za* (secondary actor's seat)
17 *Waki-bashira* (secondary actor's pillar)
18 *Shirasu-bashigo* (steps crossing the white gravel)
19 *Metsuke-bashira* (pillar on which to fix the eyes)
20 *Shirasu* (white gravel)
21 *Kagami-no-ma* (mirror room)

Figure 13. The Nō stage (after Maruoka, 1969)

2   These include the *Kandensho* (1400–18), *Kakyō* (1418–24), *Shikadōsho* (1420), *Nikyoku zantai ezu* (1421) and the undated *Kyūi shidai*. See Kunio Komparu, *The Noh Theater: Principles and Perspectives* (New York and Tokyo: Weatherhill/Tankosha, 1983), 347–50.

increasing the limitation of expressive techniques a greater emotional profundity is achieved. This difficult proposition has been aptly summarized by Kunio Komparu as 'a highly sophisticated concept that envisions the performer as one who first denies the subjective with the objective and then goes beyond the objective to find another subjective truth.'[3] Further subtlety is added to this paradox by the impression of spontaneity and of an actual liberation from restrictions which can result from intense stylization. We shall see how this central consideration is paralleled not only in the dramatic format of *Curlew River* but also in Britten's musical style, which cultivates an optimum balance between extreme economy and maximum expressiveness. In spite of intense study and inbred identification with the medium, Nō actors will never present a play the same way twice, a feature clearly retained in Britten's development of a musical idiom permitting a large degree of inter-pretative variety within the confines of its own conventions.

The Nō stage (see Figure 13) projects well into the auditorium, subtly strengthening the audience's participation in the drama. This concept of an experience shared between actors and onlookers is once again an important part of Britten's ideal in all three Church Parables, and may be traced back to the direct audience participation in *Saint Nicolas* (1948), *Let's Make an Opera* (1949) and *Noye's Fludde* (1957) – the latter a seminal work in the development of the Parable style, dating as it does from the year following Britten's visit to Japan. Colin Graham's Church Parable stage (see Figure 14) lacks the roof symbolizing the sanctity of the space beneath it in the Nō prototype,[4] but the church setting clearly has a powerful sanctity of its own. The Nō stage is made of plain cypress (*hinoki*) which is highly polished to reflect the movements of the actors' feet. The major part of the performance takes place on the *hon-butai* (main stage), but an additional side-stage (*waki-za*) to the audience's right is used by the chorus and includes its own small entrance door (*kirido-guchi*) at the rear. Behind the main stage is the *ato-za* (rear stage) reserved for the instrumentalists and property attendants. The background is undecorated except for a solitary painted pine tree (*kagami-ita*), a reminder of the original outdoor setting of the Nō theatre and said to be modelled on the Yogomatsu tree at Nara which Britten visited on 14 February 1956.[5] Representations of bamboo may also be painted at upstage left.

The entire stage has a directional orientation and faces south, relative positions being taken from the four roof corner-posts. This feature is clearly reflected in Colin Graham's production notes for *Curlew River* (see below). The stage is surrounded by a pebble moat (*shirasu*), across which runs a bridgeway (*hashi-gakari*) connecting the stage to the mirror room (*kagami*

---

[3] *Ibid.*, 17.

[4] *Ibid.*, 111–13. In the Nō theatre, the roof projects beyond the limits of the stage in order to embrace the audience symbolically.

[5] Literally 'the tree which the shades bid welcome'. It stands in the broad park surrounding the Kasuga shrine.

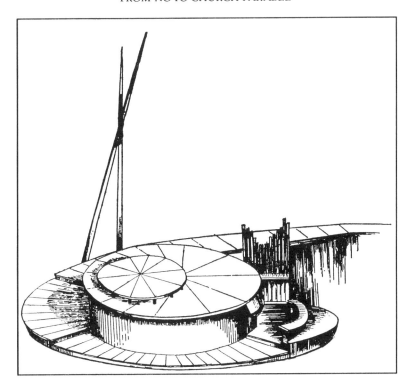

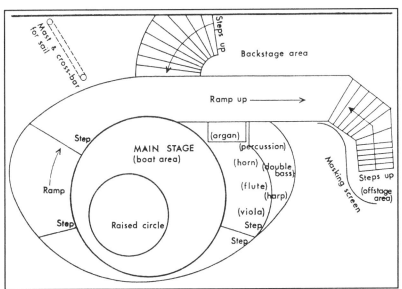

Figure 14. The Church Parable stage

133

no ma), where the participants prepare themselves for the performance. This bridge fulfils a symbolic function, representing the dream link between our world and the supernatural: the phrase *hashi-gakari* is literally translated as 'suspension bridge'. As characters enter along the bridge they are seen in stark profile, their entrance emphasized by special instrumental music. Graham's entrance ramp in his Church Parable stage is exactly analogous to this bridgeway. The function of the mirror room, where the principal actor dons his mask in order to study its reflection and where the instrumentalists play a sacred prelude (*shirabe*) before processing on stage, is replaced in Britten's Parables by the initial procession and subsequent on-stage robing ceremony which both strengthen the effect of enacting a ritual.

The central performer in Nō is the *shite*. Each play is concerned with a single event in the life of this character, and the five types of *shite* determine the five categories of Nō play: god, warrior, woman, lunatic and demon. The *shite* is generally played by a masked male actor even though the majority of roles are female. The mask (*nōmen*) identifies the spiritual state of the relevant character and denies the use of facial expression: instead, expressiveness is achieved by movement of the head or by the exaggerated features on some masks. As a foil to the *shite*, a deuteragonist (*waki*) evokes the *shite*'s thoughts by means of dialogue. *Waki* parts are always male (generally officials or priests) and played without a mask to highlight the importance of the *shite*. The *waki* is often cast as a traveller, since this allows his presence in any situation to be readily plausible. Occasionally, one or two subsidiary actors (*shite-* or *waki-tsure*) may be included. Of special significance in the present context is the *kokata* (child performer) who portrays not only children but also the sanctity of emperors and other revered characters. It seems likely that the *kokata* in *Sumidagawa* (who plays the spirit of the dead boy) was a strong attraction to Britten since he embodies many of the composer's preoccupations with youth and innocence; we have seen how his own description of the play in a letter written home from the Far East accurately identifies all the principal characters, including the *kokata* (see above, p. 120).

The individual actors are complemented by a chorus (*ji-utai*) of between six and ten men who are all Nō masters (*shite-kata*) in their own right and of the same acting school as the *shite*. They sit in two rows on the upper side-stage, entering and exiting through the *kirido-guchi*, and sing in unison chant. Their function is to keep the plot in motion, to set the scene (very necessary in the absence of realistic stage representation) and often to voice the thoughts of the *shite* or *waki*. There are three or four musicians (*hayashi-kata*), who are the first to enter and last to exit. The flute (nōkan), shoulder-drum (ko-tsuzumi) and hip-drum (ō-tsuzumi) are always employed, and several plays demand an additional stick-drum (taiko). There is, however, no taiko in *Sumidagawa*, as revealed in Prince Ludwig's description of the play. Close at hand by the musicians are the *kōken* (prompters and property attendants) whose function is preserved by the boy acolytes of the Church Parables.

The principal means of expressive representation in Nō comprise movements of the *shite*'s mask and specific gestural patterns.[6] The mask may be brightened to express joy by tilting it upwards (*omote o terasu*) or darkened to express sorrow by tilting it downwards (*omote o kumorasu*). A quick movement from side to side expresses anger (*omote o kiru*) and a slow movement from side to side indicates profundity (*omote o tsukau*). Every movement and gesture is carefully choreographed, the movement patterns (*kata*) involving details of stance (*kamae*) and carriage (*hakobi*). The basic stance requires the arms bent in a circle and the trunk tilted forwards. This position is maintained throughout movement across the stage, which is always accomplished by a gliding walk. The *kata* fall into three types: realistic, symbolic and abstract. Symbolic gestures adopted by Colin Graham for the Church Parables include weeping (*shiori*: one or both hands raised to the eyes) and worship (*ogamu*: both hands raised horizontally, the fingertips brought together). Abstract dance patterns (*mai*) frequently form the climax of a play. In addition to these techniques, simple props are employed to aid the heavily stylized representation of character and events. Again there are three types: stage props (*tsukuri-mono*), such as the framework of a boat or tomb; personal props (*ko-dōgu*) held in the performer's hand, such as the bamboo shoot denoting the mother's madness in *Sumidagawa*; and multi-purpose props (*tōyō-dōgu*).

Zeami's analysis of Nō reflects the importance of the number five in its Five Elements Theory, which calls for, amongst other things, five acting skills (Song, Dance, Old Man, Warrior, Woman) and five structural elements (Music, Dance, Acting, Gesture, Emotion). We have already seen that there are five categories of Nō play, differing in the role played by the *shite*. Traditionally, a cycle of five plays (one from each category) is presented in a single day, interspersed with Kyōgen interludes.[7] The cycle also reflects the threefold aesthetic structure known as *jo–ha–kyū*, a theoretical organization of dramatic intensity (borrowed from Gagaku) which governs every aspect of Nō drama from a single line of song to an entire play cycle. *Jo* means 'preparation', *ha* literally means 'breaking' and *kyū* may be translated as 'rapid' or 'urgent'.[8] Each Nō play is considered to have a structure which follows the same tripartite principle, and when applying these terms to matters of dramatic form Komparu elects to translate *jo–ha–kyū* as 'intro-duction–development–conclusion'.[9] The term 'development' can be mis-leading for the Westerner in this context, however, and it must be stressed that Komparu's usage signifies an intensification of mood rather than a plot development in the Western theatrical sense. However, William Malm's

---

6   See Komparu, *The Noh Theater*, 217–20 and 229–30.
7   Short comic plays providing contrasted relief. These were a contemporaneous mediaeval development: see Tatsuo Yoshikoshi, Hisashi Hata and Don Kenny, *Kyōgen* (Tokyo: Hoikusha, 1982).
8   Komparu, *The Noh Theater*, 34ff.
9   *Ibid.*, 27.

(more literal) alternative translation of *jo–ha–kyū* as 'introduction, scattering, rushing' can be equally confusing in dramatic terms since 'scattering' hardly implies this process of intensification.[10] Malm's translations are better applied to matters of musical construction; these terms were in any case originally coined to describe the accelerating tempi of a Gagaku composition.

The cycle of five Nō plays is organized in the following manner, the three plays of the *ha* group themselves following the *jo–ha–kyū* pattern:

1 God (*JO*)
2 Warrior (*jo* of *HA*)
3 Woman (*ha* of *HA*)
4 Lunatic (*kyū* of *HA*)
5 Demon (*KYŪ*)

The fourth category, with which we shall be most concerned, forms the most intense part of the cycle (*kyū* of *ha*). It consists of lunatic plays (*monoguruimono*) and madwoman pieces (*kyōjo-mono*). *Sumidagawa* is a fine example of the latter. At the beginning of the play, the *kōken* place a framework mound covered with willow branches on the stage in front of the *hayashi*. This contains the *kokata* who is to perform the part of the Ghost of Umewaka-Maru. The Ferryman (*waki*) enters to the entrance music *nanori-bue* and introduces himself (*nanori*). He reveals that a memorial service is taking place that day on the opposite side of the Sumida River, and then sits in front of the *ji-utai*. A Traveller from Miyako (*waki-tsure*) enters to the entrance music *shidai* and describes his travels (*michi-yuki*) before announcing his intention to cross the river. The Ferryman delays their departure in order to hear the singing of a demented woman who is approaching the boat. The Madwoman (*shite*) enters to the entrance music *issei* and performs a dance (*kakeri*), singing of her lost child. The Ferryman engages her in dialogue (*mondō*) and eventually agrees to take her across the river with him. During the river-crossing, the Ferryman relates at length (and without accompaniment) the story behind the memorial service. Exactly a year before, a slave-trader arrived with a twelve-year-old boy suffering from exhaustion. The slaver abandoned the child, who subsequently revealed his noble parentage before he died from illness. The local people buried him by the roadside in accordance with his wishes. On reaching the far bank, the Madwoman questions the Ferryman about the event (*mondō*) and it becomes plain that the child was her abducted son. The Ferryman leads the Madwoman to the grave, where she sings a lament (*kudoki*). The Ferryman then gives the mother a prop gong (*shōgo*) with which to beat an invocation to the child's ghost. The voice of the spirit is heard joining in with the chanting of 'Namu Amida', and the child's ghost comes out of the burial mound. In the final section of the play (*kiri*), the Madwoman

---

10   William Malm, *Six Hidden Views of Japanese Music* (Berkeley: University of California Press, 1986), 37. For further discussion of Malm's analysis of *Curlew River*, see below.

drops her gong and frantically clutches at the spirit, but the child retreats into the tomb and she is left weeping disconsolately on the ground. The performers slowly exit in silence (the actors along the *hashi-gakari*, the *ji-utai* through the *kirido-guchi*, and finally the *hayashi* along the *hashi-gakari*) and the audience is left in silent contemplation.

In *Sumidawaga*, madness 'is in reality seen as a highly spiritual state accompanied by separation from the self'.[11] In Motomasa's portrayal of grief-induced madness, the process of the mother's derangement is more important than the 'development' of the actual plot, which is customarily static. This emphasis is outlined in the preface to the authorized English translation of the play, which was employed by both Britten and his librettist, William Plomer, in the creation of *Curlew River*:

> When they are bereaved mothers, the heroines in this division are represented as abnormally sensitive and particularly susceptible to their surroundings, and fall into fits of poetic exaltation which expresses itself by frenzied gestures. When their lost ones are found, their temporary madness leaves them. In this particular piece, the heroine discovers her lost child to be dead and the play ends on a tragic note, not usual in 'mad woman' pieces.[12]

This final 'tragic note' was completely removed in Britten's version of the plot and replaced by a consolatory and cathartic ending.

II *Sumidagawa* and the *Curlew River* libretto

As it had been William Plomer who had recommended the Nō theatre to Britten in the first place (see above, pp. 115–16),[13] it was natural that the

---

[11] Komparu, *The Noh Theater*, 37.
[12] Japanese Classics Translation Committee, *Japanese Noh Drama* (Tokyo: Nippon Gakujutsu Shinkokai, 1955), 145.
[13] For definitive biographical information on Plomer, including discussion of his collaborations with Britten, see Peter Alexander, *William Plomer: A Biography* (Oxford: Oxford University Press, 1989). Britten had known the poet and novelist since 1948 when he gave a talk on Edward FitzGerald at the inaugural Aldeburgh Festival. In August 1951 the two men were thinking of working together on a successor to *Let's Make an Opera*, to be based on Beatrix Potter's story of Mr Tod. By November of the same year the plan was shelved, and their thoughts turned to a science-fiction tale provisionally entitled *Tyco the Vegan*. This project persisted until May 1952 when work began on *Gloriana*, for which Britten had selected Plomer as librettist in preference to Ronald Duncan. Following the completion of the Coronation opera, Plomer expressed his desire to collaborate again with Britten in a letter dated 23 July 1953: 'I do much hope that we shall work together again – I feel that we can really make a fire out of the right sort of spark.' They met at regular intervals and Plomer continued to contribute to the Aldeburgh Festival. In the autumn of 1954 they were contemplating another children's opera to be based on a Greek myth (possible options included the stories of Phaethon, Arion and Icarus) but it was not until Britten's visit to the Far East in 1956 that the prophesied 'spark' was generated.

composer should communicate his enthusiasm for the genre to him immediately upon his return from Japan. He wrote on 13 May 1956:

> But what compels me to write even this scribble is not my incredibly strong reaction to Japan – that really must wait until we meet . . . – but that Gloriana in her entirety has just been first performed in America . . . [I] pray we can meet – & talk about those Noh plays, that Court music (I've brought a Shō back with me), Nara,[14] that charm and bewilder-ment . . . ad infinitum. Do you know the play Sumidagawa by the way?

Plomer was quick to respond to Britten's enthusiasm, and replied by return of post on 14 May:

> it is a very great pleasure to me, and somehow not altogether a surprise, that your response to Japan was instant & strong. You see now how fortunate I was to be able to live there for a couple of years in my twenties. It struck me as a gong or bell is struck, & the vibration set up in me will last till I drop. I must hear more from you soon, viva voce.

The correspondence then remains inexplicably silent on the subject of Nō plays for over a year. On 5 July 1957 Plomer wrote to say: 'Somebody brought me a book of Nō plays from Japan the other day & I have been re-reading Sumidagawa. Have you thought at all of it again?' Britten's reply, written during the composition of his Malaysian National Anthem, reveals that the possibility of adapting the Nō play for the Western stage had already been discussed:

> The 'Sumidagawa' doesn't come into any immediate plans. I've rather put it to the back of my mind; but anytime you feel you'd like to talk about it, it can be brought forward again. It is something I'm deeply interested in, & determined to do sometime. Isn't it a curiously moving and disturbing story? I wonder which translation you've got.[15]

Plomer's response is dated 16 July 1957:

> You ask which translation of Sumidagawa I have. Well, it's good and recent, & the work of an imposing committee appointed by the Nippon Gakujutsu Shinkōkai [Japanese Classics Translation Committee], among them an old acquaintance or two of mine. It seems very well done. Some

---

14 A photograph in the Plomer collection at Durham University Library reveals that Plomer was himself at Nara in the autumn of 1926. Britten visited the area on 14 February 1956.

15 Letter dated 10 July 1957. Britten was not, in fact, the first composer to tackle an English version of *Sumidagawa*. In 1913, the year of Britten's birth, Clarence Raybould had written a one-act operatic treatment of the Nō play for the Glastonbury Festival. Raybould's libretto was prepared by Dr Marie Stopes, the renowned pioneer of birth control, who (like Plomer) had herself spent several years in Japan. Britten was unaware of the Raybould–Stopes collaboration until Plomer informed him of it in a letter dated 7 October 1958.

day, when you feel bent towards it, we might talk about it – it is strangely haunting.

The translation discussed here later proved to be the direct basis for the libretto of *Curlew River*, and Britten obtained and annotated his own copy of it.[16]

Nothing further is heard of the project for exactly one year. Then, in the summer of 1958, Britten's enthusiasm was fired once again and he wrote on 12 July: 'I can't write about the No play idea now, except to say that it's boiling up inside me, but that I have so many things to talk to you . . . about the style & all . . . before I start on it.' Britten's comment is revealing, and suggests that he had some conception of the novel Church Parable idiom much earlier than has hitherto been thought. Plans for the new work now seemed much more concrete and, sometime in the autumn of 1958, Plomer went ahead and produced his first draft libretto. This takes the form of a straightforward paraphrase of the Japanese Classics Translation Committee's authorized translation and is entitled *Sumida River*. It is handwritten throughout and differs very little from the original text. Both the Japanese names and the numbered sections of the translation are retained, the latter undoubtedly helping Britten in his perception of the play's structure. There is some versification of the original prose, but much of the phraseology is identical and many verbal expressions from the translation were retained in the final version of the libretto completed some five years later. Plomer's chorus speaks in the first person when voicing another character's thoughts: this is a peculiarity of the Nō convention which was subsequently dropped, the role of the chorus changing from identification to narration in Britten's conception of the story's dramatic presentation.

This initial draft differs from the final text of *Curlew River* in several important respects. Most striking are the absence of the quasi-liturgical framework subsequently imposed on the presentation of the story and the retention of all the Buddhist references, which were also to be modified at a later stage in the work's development. There is thus every indication that Britten and Plomer were contemplating a faithful treatment of the play reflecting its Japanese characteristics. This is also suggested by a letter from Plomer to Britten written on 2 October 1958 during the composition of the first libretto draft:

As my mind begins to run on Sumida River, I feel less inclined to shy at Japanese names & place-names. It may be that some of them will be just as useful to you musically as 'Namu Amida' &c. As you know, in Japanese all goes by syllables, and each syllable is, in theory, of equal weight, so, if Japanese words are to be sung or spoken, it is better that they should be rather formally enunciated than slurred or falsely accented. E.g. we ought to have, as nearly as possible,

---

[16] See above, note 12. *GB-ALb* 1-9501249.

Mi-ya-ko, not Miyáko
Su-mi-da, not Súmida
Mu-sa-shi, not Musáshi.

Naturally when the words are said or sung in a quick tempo, the syllables do not always seem to be equally accented: so shite, as Ezra Pound so delicately tells us, can seem to sound like shtay . . .

Don't let all this worry you, & unless you have strong feelings in the matter against my doing so, I shall proceed to make what seems judicious use of Japanese names.

In a note dated 8 October 1958 Britten scrawled in a hasty postscript: 'I am very keen on as many nice evocative Japanese words as possible!'

A more important difference from the final version arising from this faithfulness to the original text concerns the play's closing lines. At the end of *Sumidagawa*, the child is discovered to be dead and, after a brief appearance, his spirit vanishes for ever, leaving the mother weeping on the ground. Plomer's first draft corresponds closely to this conclusion:

What seemed her son is nothing but a mound,
A grassy mound alone beside a road.
Lament for a woman so bereaved,
And give her the only thing we can – our tears.

The decision to provide the story with a Christian foundation later necessitated a completely different interpretation of the play, and the inclusion of an ending which would appear more obviously cathartic to a Western audience not versed in what Plomer elsewhere termed 'esoteric Buddhism' (see above, p. 116).

The handwritten draft of the first libretto ultimately remained in Plomer's possession.[17] Britten's copy, surviving at the Britten–Pears Library, consists of a typed version of the same text probably made in November 1958.[18] This has been slightly annotated by both Plomer and Britten: the stage direction 'Entrance Music' which accompanies the first appearances of the Ferryman, Traveller and Mother is ringed by Britten at each occurrence, and other pencilled notes refer to incidental musical details. There is some confusion over the allocation of lines for the chorus, and Plomer has suggested the provision of 'Rowing music – chorus?' for the ferry's journey across the river.

The correspondence between the two men reveals that all this work must have been carried out before March 1959. On 21 October 1958 Plomer had written to Britten: 'I have made some progress with a first draft of Sumida – & find the language assuming great simplicity – as in a fairy tale or legend –

---

[17] It now forms part of the Plomer collection at Durham University Library (*GB-DRu*).
[18] *GB-ALb* 2-9100297.

& the rhythm of the language primitive or archaic.' Britten replied on 29 October, writing from Madeira while on holiday:

I long to see what you have been doing over Sumidagawa, & to talk endlessly with you about it. I am more and more excited about it, & have to keep my ideas in chains in case they don't run parallel to yours.

Britten's respect for Plomer's feelings is somewhat unusual in the context of a librettist–composer relationship of this kind: in most other cases (with the notable exception of the more idiosyncratic W. H. Auden), Britten's librettists were largely subservient to the composer's wishes. This is clearly indicative of Plomer's importance in shaping the character of the Church Parable genre from its very inception.

In the same letter Britten asks if Plomer favours the actual appearance of the spirit or of an imaginary ghost ('we saw both versions in Tokio [sic]'), and Plomer replied on 4 November to say that he preferred the boy's actual appearance. Three days later Plomer wrote again to confirm that he had completed a preliminary libretto draft and 'would much like to discuss it with you & to hand it over for you to read'. The two men met in London a week later and Britten took possession of Plomer's draft. On 16 November[19] he expressed admiration for the work that had been done:

I had hoped so much to have a chance of telling you how excited I am with your Sumida River. You have touched so many of those lame phrases to magic, & yet kept the (to me) moving simplicity & serenity of the original . . . But what a wonderful play it is, & I cannot thank you enough for working with me on it. The more I think of it, the more I feel we should stick as far as possible to the original style & look of it – but oh, to find some equivalent to those extraordinary noises the Japanese musicians made!

Britten's much later remark that 'there was no question . . . of a pastiche from the ancient Japanese'[20] must now be qualified along with Plomer's own observation that 'neither he nor I nor anybody else would want a pastiche of a Nō play, a piece of *japonaiserie*'.[21]

---

[19] Britten dates his letter 16 October by mistake.

[20] Britten's foreword to the published score of *Curlew River* (London: Faber Music; vocal score, 1965; full score, 1983), which was prepared from notes initially made by Pears.

[21] Plomer's programme note to the Church Parables written in 1968. In this same passage, Plomer recounts his initial anxiety when embarking on the venture: 'Though honoured to be asked, I thought the project hardly possible . . . As the original depended entirely upon its *mise en scène*, archaic music, all-male cast and rigidly formal production down to the last detail of masks, costume and movement, it was hardly transferable to the Western operatic stage. What was more, the language and action of the play belonged to an antique Buddhist culture and could only be properly appreciated by highly cultivated Japanese traditionalists. But, like the poets Yeats and Waley (neither of whom ever visited Japan), Britten had been enchanted by the Nō, as I had been enchanted before him, so what was the good of protesting?'

The alterations to the first draft must have been made over Christmas 1958, which Britten and Plomer spent together at the Red House in Aldeburgh. Plans were then delayed while Britten completed the *Cantata academica*, to which he refers in a letter dated 8 March 1959:

> In a month or so it should be done & I'll get to work on what really interests me. I think the Noh libretto is wonderful. I showed it to Lu Hesse & he was enraptured. He is doing a rough German translation to show to this German producer whom I hope will do it, who has such a feeling for the style.

The producer in question was Gustav Sellner, who had been responsible for a production of *The Turn of the Screw* in Darmstadt which Britten had much admired.[22] Plans to mount the new work in 1960 were certainly made at this time, but the reopening of the Jubilee Hall at Aldeburgh in that year necessitated a change of direction, as Britten explained to Plomer in a letter dated 17 August 1959. Britten originally intended Sellner to direct the première of *A Midsummer Night's Dream*, the work written for the refurbished Jubilee Hall. As it happened, this task was given to John Cranko on the recommendation of John and Myfanwy Piper, and by the time *Curlew River* was nearing completion four years later Colin Graham (then Director of Productions for the English Opera Group) seemed the most logical choice of producer.

The changes to the libretto discussed over Christmas 1958 had been incorporated into two new typed copies,[23] and Plomer was preparing to work on this new version when he received a long and very carefully considered letter from Britten written on 15 April 1959. In view of the importance of this document to an understanding of Britten's motivation in changing the entire philosophy of the original Nō play, the composer's comments deserve quotation at some length:

> I rather hope that you are feeling strong & courageous when you open this letter, my dear, because I feel it's going to be long-winded, & maybe a trifle disturbing. Anyhow it doesn't need an immediate answer – only something to think about & which we can discuss when we meet. It is about the Noh play. A new idea has come into our (Peter's & my) heads about it – put in, because for many reasons it would be best if done in one of the churches here – I won't go into the practical reasons here, which are pretty important,[24] but the artistic ones include placing of orchestra, long entrances, beauty of sound (if in Orford Church) & contact with audience. This lead [*sic*] us to the idea of making it a

---

[22] I am grateful to Colin Graham for his help in identifying Sellner in this context.

[23] *GB-ALb* 2-9100299 and *GB-DRu*. It is not clear why this version was typed twice.

[24] Both Hans Keller and Pears recalled that financial difficulties were a prime consideration underlying the development of an 'economical' style in the Church Parables.

Christian work (Here you can stop reading & have another sip of coffee to give you courage to proceed . . .). I think one of the best ways of writing what I feel about this is to weigh the matter – pros. & cons.

Pros. The little bits of Zen-Bhuddism [*sic*], which don't mean much to me could be replaced by something which <u>does</u>. The story is one which stands strongly wherever it is placed. I have been <u>very</u> worried lest the work should seem a <u>pastiche</u> of a Noh play, which however well done, would seem false & thin. I <u>can't</u> write Japanesy music, but might be led into trying if the rest of the production (setting, clothes, moves) were Japanese. <u>Masks</u> – for which no solution has yet presented itself, & remains a colossal problem for the singer. The chorus could move freely, if we wanted it.

Cons. We should lose the magic of the Japanese names, & atmosphere – obviously very dear to you, & dear to me too. No very good reason for Peter to do a female part, unless in an accepted style.

Actually, to answer the <u>cons</u>, if we made it Mediaeval, or possibly earlier, it would be accurate that no women should be used; also if the style were kept very artificial, very influenced by the Noh, then it wouldn't seem so odd for a woman to be played by a man, especially if the dresses were very carefully & strongly designed. There is nothing, I realise, to replace the magic of 'Shimosa', or 'Miyako', or even 'Namu Amida' – altho' 'Kyrie Eleison' is pretty good. But we might get a very strong atmosphere (which I personally love) if we set it in pre-conquest East Anglia (where there were shrines galore) – or in Israel, or south Italy. (We might even set it 'no-where', with 'the river', 'the village' etc. etc.)

My own mind is very fluid about the matter, altho' the pros. weigh heavier than the cons. I must confess. Please don't be too cross about it, altho' I realise that your patience will be sorely tried! It is maddening to have so fundamental a point questioned when you have done so much of the work, & so beautifully, which we all love too. Don't, as I said, bother to react on paper immediately. Wait till we can talk it over . . . Excuse long-winded & muddled letter, but I wanted to write as quick as possible about the matter.

In spite of his apologies for being 'muddled', Britten's reasoning is so logically and clearly expressed, and his ideas so apt, that it would have been hard for Plomer to object. On 17 April the librettist replied:

I have felt all along that the problems & difficulties were formidable, & with anybody but you I should have thought them from the first insuperable. But, knowing your extreme ingenuity, I allowed myself to think that you might be able to overcome them. I can't say that I'm astonished at your – I won't say throwing up the sponge, but setting fire to your – and indeed my – kimono. I really don't know <u>how</u> the piece could have turned into anything but a pasticcio grosso. But it is a little electrifying to have to think of transposing the story into Christian terms. Think I will, my first thought being that the missing child has come to be regarded locally as a saint (perhaps he could have been martyred) & that his grave has already become a place of pilgrimage.

Working on a typed version of the earlier libretto,[25] Plomer accordingly set about transposing the action of *Sumidagawa* to mediaeval England, making emendations in ballpoint pen. The result is a fascinating testament to his ingenuity in fulfilling Britten's request. It was a relatively simple matter to modify the Japanese names and place-names he had formerly favoured, but it proved rather more challenging to adjust the many Buddhist references to a Christian interpretation of the events.

On the first page of the typescript, the working title 'Sumida River' was duly deleted. The title remained problematical for several years: Plomer first suggested 'Curlew River' in a postcard dated 26 May 1959 and this seems to be the title he had in mind when preparing the modified libretto. As late as 23 October 1963, however, Britten wrote:

> We [i.e. Britten and Colin Graham] did discuss (& with Peter) the title idea & hit on one which struck us as good, & I long to know how you react. 'The other side of the River.' That seemed to be the best use of the 'River' which seems to us to be such an important part of the whole business.

Other alternatives were 'Across the River' and 'Over the River'. On 4 January 1964 Britten wrote that 'the title remains a great problem', and the matter was only fixed on 15 February 1964: 'Oddly enough, as the work progressed the Curlew grew in significance; & my inclination is to go back to Curlew River as a title!! Colin (who is here now) agrees, & Peter, not wholly.'[26] 'Curlew' was Plomer's substitute for the Japanese 'Miyako bird' and it was to become an important verbal and musical leitmotif in Britten's setting of the text.

On a handwritten page inserted at the beginning of Plomer's modified libretto, the first indication of a possible prologue to the work is found in a note which reads:

> CURLEW RIVER
>
> (Entrance music.)
> Headed by their Abbot, a party of
> monks in single file approach the
> stage. The Abbot comes forward,
> centre, to ~~speak deliver~~ sing a short
> prologue. While he is singing, the

[25] *GB-DRu.*
[26] Letter written from Venice on 15 February 1964. One further variant, 'Crossing the River', had been considered in January 1964 and this wording found its way onto some of the scenery used in the first production: see Alexander, *William Plomer*, 305; 379, note 87.

> monks who are to take the parts
> of the Ferryman, the Traveller, and
> the Madwoman prepare themselves.
> The others dispose themselves as the
> Chorus.

The provision for 'Entrance music' (not at this stage conceived as a plainsong processional) recalls the Nō convention, but the robing of the acting monks has not yet been separated as an act of ritual significance. Plomer's note continues:

> The scene is East Anglia a
> thousand years ago, on the west bank of
> ~~of a river then known as~~ the
> Curlew River. ~~The only scenery is a
> grassy mound surmounted by a cross,
> in front of which two or three
> candles are burning.) It is morning.~~
> A morning in autumn.

The season has for some reason been changed from spring to autumn, and an element of the original Nō staging has been eliminated.

Plomer systematically changed the words of the chorus, writing a marginal note on p. 5 to remind him to use the third rather than first person. Where the 'two provinces' are mentioned, Plomer suggests '?E + W ?Fenland' as alternatives, and the 'pine tree standing all alone' becomes '?reeds'. The kidnapper of the boy is variously 'a Dane', 'a Norseman', and finally 'a Northman'. 'Miyako' becomes 'west country', and 'willow tree' is deleted in favour of 'yew tree'. For the Mother's song on arriving at the far bank, Plomer directs himself to 'expand with fenny details', and one lengthy passage is marked 'de-jap a bit'. The mourning gong[27] becomes a chapel bell, tolled not by the Mother but by a Priest. The final chorus section is entirely deleted and the Spirit is given new closing lines in the more optimistic vein required by the Christian interpretation of the action. Alterations necessitated by the direct references to Buddhist philosophy include the emendation of: 'Ah, but the bond of parenthood/Cannot survive the grave' to 'But that would not diminish/Her yearning for her child.' The spiritual implications of the new version are therefore almost diametrically opposed to those of the original. As Britten suggested, 'Namu Amida' is universally replaced by 'Kyrie eleison', and where the Traveller suggests a prayer to 'the unknown world' the image is altered to 'God in heaven'. The passage that follows is simply marked 'Christianize' by Plomer:

---

[27] Transliterated 'shōgo' in the text of *Sumidagawa* (cf. Malm, *Six Hidden Views*, 191). A similar gong (shōko) is used in Gagaku.

O worship the numberless
Millions of Buddhas
In the Western Paradise,
Abode of the blessèd,
Sphere of Eternal
Peacefulness, happiness!

This later became:

And her prayers go straight to heaven
And, o, to the numberless
Holy and glorious
Saints and martyrs,
All the company
Holy and glorious
There in the blessèd
Abode of eternal
Peacefulness, happiness.

There is no text given for the Abbot's prologue or epilogue, but the latter is indicated by an amusing note which reads '?Abbot winding up – a little preachment'.

A further addition made at this stage is the Mother's 'mad song' ('You mock me . . . I turn me away'), which was inserted on another handwritten page. This neatly dovetails her entrance with the Ferryman's curiosity about the approaching 'strange noise', and corresponds to the stage direction in *Sumidagawa* which requires the Madwoman to pause on the *hashi-gakari* while she delivers her opening lines.[28]

It was noted above that plans to mount *Curlew River* in 1960 were eventually abandoned. Britten explained the reasons for this in a letter to Plomer dated 17 August 1959:

I fear I must postpone this piece, still near to my heart, for a year. For many reasons. Partly time; because of my change of location, moving it from Japan to Mediaeval England, we are well behind our schedule. I'm not complaining about this, because I know that this re-orientation must happen slowly . . . [Concerning the opening of the Jubilee Hall:] The 'River', being for a church, wouldn't do, also, it is scarcely Festive.

During the composition of the new opera for the Jubilee Hall, Britten's thoughts were not far from the Nō project. He wrote to Plomer on 23 November: 'Even when deep in the Midsummer Night's Dream I cast nostalgic glances into the future towards 'The River' – still very strong in my fancy & inclination.' The correspondence is then silent on the subject until after the 1960 Aldeburgh Festival. Britten reopens it in a letter dated 4 August of that year, saying: 'I'd

[28] Japanese Classics Translation Committee, *Japanese Noh Drama*, 149.

146

love to talk about one or two bits fairly soon, but it is thrilling that it is all so beautifully & convincingly shaped now.'

Britten spent Christmas 1960 at work on his C major Cello Sonata for Rostropovich and was then fully occupied until December 1961 with the composition of the *War Requiem*. Although *Curlew River* is mentioned in several letters from this period (on New Year's Day 1961, for instance, Britten wrote 'I've had one or two interesting ideas about it musically. But I'm worried about a producer'), it was not until Britten and Plomer spent Christmas 1961 together at Aldeburgh that talks were resumed. Even then, Britten could find no time to devote to the project and Plomer wrote to him on 8 November 1962 to say: '[I] am of course happy to think that Curlew River is flowing steadily along under your surface: I know you have many & weightier obligations.' In July 1963 Britten discussed *Curlew River* with the Hesses at Schloss Wolfsgarten and decided upon Colin Graham as the ideal producer.[29] A première at the 1964 Aldeburgh Festival was scheduled, and work on the long-delayed project was at last resumed in earnest. Much of the remaining work on the libretto was carried out over Christmas 1963, and on 4 January 1964 Britten wrote thanking Plomer for his gift of a set of Japanese prints of scenes from Nō plays:

> They are beauties – dangerously so, because it is risky that they may lead us back to Japan, already a strong influence in the 'River' (or whatever). I'm not serious, because there is really no danger of a pastiche & one can always learn from an art so firm and universal (I find) . . . I have had some excellent talks with Colin Graham . . . He is getting on well with his ideas, & I think they are good. One scheme we have developed is this: the Chorus, seated at one side, is going eventually to give the appearance of being in the boat. There-fore, on arrival on the other side they all will get out & cross to a new position around the Shrine. This will happen on page 15 (typed script) after 'For this boy he never knew.' Could there be a few lines of verse for them to sing as they cross . . . 'Let us go and pray ourselves etc.'??

Plomer produced a new version of the modified libretto he had made in 1959, and this was subsequently annotated by Britten.[30] The Abbot's prologue and epilogue were included in full, Britten adding as an afterthought the chorus's echoes of certain of his lines. At the end of the prologue, Britten pencilled in 'Ceremonial Robing' before the entrance of the Ferryman. The 'Entrance music' for the Abbot is altered to an 'Entrance Hymn – 3 verses', an indication that Britten had now conceived the plainsong processional on 'Te lucis ante terminum'. The locations mentioned in the text are made much less specific, 'Cornwall' becoming 'the Westland' and the 'Marches of Wales' being replaced by the 'Black Mountains'. Britten himself put the finishing touches to

29 See Britten's letters to Plomer dated 17 July and 24 September 1963.
30 *GB-DRu.*

the libretto when working on the music at the Palazzo Mocenigo in Venice during February 1964:

I will . . . give you a brief account of the progress of the opera. As I said, it has come 'easily' – except for the very start. When we arrived I was tireder than I thought . . . & honestly I still couldn't quite see the style of it all clearly enough. I was still very drawn towards the Nô, too close for comfort. However, a few days here, although Arctic in temperature, the Gothic beauty & warmth, and above all the occasional Masses one attended, began to make their effect. It was a slow start, but after that it rushed ahead, & after little more than a month I am well towards the end. Apart from the usual bits that need clarifying, I am very pleased with it. Honestly I would have loved to have you at my side all the time; there have been so many problems. But you have other things to do, & so I have made my own changes, & we must just work at them together at the earliest moment, & see that we are both happy. There is nothing major at all. It has only been the infinite little details, which, until the music begins to take over, one can never anticipate – lengths of line & verses, forinstance . . .

A few points. The Ceremonial robing now takes place after the Abbot's prologue (reasons are mostly practical). I've referred to the Land of East (or West) rather than Kingdom (rhythmic problem). To emphasise the river, & Curlew, idea, I like to refer to the River people, as opposed to Village p. (less contemporary too, I feel). I liked the idea of keeping the mystery a little longer, & so on page 2 & 3 (typed script), I have kept the burial anonymous (no boy mentioned yet). In the great narration on the boat – I've inserted a reference to the boy as being a Christian – & therefore the Northman as a pagan. Do you mind?

As you obviously didn't have time to do me a new piece for the Chorus getting out of the boat I used the river chorus from page 12 again, & it works well. I am sorry to have bothered you about this, because I ought to have spotted it before, as the best solution.

I have omitted referring to the boy's name (Siward) anywhere – it didn't seem necessary . . .

I have had to concoct a big ensemble after her revelation on page 17 – which I've done with Colin's help, mostly from phrases used elsewhere. Similarly I have concocted a big really Crazy scene for Madwoman on top of 18 – but used nothing, I think, which hasn't appeared before, except one idea pinched from the Nô. I have made her confuse the Curlew river with the bird, & suggested the boy has flown away with the young Curlew birds – 'like the four young birds that left their nest.' (Nô) But of course it can be changed if you object.

I have a big new idea, which I think is good – I am just approaching the big moment round the Tomb. I would like to use one of those great Gregorian plain-chant tunes. It will somehow tie the whole thing together, & match the entrance & exit chant, (for which I am using 'Te lucis ante terminum'). The one I have my eye on is: 'Custodes hominum' from the Feast of the Holy Guardian Angels, a magnificent tune & suitable too. If you agree with our feeling that it should be sung in English could you possibly do a translation – It is quite short, needs to be metrically exact, but not rhyming – ?[31]

Plomer may have advocated retaining the original Latin text of 'Custodes hominum', since it appears in this form in the final version of the work even though typescript translations survive.

On 2 April, Britten consulted Plomer on the question of a subtitle for the work ('we all like the parable-idea') and then the librettist's task was at last complete after nearly eight years of protracted discussion and conceptual development. *Curlew River* received its first performance in Orford Church on 13 June 1964 during the Aldeburgh Festival. Uncharacteristically, Britten made significant musical alterations to the ending of the work during rehearsals: Oliver Knussen has revealed that in the original version the Madwoman was made to clutch frantically at the spirit of her son, as she does in *Sumidagawa*.[32]

The phraseology of Plomer's final libretto remains close to that of the original Nō play in spite of the change of locality from Japan to mediaeval England. The following lines, for example, are retained verbatim from the 1955 authorized translation:

'Mark this well, all of you!' (Ferryman)
'And now I have reached the ferry' (Traveller)
'I see the ferry-boat about to leave' (Traveller)
'But first may I ask you?' (Ferryman)
'I will delay the ferry-boat' (Ferryman)
'Shall I ask these travellers?' (Madwoman)
'Let me get into the boat!' (Madwoman)
'Living in this famous place' (Ferryman)
'He spoke these words calmly, like a man' (Ferryman)
'Since then have neither/Of his parents been here?' (Madwoman)
'He was the child . . . Is this a dream?' (Madwoman)
'Now let me show you where the boy is buried' (Ferryman)
'He whose life was full of promise' (chorus)
'The moon has risen,/The river breeze is blowing' (chorus)
'We shall keep silent' (Ferryman)
'Say your prayer alone' (Traveller)
'Is it you, my child?' (Madwoman).

Many lines are only slightly altered: the Traveller's 'Tedious days of travel lie before me' in *Sumidagawa*, for instance, becomes 'Weary days of travel lie

---

[31] Letter dated 15 February 1964. In this same letter the final form of the work's title was established: see above, p. 144.
[32] Carpenter, *Benjamin Britten*, 438–9.

before me' in *Curlew River*. Plomer often expands small sections of the Nō text, filling in circumstantial details which hint at a realism somewhat removed from the Nō aesthetic. This is seen in the Ferryman's opening lines:

Sumidagawa

I am he who rows the ferry across the Sumida in the province of Musashi.

Curlew River

I am the ferryman.
I row the ferry boat
Over the Curlew,
Our wide and reedy
Fenland river.
In every season, every weather,
I row the ferry boat.

Most of the important divergences from the original were, of course, necessitated by the Christian interpretation. The following lines are entirely Plomer's invention:

Ferryman:	[There the folk are gathering] To pray before a grave, As if it were a shrine . . . The river folk believe Some special grace is there To heal the sick in body and soul.
Traveller:	May God preserve wayfaring men!
Ferryman:	But the Devil himself . . . God have mercy upon us!
Ferryman:	. . . a gentle boy . . . and a Christian . . . Then he said a prayer: 'Kyrie eleison! Kyrie eleison!'

[Replacing: '[he] invoked Amida Buddha several times']

Ferryman:	The river folk believe The boy was a saint. They take earth from his grave To heal their sickness. They report many cures. The river folk believe His spirit has been seen.
Ferryman:	And, O, to the numberless . . . Peacefulness, happiness. All angels, all martyrs,

All saints, pray for us.
Christ have mercy upon us.

Spirit: Go your way in peace, mother.
The dead shall rise again
And in that blessèd day
We shall meet in Heaven . . .
God be with you all . . .
God be with you, mother.

Clearly, Britten's decision to Christianize the plot of *Sumidagawa* marks a significant and philosophically radical departure from the aesthetic effect of the Japanese original. To the uninitiated Westerner, many Nō plays seem highly static in their dramatic effect because stage action and plot developments are less important than the philosophical contemplation expected from cognoscenti of the genre. The aesthetic principles of Nō theatre are both complex and subtle,[33] and are based on three categories of artistic 'beauty' termed *hana*, *yūgen* and *rōjaku*, which are expressed through a sophisticated process of dramatic symbolism.[34] Britten evidently had little interest in this fundamental dimension of Nō, and his attempt to replace it with a dramatic momentum more typical of Western theatre might well disappoint a connoisseur of Nō aesthetics. Indeed, his apparent trivializing of the 'little bits of Zen-Buddhism, which don't mean much to me' and Plomer's reference to 'esoteric Buddhism' might be taken to indicate a somewhat cavalier attitude to their literary source.

William Malm's study of the dramatic and musical parallels and contrasts between *Sumidagawa* and *Curlew River* goes to some lengths to explain the dramatic strengths of the original Nō play.[35] He describes *Sumidagawa* as a 'powerful Buddhist story of the evanescence of life' and offers some interpretation of textual symbols and literary allusions which were clearly not important to Britten and Plomer. (We have even seen how Britten went so far as to describe some of the *Sumidagawa* text as 'those lame phrases'.) Malm notes that at one point in *Curlew River* a passage of 'Buddhist message' which lasts five minutes in a performance of the Nō play is drastically reduced to a mere four lines of alternative text. Particularly perceptive is his frequent observation that Britten and Plomer incorporate textual (and therefore often

---

[33] Summarized in Shigeo Kishibe, 'Japan, III: Theatrical and Courtly Genres', in Sadie (ed.) *The New Grove Dictionary*, IX, 519, and the same author's *The Traditional Music of Japan* (Tokyo: Japan Foundation, 1984), 54.

[34] For a full discussion, see Komparu, *The Noh Theater*, 10–15.

[35] Malm, *Six Hidden Views*, 151–97. Malm's essay is not always reliable. He states that *Curlew River* was completed 'in Vienna' (p. 152), not Venice, and it is curious that so renowned an authority on Japanese music should neglect to mention the obvious derivation of what he terms 'soft tone clusters on the organ' (p. 162) from the shō. In addition, Malm attempts little critical evaluation of Britten's enterprise and is mostly content to discuss the two versions of the story in parallel.

musical) recapitulations, which are characteristically absent in *Sumidagawa*, in order to achieve a sense of completion and structural balance more comprehensible to a Western audience.

However, Malm is also able to talk of the 'great respect' with which Britten handles the bulk of the original text, and his interpretation of the story is never criticized: rather, the composer's 'Western' approach is shown to have a dramatic cogency equal to that of *Sumidagawa* if based on entirely different aesthetic principles. In fact, Plomer's Christianized text has a dramatic shape of its own which is not discussed by Malm. In *Curlew River* the Mother makes no reference to God or Heaven until she is freed from her madness by the apparition of the Spirit and sings 'Amen'. Britten's drama may therefore be seen as a spiritual progression towards this climactic and cathartic moment (a familiar scheme in the composer's operatic output), a tangible dramatic momentum greatly aiding the Western audience's appreciation of the story. The initial alienation of the Mother from the Faith which lies at the heart of *Curlew River* is strengthened by the many references to God, Heaven, saints, martyrs and prayer by the characters around her – a sharp contrast to her brooding melancholy. At the same time, her final transfiguration is doubly emphatic in the context of the humility of the Ferryman and his passengers at the graveside.

The original ending of *Sumidagawa* is very powerful in performance, and the audience sits in silent contemplation while the performers exit.[36] (In *Curlew River*, Colin Graham's direction that 'no lights should be turned on in the church at the end of the piece until after an appreciable pause, particularly if the performance is an evening one and the church is in darkness' undoubtedly reflects Britten's desire to emulate the profound conclusion of the Nō play.) In spite of this, one can appreciate why the composer felt the need to present his audience with a more Westernized dramatic preparation for the moment of climax, and why he replaced the climax itself with an overtly expressed spiritual transformation.

We shall return to the implications of these aesthetic departures later. In the present context, it is important to add that Britten's Christian Parable opened up possibilities for the treatment of further, biblical, stories and thus created a new dramatic convention in a way which would have been difficult to envisage if the Buddhist apparatus of *Sumidagawa* had been firmly retained. The libretti for *The Burning Fiery Furnace* (1966) and *The Prodigal Son* (1968)

---

[36] The author is grateful to Prof. Kazuo Fukushima of Ueno Gakuen College, Tokyo, for his assistance in making available a video recording of his institution's production of *Sumidagawa*, which provided a useful comparison with the live performance of the play seen by the author at the Otsuki Nōgaku Kaikan in Ōsaka on 7 September 1986. More recently, *Sumidagawa* was presented at the 44th Aldeburgh Festival in Snape Maltings on 7 June 1991 in a double bill alongside a Japanese production of *Curlew River*. This was not, in fact, the first performance of the Nō play to be seen at Aldeburgh: it had been staged as part of the 1973 Festival, three years before Britten's death.

occasioned Plomer far fewer problems than *Curlew River* had done, but the protracted gestation of the first Parable for Church Performance was a necessary stage in the formulation of a dramatic style marked by its originality and effectiveness.

III *Curlew River* and the dramatic style of Nō

The stylized dramatic presentation which characterizes Britten's Church Parables is a synthesis of elements borrowed from two mediaeval dramatic genres, the Nō theatre and the European liturgical drama and mystery play. Britten was clearly interested in both areas immediately after his return from the Far East: 1957 saw not only the first discussions of *Sumidagawa* with Plomer but also the composition of *Noye's Fludde*, a setting of the Chester Miracle Play. The extent to which the theatrical style of *Curlew River* was influenced by both genres may be seen through an examination of its dramatic idiom as exemplified by the first production in 1964, in every detail of which the composer took an active interest.

The first performance of *Noye's Fludde* at the 1958 Aldeburgh Festival had been produced by Colin Graham, who also designed the setting. Graham first worked for Britten in 1954 as assistant producer (to Basil Coleman) in *The Turn of the Screw*; from 1961 to 1975 he was Director of Productions for the English Opera Group, and from 1969 an Artistic Director of the Aldeburgh Festival. He was therefore the most obvious choice of producer for *Curlew River* when the plans to employ Gustav Sellner fell through after 1960. There can be little doubt that Graham's knowledge of the mystery play and subsequent research into the Nō theatre formed a major contribution to the success and originality of Britten's dramatic achievement in the Church Parables.

Graham's correspondence with Britten throughout 1962 is principally concerned with preparations for a forthcoming production of Purcell's *Dido and Aeneas* and discussions of Graham's libretto for the projected opera *Anna Karenina* (destined never to be composed). The first reference to *Curlew River* is found in an undated letter written by Graham in 1963:

> Just a line to thank you not only for having me at the weekend – which I enjoyed very much – but also for asking me to do 'Sumidagawa': the whole idea is very exciting and challenging & I look forward to working on it with you enormously . . .
>
> I have written to the cultural attaché of the Japanese Embassy to ask if he can lay his hands on any film of Noh which would be useful. Also to ask for any books on the actual <u>technique</u> which is not gone into in any detail in the books I have seen so far. This worries me a good deal – especially if there is no film available.

153

Graham has shed further light on his preparations for the new production:

> When [Britten] asked me to do the opera, he also particularly asked that
> I should read as much as I could about Noh plays but UNDER NO
> CIRCUMSTANCES go to see one as he wanted our stylised movement to
> have its own style and not be a pastiche – thus echoing his musical
> approach. I did of course comply with both requests, but took every
> opportunity I could to ascertain all factors in the Noh philosophy of
> approach. Subsequently (before Burning Fiery Furnace . . .), I got a
> special grant to go and study the various branches of Japanese Classical
> theatre and have put a lot of my (subsequent) 20 years of study and
> research into my own work as a stage director, designer, and librettist.[37]

In the same letter Graham recalls that final details of the music were worked
out simultaneously with the dramatic ideas (in Venice during February 1964)
and that Britten had a model of the stage set constantly by his side during the
process of composition. Graham's published account of the preparations for
Curlew River confirms that he had not, in fact, seen a Nō play prior to the first
production.[38] Although the performance convention he created incorporates
much from his literary research into the Nō theatre, this deliberate neglect
compelled him to achieve a far more flexible dramatic style than might
otherwise have been possible after direct contact with Nō in live performance.

The economical and versatile stage set evolved by Graham for the Church
Parables perfectly captures the unelaborate functionality of the Nō prototype
(see Figure 14). The ramp to the rear of the main circular construction leads
off-stage to the audience's right and strongly recalls the *hashi-gakari*: both the
Traveller and the Madwoman enter along this ramp in a fashion analogous to
the Nō convention. The main stage is made of highly polished redwood and
the remainder of the set from natural whitewood, recalling the plain cypress
of the Nō stage. A small circular construction is raised above the main acting
platform and reserved exclusively for the three principal characters. This is an
intriguing idea which helps to strengthen the importance of the *shite, waki*
and *waki-tsure* (the Madwoman, Ferryman and Traveller respectively) and
suggests the concept of the sanctity of stage space which is fundamental to the
Nō aesthetic. Such a raised podium is necessary in *Curlew River* to isolate the
principals from the chorus, who move about the main stage in their role as
pilgrims. This situation does not arise in *Sumidagawa*, where the chorus is
constantly separated from the actors by remaining on its own *waki-za* (side-
stage). Graham's set includes no background pine tree, but the concept of an
unchanging feature at the rear of the stage is retained in the solitary pole
which supports the sail in *Curlew River*, the image of Merodak in *The Burning
Fiery Furnace* and the representation of the sun in *The Prodigal Son*.

[37] Letter to the present author, 24 January 1986.
[38] Colin Graham, 'Staging First Productions, 3', in David Herbert (ed.), *The Operas of
Benjamin Britten* (London: Hamish Hamilton, 1979), 49.

The church location captures several characteristics of the Nō theatre. It strengthens the concept of the sanctity of the acting area; indeed, for the Western audience of *Curlew River* the effect is much stronger than for the Japanese audience of *Sumidagawa*. Because of this, the stage needs no roof to symbolize the purity of the space beneath it. Church acoustics also capture the reverberation caused by the resonance cavities built into the Nō stage and render such an elaborate measure unnecessary. The use of the aisle in the procession and recession of the instrumentalists and actors at the start and conclusion of each performance recalls the *hanamichi* ('flower way') of the Kabuki theatre. The latter consists of one (or two) apron stages which pass through the auditorium near the left wall (or both walls) and suggest the process of intimate communication between actors and audience. In both Kabuki and the Church Parables, therefore, there exists a blurring of the distinction between the stage and real worlds. The treatment of the church aisle as a type of *hanamichi* is most strongly suggested in *The Prodigal Son*, where the Tempter's appearance along it after the main procession has reached the stage further confuses the audience's conception of reality and stage convention.

The use of a mask by the *shite* is extended to the *waki* and *waki-tsure* in *Curlew River* so that all three are effectively isolated from the rest of the performers. There seems to be no very clear reason behind this extension of the Nō principle, and when Japanese productions of the Church Parables were televised in Tokyo during March 1979 the original Nō convention was reinstated so that the Madwoman gained extra importance as the only masked character. The masks used in the Church Parables differ from their Nō counterparts by covering only the upper part of the face, a design allowing for comfortable vocal delivery (see Plate 8). This practical consideration is not found in the full-faced Nō mask, since aural comprehension of the text is not a prime factor in the artistic symbiosis of the Nō theatre. The Madwoman's mask in *Curlew River* is described as 'noble and tragic',[39] characteristics of the *fukai* ('deep well') mask worn by the *shite* in *Sumidagawa* to represent a middle-aged woman whose perfect beauty is shattered by a sorrow bordering on madness.[40] The extra masks used by the Ferryman and Traveller preserve a similar degree of characterization, the former described as 'bluff but like-able' and the latter wearing the mask of an 'older, experienced and kindly man'.

The stage properties in *Curlew River* are as economical as possible and well inside the Nō tradition. The bamboo branch carried by the *shite* to symbolize her madness is not retained (presumably because the symbolism is meaningless to an uninitiated audience), but it is interesting to note that this was another missing detail reintroduced in the 1979 Tokyo production. For

[39] Benjamin Britten, William Plomer and Colin Graham, 'Production Notes and Remarks on the Style of Performing *Curlew River*' in the published full score of the work, 145.

[40] A *fukai* mask is preserved in the Pitt Rivers Museum of Anthropology at the University of Oxford.

155

similar reasons, the small hand gong (shōgo) tolled by the *shite* at the grave-side in *Sumidagawa* is replaced in *Curlew River* by an acolyte's symbolic tolling of the chapel bell, represented by a simple rope suspended from the background mast. The Ferryman carries a punting pole symbolic of his trade, as in the original Nō play, and the Traveller's staff fulfils the same function.

In *Sumidagawa* the boy's burial mound is visible on stage from the very beginning of the play, and the *kokata* who is to perform the role of the boy's spirit is hidden inside it. In *Curlew River* the tomb is revealed only as the sail is lowered after the river crossing, and it consists of a set of steps surmounted by a cross to further the Christian dimension in Britten's adaptation of the story. The three benches for the chorus, the Abbot's stool, the low bench for the protagonists and the boat's sail are all elements added by Graham to increase the realism of a river-crossing which is entirely mimed in *Sumidagawa* and does not involve the chorus.

The costumes for the three principal characters are generally simpler in *Curlew River* than in *Sumidagawa*, where the Nō tradition dictates the use of revered robes often surviving from mediaeval times. The Ferryman's striped kimono is replaced by a 'surcoat of blue/green' and the Traveller's kimono by an 'impressive' travelling robe. The Traveller wears a hat (the *waki-tsure* in *Sumidagawa* similarly sports a traditional mushroom hat) and the Ferryman has a simple cap. The greater simplicity of the costume designs in *Curlew River* is best illustrated by the treatment of the Madwoman. In *Sumidagawa*, the *shite* wears a painted gold under-kimono in conjunction with an embroidered *koshimaki* (outer kimono). Over this is worn a broad-sleeved robe, and the outfit is completed by a wig, mushroom hat and the bamboo spray signifying her madness. In contrast, the Mother in *Curlew River* wears a 'simple but elegant robe' with a stylized wig and head-dress.

Although the decision to cast the actors as a party of monks enacting a parable might at first appear to be a radical departure from the traditions of Nō, it allows the costumes to achieve a significance similar to that of the costumes employed in Nō plays. The on-stage robing ceremony is foreign to Nō, and Graham recalls how the idea was originally conceived:

> While working on the opera in Venice [in February 1964], we attended mass given in their own chapel by the monks of San Giorgio Maggiore. We were impressed and moved by the ritual robing of the Brother of the Day who was to celebrate the mass – the robes were unfolded from a linen chest with extreme delicacy and reverence. This led Britten to follow the Abbot's address in the Parable with a robing ceremony . . .[41]

This robing ceremony not only emphasizes the distinction between the outer robes (representing character) and the undergarments (monks' habits), which is an important feature of the multi-layered costume design in Nō, but it also

---

[41] Graham, 'Staging First Productions, 3', 48.

reflects the ritual significance of the initial robing performed by the Nō actors in the *kagami no ma* (out of sight of the audience) before they enter on to the stage along the *hashi-gakari*. The choice of monks as actors is itself not as surprising as it might at first seem, as Graham points out:

> The Noh plays are of Zen-Buddhist origin and were originally performed by the monks themselves: the action is extremely stylised and the women's roles were also played by the monks. (Some years later, on a visit to Kyoto, I was entertained at a monastery by the Abbot, who amazed me by reciting from memory long stretches of the Ferryman's role.)[42]

Graham's production notes for *Curlew River* are of necessity much more detailed than the stage directions for *Sumidagawa*, since no knowledge of Nō conventions can be assumed on the part of performers coming to the work for the first time. There are, however, many indications that he based his work firmly on the authorized translation of the *Sumidagawa* text published by the Japanese Classics Translation Committee in 1955, copies of which were owned by both Plomer and Britten (who acknowledged their source in the published score of *Curlew River*). The translation is illustrated throughout by miniature diagrams depicting movements on stage, and Graham's notes for all three Parables included in the published scores are profusely illustrated by sketches in much the same spirit.

A comparison of the principal stage directions in *Curlew River* with those in the *Sumidagawa* text reveals a more fundamental debt to the translation. In both, the Ferryman turns to face the audience at the start of the story (see Figures 15a–b),[43] and sits down in front of the chorus at the end of his introductory speech. The Traveller enters along the ramp/*hashi-gakari* and, after his travelling song, the Ferryman rises. Both characters sit after the ensuing dialogue, and Graham makes it clear in his version that the Traveller is now in the boat. In *Sumidagawa* the Madwoman stops on the *hashi-gakari* to deliver her opening lines (see Figure 15c), an idea retained in *Curlew River*, where she is instructed to pause at the top of the entrance ramp. Her final entrance on to the *hon-butai* is reflected in the Parable by her movement on to the raised circle. The Madwoman's first song of grief is followed in both versions by weeping. The stillness following the Ferryman's raucous demands to hear her sing is broken in *Curlew River* by a movement of the Ferryman away from the raised circle, turning towards the Traveller who sits once more. The Madwoman then moves towards the Ferryman to remind him of the local riddle. This set of movements clearly derives from the corresponding point in the *Sumidagawa* text (see Figure 15d).

When the Madwoman in *Curlew River* begins to relate the flight of curlews to the disappearance of her son, she moves round in a circle as if to follow

---

[42] *Ibid.*
[43] In *Sumidagawa*, he takes up his pole only at the beginning of the river-crossing.

Figure 15. Production sketches from *Sumidagawa* and *Curlew River*

them and stops at the top of the entrance ramp. In *Sumidagawa* the same movement occurs as the *shite* moves to the First Pine on the *hashi-gakari* and gazes into the distance. Her subsequent supplication to the Ferryman and entry into the boat is identical in both versions. The Madwoman weeps during the relation of her son's fate in *Sumidagawa* by raising one hand to her eye in the movement known as *kata-shiori* (see Figure 15e); the stage directions at this point in *Curlew River* call for her to raise her left hand to the right side of her face. In both versions the Ferryman discards his pole after the crossing, helps the Madwoman out of the boat and leads her forward a few paces (on to the raised circle in *Curlew River*). At the conclusion, everyone turns towards the burial mound in prayer. We have already noted that the ending of Britten's version of the story is markedly different from the Japanese original, and this prevented Graham from retaining the Nō play's striking final image of the Madwoman clawing vainly at thin air in a frenetic attempt to detain the spirit of her son as it vanishes. He did, however, incorporate this gesture earlier in the Parable when the Madwoman sings 'Torn from my nest . . .'[44]

In addition to these direct parallels with the *Sumidagawa* text, many of the movements which make up the vocabulary of hieratic gestures in the Church Parables are borrowed from Nō conventions. As we have seen, weeping is represented by raising one hand to the eyes (*kata-shiori*) or by raising both hands (*moro-shiori*) as illustrated in Figure 15f. Abstract movements to either side (*sayū*) are employed when the Madwoman first steps on to the raised circle (see Figure 15g). The gesture for prayer consists of a horizontal raising of the arms (see Figure 15h) derived from the Nō movement known as *ogamu*. The complete form of this gesture, in which the hands finally meet and touch fingertips, is found in *The Prodigal Son* as the 'Gesture of Harmony', and the prayer variant is also retained in *The Burning Fiery Furnace*. In his introductory notes to the score of *Curlew River*, Graham comments that 'with every angle or tilt of the head a well-designed mask can take on a life of its own', and this quality is exploited throughout the work. At least one specific mask movement is directly derived from Nō procedures, the Madwoman's tilting her head from left to right (production cue 59), recalling the searching movement termed *omote o tsukau*.

In spite of these obvious similarities to Nō conventions and a pervasive desire for gestural economy, several of Graham's stage directions are far more detailed and realistic than the Nō allows. This is particularly evident when the Madwoman is instructed to heave her shoulders up and down as she weeps and in the swaying motion of the chorus depicting the rocking movements of the ferry as it crosses the river. These anomalies may perhaps have arisen from a fear that certain highly symbolic Nō gestures may not in themselves contain enough indications of their meanings to satisfy an uninitiated audience.

---

[44] See, however, p. 149 for Britten's original (abandoned) attempt to include the Madwoman's frantic snatching movements at the end of the Parable.

IV *Curlew River* and European mediaeval drama

The mediaeval European religious drama which constitutes the second principal influence on the dramatic style of the Church Parables was a development approximately contemporaneous with the Nō theatre and having many features in common with it. It may be subdivided into two distinct categories, both of importance to an understanding of *Curlew River* and both fully developed by the turn of the fifteenth century.

In its original form, the religious drama was designed specifically for ceremonial performance in the cathedrals and larger churches. Simple tableaux were enacted in Latin by the clergy with music, costumes and processionals enhancing the festal atmosphere. This type of play is generally termed 'liturgical' since the events portrayed were strictly related to the church calendar and performed only at the appropriate feasts. Although the genre was well established on the Continent by the end of the twelfth century, a notably early example survives from eleventh-century England: the *Regularis concordia* of St Ethelwold records how the encounter between the three Marys and the Angel at the sepulchre was to be represented at Matins on Easter Day by four brothers in costume. The liturgical drama was to remain primitive and ritualistic, maintained within the church by the clergy. Another twelfth-century theatrical development, however, became increasingly important outside the confines of the ecclesiastical institutions. This also had its basis in religious didacticism, but its nature was unceremonial, its language was the vernacular and a much greater degree of realistic histrionic detail was permitted. Dramatic realism was combined with religious symbolism: Adam's sumptuous costume might be replaced by pauper's clothes after the eating of the forbidden fruit (as in the twelfth-century *Jeu d'Adam*), a situation which is recalled in the treatment of the Younger Son's portion robe in Britten's *The Prodigal Son*. Raised staging was often employed, either as a static fixture or as a mobile pageant wagon, and the stage sets were often highly elaborate.

The establishment of the Feast of Corpus Christi by the Council of Vienne in 1311 acted as a powerful catalyst on the development of these civic dramas, since the new feast (occurring on the Thursday after Trinity Sunday) had no specific reference to the church calendar but clearly demanded extensive celebration. Corpus Christi generally fell during June, when the days were long and the festive spirit high, and a tradition evolved in which the Christian story from Adam and Eve to Judgement Day was presented in the form of a cyclic drama. In England, these 'mystery play' cycles survive from York (48 plays; earliest date 1378, surviving manuscript *c.*1430), Chester (24 plays: *c.*1375, principal manuscript source *c.*1607), Wakefield (the 32 plays in the Towneley cycle; surviving manuscript *c.*1450) and in the *Ludus Coventriae* (42 plays; manuscript dated 1468). The English mystery play flourished until the Reformation, when it was systematically repressed because it was considered contrary to the new religious doctrines.

Britten's interest in the English mystery play is well known, primarily through his direct setting of a Chester text in *Noye's Fludde*. The libretto was prepared from A. W. Pollard's *English Miracle Plays, Moralities and Interludes*, a source acknowledged in the published score.[45] The text was notably condensed, but otherwise unaltered. Britten's annotations to his copy of Pollard indicate musical sections ('Ensemble', 'Recit.', etc.) and provide marginal glosses on unfamiliar or archaic words and phrases. The score was composed at some speed less than two years after the composer's return from the Far East, and there are several prominent Balinese influences in its instrumentation. There are also dramatic parallels with the Nō theatre: Noye is a strong character of obvious virtue and tenacity (an archetypal *shite*), the text calls for mimed representation of the building of the Ark, and Britten's cast list requires four property men who fulfil a function identical to that of the *kōken* in Nō. The first production of *Noye's Fludde* was directed by Colin Graham, and it is therefore not surprising to find features which look directly ahead to the dramatic style of the Church Parables. The action takes place 'on rostra, but not on a stage removed from the congregation', and there should be 'no attempt to hide the orchestra from sight'.[46] The animals are organized in an elaborate procession to, and recession from, the Ark, and their singing of 'Kyrie eleison' is not to be found in the Chester text. (In *Curlew River* Britten was to include the same words to replace the Japanese phrase 'Namu Amida'.) The congregational participation is most effective at the climax of the storm passacaglia, and the use of familiar hymn tunes as a symbol of faith (an idea first appearing in *Saint Nicolas* in 1948) looks directly ahead to the use of plainsong in the Parables.

Towards the end of his life, Britten was also contemplating setting a text derived from the Nativity plays in the Chester cycle. This was to have been commissioned by Pimlico School (where Kathleen Mitchell was headmistress), and a typed libretto survives which is dated 5 October 1974. This was clearly prepared from Britten's own annotations to the original text, for which he consulted the 1959 edition of the Chester plays by H. Deimling.[47] The project was to consist of five tableaux presenting 'The Salutation', 'The Nativity', 'The Shepherds', 'The Magi' and 'The Innocents'. There is a long cast list which includes King Herod, a character who particularly fascinated Britten. Many features of the work were retained from *Noye's Fludde*, notably in the provision for the congregational singing of various hymns ('O come, O

---

45 Alfred W. Pollard (ed.), *English Miracle Plays, Moralities and Interludes: Specimens of the Pre-Elizabethan Drama* (Oxford: Clarendon Press, 8th edn 1927). Britten's copy is preserved in *GB-ALb* 1-9300358.

46 Introductory note to the full score of *Noye's Fludde* (London: Boosey & Hawkes, 1958).

47 Hermann Deimling (ed.), *The Chester Plays*, 2 vols. (London: Kegan Paul, 1892–1916). Britten's copy of Part I is preserved in *GB-ALb* 1-9400207.

come Emmanuel', 'Es ist ein' Ros' entsprungen', 'While shepherds watched', 'Lulla, lulla, thou little tiny child' and 'In dulci jubilo') at relevant dramatic points. More interestingly, the work was to commence with the singing of the plainsong 'Nunc sancte nobis spiritus' by boy angels, a clear derivation from the format of the Parables. Most striking of all is the suggestion that dancers should portray the animals around the crib, the sheep in the pasture, the crowds, soldiers and the boy innocents – a balletic element retained from *Death in Venice*, which had been completed in the previous year. A handful of fragmentary musical sketches for the work survives,[48] but Britten's failing health prevented him from undertaking a composition of this size.

The church environment of the three Parables suggests a stronger affinity with the somewhat earlier liturgical drama than with the mystery play, and Britten's knowledge of the former is demonstrated by his extensive annotations to the two volumes of Karl Young's *The Drama of the Mediaeval Church* which probably came into his possession in the mid-1950s.[49] Passages are emphasized with marginal pencil lines and the relevant page corners turned down. On the rear flyleaf of each volume Britten drew up a personal index pointing himself towards features he found to be of particular interest. The many passages marked by Britten may with hindsight be seen to have been influential on the dramatic style of the Church Parables, and the following account isolates the most important features of the liturgical drama to be found in *Curlew River* and its successors.

Several annotations are concerned with the practicalities of a church location for dramatic presentation and the methods of staging feasible within an ecclesiastical context. The action of the liturgical dramas was generally centred around a *platea*, an open playing-space corresponding to the circular set of Britten's Parables. In certain plays, the spaces to either side of the *platea* represented specific locations: one example marked by Britten from the Conversion of St Paul performed at Fleury suggests the site of Jerusalem to one side and of Damascus to the other.[50] Directional symbolism is also important in Nō and very strong in the river-crossing which takes place in *Curlew River*. In *The Burning Fiery Furnace*, the Jews' God is worshipped in a direction diametrically opposed to the image of Merodak. By the time of *The Prodigal Son*, Graham found it necessary to provide a specific note outlining the directional orientation of the drama:

> *Locations.* As in *Curlew River* it is important to establish the exact location of certain elements.

[48] *GB-ALb* 2-9300010.
[49] Karl Young, *The Drama of the Medieval Church*, 2 vols. (Oxford: Oxford University Press, 1933). Britten's copies (*GB-ALb* 1-9400202) are undated but from the 1951 reprint; they are now beginning to yellow. It is most likely that they were obtained before the composition of *Noye's Fludde* in 1957.
[50] *Ibid.*, II, 223.

1. For the opening and closing sections of the work, God, or Heaven, was placed high up on the left side of the church, a little way down the Nave. It is advisable to pin-point an exact position so that eye-lines will be consistent.

2. In the first scene, the City is taken to be far away on the front right of the stage. When the Younger Son journeys to the City, he starts plodding in this direction: during the walk his eye-line changes across the front of the stage until he views the distant towers on the horizon to his left. This process is of course reversed on the way home.

3. During the City scenes, 'Home' is far away on the left, thus being opposite to the direction of the City in the Home scenes.

Britten's markings in Young also refer to the additional use of positions in various parts of the church, an idea exploited in the instrumentalists' procession in *The Burning Fiery Furnace* and the Tempter's insinuating wanderings in *The Prodigal Son*. The provision of processional introits in certain liturgical dramas is also discussed by Young and marked by Britten.[51]

The adaptation of religious vestments to create symbolic costumes is twice isolated by Britten,[52] and the idea is retained not only in the monks' habits in the Parables but, much more importantly, in the function of the portion robe in *The Prodigal Son* which we have already related to the symbolic costume-change representing the fall of Adam. Britten marks one passage concerning the Rouen nativity play *Officium pastorum* which is of particular interest:

During the singing of the *Te Deum* which immediately precedes this play seven youths costume themselves with amices, albs, tunics, and staffs, to represent shepherds. As they take their places in church at the beginning of the action, a choir-boy stationed aloft, costumed as an angel, announces the Nativity to them.[53]

Here we encounter not only a strong suggestion of the accompanied robing in the Parables, but a clear precedent for the use of a boy to represent an angel. The *kokata* of *Sumidagawa* becomes the angel of *The Burning Fiery Furnace* in a dramatic procedure common to both Nō and liturgical drama.

The simple use of props is also found in both dramatic genres: Britten marks a section where Young describes how two disciples are represented as pilgrims, carrying staffs to signify their itinerant status in a fashion not unlike that which distinguishes the Traveller in *Curlew River*.[54] Masks were used in the mystery play to portray devils, and many rubrics prescribe the actors' gestures with some care. Other incidental details in Young (all marked up by Britten) found their way into the composer's own dramatic projects.

---

51 *Ibid.*, I, 324–5.
52 *Ibid.*, 244, 252.
53 *Ibid.*, II, 13.
54 *Ibid.*, I, 463.

Descriptions of *imago* ceremonies recall the treatment of the idol-god Merodak in *The Burning Fiery Furnace*:

> A far more ambitious ceremony is described in a sixteenth-century ordinary from Bamberg. It occurs after the office of None, and centres in the lifting up of an image of Christ. This *imago* is placed upon a *mensa*, or platform, in front of the choir, and after a short liturgical observance, including censing and sprinkling, the officiating priest and his ministers raise it aloft a short distance, singing *Ascendo ad Patrem*, and then lower it again . . . After this raising and lowering has been done three times, the *imago* is slowly and finally drawn up through an opening in the roof . . . Ceremonies of this sort seem to have been not uncommon in the fifteenth and sixteenth centuries, and perhaps earlier, in Germany.[55]

The attention which Britten pays to the comic portrayal of King Herod in the Freising Magi play,[56] with his impulsiveness, naïvety and arrogance, is unmistakably reflected in the presentation of Nebuchadnezzar in *The Burning Fiery Furnace*, itself a notable departure from the austere characterization in *Curlew River*. The comic diversion provided by Noye's wife in the *Fludde* may be seen to reflect a similar desire for parodistic character portrayal on the part of the author of the Chester cycle.

Congregational participation is described by Young in a passage predictably highlighted by Britten: 'A conspicuous feature of a considerable number of the plays of the general type now before us [i.e. Resurrection and Passion plays] is the congregational singing at the conclusion.'[57] While this suggestion is clearly more relevant to *Noye's Fludde* than to the Church Parables, the involvement of the congregation outlined in a later section is fundamental to the didactic nature of the trilogy: 'The conclusion of this scene [in the Fleury Magi] is unique in that after adoring the Child themselves, the shepherds invite the congregation to do likewise.'[58] Although uncommon in the liturgical drama, the exhortation of the audience to reverence and piety is a feature prevalent in the mystery play, and it undoubtedly influenced the style of the Abbot's prologue in the first two Parables, and of the epilogue in all three. The mystery play itself is primarily a didactic tradition, a consideration well illustrated in the following extract from the Banns prefatory to the Chester cycle:

> Whoo so comyth these plays to see,
> With good devocion merelye,
> Hertely welcome shall he be,
> And have right good chere . . .

---

55 *Ibid.*, 484.
56 *Ibid.*, II, 99.
57 *Ibid.*, I, 320.
58 *Ibid.*, II, 89.

Now have I done that lyeth in me
To procure this solempnitie,
That these playes contynued may be
And well set forth alway.
Iesu Crist that syttys on hee,
And his blessyd mother Marie,
Save all this goodely company
And kepe you nyght and day.[59]

In mediaeval religious drama, the didactic element became concentrated in the so-called 'morality' plays, which had originated as interludes to the mystery plays performed by travelling players and involved abstract personifications of vices and virtues. The allegory represented

a descent out of innocence into sin, and an ascent out of sin to salvation. The morality play . . . acts out and moralizes three interrelated stages of human existence. The life of humanity is seen to begin in a potential state of innocence but to lapse in the course of experience into an actual state of sin. This state of sin, in turn, is seen to lead by its own contradictions toward the possibility of a state of repentance.[60]

This allegory of innocence and corruption is very close to Britten's dramatic preoccupations in all his major stage works, and its presence in the more overtly didactic Church Parables is not surprising. Britten's use of the subtitle 'Parable' itself suggests that the allegorical element is an important one, and we shall later see how this is corroborated by the stylized presentation of sin and redemption in the two later biblical parables.[61]

V The musical style of *Curlew River*: Nō and Gagaku

When Britten attended the first of the two performances of *Sumidagawa* he saw in Tokyo in February 1956, his initial perplexed reaction to the genre must largely have been influenced by the nature of the play's musical accompaniment. The music of Nō has little to offer the uninitiated Western ear and certainly has nothing of the colourful appeal of the Balinese gamelan. We have seen that Prince Ludwig's description of the performance refers to the

---

[59] Peter Happé (ed.), *English Mystery Plays* (Harmondsworth: Penguin, 1975), 48.
[60] Robert Potter, *The English Morality Play: Origins, History and Influence of a Dramatic Tradition* (London: Routledge and Kegan Paul, 1975), 190.
[61] Important research into Britten's involvement with religious drama has recently been carried out by Stephen Arthur Allen in connection with his D.Phil. dissertation 'Britten and Christianity' (Somerville College, University of Oxford; in progress). Mr Allen has drawn attention to Britten's creative reaction to the Beauvais *Play of Daniel* (seen by Britten in a performance by the New York Pro Musica at King's Lynn in 1960), and made a detailed assessment of the composer's debt to Karl Young's *The Drama of the Medieval Church*.

'curiously strained and strangled' vocal quality and the 'nonsensical' recitation, but there is no further mention of the music. On the evidence of the score of *Curlew River* and Britten's correspondence with Plomer, it seems probable that the composer was primarily attracted by the dramatic qualities of Nō and not by its musical idiom. This is not to say that there are no traces of Nō music in the work: certain characteristics are emulated by Britten, if only at a fairly superficial level. Much more seminal Japanese influences on the musical style of *Curlew River* were the category of Gagaku known as Tōgaku, a genre in which Britten took an active interest, and the simple style of two-part heterophony to be found in traditional vocal music with shamisen accompaniment.

Britten made no sketches from Nō music to correspond to the detailed manuscript he had compiled in Bali. This is hardly surprising, since the fluctuating pitches and sometimes freely superimposed rhythms of Nō music make it notoriously difficult to transcribe in Western notation. He did, however, go to the trouble of obtaining a reel-to-reel tape recording of *Sumidagawa* (CD track 9).[62] The tape is entitled 'Sumi-Kawa', and was acquired by Reginald Close at Pears's request and subsequently taken back to London in person by Lady Gascoigne. The recording is of a live performance which has been edited, and the total duration is 95 minutes. There are no specific correspondences between the music of *Sumidagawa* and the music of *Curlew River*, and the tape appears to have been little used.[63] The intensely portrayed grief of the *shite* is vividly captured, however, and the recording must have served as a useful reminder of the highly charged atmosphere of the Tokyo performances.

The most obvious debt to Nō music in *Curlew River* is in the vocal and instrumental forces required for performance. All the singing parts are male (tenor *shite*, baritone *waki* and *waki-tsure*) and the chorus consists of a leader (Abbot) and eight voices, an ensemble corresponding to the average size of the *ji-utai*. The most prominent members of Britten's instrumental septet are the flute and drums, a direct parallel with the only types of instrument employed in Nō. Although the remaining instruments are not derived from the Nō tradition, we shall later see that their choice was partly dictated by the influence of other Japanese musical ensembles.

The single flute employed in Nō (nōkan) is a transverse bamboo instrument with seven fingerholes. It is the only melodic instrument in the *hayashi* (instrumental ensemble), and its melodic material is quite independent of that of the vocal performers. In *Curlew River*, Britten's Western flute is accorded an importance commensurate with the status of the nōkan, but without emulating the musical functions of the Nō prototype in detail. It is mostly

---

[62] *GB-ALb* 3-9401064.
[63] When examined for the first time in 1985, the casing showed few signs of wear and tear nearly 30 years after it was obtained.

associated with the Madwoman, and after the robing music preludial to the drama its use is therefore reserved until the first mention of the Madwoman's singing at fig. 19, where it provides a canonic accompaniment to her off-stage lines. This use of canonic technique may be related to Britten's interest in heterophony or to a particular type of Tōgaku piece examined below, but the nōkan never plays the same melody as sung by the vocalist and heterophony is therefore not a technique encountered in Nō music. A flute cadenza accompanies the Madwoman's eventual arrival at the bottom of the entrance ramp (fig. 25), the liberal flutter-tonguing probably intended to capture something of the distinctive tone quality of the Japanese instrument, which is characterized by wide vibrato and often harsh overblowing. In later passages, a descending portamento effect recalls the glissandi prominent in nōkan music (see Ex. 6.1).

Ex. 6.1

Although specific parallels between genuine nōkan music and Britten's flute part are few, the significant function of the instrument in creating atmosphere was clearly inspired by Nō. Zeami wrote in his *Sixteen Essays*:

> In the theatre it is the flautist who has the important rôle of setting the tone of the nuances of the entire play. Before the Sarugaku [an ancient form of Nō] begins, it is for the flautist to prepare the audience by playing several preliminary measures in a manner to render them immediately receptive to the first offerings. As soon as the dancing and singing begin, the flautist must adapt himself to the voice of the *shite* while enhancing and shading his performance.[64]

Surprisingly, however, the flute and drums are never heard in isolation together in *Curlew River* and the most distinctive Nō sonority is therefore lost. The texture closest to Nō is that found at fig. 81, where the Madwoman's soliloquy is accompanied only by the solo flute, a sparse effect allowing maximum impact when four other instruments enter on the word 'grave'. Throughout the work, the flute is given an increasingly abstract significance as a symbol for the curlews with which the Madwoman becomes obsessed.

[64] Quoted in Akira Tamba, *The Musical Structure of Nō* (Tokyo and Paris: Tokai University Press, 1974; repr. 1981), 35.

The motif representing the bird is frequently allocated to the instrument, and there are many passages where its sonority directly suggests bird-calls.

The set of five untuned drums which dominates the textures of the three Church Parables is clearly inspired by the three drums which, together with the nōkan, make up the complete *hayashi* ensemble. Every Nō play requires at least two of these drums, the ko-tsuzumi and ō-tsuzumi. Both have twin skin heads and a wooden hour-glass body. The shoulder drum (ko-tsuzumi) is of variable pitch, the tension of the heads being regulated by tuning chords (*shirabe*) which are grasped by the left hand. These tuning chords are carefully described by Prince Ludwig in his account of the first *Sumidagawa* performance. The drum is struck by the right hand at shoulder level and the timbre is further varied by different methods of striking the head. The hip-drum (ō-tsuzumi) is of fixed high pitch in spite of its retention of ornamental *shirabe*. It is played at hip level, the striking hand protected by parchment or leather thimbles (*yubigawa*). About half of the extant Nō repertory requires the use of only two drums, and these plays are termed *daishō-mono*. In principle, all second-group warrior plays and fourth-group madness plays are *daishō-mono*, *Sumidagawa* belonging to the latter. The third drum, found only in the remaining plays, is the taiko – a horizontal drum played with two wooden sticks (*bachi*). Although this instrument is not found in *Sumidagawa* (and Prince Ludwig's description therefore mentions only two drummers), Britten would have been familiar with its cousins the kakko and taiko of Tōgaku.

Britten's percussion adviser for the Church Parables was James Blades, who had already aided the composer with the scoring of the gamelan passages in *The Prince of the Pagodas*. Blades supplied a set of five Chinese drums which are played with a wide variety of techniques in an attempt to capture something of the sonorities of the Nō originals. The score calls for several different methods of striking: with fingers, with the flat of the hand, with thimbles, with soft and hard sticks, on the edge of the head and in the centre of the head. The use of thimbles clearly suggests the Nō *yubigawa*, the hard sticks recall the taiko, and different numbers of fingers and varying strike points are used on the ko-tsuzumi. Britten's drums are most prominent in the Abbot's prologue and epilogue, where their unusual accelerating tremolo effect is derived both from the Balinese gamelan and from Tōgaku kakko techniques. They tend to assume a solo role at key dramatic moments, the most effective example occurring during the Madwoman's cross-examination of the Ferryman, where they represent his irritation at her persistence (fig. 72[1]). The increasingly dense harmonic conflations which support the Madwoman's lines provide an excellent contrast to the stark rhythms of the Ferryman, whose gruff nature is frequently portrayed by the drums. The rhythmic organization of Nō music is extremely complex and has no specific relevance to the score of *Curlew River*. In general, drum strokes are much more sporadic in Nō than in Britten's Parables, where the drums are employed pervasively and in relatively straightforward metrical patterns with notable linear continuity.

The vocal music of Nō (*utai*) falls into three principal categories: non-rhythmical/non-melodic prose, non-metrical chanted verse and metrical chanted verse. The first of these (*kotoba*), which is employed only by the actors and never by the chorus, consists of intoned speech and is often found in the *waki*'s lines of self-introduction (*nanori*). Something of this style may be present in Britten's monotone recitation, a technique which was in any case encountered frequently in his operatic output before he visited Japan. In *Curlew River*, however, the technique is applied equally to the chorus in an unmeasured, parlando style (e.g. fig. 22). A single reciting tone is common in *utai*, but Britten acquired only scant knowledge of the complexities of Nō chant and these examples may well be merely coincidental.

Ex. 6.2

However, one feature of the vocal writing in *Curlew River* which must certainly have been derived from *Sumidagawa* is the prominent portamento. In Nō, the vocal attack at the beginning of every melodic phrase commences with an upward glissando; a descending glissando is termed *osae*. An example of portamento quoted by Eta Harich-Schneider (see Ex. 6.2a)[65] is remarkably close to the motif which pervades the Madwoman's relation of her history (see Ex. 6.2b). The later imitative fragmentation of this idea by the voice and solo flute creates a short passage in which the debt to Nō is strong (see Ex. 6.3). The most important motif in *Curlew River* is also coloured by ascending and descending vocal glissandi. It represents the mother's madness and her later preoccupation with the curlew, and is first heard in her very opening line. In its subsequent occurrences, the portamento is treated in

---

65 Eta Harich-Schneider, *A History of Japanese Music* (London: Oxford University Press, 1973), 440, from the Nō play *Momijigari*. Reproduced by permission.

Ex. 6.3

Ex. 6.4

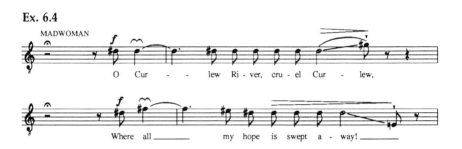

a fashion which would not be entirely out of place in the Nō vocal style (see Ex. 6.4). A major difference from Nō is the deliberate restriction of this effect to a single specific musical symbol. This is more an advantage than a draw-back, however, since even the most fleeting reference to the motif can suggest a depth of meaning quite incommensurate with the means employed. The most striking example occurs when the Madwoman sees the spirit of her child for the first time (fig. 209): because this tiny melodic fragment is instantly recognizable as part of the 'madness' theme (and occurs, enharmonically respelt, at the same pitch), the moment of recognition effectively equates the visionary curlews with the plight of the Madwoman's child and unites them as the common cause of her lunacy.

A height of vocal stylization is achieved in the lengthy soliloquy which the Madwoman delivers on arriving at the tomb (fig. 81). This passage has already been cited for its *shite*/nōkan significance, and Malm comments that 'the wavering [vocal] line does remind one of the wide, slow vibrato of Nō music'.[66] More importantly, its construction from a semitonal cell which bears little relation to the individual words of the text is unusual in Britten, a composer for whom the suggestions offered by the words themselves are usually of paramount importance. Even if the reiteration of the cell was suggested by the image of wandering in the libretto, its exhaustive application suggests the composer's desire to achieve an austere and highly stylized vocal delivery. This approach is not without precedent in Britten's

---

[66]   Malm, *Six Hidden Views*, 185.

Ex. 6.5

oeuvre,[67] but its use may have been encouraged in this context by his own perception of Nō vocal music as a highly stylized phenomenon.

The chorus in *Curlew River* is predominantly monophonic, and the frequency of unison chant in the work clearly reflects the completely monodic basis of the *ji-utai* in Nō. There are only two chorus passages in real polyphony ('Birds of the Fenland', fig. 49, and 'Lady, let him guide you to the tomb', fig. 80), and these are doubly effective for their rarity, providing important points of structural focus. Monophonic plainchant is, of course, first heard at the very opening of the work and provides both the melodic basis for the entire Parable and a convenient link between East and West. Many other notable themes are presented by the chorus in unison. The most common variant of simple monody in *Curlew River* is the heterophonic elaboration of a single melodic line. This may be seen in the prologue and epilogue (see Ex. 6.5) and in the theme associated with the river (fig. 9), which is itself a variant of the Ferryman's motif. As already noted, heterophony is not encountered in Nō music, but its presence in *Curlew River* may still be related to Britten's experience of other Japanese genres and to his continuing involvement with gamelan music. The fundamentally monodic conception of the chorus music in *Curlew River* is unique in the Parable trilogy: both *The Burning Fiery Furnace* and *The Prodigal Son* contain much more polyphonic choral writing, and *Curlew River* therefore exhibits a greater debt to the Nō model. Also unique to *Curlew River* is the function of the chorus as the principal commentator on the action. Its role is exactly analogous to that of

---

[67] Cf. 'O might those sighes' from *The Holy Sonnets of John Donne* (1945) – an instance already cited for its heterophonic displacements – and Quint's hypnotically melismatic elaboration of the name 'Miles!' in *The Turn of the Screw* (1954).

the *ji-utai* in *Sumidagawa*, which describes the setting, the time of the action and the feelings of the *shite*. If the chorus in *The Burning Fiery Furnace* and *The Prodigal Son* does not fulfil the same function, we must remember that *Curlew River* is the only one of the three Parables to take a Nō play as the direct basis for its libretto. The principal difference in Britten's treatment of the chorus in the work is the freedom with which it takes part in the physical action of the Parable. In Nō, the chorus remains sitting on the *waki-za* for the duration of the play. The still greater participation of the chorus in the dramatic action of the two later Parables (as courtiers, workers, revellers and beggars) is a further move away from the aesthetic principles of the Nō theatre.

In several respects, the musical structure of *Curlew River* reflects the 'number' structure of the Nō play on which it is based. Every Nō play falls into structural subdivisions called *shōdan*,[68] of which there are four categories:

1 *katari-goto* (spoken pieces in prose);
2 *utai-goto* (chanted pieces in verse);
3 *hayashi-goto* (instrumental pieces);
4 *shijima-goto* (silent pieces).

The most significant category as far as *Curlew River* is concerned is the *hayashi-goto*. We have already seen that Britten makes comparatively little use of Nō vocal prototypes, and it is in his positioning of passages for instruments alone that we see the clearest influence of Nō structure. The *hayashi-goto* may be grouped into five further subdivisions:

1 *iri-goto* (entrance pieces);
2 *de-goto* (exit pieces);
3 *tsunagi-goto* (linking pieces);
4 *hataraki-goto* (descriptive pieces);
5 *mai-goto* (dance pieces).

The various *shōdan* which make up a Nō play are generally grouped into a structure of five *dan*, organized according to the progressive intensity of the *jo–ha–kyū* principle. These three terms were originally borrowed from Gagaku, where they are used to indicate the three sections of increasing tempo into which an instrumental piece traditionally falls. The five *dan* in a typical Nō play are grouped in the manner shown in Table 2. The three *dan* of the central *ha* section are themselves conditioned by their own *jo–ha–kyū* structure. We have also seen that the concept of *jo–ha–kyū* governs the five-play Nō cycle: as a fourth-category play, *Sumidagawa* occurs in the final *ha* level (*kyū* of *ha*) and is therefore very intense. The structure of *Sumidagawa* is summarized in Table 3.[69] Plomer's retention of the exact shape of the *Sumidagawa* text ensures that this scheme is fully preserved in *Curlew River*.

---

[68] Komparu, *The Noh Theater*, 204–6, 282–8.
[69] Cf. Malm, *Six Hidden Views*, 159–60.

Table 2. The five-*dan* structure of Nō plays

JO	Introduction	1st Dan	slow tempo
HA	Development	2nd Dan (*jo* of *HA*) 3rd Dan (*ha* of *HA*) 4th Dan (*kyū* of *HA*)	faster tempo
KYŪ	Conclusion	5th Dan	fast tempo

Table 3. The structure of *Sumidagawa*

JO	Introduction	1st Dan	Entrance of *waki* (Ferryman) Entrance of *waki-tsure* (Traveller)
HA	Development	2nd Dan 3rd Dan 4th Dan	Entrance of *shite* (Madwoman) *mondō* (interrogation) *kudoki* (lament) climax
KYŪ	Conclusion	5th Dan	*machi-utai* (waiting song) *mai* (dance) *kiri* (conclusion)

Jean Hodgins first drew attention to certain similarities between the structures of *Sumidagawa* and *Curlew River*, most of which arise directly from the text and not from specific musical parallels.[70]

Certain types of *hayashi-goto* are more clearly reflected in the structure of *Curlew River*. The notion of entrance music (*iri-goto*) is preserved for each of the three principal characters. The *nanori-bue* ('name-saying flute') of the *waki* becomes the Ferryman's brash music for horn and drums (fig. 8). There may be no formal introductory passage for the instruments alone, but this sonority is so immediately distinctive that a single note on the horn can later instantly herald the Ferryman's appearance. The *shidai* ('next in order') of the *waki-tsure* consists of a more formal introduction of the Traveller by harp and double-bass (fig. 13). This is the only passage in the work where Western triadic harmony is overtly emphasized, perhaps a deliberately ironic touch suggested by the Traveller's first words ('I come from the Westland'). The Traveller's aria corresponds to the *michi-yuki* ('travel song') in the Nō play, and his solo concludes at fig. 17 with the *tsuki-zerifu* ('arrival lines'). The entrance music for the Madwoman has already been discussed for the nature of its flute accompaniment, and this corresponds to the *issei* ('one voice')

---

[70] Jean Hodgins, 'Orientalism in Britten's *Curlew River*' (M.A. dissertation, University of British Columbia, 1981).

173

which begins the *ha* section in *Sumidagawa*. On Britten's copy of Plomer's first libretto (the version prepared directly from the Japanese translation), the composer ringed in pencil the stage directions calling for 'Entrance Music' which the librettist had placed above the opening lines of each of the three main characters. This first version of the text preserves the numbered sections of the Japanese Classics Translation Committee's translation on which it is based, thus giving a clear indication of the constituent elements in the play's overall structure.

Ex. 6.6

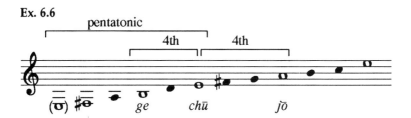

In view of the notational problems and pitch complexities of Nō, it should come as no surprise to learn that Britten made little attempt to appropriate the modal system employed in Nō music. It is, however, possible that the perfect and augmented fourths prominent in the 'curlew' motive were suggested by the melodic mode in Nō singing known as *yowa-gin*. This scale is reproduced in Ex. 6.6 and consists of three axial pitches a perfect fourth apart: high (*jō*), middle (*chū*) and low (*ge*). A number of auxiliary notes supplements this basic framework. Harich-Schneider describes how leaps between the axial pitches can be made as rising perfect fourths or tritones,[71] a technique which may have inspired Britten's 'curlew' motif. As we saw earlier, however (cf. Ex. 2.4c), melodic and harmonic configurations involving perfect fourths and tritones were frequently used by Britten in contexts suggesting anxiety or fear well before his direct acquaintance with oriental music.

Since the flute and voice are the only pitched elements in Nō music, there is no real harmonic dimension. Clearly this is an important observation in terms of the sparse harmonic idiom which is one of the most immediately obvious features of *Curlew River*. A closer model for this new approach to harmony is to be found in Gagaku, where heterophonic techniques dominate the textures of a much larger instrumental ensemble. Gagaku ('elegant music') is the oldest form of traditional Japanese music and is generally agreed to be the earliest orchestral genre to have survived as a living tradition. During the period from the fifth century AD to the beginning of the ninth, indigenous Japanese music was strongly influenced by instrumental

---

[71] Harich-Schneider, *A History of Japanese Music*, 436.

Plate 7. The Nō play *Sumidagawa*

Plate 8. Peter Pears as the Madwoman in *Curlew River*, 1964

dances and music imported from China and Korea. The eclectic Chinese music of the T'ang dynasty (reflecting aspects of Indian, Iranian and central-Asian music) supplied Japan with the hemitonal scale forming the basis of Tōgaku, the so-called 'Left' school of Gagaku. Court music from Korea and Manchuria provided the foundation for Komagaku, the 'Right' school. These two subdivisions of Gagaku were rationalized during the Heian Period (794–1192) and involve quite distinct instrumentation, the Left school requiring more impressive instrumental forces. The following discussion will be principally concerned with the category of Tōgaku known as Kangen, which consists of purely instrumental music (the term literally means 'wind and strings').

Britten is likely to have heard Kangen pieces on his two visits to the Music Department of the Imperial Household Agency in Tokyo. As we have seen, the date of one of these visits is unknown; the other took place on 18 February 1956, on which occasion a musical performance was especially arranged for his benefit. Britten was certainly captivated by the sonorities of Tōgaku (an enthusiasm apparently not shared by Pears!), and went out of his way to obtain his own shō from Satake's music shop in Kyoto. Peter Kurosawa's photographs from the tour show Britten carrying the instrument with great care as he left Haneda Airport at the end of his stay in Japan (Plate 6). He also purchased two recordings of the Tōgaku ensemble he had witnessed at the Imperial Household. These are both Columbia long-playing discs, numbered BL28 (containing pieces entitled 'Etenraku', 'Bairo' and 'Chogeshi') and BL29 (the entire record devoted to 'Taiheiraku').[72]

While Britten was making use of Tōgaku-inspired techniques during the composition of *Curlew River*, he was not the only composer to be interested in the genre. When Messiaen attended the first Japanese performance of his *Turangalîla-symphonie* in 1962, he conceived a set of 'Esquisses japonaises' which subsequently became the *Sept haïkaï* for piano and small orchestra. The central movement of the seven is entitled 'Gagaku' and is an enterprising attempt to evoke the atmosphere of the Japanese orchestra. The chords played by the shō are imitated by eight solo violins *sul ponticello*, and the hichiriki by trumpet, two oboes and cor anglais. (Both Japanese instruments are described below.) Messiaen adds a great deal to the rather lean Japanese sonorities, notably a tuned percussion section alien to Gagaku instrumentation. It is, however, highly unlikely that Britten was at all influenced by the *Sept haïkaï*: Messiaen's work was not performed until 30 October 1963 (Britten was by this time deeply involved with planning *Curlew River*, and the Messiaen première had taken place in Paris), and Britten's own direct experience of Gagaku had in any case occurred some six years earlier.

The Tōgaku piece entitled 'Etenraku' (CD track 10) which begins one of Britten's recordings (BL28) is perhaps the most popular composition in the

---

[72] *GB-ALb* 3-9401032–9401041 and 3-9401031 respectively.

Ex. 6.7

179

entire court-music repertory. It is familiar to many Westerners and provides a clear illustration of the musical techniques peculiar to the Tōgaku style. The first section of the piece is reproduced in Ex. 6.7.[73] The opening melodic motif is presented by a solo ryūteki, a transverse bamboo flute with seven fingerholes closely related to the nōkan. Shiba's transcription does not indicate the ubiquitous portamento style of ryūteki technique: in Britten's recording of 'Etenraku', prominent glissandi are to be heard between virtually all the notes of the melody. To Britten, this would have clearly resembled the nōkan portamento which, as we have already seen, had some impact on the flute writing in *Curlew River*.

In bar 9, the three hichiriki enter to reinforce the melodic line. There is no equivalent to the piercing sound of these bamboo shawms in Britten's Parable (and to suggest that the inclusion of a trumpet in *The Prodigal Son* derives from Tōgaku instrumentation is to take the oriental parallels to extremes, even though Messiaen used the trumpet for that identical purpose). The hichiriki are also characterized by portamento playing of a kind known as *enbai*. Of greater interest is the interplay between the two simultaneous versions of the melody, the ryūteki adding extra decorative patterns once the hichiriki have entered with the thematic outline. This is a conspicuous example of melodic heterophony and a possible source of inspiration for the robing music in the Church Parables. It will also be noted that the parts for koto and biwa are variants of the fundamental melodic line, the koto restricted to pentatonic accompanimental patterns. These two stringed instruments (the koto a thirteen-string zither played with three bamboo plectra, the biwa a four-string lute also played with a plectrum) both support the melody of the wind instruments, and their heterophonic function must also have been a significant influence on the organization of much of the music in *Curlew River*. The sonorities of the koto and biwa probably influenced Britten's choice of the harp as one of the two main harmonic instruments in the Church Parables, even though he had already displayed a natural affinity for it in many earlier works. There seems to be no good reason for the harpist to play *près de la table* with the fingernails for the Traveller's entrance music (fig. 13) unless Britten was directly recalling the metallic sonority of both koto and biwa, or perhaps the shamisen he knew from his visits to geisha parties and the Kabuki theatre.

The percussion section of the Tōgaku orchestra provides a colotomic rhythmic foundation for each piece in a fashion not entirely dissimilar in principle to that of the Balinese gamelan. In Ex. 6.7 the simple colotomic pattern in 'Etenraku' is provided by the kakko (a barrel-drum with twin heads played with two sticks), the shōko (a small gong played with two

---

[73] The transcription is taken from Sukehiro Shiba, *Gosen-fu ni yoru Gagaku sō-fu* (Tokyo, 1972), II, 67. For further information on Gagaku techniques, see Robert Garfias, *Music of a Thousand Autumns: The Tōgaku Style of Japanese Court Music* (Berkeley: University of California Press, 1975).

mallets), and the taiko (a barrel-shaped counterpart of its Nō namesake). Peter Kurosawa recalls that Britten was particularly impressed with the two gigantic dadaiko, much larger versions of the taiko not used in 'Etenraku' (and in fact only employed in danced pieces falling into the category of Bugaku) but seen by Britten at the Imperial Household.

Ex. 6.8

Ex. 6.9

* Indicates tremolando with gradual, unmeasured accelerando

An instantly recognizable parallel between Tōgaku percussion techniques and Britten's use of the percussion in *Curlew River* is the accelerating kakko pattern heard throughout 'Etenraku', notated by Shiba in Ex. 6.7 as a roll but producing in performance the effect shown in Ex. 6.8.[74] This technique is known as *nagashi*, and it is the most obvious model for the accelerating drum beats employed in the prologue and epilogue of *Curlew River* (Ex. 6.9). A similar kakko pattern termed *katarai* is also commonly found in Tōgaku. Britten had already encountered an accelerating tremolando in the Balinese *kebyar* style, found in the composer's gamelan-inspired music from *The Prince of the Pagodas* onwards and resulting in the evolution of the notation employed in the 'Sanctus' of the *War Requiem* in 1962 (see below, p. 225). The gamelan parallel is retained in *Curlew River*, where the accelerating rhythms appear on the set of small bells at fig. 87. This device is employed in the prologue to *The Prodigal Son* on a suspended cymbal, which replaces the drums and creates a more distinctively gamelanesque sonority. In contrast to its accelerating patterns, the Tōgaku kakko also frequently plays regular repeated notes (*mororai*). A similar effect is found in *Curlew River* (fig. 73[1]) and subsequently in *The Burning Fiery Furnace* (fig. 70[4]).

To the Westerner, the most intriguing instrument in Gagaku is likely to be

[74] From a transcription of 'Etenraku' by Hisao Tanabe in his *Japanese Music* (Tokyo: Kokusai Bunka Shinkokai, 1959; 3rd edn, 1960), 62.

the shō, which is unique to the Tōgaku repertory. Britten was clearly fascinated by it, and his understanding of the instrument contributed significantly to the unusual style of the music for the chamber organ in the three Parables. It will be recalled that Britten obtained his own shō from Satake's instrument shop in Kyoto, and Plate 6 shows him clutching the instrument in a brown-paper parcel on the day of his departure from Tokyo's Haneda Airport; as we have seen, Britten also learnt to play the instrument (Plate 5). The shō is a mouth organ in the form of a wooden windchest supporting seventeen thin bamboo pipes, each with its own metal reed except for two curious mute pipes. The instrument is blown through a mouthpiece leading to the windchest, and the pipes are activated by the player covering the holes at their base with his fingers. In Tōgaku, the shō uses eleven chords of five or six notes each, termed *aitake* ('complementary bamboos'). The instrument plays only chords, the lowest notes of which are directly related to the thematic material of the other instruments. The pipes are located in an arrangement facilitating the selection of the combinations required for the eleven *aitake* chords, which are shown in Ex. 6.10. Five of these chords (*kotsu, bō, ichi, otsu* and *takai-jū*) may be used to end a piece, and they are all pentatonic in construction.[75] Britten seems to have been aware that chord *bō* might be used as a point of repose: he was well acquainted with the *aitake* from the chart listing these chords in his printed volume of Tōgaku transcriptions,[76] and probably inferred the significance of *bō* merely by listening to his gramophone recordings.

Ex. 6.10

(sempre 8va)

takai- jū   ge   otsu   kū   bi   ichi   gyō   bō   kotsu   hi
jū

Shiba's 'Etenraku' transcription (Ex. 6.7) gives some idea of the subtle transitions from one chord to the next. The player's fingers slip away from the holes of the pipes sounding the first chord and then up again to cover those of the next, the movement being made in a precisely prescribed order which

[75] The theoretical basis behind the function of the *aitake* chords is complex, and concerns the six heptatonic scales (*chōshi*) employed in Gagaku. Each scale contains two auxiliary notes (*hennon*) which may be omitted to produce anhemitonic pentatonic patterns coincidentally similar to the Indonesian *slendro* scale shown in Ex. 1.1. For a discussion of the concept of 'consonance' and 'dissonance' in Gagaku, see Garfias, *Music of a Thousand Autumns*, 65–6.

[76] Shiba, *Gagaku*, I.

Ex. 6.11

otsu   *ichi*

Ex. 6.12

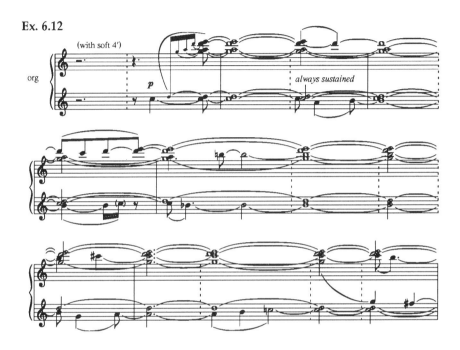

ensures that between three and five complementary pipes continue to sound during the changeover. This technique results in what Harich-Schneider calls an 'anticipated ligature' between any two chords; she provides a transcription of a typical example (see Ex. 6.11).[77] The opening of the organ part in *Curlew River* (see Ex. 6.12) demonstrates Britten's impressive understanding of this procedure. The arpeggiated first chord emulates the arpeggiation with which the shō always enters in Tōgaku. Britten's version of shō technique is disconcertingly authentic: the timbre of the chamber organ used in the original recordings of the Church Parables is uncannily close to the sonority of the original instrument, and several of the chords in Britten's harmonic vocabulary are identical with *aitake* patterns. Ex. 6.13 gives a harmonic reduction of the organ part for the entire prologue, indicating the complementary ligatures as tied notes. A comparison with Ex. 6.10 reveals

---

[77]   Harich-Schneider, *A History of Japanese Music*, 130. Reproduced by permission.

Ex. 6.13

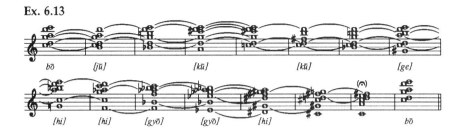

several correspondences. Most striking is the use of chord *bō* (transposed down a tone) to begin and close the progression, fully in keeping with its status as one of the five *aitake* 'consonances'. The second chord is related to *jū*, the ninth and tenth to *hi*, and the fourth and sixth to *kū*. These relationships are clarified in the comparative chart in Ex. 6.14. The influence of *kū* is to be felt in the chords used to represent the Madwoman, which again recall the shō in their organ scoring (fig. 29) and are also related to the 'curlew' motif. It is also prominent in the chord progression underlying the epilogue. The organ clusters accompanying the line 'Dew on the grass' (fig. 30) recall the conflated structure of *hi*. *Bō* recurs throughout the work in a simplified form as the static harmonic basis for the 'river' motif (fig. 9), where it is embellished by an independent inner line in the organ part. Dense harmonic configurations such as these constitute a new aspect of Britten's harmonic language, and there can be little doubt that they were directly inspired by the shō *aitake*.

Two further aspects of Tōgaku must finally be mentioned. The concept of a ritual prelude (*netori*) before every performance is reflected in the importance attached by Britten to the preludial robing music in the parables.

Ex. 6.14

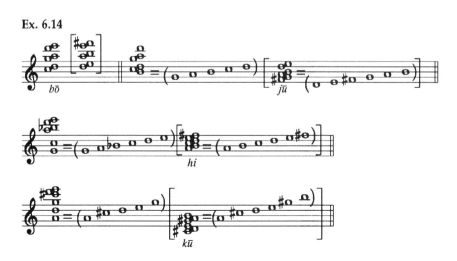

In addition, there is a special type of Tōgaku construction described by Shigeo Kishibe as an example of 'chaophony'.[78] This is sometimes used for the entrance and exit of Bugaku dancers and consists of a canonic ensemble initiated by the three shō in turn, followed by three hichiriki and three ryūteki. The overall effect is, according to Kishibe, based on an 'elastic discrepancy' between the canonic parts, and it is described in greater detail by Garfias:

> For a Bugaku performance the prelude, netori, is not usually employed. Instead a considerably more complex form of introduction known as *chōshi* is played. The name for this Bugaku prelude is the same as the word that describes the concept of mode, *chōshi*. The Bugaku *chōshi* begins, like the netori, with a solo shō. However, the *chōshi* is played by the entire ensemble and thus after the short shō solo the remaining shō players enter, one at a time, playing the same figure in strict imitation, a style known as *kake-buki*. The shō players continue in this fashion until, one by one, the hichiriki players all enter playing in imitation a figure different from that of the shō. . . In [a] longer version of the *chōshi*, the shō players continue after the hichiriki players have stopped. The fue [i.e. ryūteki] player then begins the netori. After the netori is completed all three groups begin again and continue the *chōshi* in *oi-buki*, a style in which the entrances of the instruments are much more closely spaced than in *kake-buki*.[79]

If Britten knew this type of piece, it may have provided a direct model for his own canonic ensembles such as 'Birds of the Fenland', particularly since it is one of the very few pieces in the Tōgaku repertory not to be composed in congruent metrical rhythms. Transcriptions of these distinctive *chōshi* prepared by Sukehiro Shiba show how complex the superimpositions can become when the groups of shō, ryūteki and hichiriki are all participating with independent canons set against an unrelated kakko rhythm.[80] The free rhythmic superimpositions in these examples are strikingly similar to Britten's procedures in *Curlew River*. It is plausible that he might have perceived asynchronous canonic superimposition of this type to be related to the heterophonic 'displacement' techniques he had already explored in a number of earlier works.

We have already seen that Britten elaborated melodic lines heterophonically many years prior to his Far Eastern tour, and that this technique is not found in Nō but is present to some extent in the melodic interplay between the ryūteki and hichiriki in Tōgaku. An even more striking example of the heterophonic 'blurring' of a single melodic line is to be found in traditional Japanese vocal music with accompaniment on the shamisen (a

[78] Kishibe, *The Traditional Music of Japan*, 27.
[79] Garfias, *Music of a Thousand Autumns*, 76.
[80] Shiba, *Gosen-fu nī yoru Gagaku sō-fu*, IV, 160ff., 172ff.

Ex. 6.15

three-stringed banjo played with a large hand-held plectrum). A representative example of the genre *ha-uta* is given in Ex. 6.15[81] and may be compared directly with Britten's own heterophonic techniques. Britten undoubtedly heard this style of Japanese music on his visit to the Kabuki theatre and when entertained by geisha women.

It has been the heterophony of *Curlew River* which has excited most critical attention. Peter Evans comments:

> Most of the talk about exoticism was prompted by the heterophony of the instrumental interludes of the inner frame. Now it is true that the techniques of anticipation by which a single melodic line is rendered as several asynchronous lines may be found in the traditional music for voice and koto [or shamisen]; and the fascinating mist of ornamental quaverings and slides that blur the plainchant here is certainly remembered from Japanese models. However, Britten's interest in heterophonic presentation of a line can be traced back to examples as diverse as the witty one-part fugal exposition of the Frank Bridge Variations, the third Chinese Song, and the piccolos' ornamentation of the Saraband in *A Midsummer-Night's Dream*. And in the first two of these we can also find precedents (to which innumerable others could be added) for that renunciation of harmony as a primary phenomenon which is so arresting a feature of *Curlew River*.[82]

Many of these stylistic precedents have already been examined in Chapters 2 and 4, and the extract from the robing music reproduced in Ex. 6.16 may be constructively compared with Exx. 2.9–11 above.

Malm, however, goes as far as to make a direct comparison between the robing music and the *nanori-bue* which occurs at the analogous juncture in *Sumidagawa*:

[81] Tanabe, *Japanese Music*, 71. The song is entitled 'Haru-same'.
[82] Peter Evans, *The Music of Benjamin Britten* (London: Dent, 1979; 2nd edn, 1989), 469.

Ex. 6.16

slowly moving The MONKS who are to play the
andante lento MADWOMAN, the TRAVELLER and the
FERRYMAN are ceremonially prepared.

the highly fluid linear style of the Noh version is effectively matched, for all the instruments in Britten's passage are equally linear and their total sound is deliberately blurred . . . This section in both pieces is designed to give the listener time to enter into the mood of the play through transparent textures.[83]

The first part of this statement is surprising: the strong metrical framework of Britten's robing music is in effect quite unlike the corresponding passage in the Nō play, and there can be little doubt in view of the absence of heterophony in Nō that this section of *Curlew River* was not inspired by that genre. As Evans suggests, it would seem more appropriate to view the heterophonic elaboration of the plainsong as an extension of a stylistic preoccupation already prominent many years before Britten's encounter with Japanese music. Nevertheless, Malm's interpretation of the intention behind the robing music is pertinent.

We saw earlier how Britten's interest in linearly conceived textures significantly affected his approach to harmonic progression, and a parallel was drawn with the gamelan where any chords present are mostly a by-product of the interaction between the melodic lines. The renunciation of conventional harmonic organization is taken much further in *Curlew River*, and is significantly affected by Britten's experiments with rhythmic techniques. The work has often been praised for its meticulously organized ensembles in free rhythmic superimposition. We saw in Chapter 2 how Britten's liberation of rhythm from metrical simultaneity had been foreshadowed by his recitative-ensemble style as early as *Albert Herring*, and his experience of heterophonic techniques now allowed him to rationalize disparate rhythmic elements by employing a common harmonic basis. It should be emphasized, of course, that the method bears no resemblance to Nō music, which is (as we have frequently observed) entirely anharmonic. But the interplay in Gagaku, where all participating instruments are related to an underlying melodic pattern, was clearly a prime influence. The finest example of this asynchronous style in *Curlew River* is unquestionably the climactic 'Birds of the Fenland', the poignant ensemble which moves the Ferryman to allow the Madwoman aboard his boat (figs. 49–51). In contrast, the Madwoman's little pentatonic dance, accompanied by regular ostinati in the flute, viola and harp, demonstrates the flexibility of Britten's method of harmonic-temporal suspension at its simplest (fig. 27). Britten frequently accompanies a single melodic line with a sustained chord derived from the contours of the theme, a procedure seen most conspicuously when the boy's spirit addresses his Mother towards the close of the work (fig. 96).

Although Britten clearly made no attempt to study or emulate in specific detail the complex rhythmic procedures of Nō music, it is possible that his

[83]   Malm, *Six Hidden Views*, 165.

liberation of rhythm in *Curlew River* was inspired by the sense of rhythmic freedom which will strike any Westerner listening to a Nō play for the first time (the product of a complex theoretical system 'following the fluid rhythm of life and avoiding mechanical arrangement').[84] Britten might well have been aware that Nō music employs a system of rhythmic superimposition without having the slightest understanding of the principles behind it. Malm makes an analogy between the rhythms of Japanese music and a system of independently sliding doors restricted by a single track:

> If there are two or more doors in a frame, each has a specific size and each has a track parallel to that of the other doors. However, when the doors move along their tracks they may start from different positions. They usually come to an equal, parallel position only at the end of the track (the cadence?). The 'sliding', disjunct phrases in Japanese music are one of the hidden devices that contribute to the sense of forward motion in time.[85]

This image might equally well be applied to the rhythmic organization of *Curlew River* where individual lines are carefully regulated by the specially invented 'curlew pause' ($\frown$). Britten's rhythmic experiments are perhaps the best illustration of what Malm terms the work's 'ability to capture the spirit of Noh and to respond to its musical essence without direct imitation'.[86]

Britten's first Church Parable embodies both highly specific Japanese allusions (notably to the shō *aitake*) and a musical style which acknowledges the general debt to Japanese music as a catalyst stimulating the development of important compositional tendencies already inherent in Britten's earlier style. In turning our attention to the two later Church Parables, we find the Japanese allusions becoming increasingly less prominent as the composer sets out to develop the musical and dramatic possibilities of his new operatic genre.

---

84 Komparu, *The Noh Theater*, 190.
85 Malm, *Six Hidden Views*, 42–3.
86 *Ibid.*, 153.

7

The Later Church Parables

I *The Burning Fiery Furnace*

Less than one month after the first performance of *Curlew River* in Orford Church, Britten was contemplating a possible successor to the work. On 9 July 1964 he sent a postcard to Plomer from Amsterdam, where he was on tour with the English Opera Group, to say: 'Just done Curlew River here . . . Got a good idea for another opera in the same style – so be prepared!!' In a letter dated 8 September of the same year, Britten was able to be more specific about the subject matter he had in mind for the new work: 'I think a lot about Church Parable II – and long to discuss Shadrach, etc. . . . or possibly Tobias and the angel. Do you have any feelings?'[1] It therefore seems that the two men were contemplating a biblical story as the basis for the second Parable from the very start.

On 16 October Plomer sent Britten a carefully considered letter in which he discusses the relative merits of the two stories suggested by the composer:

> You can't – or can you? – have had much chance to think any more about Church Parable II. I warmed at once to your suggestion about Tobias & the Angel, a story I'm very fond of, but the problems of making it presentable in the convention of Church Parable I seem, at first sight, rather daunting. Shadrach & company would be surely much more manageable (though much less impressive, lighter, slighter), as being nearer to the Nō tradition of a single magical episode or situation. I see Tobias as almost like a novel or (Western) play, with a story, a variety of characters, & two different places that have to be journeyed between. I don't believe that the problems of dealing with Tobias in this new convention are insoluble, though they seem rather formidable: and, as you can perhaps guess, I should myself feel much more drawn towards Tobias than to Shadrach. Do let me know how your thinking goes on the matter, and if it goes, as I hope, Tobias-wards, I will begin gradually to work out a possible basic form for gradual manipulation.

---

[1]   The story of 'Shadrach, etc.' is recounted in the first three chapters of the Book of Daniel, and was soon accepted as the plot for the new work. The tale of Tobias and the Angel is found in the Book of Tobit, which forms part of the Apocrypha. It has a far more complex plot and was therefore less suitable for the Parable medium, as Plomer was sensibly to point out.

Clearly the requirements of the dramatic convention established by *Curlew River* were to be the fundamental consideration in the choice of the new story, and it is significant that the subsequent correspondence makes repeated reference to the Nō theatre in spite of the biblical subject-matter.

The two men must have spent part of Christmas 1964 or New Year 1965 together in order to discuss the project, since on 10 January 1965 Plomer wrote to Britten:

> It was very exciting to feel . . . the New Nō beginning to come into focus, & as you can imagine I begin to hear the beginnings of utterances and to think I hear with them the first stirrings of 'the cornet, flute, harp, sackbut, psaltery, & dulcimer, & all' (well, not quite all) 'kinds of music'.

Their meeting had obviously resulted in the decision to take the story of 'Shadrach and company' as the basis for the new libretto, and Plomer confirms this in a letter dated 18 April ('I have indeed thought about the Boys in the Fire, & could almost pass an exam on the Book of Daniel . . . I have made notes but have nothing really shaped or demonstrable yet'). On 24 May Plomer wrote that 'The Jew Boys now begin to be visible & almost audible', and six days later Britten informed his librettist that Colin Graham was arriving in order to go through the synopsis of the new work. The producer was thus called in at a much earlier stage than he had been during the composition of *Curlew River*, a clear acknowledgement of the role he had played in shaping the dramatic style of the Parable genre. Graham later recalled that the story of the 'Boys in the Fire' was originally suggested to Britten by a sculpture of Nebuchadnezzar he saw in Chartres Cathedral, where the impressive stained-glass windows were also to inspire the work's colourful and vivid stage presentation.[2]

On 13 July 1965 Plomer began what was to be a lengthy debate on possible titles for the new piece:

> I think you will like to know that I have completed a basic rough draft for the New Nō, which I have provisionally labelled Strangers in Babylon . . .
> I turn over titles but never care for them much. The Fourth Man occurred to me, but I don't think it would do, for various reasons.

Two days later Britten confirmed his own indecisiveness: 'Titles completely evade me too – it's getting called Fiery Furnace in discussions, but that need not worry us. I like 4th Man but fear it's a bit filmish(?!)' On 16 July Plomer sent Britten the first draft libretto for his comments.[3] On the next day he wrote to his lifelong Japanese friend Taro Shiomi:

---

[2] Graham, 'Staging First Productions, 3', 49.
[3] Now in the Plomer Collection at Durham University Library.

I have been working very hard on the new libretto for Britten. He is taking it with him to Russia next month, where he is going for a holiday with some Russian friends – the great cellist Rostropovitch and his wife.

Before Britten left for Russia he found time to look in detail at Plomer's first draft, and communicated some thoughts to him in a letter dated 28 July. These are worth quoting at some length to illustrate Britten's highly practical approach to the problems of the self-imposed dramatic convention in which they were working:

> I am so sorry not to have written before about <u>Strangers in Babylon</u> or <u>The Fourth Man</u> or <u>The Fiery Furnace</u> – incidentally my preference is still for the last . . .
> I am afraid there is one great problem, which I thought I had mentioned to you, but obviously in my stupidity or abstraction forgot. I fear there is not room on our little stage for more than Nebuchadnezzar, the Soothsayer, the three Children, Abbot and Chorus . . . So I fear we must lose Arioch [see below] and give his pronouncements to a Herald, who can be a member of the Chorus. This will mean a few little adjustments, but personally I do not regret it since he does not, as far as I can see, play a large part in the opera that cannot be easily done by the Soothsayer or a Herald.
> That brings us to the Soothsayer, which will have to be played by the Abbot. I think we agreed that it did not matter the Abbot impersonating a sinister character. Would you perhaps like him to make a passing reference to this in his first address to the Congregation – it could be either in general or particular?
> . . . (Colin has nice ideas of the Acolytes singing and tumbling, which may need some words, but we can leave that for the moment. I hope you know some nice Babylonian folk songs).
> . . . The plan for the musicians' procession at the moment is like this: they leave their seats, process as far round the church as possible, to be joined by the Chorus, Abbot and Soothsayer at various points, they arrive back on the plate [i.e. the raised circle on the stage platform] where Nebuchadnezzar meets them, at which point the image rises in the background. Could we have a few sentences for the singers to chant as they follow the procession?
> . . . The song of the Three, eventually Four, may need a little musical adjustment. Certainly they must all sing the Benedicite, and if we decide the Abbot and Chorus should join in with the latter, I feel they should do it quietly, almost subconsciously. But I am not clear in my mind yet about the end of the whole opera; whether this is the musical climax, or after Nebuchadnezzar's change of religious heart.

The desire for a single climactic moment reflects the continuing influence of the Nō aesthetic that had been emulated in the dramatic structure of *Curlew River*.

Two days after receiving this long letter, Plomer wrote to Britten to say that his suggestions would be 'duly pondered'. In September, Plomer sent him a typescript of a new libretto version[4] and Britten appears to have started the composition of the music in October. Writing on 27 October, Britten declared: 'I have now got down to the B[urning] F[iery] F[urnace] & although I am enjoying it can't be really said to have caught fire yet.' In the same letter Britten suggested further alterations which Plomer supplied on three hand-written pages in a letter dated 1 November. On 24 November, Britten still appears to have been making comparatively slow progress with the score: 'I had a nice day – with the usual slogging at B. F. Furnace: I think it is coming along a bit, but it is far from worthy yet of you & the wonderful subject.' On 6 December, Britten told Plomer that 'about half the music is sketched out' and finally informed him in a letter dated 2 February 1966 that the composition sketch was complete.[5] It seems that the scoring was undertaken rapidly, since Plomer wrote to Britten as early as 14 February to praise him for having completed 'half the score' in spite of a recent operation for diverticulitis. The full score[6] was completed on 5 April and *The Burning Fiery Furnace* went into rehearsal on 16 May, the first performance taking place in Orford Church on 9 June as part of the Nineteenth Aldeburgh Festival.[7]

The source material for Plomer's libretto survives complete, and the various documents may easily be fitted into the chronology established by the correspondence examined above. Plomer began by making an outline sketch of the work in an exercise book[8] which contains little of interest apart from a preliminary attempt to establish a working title, which reads:

– ?Something about Babylon –

STRANGERS IN BABYLON

GOLD IN THE FIRE

THE FOURTH MAN

The first manuscript rough draft[9] is entitled 'Strangers in Babylon' and is generally close to the final libretto in all important respects. (It is presumably this document to which Plomer alludes in his letter of 13 July 1965.) The fact

4   *GB-ALb* 2-9500545.
5   *GB-ALb* 2-9500543.
6   *GB-ALb* 2-9500544.
7   For an account of the endearing circumstances in which Britten came to dedicate the work to Donald and Kathleen Mitchell, see Mervyn Cooke, 'From Nō to Nebuchad-nezzar', in Philip Reed (ed.), *On Mahler and Britten: Essays in Honour of Donald Mitchell on his 70th Birthday*, Aldeburgh Studies in Music, 3 (Woodbridge: The Boydell Press, 1995), 137.
8   Now in the Plomer Collection at Durham University Library.
9   Now in the Plomer Collection at Durham University Library. Three draft scenarios in Britten's hand pre-date Plomer's first manuscript draft, and survive in one of the composer's old school exercise books (*GB-ALb* 2-9500557) which he sometimes pressed into service during the process of planning a new work.

that little reshaping of the text proved to be necessary is an indication not only of the suitability of the story for the Parable medium but also of the increased confidence of composer and librettist after the success of *Curlew River*. The initial eight years of gestation which had led to the creation of the new idiom allowed the subsequent members of the trilogy to be conceived and executed at a far greater speed.

The cast list attached to this first draft includes the character of Arioch, who is described as 'Captain of the King's Bodyguard'. He survived a mere fortnight before Britten's letter of 28 July resulted in his permanent removal from the plot for practical reasons. As the correspondence reveals, Arioch's lines were later assigned to a Herald who was taken from the chorus in an effort to economize on the available stage space. The 'Soothsayer' who appears in this draft was later to be renamed 'Astrologer'. At the beginning and end of the text, Plomer made provision for an 'Entrance Hymn' and a 'Terminal Hymn' in an obvious response to the precedent of *Curlew River*; Britten proceeded to select an appropriate plainsong before beginning the composition of the music. The most significant difference between this initial draft and the final libretto is the complete absence of the entertainment later to be provided by the boy acolytes at the feast (which Plomer wryly came to call the 'cabaret'). This was another modification first mentioned by Britten in his letter of 28 July where he states 'Colin has nice ideas of the Acolytes singing and tumbling, which may need some words.' The only other feature of the first draft worthy of mention is Nebuchadnezzar's question to the abstaining Jews 'Are you all on a diet?', a humorous stylistic lapse which was removed in subsequent versions of the text.

A typescript top copy of the first draft survives at the Britten–Pears Library with a number of interesting pencil annotations in Britten's hand.[10] The Herald is added to the cast list and the Chorus Leader (originally intended to have portrayed the Abbot as in *Curlew River*) is deleted, the Abbot doubling as Soothsayer instead. The opening speech formerly given to Arioch is heavily cut and reassigned to the Herald, who announces the impending royal feast. This pruning is significant, as Arioch's longer passage had been a self-introduction in exactly the same spirit as the Ferryman's *nanori* in *Curlew River*, and the new version therefore departs from a Nō convention it had originally been the intention to retain.

A handwritten insertion provided by Plomer is also intriguing:

Note on pronunciations, which I have looked up.

Merodak = Merōdak, with a long ō. This was the Babylonian god. He was sometimes called Marduk, but that seems to me ugly.

Plomer's comment was directly to inspire Britten's musical setting of the god's name.

[10] *GB-ALb* 2-9500545.

Other annotations to the typescript added by Britten include a note suggesting:

Chorus of preparing & eating.
Song (Babylonian) for Acolyte.
Dance of Acolyte

When Nebuchadnezzar decrees a general monotheism as a result of what he has witnessed in the Furnace, a pencilled note reads 'Latin Hymn for all'. This later became the setting of the 'Benedicite', which thus appears to have been conceived as a parallel to the hymn 'Custodes hominum' in *Curlew River*. Once again, the concept of a convention appears to be uppermost in the composer's mind. Minor differences from the final libretto include the spellings Hananiah, Mishael and Azariah and the provision for the image of Merodak to rise in the background during the instrumentalists' procession rather than after it. An early reference in the text to Merodak was later cut, perhaps to delay mention of the god for as long as possible in order to achieve greater dramatic effect.

A carbon copy of this typescript at Aldeburgh bears further annotations and additional material in Plomer's hand.[11] The title is now established as *The Burning Fiery Furnace*, and Plomer added the lines for the Abbot requested by Britten in his letter of 28 July on a slip of paper sellotaped to the bottom of a page:

> We all shall play our parts,
> And I, your Abbot, must appear
> A heathen, and an evil man:
> It is all for the glory of God.

The first line of this insert was an afterthought added in black ballpoint, the remaining three lines having been written in Plomer's blue ballpoint. A new page in Plomer's hand bears the Herald's revised *nanori*, which begins with the phrase 'I am the Herald' in an obvious allusion to the convention established by the Ferryman's *nanori* in *Curlew River*. Even this modestly Nō-inspired line was later to be removed from the text to make the Herald's proclamation still less like that of the Ferryman's. A first version of the Acolytes' 'cabaret' was also inserted into this copy of the text on two further pages in Plomer's hand.

A new typescript was compiled from this revised version[12] and contains annotations dated 5 January 1966, mainly minor corrections such as the standardization of the spellings for the three Jews' names, the reassignment

11 *GB-ALb* 2-9500546.
12 Two copies survive at the Britten–Pears Library, one annotated by Britten (2-9500547) and the other by Britten and Colin Graham (2-9500548). An unmarked carbon copy of the first sixteen pages of this version also survives (2-9500549).

of certain lines given to the Herald and the Soothsayer and several unimportant alterations to the 'cabaret'. A more significant departure is the rewriting of the Herald's proclamation prior to the instrumentalists' march so that the phraseology corresponds directly to that of his announcement at the opening of the work. This enabled Britten to incorporate a logical and structurally effective recapitulation of the music from the Herald's first passage at this, the turning point of the drama (cf. figs. 7 and 52). The line 'Lord, help us in our loneliness' is now included as a refrain to the words sung by the Jews as they anxiously await the return of Nebuchadnezzar, and during the invocations of 'Merodak!' Britten marks the long 'o' with a stress mark in direct response to Plomer's 'Note on pronunciations'. The removal of the Image is now also included: this had not been specified in the earlier versions of the libretto.

The third version of the text was retyped[13] to include the words of the entrance plainsong (the hymn 'Salus aeterna') and to incorporate a major reallocation of the lines in the 'Benedicite' ensemble. A carbon copy of this document was corrected by Plomer, Colin Graham and Rosamund Strode on 2 February.[14] Many of the annotations refer to the version of the text Britten had included in his composition sketch, and a final late addition is the provision for the instrumentalists to 'warm up' on their parts for the processional march during the final prayer of the three Jews (figs. 56–8). This striking and humorous effect must therefore have been conceived by the composer only when he arrived at that point during the composition of the music. A final typescript was then duly prepared from this version, differing only in the correction of minor errors in punctuation.[15]

Plomer's opinion of *The Burning Fiery Furnace* was high, as shown by his remarks in a letter to Britten dated 26 March: 'I'm only a precursor of many who will be filled with fascinated admiration at the richness of invention & effect you've achieved within the strict limits laid down by what is now the precedent of Curlew R.' Once again Plomer's remark reveals the importance of the 'precedent', but in several significant respects the new work constituted a departure from the dramatic conventions established by the first Church Parable. As Graham commented:

> If *Curlew River* had been introvert in the Zen sense, *The Burning Fiery Furnace* was outgoing, fantastic and colourful. It follows the same pattern and convention and is also a story of faith. William Plomer developed the style 'authentically': here the Protagonist is threefold – Ananias, Azarias and Misael, the favourites of the King – and the Antagonist is dual and more dangerous – the mad Nebuchadnezzar and the Astrologer who pits his idolatrous beliefs against the steadfast faith

13 Copies are preserved at both Durham and Aldeburgh (2-9500550).
14 *GB-ALb* 2-9500555.
15 *GB-ALb* 2-9500556.

of the three young Jews. The same triptych form is there: after the first clashes of will at the Feast, the three young men deliberate with anxiety on their future, at the same dramatic point as the Ferryman had told his tale in mid-stream, in a trio based closely on the opening plainchant melody 'Salus eterna'. The dramatic happenings at the tomb of the Madwoman's son and her faith's reward of peace and sanity are here paralleled by the raising of the Image of Gold and the appearance of the Angel in the Furnace. Here the resolution is the conversion of Nebuchadnezzar.

Both the Acolytes (trebles) and the players take a more active part: the boys provide an entertainment at the Feast – thought by many to be unsatisfactory and unnecessary – as well as the dazzling Angel in the Furnace. The players . . . have a pagan march to play as they parade round the church while Merodak, the Image of Gold, is raised.[16]

These remarks isolate the most important points of resemblance between the *Furnace* and *Curlew River*, but they demand a certain amount of amplification and qualification. The *Furnace* is certainly much more extrovert than its predecessor, and this is clearly the most significant departure from the emotional restraint and aesthetic consistency which had made *Curlew River* such a powerful dramatic experience. This is not to say that the second Parable is less powerful as a result of its new vitality; it is simply a necessary shift in dramatic emphasis which prevents the *Furnace* from becoming a pale imitation of its model. There is a strong vein of humour in the work (vividly present in the deleted line 'Are you all on a diet?'), not only in much of the phraseology but also in the characterizations of Nebuchadnezzar and the Astrologer, which border on the satirical. We saw earlier that Britten seems to have based his treatment of Nebuchadnezzar on the lively characterization of King Herod in mediaeval church drama.

Clearly this is a radical departure from the conventions of Nō. It seems more likely that the spirit of *The Burning Fiery Furnace* derives from Kabuki, thus preserving the debt to Japan but allowing maximum possible contrast to *Curlew River* without leaving the dramatic conventions entirely behind. Kabuki might well be described as 'outgoing, fantastic and colourful', and it contains a very strong element of humour. Pears confessed to having been 'knocked sideways' by the medium when the tour party saw it in Tokyo on 17 February 1956,[17] on which occasion Britten described Kabuki as 'madly exciting', and Pears's interpretation of the role of Nebuchadnezzar would not be out of place on the Kabuki stage. As Donald Mitchell recalled, the impersonation

included the splendid miming of P.P. in the Babylonian feast, which the small boys later satirise. He brought to a very fine art indeed his

16 Graham, 'Staging First Productions, 3', 49–50.
17 Personal communication.

simulated munching and drinking, above all the plucking of the imagined grapes from the imagined bunches, each grape held fastidiously between finger and thumb, appraised and fastidiously gobbled.

This scene was astonishingly evoked [in 1971] one night in New York (an improbable setting), when B.B., P.P., Sue [Phipps], Kathleen and I were taken off to a Japanese restaurant by our generous New York friend, Laton Holmgren . . .

We had here of course a special combination of circumstances: an explicit link with Japan (shades of the Nō-play!), a feast of no less than Babylonian proportions, and a compulsory silence [Pears had lost his voice] which made mime a convenient substitute for speech. At any rate, the next time I looked across at P.P. I was amazed to find that he had vanished and Nebuchadnezzar sat in his place, going through his Babylonian gobbling routine with inimitable verve, plucking food out of the air, and consuming it with evident satisfaction, much to the mystification of the New Yorkers by whom we were surrounded. It was not a long display but I think we were all transported back to Suffolk and Orford Church in a matter of seconds; and I remember it struck me at the time that this brilliant bit of impromptu stage business only went to show how P.P. carries the art of impersonation around with him at his very fingertips.[18]

The Acolytes' 'cabaret' seems also to be part of the same tradition, particularly since Graham suggests in the production notes printed in the full score that the boys should perform in a 'slightly grotesque' fashion. In a Japanese performance of *The Burning Fiery Furnace* televised in Tokyo during March 1979 the entertainers used the main aisle of the building as a Kabuki *hanamichi*, as did Nebuchadnezzar and the Astrologer when they receded down it at the centre-point of the work.[19] In *The Prodigal Son*, too, the *hanamichi* is clearly emulated in the unexpected first appearance of the Tempter at the back of the church.

In spite of this fundamental divergence in spirit, the dramatic shape of the *Furnace* libretto is close to the Nō-derived structure of *Curlew River*. The *jo–ha–kyū* shape (presumably the 'triptych form' mentioned by Graham) conditions the action and promotes dramatic simplicity in exactly the same manner. The *jo* section begins with the Herald's *nanori*, which leads to the appearance of Nebuchadnezzar (accompanied by entrance music recalling the *shidai* convention in *Curlew River*). The beginning of the central section (*jo*-of-*ha*) is marked by the name-giving ceremony and includes the 'cabaret'. The Jews' abstention at the Feast begins *ha*-of-*ha*, and the episode where they

---

[18] Donald Mitchell, 'Double Portrait: Some Personal Recollections', in Ronald Blythe (ed.), *Aldeburgh Anthology* (London: Faber Music/Snape Maltings Foundation, 1972), 435; repr. in Donald Mitchell, *Cradles of the New: Writings on Music, 1951–91*, selected by Christopher Palmer, ed. by Mervyn Cooke (London: Faber and Faber, 1995), 486–7.

[19] A videotape recording of this performance is preserved at *GB-ALb* 3-9700528.

pray aloud after Nebuchadnezzar has withdrawn with his adviser forms a static centre-point which, as Graham observes, is related to the river-crossing in the earlier work. Nebuchadnezzar's absence from the stage at this point may be compared to the convention by which the *shite* withdraws between the two distinct halves of many Nō plays, leaving the *waki* (in this case, a composite character comprising the three Jews) on stage to provide interludial comment. The closing part of the central section (*kyū*-of-*ha*) is represented by the raising of the Image and the worshipping of Merodak. This corresponds directly to the revealing of the tomb in *Curlew River*. The concluding *kyū* section consists of the miracle in the Furnace and Nebuchadnezzar's subsequent conversion. The appearance of the Angel is an obvious parallel to the vision of the child's spirit in *Curlew River* (both are played by boys after the Japanese *kokata* convention), and Nebuchadnezzar's conversion corresponds to the cathartic effect of the boy's spirit on his mother's madness in the earlier Parable. The strongest connection between the plots of the two works is the concept of renewed (or new) faith. It is important to note that this crucial factor in the Parable convention is entirely unrelated to Nō and was the one significant addition which had to be made to the *Sumidagawa* story.

Graham's description of the functions of the principal characters in *The Burning Fiery Furnace* is more problematic. He describes the three Jews as the 'Protagonist', thus implying that they fulfil the role of the *shite* and therefore correspond to the Madwoman in dramatic importance. The 'Antagonist', according to Graham, is principally Nebuchadnezzar, who 'pits his idolatrous beliefs against the steadfast faith of the three young Jews'. This interpretation is misleading in the context of the Nō conventions from which the character-izations are still essentially derived. The single most important character is undoubtedly Nebuchadnezzar, since he is the only figure to undergo any kind of transformation (and the process of transformation is fundamental to many *shite* roles in Nō). The three Jews are indeed a composite single character, albeit with individual musical idiosyncrasies like the Rustics in *A Midsummer Night's Dream*, but their outlook remains static and it is rather they who 'pit their beliefs' against Nebuchadnezzar. In doing so, of course, they ultimately bring about the transformation in the King's faith which is the climactic moment of the drama. It is therefore more appropriate to talk of Nebuchadnezzar as the *shite* and the Jews as a composite *waki*: as in Nō, the *waki* is present to elicit a specific response from the *shite*, often a trans-formation or explication of dramatic circumstance. The Jews may therefore also be viewed as the 'Antagonist' because their dramatic function is active and steadfastly combatant. The most significant indication that Nebuchad-nezzar must be regarded as the *shite* is the direct parallel between his conversion and the transfiguration of the Madwoman in *Curlew River*. In this interpretation the Astrologer may be seen as a straightforward *shite-tsure*.

It is certainly true that the actors and instrumentalists take a much more active part in the dramatic presentation of *The Burning Fiery Furnace* than they had done in *Curlew River*. We have already seen that the instrumentalists' procession may well have been inspired by the procession of a Balinese gamelan Britten had witnessed on 14 January 1956:

> Beneath the roof of the meeting place, in front of the entrance to a complex and highly ornate temple, sits a gamelan – that is to say, an orchestra which has at least one gong and one drum. There are about twenty instruments: metallophones, gongs, drums. [The musicians] play beautiful, complicated music without looking at each other – they have the confidence of sleepwalkers, and smoke cigarettes. The gamelan gradually gets to its feet and moves off in a small procession round the area. An old priest mumbles nasally from a high bamboo stall in front of the temple. He plays skilfully with his fingers, spraying water from stalks of flowers and ringing a small handbell here and there.[20]

The religious context of this incident strengthens the suggestion that it provided the stimulus for Britten's 'temple ceremony' in *The Burning Fiery Furnace*.

The increased dramatic importance of the chorus is of greater significance than the novelty of the instrumentalists' participation in the Parable's action. In *Curlew River*, Britten was aware that he was departing from the conventions of Nō by making the chorus portray a band of pilgrims taking part in the river-crossing (cf. his letter to Plomer quoted above, p. 147). In Nō, the *ji-utai* remains sitting on its side-stage (*waki-za*) for the duration of the play and never takes part in the action. *The Burning Fiery Furnace* marks a further step away from the Nō model. Here the chorus forms a band of subservient courtiers who mindlessly echo the King's words (and therefore neatly retain the Nō convention of voicing the *shite*'s thoughts) but also take an active part in the feasting and idolatry. They are given specific stage directions (e.g. 'During this ensemble the Courtiers sway on the strong beats in strong stylised movement of greedy conviviality') and follow the general trend of increased movement around the stage in contrast to the more static positions of all the characters in *Curlew River*. As we shall see, the more active function of the chorus in the *Furnace* is part of a general move away from specific Nō conventions which is taken still further in *The Prodigal Son*, where the chorus represents several contrasting groups of characters in successive 'scenes'.

The stage used for the first production of *The Burning Fiery Furnace* was identical to that created for *Curlew River* (Figure 14), thus preserving the important visual link with the Nō theatre. The props for the new Parable were also designed in the same spirit as those in *Curlew River* and continue to reflect the Nō influence. The Astrologer and Herald both carry a simple staff to signify their official status, while Nebuchadnezzar holds a regal orb.

---

[20] Prince Ludwig of Hesse, *Ausflug Ost*, 43–4.

Nebuchadnezzar's throne occupies the predominant position on stage. The situation of the image of Merodak corresponds directly to that of the tomb in *Curlew River*, and it is raised by means of the same pole on which the sail hiding the tomb was hoisted. The most interesting of the new props devised for *The Burning Fiery Furnace* is the fire itself, which both in its extreme stylization and in its requiring two attendants (= *kōken*) to operate it is very close to Nō:

> This is a screen made of very light silk, with hundreds of attached, floating flame-pieces; the whole in variegated flame-colours, and supported between two bamboo poles by two Attendants. It should be translucent but *not* transparent. It is operated by the two poles being set in motion in opposite directions, forward and back.[21]

Rather less is owed to Nō by the costumes, which, although certainly stylized and still symbolic of character (especially in the contrast between the extravagant Babylonians and simple Jews), are much more opulent than those in *Curlew River*. This development may be seen as part of the process of revitalization which distinguishes the two works. A more colourful approach is immediately apparent:

> Gold, synonymous with Power, and therefore with Babylon, and eventually epitomized by the Idol, is an important motif, and generous use was made of it in the costumes and in the gilded throne that confronts the audience on their arrival in the church.[22]

Masks are retained for Nebuchadnezzar (as *shite* – a golden mask to emphasize his artificiality) and the Astrologer (as *shite-tsure*), but not for the three Jews, another difference from *Curlew River* which allows the human appearance of the Jews to create a pointed contrast to the Babylonians. Again, this suggests that the Jews should be regarded as a composite *waki*, since the latter does not wear a mask in Nō.

As in *Curlew River*, Graham continued to use production diagrams inspired by the sketches in the authorized translation of *Sumidagawa*. One authentic Nō gesture is retained (production cue 158): this is *ogamu*, the *kata* signifying prayer. Three new gestures were created for the work, clearly inspired by Nō if not actually authentic. These are the gestures of Power, Authority and Refusal (see cues 16, 42 and 53 respectively), the first two signifying concepts rather less tangible than the original Nō *kata*. Most of the gestures employed in *Sumidagawa* and retained in *Curlew River* are, however, inappropriate to the new work, and the invention of a new set of movement patterns was a logical step. In some respects, the dramaturgy of the *Furnace* is even more stylized than that of *Curlew River*, as is illustrated by the stage

---

[21] Colin Graham, production notes to *The Burning Fiery Furnace*, full score, 203.
[22] *Ibid.*, 201.

direction at cue 14: 'The Courtiers turn slowly to face the congregation, assuming artificially characterised attitudes as they turn.' Finally, the concern for clear directional orientation found in the presentation of the river-crossing in *Curlew River* is retained in Graham's careful instructions that 'God' should be consistently located by the performers on a specific eye-line (cf. cue 77: 'The Three turn slowly from Nebuchadnezzar towards their own God, who is always imagined as being in front of the stage to the left, i.e., diametrically opposite to the Throne and, later, the Image').

Britten was clearly as concerned with developing the musical conventions he had created in the first Parable as with reworking its dramatic formulae. Several external features which had appeared in *Curlew River* under the direct influence of Nō, Gagaku and traditional Japanese vocal music are still present in *The Burning Fiery Furnace*. The concept of specific entrance music is retained, most notably in the lengthy entrance of Nebuchadnezzar, which parallels the *shidai* of the *shite* in *Sumidagawa* and *Curlew River*. The formal song of greeting sung by the courtiers immediately afterwards also fits comfortably into the Japanese tradition. At the static centre of the drama the Jews are given a waiting-song (*machi-utai*), also to be found in *Sumidagawa*. The symbolic movements of the flames in the Furnace, corresponding to the appearance of the Spirit in *Curlew River*, may be interpreted as a concluding *mai*.

The Herald's opening proclamation (conceived in the dramatic style of the Ferryman's *nanori*) owes an additional musical debt to the Ferryman. The stark horn is now replaced by the alto trombone, similarly shadowed by viola and double-bass, and D is again the note chosen for the opening declamation (fig. 7). The alto trombone supersedes the flute as the principal instrumental sonority in the work, although its function in terms of characterization is not so clearly established. It is associated with the Babylonian court in a general sense, unlike the horn in *Curlew River*, which consistently represented the Ferryman, and the flute, which constantly attended the Madwoman. Flute and drums remain prominent in the score in a continuing reflection of the initial Japanese stimulus (the flute doubling piccolo towards the end of the work in a clear parallel with *Curlew River*). The other percussion instruments are much more specialized (see p. 226 below) and it is conceivable that the 'multiple whip' reflects the influence of the Japanese shakubyōshi, a whip-like instrument employed in some Gagaku pieces and Shinto ceremonies. Britten had used the Western orchestral whip in numerous earlier scores, and its use in Gagaku is unlikely to have escaped his attention.

The *Furnace* contains a single instrumental set-piece, as *Curlew River* had before it: the march prior to the raising of the Image corresponds directly to the instrumental fantasy after the sail is lowered in *Curlew River*, the two passages occurring at analogous dramatic junctures. A more esoteric connection is to be found in the music at fig. 53, where the Herald describes the Image to the accompaniment of an expanding cluster of tones and

Ex. 7.1

Ex. 7.2

The ABBOT comes forward to address the congregation.

semitones, a procedure identical to that found during the Madwoman's inter-rogation of the Ferryman (i.e. *mondō*) in *Curlew River* (figs. 72–4).

The closest similarity between the first two Parables lies in the music for the Abbot's prologue and epilogue and in the ceremonial robing music. It is the framework set up by these symmetrically placed events which most firmly establishes the Parable idiom as a unique genre, and the Japanese influences remain most acute in these portions of the score. Britten's first sketch for the very opening of the Abbot's address in the *Furnace* (see Ex. 7.1) is notably close to the beginning of *Curlew River*. In the final version the accelerating rhythm was replaced by a new decelerating pattern in an attempt to make the comparison less exact (see Ex. 7.2). The organ begins the work with the flourish which had originally been suggested by the initial arpeggiation of the shō in Tōgaku, but the harmony moves much more rapidly than it had in *Curlew River* and the chords are less closely related to the Japanese *aitake*. Although the ligatures joining adjacent chords are faithfully preserved, the chords themselves may be only loosely related to the *aitake* by the idiosyncratic combinations of seconds and thirds they embody and none of them corresponds exactly to any member of the shō's harmonic vocabulary. The organ itself is accorded a melodic importance quite absent from its opening passage in *Curlew River* (cf. Ex. 6.12) and it is perhaps more than just coincidence that the opening theme, which is immediately repeated in decorated form, bears a close resemblance to the first phrase of the chant 'Te lucis ante terminum' which had constituted the principal leitmotif in *Curlew River*. By fig. 2 the shō style has disappeared completely, the ligatures now abandoned and the harmony still more alien to the *aitake*. Little needs to be said about the new robing music. The heterophonic treatment of the plainchant is virtually identical to that in *Curlew River* apart from the addition of triplet decoration in the harp part. The number of real sounding parts remains the same, as does the underlying five-beat drum ostinato. When the music deviates chromatically from its diatonic beginning, as it had in *Curlew River*, precisely the same inflections are stressed (principally B♭ and A♭).

In an early review of *The Burning Fiery Furnace*, Edward Greenfield wrote:

> Britten has attempted a cross-fertilization from Oriental music more striking than in *Curlew River*. No doubt the avant-garde will condemn the experiment for its 'reactionary' qualities, but in some ways Britten is here as close as any of the avant-garde . . . to achieving the new 'complex of sounds' which is the confessed ideal of Pierre Boulez.[23]

Michael Kennedy declared that 'The resulting sonorities are more oriental, appropriately enough, than any in *Curlew River*',[24] a comment referring to the instrumental march in particular. It is ironic that a passage in which the specific debt to Japanese or Balinese music is actually negligible should have led both critics to speak of a greater debt to Asian music in the second Parable. It may well be that the lyra glockenspiel, small cymbal and 'Babylonian' drum create an exotic atmosphere far more colourful than anything in the instrumentation of *Curlew River*, but this superficial resemblance to an imaginary 'gamelan' is certainly not indicative of a 'cross-fertilization from Oriental music more striking' than in the earlier work.

The depth of Britten's debt to Eastern music is rather to be found in the completely natural manner in which the techniques of heterophony and superimposition are deployed throughout the entire score. The debt is no longer a striking one in surface terms – after all, the techniques are thoroughly familiar from *Curlew River* – and might not be singled out for comment at a first hearing. Yet it demonstrates the consistency of Britten's procedures and

[23] *Guardian*, 10 June 1966.
[24] Michael Kennedy, *Britten*, Master Musicians (London: Dent, 1981; 2nd edn, 1993), 220.

suggests once more that many of the methods stimulated by his contact with Asian music were already inherent features of his style.

The Burning Fiery Furnace demonstrates an even closer link between the stylized, hieratic gestural language of the stage action and formularized musical construction. This more detailed integration of the visual and aural elements in the drama, itself redolent of the Nō tradition, possibly constitutes the work's most important development from *Curlew River*. An excellent illustration is the passage where Nebuchadnezzar makes his initial entrance. At production cue 25 the instrumental flourishes match Nebuchadnezzar's greetings to the crowd. Later (cue 27) the same phrase is appropriately adopted by the vocal parts for the greetings showered on the King by his courtiers. These two incidents are separated by the three anvil strokes which mark the three steps Nebuchadnezzar takes to ascend his golden throne (cue 26), and with typical symmetry these anvil strokes return after the courtiers' song of greeting to depict the movement of the three Jews on to the raised acting circle (cue 34). Another well-integrated passage of more abstract construction occurs when the Jews are left to deliberate on their plight. At cue 86, 'each time a similar phrase for the drum occurs . . . they move, turning towards the instigator of each utterance. During the horn passages they remain absolutely still, thinking.' When they 'separate, disturbed' at cue 91, the music is suitably enough in three widely contrasted vocal parts. United again at cue 94, they sing the same melody in heterophonic elaboration. Similar integration of action and music is found at cue 121, where 'the moves are made on the instrumental phrases and are halted each time by the drum'.

Although there are several notable instances of similar connections between drama and music in *Curlew River*, the parallels rarely extend to apparently trivial dramatic details as they do in the second Parable. It seems highly unlikely that these dramatic correspondences were grafted on to the music by Colin Graham after the composition was complete, since it is known that Britten took a very active part in the production details and called his producer in at a much earlier stage than he had during the composition of *Curlew River*. We have seen that Graham had studied Japanese theatre more thoroughly at some point between the first productions of the two Parables, and it is not surprising that work on the dramatic style of the second piece should have involved a more detailed attempt to unite specific details of music and drama.

II *The Prodigal Son*

On 30 December 1966 (while celebrating the New Year in Russia with their Soviet friends Shostakovich, Rostropovich and Richter), Britten and Pears visited the Hermitage Gallery in Leningrad and saw Rembrandt's painting

'The Return of the Prodigal'.[25] As had been the case in *The Burning Fiery Furnace*, with its inspiration drawn from the stained-glass windows in Chartres Cathedral, *The Prodigal Son* appears to have been conceived from a specific visual stimulus. Britten no doubt recalled the significance of his visit to Leningrad when he decided to dedicate the third and final Church Parable to Shostakovich.

Writing to Plomer on 6 January 1967, shortly after his return from the USSR, Britten added a hasty postscript: 'P.S. Does the idea of the Prodigal Son attract you for a new Ch. Par. – inspired by a fabulous Rembrandt in the Hermitage?' Plomer responded positively on the following day ('The idea of the Prodigal Son attracts me strongly – much more than Tobias & the A. It's a wonderful idea') and on 17 March Britten decided to commit himself to the project: 'For several reasons (which I won't bore you with now) I do want to do it for next year – it would be wonderful to complete the trilogy when one's mind is working in this direction.' Three days later, Plomer communicated his initial thoughts to the composer as his mind began to run on the dramatic possibilities offered by the story:

> I hadn't realized that there was a likelihood of your beginning to plan the Prodigal Son so soon. I'm very glad you are . . . Think, for instance, about the Prodigal's brother. Ought he not to be fairly important, more than he is in the original? Ought his mother to figure in the proceedings? If so, in a mostly silent, miming way, or not? Can the Prodigal, at his lowest ebb, have a few moments absolutely alone?

The suggestion that the Prodigal's mother should be included as a mimed, silent part (an idea not subsequently taken up by Britten) is an interesting glance ahead towards the dramatic style of *Death in Venice*.

On 27 July, Plomer sent Britten a 'first rough version' of the libretto for *The Prodigal Son*.[26] The composer was enthusiastic ('The Prodigal Son has arrived & I am studying him with the greatest excitement,' he wrote two days later) and must have responded with his own suggestions since Plomer dispatched a fair copy of a revised libretto on 16 August.[27] Britten again replied with enthusiasm on the following day ('I am so grateful to you for having worked so hard & so promptly on the Prod. Son revisions – it is really splendid'), and work on the music began in November. Britten wrote on 22 November, his fifty-fourth birthday:

> I am launched on the Prodigal – i.e. I have found a splendid Plain-song to start me off, & useful ideas are popping up. I am having a meeting

[25] For Pears's account of the visit, which was subsequently published in his *Moscow Christmas* (Colchester: Benham and Co., 1967), see Reed (ed.), *The Travel Diaries of Peter Pears*, 145–6.

[26] *GB-ALb* 2-9700609.

[27] *Gb-ALb* 2-9700610.

with Colin, early in December, & I & he have several matters we want to discuss . . . My chief worries are still the nature & presentation of the temptations, & the character of the Tempter which I still haven't found the exact prototype for.

Britten travelled to Venice in the winter to recapture the inspiration his favourite city had afforded him during the composition of *Curlew River*. He wrote to Plomer from the Palazzo Mocenigo on 20 January:

I have started my routine of working all the morning, & in the after-noons wandering, looking into churches (when they are open: not very often, I fear), & generally fascinated by this beautiful, but very much lived in, museum of a city. The P.S. is going along fairly fast, & I am on the whole pleased . . .
Colin arrived 3 days ago, and we started discussing the Temptations immediately. He is writing the details of our conclusions with this [i.e. a separate letter was enclosed], & I hope you will like the suggestions. They are much bigger & more important than they were previously – right, I am sure, for the shape of the work. I had the idea of seductive acolyte, voices 'off' to add to the night-mare atmosphere.

Partly due to illness in the spring, and perhaps partly due to a growing realization that the score contained uncharacteristic moments of musical and dramatic weakness, Britten's initial enthusiasm for the project seems to have evaporated towards the final stages of composition. He wrote to Plomer on 29 April:

By breaking all doctors' orders, & really thrashing my poor old self I have finished Prodigal Son – score & all. I hope it's all right, worthy of the wonderful subject & you, but under the circumstances I've done all I can & I hope you & God will forgive any inadequacies (of which I fear there are many).

The correspondence on the subject of *The Prodigal Son* then comes to an end, having revealed far fewer details than the letters relating to *Curlew River* and *The Burning Fiery Furnace* had done in previous years. This suggests that many specific points were discussed orally, and perhaps that the planning and execution of the libretto for the final Church Parable was a much smoother affair. The source material surviving for the libretto tends to confirm the latter interpretation. As with *The Burning Fiery Furnace*, Plomer began work with a rough outline sketched in a notebook which contains a cast list including the Prodigal's mother.[28] He then appears to have produced a hand-written draft, which now survives at Aldeburgh, annotated by Britten.[29] The

[28] Now in the Plomer Collection at Durham University Library.
[29] See note 26 above.

most interesting of the librettist's suggestions occurs at the very beginning of the script where he queries the first entrance of the Tempter:

> Problem here: – At what point does the TEMPTER appear at the back of the church and begin to address the congregation? Before, during, or after they prepare themselves to represent the various characters? The TEMPTER's opening words can be altered accordingly.

Before the Tempter's line 'You are about to see . . .', Britten suggests the inclusion of 'A cry? Good friends?' Plomer adopted this idea with the words 'Ah you people, listening here today,/Do not think I bid you kneel and pray . . .' The Tempter sings these lines as he progresses down the aisle, thus strengthening the parallel with the use of the *hanamichi* in Kabuki for entrances in the midst of the audience.

Britten deleted the following passage, which Plomer had given to the chorus on the first appearance of the Tempter:

> Who is this evil one?
> Never seen him before!
> Why doesn't he speak to us?
> What is he doing here?
> Where is he going now?
> Never been here before!
> Who is this evil one?

This is certainly not an inspired example of Plomer's literary abilities, but Britten's removal of the passage is significant for the light it sheds on his attitude towards the chorus in *The Prodigal Son*. As we have remarked before, the chorus in the third Parable has progressed well beyond its Nō prototype by taking a very active part in the stage presentation of the drama, a development already present in *The Burning Fiery Furnace*. The chorus no longer provides direct comment on the action: in *The Prodigal Son* this function is fulfilled by the Elder Brother. Britten's decision to cut the passage quoted above is clearly related to this new approach. In any case, it is dramatically more effective to have the Tempter visible only to the Younger Son, since he functions as an externalization of the latter's internal longings. The words originally given to the chorus, even if inspired by the Nō convention in which the chorus assumes the first person and thus voices the emotions of the *shite*, can only suggest that the farm labourers are also aware of the Tempter's presence.

In the first draft there is no provision for the Younger Son's portion robe, and the temptations exist in a very primitive state. A second handwritten draft, also preserved at Aldeburgh,[30] incorporates a stage direction relating to the portion robe ('Robing ceremony, to indicate the handing over of the

---

[30] See note 27 above.

YOUNGER SON's share of the inheritance'), but the temptations remain as they stood in the original. It was not until the third, typescript, version that they were substantially modified.[31] The only major alteration left to be made prior to the typing of the fourth version[32] was the expansion of the passage relating the delights of the city (referred to by Britten in his letter of 20 January 1968 with its mention of 'acolyte voices "off"'). A carbon copy of the fourth version was given minor corrections by both Britten and Rosamund Strode before publication.[33] (It is interesting to note in passing that even on the final version of the libretto, as in the composition sketch,[34] the list of instruments stipulates a conventional flute and not the distinctive alto flute which was to transform the sonority of the score.) On the printed proof of the libretto,[35] the word 'stage' has been replaced by 'acting area' in a rather self-conscious bow to the conventions of the Parable genre.

The tale of the Prodigal Son was an appropriate choice for the last member of the Parable trilogy. It is strictly the only one of the three stories to be a 'parable' as such, and its origin in St Luke (Chapter 15) neatly completes a tripartite scheme in which the first story is drawn from Nō theatre, the second from the Old Testament and the third from the New Testament. Plomer fitted the plot to the confines of the trilogy's dramatic conventions with ease, and managed to preserve several features which originated in *Curlew River*. The most immediately striking departure is the first entrance of the Tempter, which we have already compared to the use of the *hanamichi* in Kabuki plays. In spite of this apparently sharp divergence from the format of the Abbot's prologue in the first two Parables, Plomer cleverly retains the linguistic style of the Abbot's earlier introductions. After his opening lines, the Tempter sets the scene:

> You are about to see
> A country patriarch,
> A father with his family.
> With property and progeny
> In order,
> So orderly, so dutiful,
> He enjoys
> The harvest of a well-spent life.

This corresponds to the scene-setting in *The Burning Fiery Furnace*:

> We show how three young men
> Of Israel
> By steadfastness

---

[31]   *GB-ALb* 2-9700611.
[32]   *GB-ALb* 2-9700612.
[33]   *GB-ALb* 2-9700614.
[34]   *GB-ALb* 2-9104583.
[35]   *GB-ALb* 2-9300038.

> Rose in a single day
> Into the light of lasting fame . . .
> How could they know
> What testing lay ahead?

Neither passage is as atmospheric or resonant as the prologue to *Curlew River*, and the language of the two passages quoted above appears dull by comparison to the earlier libretto:

> As a candle-shine
> In a dismal place,
> A freshet spilt
> In a desert waste,
> As innocence
> Outshineth guilt,
> A sign was given
> Of God's good grace.

In the introduction to *Curlew River* Plomer had carried over elements of nature symbolism borrowed from *Sumidagawa*, but these were abandoned in the more prosaic style of the later prologues.

The scene-setting function of the prologue to *The Prodigal Son* is, therefore, essentially identical to that of the two earlier introductions. The difference lies in the irony of the situation: the speaker will take an active part in destroying what he describes and the effect of the address on the audience is correspondingly more subtle. Because the opening passage still corresponds to the dramatic convention, the monks can complete the prologue with their prayer 'Deliver us, O Lord, from the evil man . . .' (as they had in the two earlier Parables) with no apparent incongruity. In fact, this closing prayer is more effective than those in *Curlew River* and *The Burning Fiery Furnace* since it is said in the stage presence of the sinister 'evil man' himself.

The Father's opening words, 'I am father to you all', continue the convention of self-introduction derived from the *nanori* in Nō. The remainder of the text contains fewer specific correspondences to Nō models, although the libretto's structure still conforms to the *jo–ha–kyū* principle: the opening scene at the Father's estate is equivalent to *jo*, the Temptations to *jo*-of-*ha*, the portion-robe ceremony and journey to the city to *ha*-of-*ha*, the urban hedonism to *kyū*-of-*ha* and the reconciliation and celebration of the Prodigal's return to *kyū*. The lengthy final dance corresponds more closely to the *mai* in Nō than the conclusions of either of the two earlier Parables, and the earlier formal withdrawal of the Tempter suggests the objectivity of Japanese theatre:

> Now –
> I have done
> What I said I would do . . .
> I have broken up that family

210

Before your eyes.
See how I broke it up!
(*Gracefully bowing, the Tempter leaves the stage*)

In literary terms, the temptations themselves constitute the most interesting passage in the libretto. The concept of an externalized Tempter is derived from T. S. Eliot's play *Murder in the Cathedral* (1935), in which Archbishop Thomas à Becket is confronted by Four Tempters who function as dramatically effective externalizations of Becket's own history and of his sub-conscious desires. Plomer's Tempter fulfils precisely the same dramatic function, and the phraseology recalls Eliot directly in at least two instances:

Eliot

THOMAS:	Who are you?
4TH TEMPTER:	As you do not know me, I do not need a name,
	And, as you know me, that is why I come.
	You know me, but have never seen my face.
	To meet before was never time or place.
THOMAS:	Say what you come to say.

Plomer

YOUNGER SON:	Who are you? . . . I do not understand you.
TEMPTER:	Ah, but I think you do . . .
	I am no stranger to you,
	You know me very well,
	I am your inner voice, your very self.
YOUNGER SON:	What right have you – ?

Eliot

THOMAS:	No!
	Who are you, tempting with my own desires? . . .
	What do you offer? what do you ask?
4TH TEMPTER:	I offer what you desire. I ask
	What you have to give.

Plomer

YOUNGER SON:	How can he be informed
	Of my most secret longings in this way,
	Giving them shape as I have never dared to do?
TEMPTER:	Act out your desires!

If the dramatic parallels with Nō are to be pursued in the third Parable, then the Younger Son must be viewed as the *shite* and the Tempter as the *waki*, since it is the latter whose function is to elicit a specific response from the former. As had been the case in *The Burning Fiery Furnace*, this parallel is probably not intentional and is in any case not especially convincing. *Curlew River* owes the strongest dramatic debt to the *shite/waki* convention, since it is the only one of the three Parables to take a Nō play as the basis for its libretto; there is no inherent need for *The Prodigal Son* to follow the same stylized character types.

As remarked earlier in this chapter, the most radical departure from Nō dramaturgy in *The Prodigal Son* lies in the highly mobile treatment of the chorus. Plomer draws attention to this feature in his introduction to the published libretto:

> Those familiar with the first two of these works will be able to discern how *The Prodigal Son*, while remaining within similar limits, has in various ways developed beyond them, notably in the much fuller function given to the chorus.[36]

Colin Graham also stresses the chorus's new significance in a note on the first scene (in which they take the role of workers on the family estate):

> The intensity of involvement of each member of the chorus in what is being said and done in this scene is vital. Their whole contribution to this Third Parable is considerably more responsible and involved than in the First and Second.[37]

It will be recalled that in Nō the *ji-utai* remains stationary on the *waki-za* and takes no active part in the dramatic events depicted on the main stage, providing narrative and interpretative commentary at appropriate moments. In *Curlew River* Britten's chorus retained the commentating function as a result of the heavy dependence of the libretto on the *Sumidagawa* text, but began to be more involved in the stage action than its Nō prototype by representing a band of pilgrims in the Ferryman's boat. The chorus took a more colourful part in *The Burning Fiery Furnace* by representing Nebuchadnezzar's henchmen and courtiers, a role which involved them in more active movement around the stage. In *The Prodigal Son* this transformation is completed by their assumption of three different dramatic roles: labourers in the first and fourth scenes (the family estate), parasites and hedonists in the second (the city) and beggars in the third (the journey homewards). From this brief résumé of the respective scenes it will also be observed that the scope of location in the story is far greater than in the earlier two Parables, although we have seen that Graham preserves the strong directional orientation which had first been important in the staging of *Curlew River* as a feature directly emulating both Nō and European liturgical drama.

[36] Reproduced in Herbert (ed.), *The Operas of Benjamin Britten*, 311.
[37] *The Prodigal Son*, full score, production cue 37.

The stage used in the first production of *The Prodigal Son* remained basically the same as that employed in the earlier Parables, the pulley/mast mechanism in the background (originally inspired by the Nō pine tree) now supporting the Sun, the movement of which symbolically represents the nadir and zenith of the Younger Son's progress. We have several times drawn attention to the influence of Kabuki (which Graham studied after completing his work on *Curlew River*) on the Tempter's first entrance. Graham himself mentions the further influence of Kabuki on the treatment of the raised stage circle as 'a special, almost sacred area'.[38]

The production notes are less emphatic than formerly on the subject of masks for the principal characters. These had not proved to be an entirely successful innovation and are often abandoned in performance, as they were even in the Japanese televised productions of the Parables in 1979, which added many Nō details missing in the original Graham productions. The costumes deliberately depart from Nō in being based upon Islamic art; in this context it is perhaps also significant that the concluding dance is to be 'strictly stylised like a Greek or Israeli formal dance'.[39] The dependence of the concept of portion robes on the mediaeval tradition of Adam's symbolic costume has already been noted. The intention that the Younger Son 'must give indications of moral as well as physical deprivation with each removal of garment'[40] reflects Adam's transition from finery to pauper's rags after his acceptance of the forbidden fruit. The vocabulary of stylized gestures which originated from Nō in *Curlew River* is now extended and expanded so that a wide variety of emotions can be expressed by different movements. The gestures of Longing, Argument and Prayer had already appeared in the first two Parables, and to these are added movements representing Harmony, Evil, Frustration and Repulsion. The Nō tradition behind them is emphasized when Graham directs that the hands should never touch.

In general, the musical idiom of *The Prodigal Son* makes no significant advance on that established by *Curlew River* and developed in *The Burning Fiery Furnace*, and it will not be necessary to illustrate Britten's continued (and here sometimes mechanical) use of heterophony and layered textures. The introduction of *Sprechstimme* for the Tempter during the city scene is notable: it will be recalled that in his description of the Tokyo performance of *Sumidagawa* in 1956, Prince Ludwig described the vocal quality of the *shite* as a 'high, swelling *Sprechstimme*'. The work's instrumentation continues to reflect oriental influences, including two percussion instruments recalling the gamelan: the 'small Chinese cymbal' which performs the accelerating rhythmic effect in the prologue formerly given to the drums (here strongly reminiscent of the Balinese *kebyar* accelerando) and a small gong tuned to

---

[38] *Ibid.*, 155.
[39] *Ibid.*, production cue 137.
[40] *Ibid.*, production cue 105.

F which provides a colotomic punctuation for the seductive parasites' ensemble 'Nights are days' (figs. 47–50).[41]

There is, however, a new and specific Asian influence in the score which is well worth examining in some detail. It came to light as a result of a sketch for the third Parable brought to the present author's attention by Philip Reed in March 1986,[42] and it constitutes the only known example in Britten's output of the appropriation of material borrowed directly from Indian music.

Ex. 7.3

As with Balinese and Japanese music, Britten had first come into contact with Indian music as a young man in the 1930s (see above, p. 24). During the 1956 world tour, he was greatly impressed by the Indian music he witnessed on several occasions, and brought back with him a tape of the 'magnificent' Singalese drumming from Kandy. In the 1958 Aldeburgh Festival, the Asian Music Circle presented a programme of Indian music and dance at the Jubilee Hall on 14 June. Although Britten was never to return to Bali or Japan after 1956, he did find the opportunity to travel once more to the Indian sub-continent for a holiday in the spring of 1965. Amongst the fragmentary material for *The Burning Fiery Furnace* he sketched out at the end of the year, there exists a curious passage marked 'Toda welcome song' (see Ex. 7.3).[43] This theme was not incorporated in the second Parable, or apparently anywhere else in Britten's output, but it was certainly derived from Indian sources since the Toda are a southern Indian people. Pears described the tribe in a letter to Helene Rohlfs on 7 February 1965:

> We went to visit a settlement of ancient aboriginal people, the Todas, in appearance similar to the Indians but taller and with more aquiline features. They worship no images, only the spirits of nature, and build circular covered cones of bamboo & grass in which a priest lives (chosen by the month, I think) with a buffalo, the chief supplier of their food. They are pastoral & eat only milk fruit nuts and millet, a charming simple peaceful people. (Their buffaloes are especially splendid.) Of course they will disappear. Their land, the grazing downs, are being planted with quinine trees by the government & they won't be able to wander as they used to. There are only 1600 of them left. Sad.

---

[41] The instrumentation list in the published full score incorrectly describes it as 'large'.
[42] *GB-ALb* 2-9700617.
[43] Composition sketch, discarded sketch 'A'. *GB-ALb* 2-9700617.

In a letter written on 9 February to John Newton, Britten recounted the Toda tribe's performance of the welcome song he transcribed:

The women, who wear their black hair done in ringlets, sang a song of welcome to us: the tune (repeated over and over again) . . . I couldn't catch the words, I'm afraid which were in one of the 225 quite independent languages which they have in India![44]

Four months after this encounter, a further evening of Indian music took place at the Aldeburgh Festival when the dancer Balasaraswati appeared at the Jubilee Hall in a programme of Bharatanatyam (classical dance of southern India) on 21 June 1965.

Britten's latent interest in Indian music must have again been revived at some point prior to work on *The Prodigal Son*. Amongst his collection of ethnic gramophone recordings is a disc (EALP 1252) of the famous Indian flute-player Pannalal Ghosh performing two ragas: 'Yaman' and 'Shri'.[45] Ghosh was an East Pakistani musician (1911–*c*.1960) who, according to the biographical note on Britten's recording, was responsible for raising the status of the humble bamboo folk-flute to that of a fully-fledged concert instrument:

It is an outsize flute about 32" long and the seven holes on it are so wide apart that no ordinary flute player can play on it with [the] ease and proficiency that this gifted Flutist exhibited in his playing whilst weaving intricate patterns in the course of elaboration of a Raga.

Britten was so captivated by side 1 of this recording, 'Raag Yaman' (CD track 11), that he incorporated sizeable portions of Ghosh's melody in the music for *The Prodigal Son*. Transferred to the alto flute (the instrument closest to the sonority of the mellow Indian instrument),[46] the languid and repetitive patterns create the tranquil, pastoral atmosphere at the father's estate. The sleeve note on 'Raag Yaman' reads as follows:

This is a most popular Raga having all the 7 notes both in Ascent (Arohana) and Descent (Avarohana). The usual practice is to expound this Raga in the evening or early part of the night. It creates a very quiet and subdued atmosphere and is very serene in character. The slow moving flow of the exposition unfolding the ever surpassing beauty of the melody in the process of elaboration speaks volumes for the imagination and skill of the artiste. The first part is confined to a Tal (Rhythm) known as 'Zoomra'. This consists of 14 equal beats divided into two equal parts of 7 each. This is followed by a melody in the same Raga but in a faster tempo and is confined to the Tal (Teental) consisting of 16 equal beats divided into four groups.

---

[44] Reed (ed.), *The Travel Diaries of Peter Pears*, 94–5.
[45] GB-ALb 3-9302387, 3-9302388.
[46] In the composition sketch and libretto materials, however, a conventional flute is specified.

Figure 16. Britten's sketches from 'Raag Yaman', p. 1

Figure 17. Britten's sketches from 'Raag Yaman', p. 2

217

Ex. 7.4

[p. 31]

[p. 32]

Colin Matthews, who was Britten's amanuensis in the 1970s (and whose brother David fulfilled the same function during the composition of *The Prodigal Son*), recalls that the composer was constantly listening to a certain recording at the time he was working on the third Parable.[47] Although its identity had long been forgotten, this must surely have been the recording of 'Raag Yaman'. At some point in 1968 Britten purchased a copy of Alain

---

47 Personal communication.

Daniélou's newly published study *The Râga-s of Northern Indian Music*. This explains how the title 'Yaman' is derived from the Sanskrit word 'Yamunâ', a 'mother of voluptuousness [resting] in the arms of the vanquisher of demons'.[48] It also gives the ascending and descending forms of the scale on which the raga is based (in more correct spelling, 'Âroha' and 'Avaroha' respectively) and describes its expression as 'joyful and contented'.

Figures 16–17 reproduce the sketches Britten took down from the recording of 'Raag Yaman', which are found on pp. 31–2 of the small sketchbook he was using at the time of the composition of *The Prodigal Son* (see above, note 42). These are transcribed in Ex. 7.4. The music is notated in a scale equivalent to B major, which approximates to the pitches of Ghosh's performance, although the melodic material was subsequently transposed into B♭ for the alto flute in *The Prodigal Son*. The relationship between the melodic material of *The Prodigal Son* and the sketches from 'Raag Yaman' is show in tabular form in Ex. 7.5, in which page numbers refer to the full score.

Ex. 7.5

---

[48] Daniélou, *The Râga-s*, 269.

8

Stylistic Synthesis: *Death in Venice*

Although Britten's Far Eastern interests were largely focused on Japanese models during the creation of the Church Parable trilogy, which occupied his thoughts from as early as 1957 until the completion of *The Prodigal Son* in 1968, he had in the meantime continued to assimilate into his compositional style those features of Balinese gamelan music emulated so authentically in *The Prince of the Pagodas* under the direct influence of his trip to Indonesia. In Chapter 2 it was stressed that the incidence of heterophonic techniques, polyphonic stratification, colotomic percussion patterns and scales resembling the two Balinese tuning systems in works composed before 1956 could in many cases be viewed as a product of the composer's subconscious. Those features recalling the early stimulus provided by McPhee's *Balinese Ceremonial Music* were in fact inherent characteristics of Britten's compositional style well before his initial contact with Balinese music. One reason for his intense involvement with the gamelan in 1956 must therefore have been his realization that certain Balinese musical procedures paralleled his own stylistic preoccupations at the time. There seems little doubt, however, that the notable intensification of these devices in Britten's music after *The Prince of the Pagodas* must represent a more conscious application of Balinese devices on the composer's part.

Following the ballet's première, Britten had immediately devoted his attention to two new works for the 1958 Aldeburgh Festival: the *Songs from the Chinese* for high voice and guitar, and the setting of the Chester miracle play *Noye's Fludde*. In both pieces, the recent experience of working at close hand with Balinese music has clearly left its mark. The *Songs from the Chinese* (composed in the autumn of 1957) are appropriately dedicated to the Prince and Princess of Hesse, Britten's travelling-companions on the recent Far Eastern tour. Perhaps on account of its relatively unusual scoring, the cycle has remained a neglected work in spite of its stature as one of Britten's finest solo vocal compositions. The songs consist of six settings of Chinese lyrics in the famous translations by Arthur Waley. Britten's copy of Waley's published texts was inscribed by Imogen Holst in 1947;[1] the song-cycle of ten years later thus represents the renewal of a much earlier interest in oriental cultures on

---

[1]   Arthur Waley (trans.), *Chinese Poems* (London: George Allen and Unwin, 1946). Britten's copy is preserved in *GB-ALb*, 1-9600214.

the composer's part, an interest of the kind that Waley's work did much to foster in the English-speaking world in the immediate post-war years. In spite of their promising title, however, the *Songs from the Chinese* may prove disappointing to the listener expecting an overtly oriental flavour. As Peter Evans has observed, 'in the precise, laconic language of Arthur Waley's translations, these poems do not invite a treatment that would give more weight to their exotic origins than to their oblique but universally relevant illumination of the human condition'.[2] The significance of the cycle lies in the manner in which Britten's music begins to achieve a workable synthesis between those Balinese elements employed almost as a special effect in *Pagodas* and compositional procedures more typical of Western music. Familiar heterophony appears in the accompanimental elaboration of a single melodic line, and certain tonal configurations continue to suggest the influence of the pentatonic scale *selisir gong* (Ex. 1.3). An impressive example of tonal stasis is the setting of 'The Old Lute', which attempts to capture the atmosphere of 'Ancient melodies – weak and savourless,/Not appealing to present men's taste'. Britten's setting is in the Lydian mode on E (we have already noted the likelihood of his perceiving Lydian implications in *selisir*), and the extraordinary guitar accompaniment consists of a series of elaborations of a four-part texture in which each voice is restricted to three or four notes of the mode. This produces an effect of suspended tonality in which the different possible vertical combinations of notes within the confines of the mode are continually exploited. There can be no doubt that Britten's approach to modality as exemplified in this song is remarkably close to the static effect Balinese scales appear to embody for the Westerner, and reflects his awareness of the gamelan's harmonic dimension as a direct by-product of linear counterpoint.

Noye's Fludde, the composition draft of which was completed in December 1957, cultivates a new dramatic style which looks ahead to the world of the three Church Parables. The ritualistic presentation suggests an obvious parallel with Nō, but a parallel may also be made with the religious functions of music, dance and drama in Balinese society. In the cultures of both Bali and Japan, music is an essential part of religious devotion and is inextricably linked to any elements of dance and theatre which may form part of the presentation. Both the gamelan and Nō *hayashi* take an active visual part in the proceedings, performing on the same level as the action and in full view of the spectators. That Britten had this practice in mind when establishing the performing convention for *Noye's Fludde* is suggested by his introductory notes to the published full score which specify that

Some big building should be used, preferably a church – but not a theatre – large enough to accommodate actors and orchestra, with the

---

2   Evans, *The Music of Benjamin Britten*, 362.

action raised on rostra, but not on a stage removed from the congregation. No attempt should be made to hide the orchestra from sight.

Noye's Fludde is an obvious attempt to fuse theatre, movement, gesture, music and religious devotion by combining elements from the mediaeval mystery play and Japanese theatre. It is significant that in 1957 Britten was already contemplating his operatic adaptation of *Sumidagawa*.

The closing pages of *Noye's Fludde* form an excellent illustration of the extent to which Britten's methods reflect the experience of his Balinese visit some eighteen months previously. The introduction of twelve handbells for God's final speech at fig. 111 creates an unmistakable 'gamelan' sonority which emphasizes the ritual significance of the spreading of a symbolic rainbow across the stage. The techniques of handbell-playing here reflect the interrelationship between melody and harmony we have already noted as a similarity between Britten's compositional proclivities and gamelan music. Before fig. 113 the bells build up a pentatonic cluster which punctuates the first two verses of Tallis's Canon in a veritable combination of Eastern and Western musical material. Independent punctuation is provided by double-bass and cello, and this texture once more recalls the colotomic structure of gamelan music. At the climax of the final hymn, the handbells re-enter with recorders, percussion and piano in a blaze of colourful pentatonicism which is organized into an ostinato structure and pursued independently from the hymn in a texture reminiscent of the stratification of gamelan polyphony (fig. 118). The work concludes with a heterophonic accumulation of this pentatonic motive and a memorable cadence in which the polytonal combination of G major and B♭ (pentatonic) creates an effective tonal ambiguity.

In the *Nocturne* (1958) Britten further explored the possibilities of his distinctive brand of heterophony in a context where harmony and melody are different manifestations of a limited tonal area. This may be seen in the Wordsworth setting (accompanied by timpani obbligato), where the opening and closing sections consist of a wide-ranging vocal melody, each note sustained by the strings to provide an accompaniment literally derived from the theme – a procedure closely foreshadowing the harmonic style of the Church Parables. Simple heterophony between voice and strings is encountered in the cycle's concluding Shakespeare setting, which constitutes Britten's most extended heterophonic exercise before *Curlew River*. Straightforward heterophonic displacements of this kind now become ubiquitous in Britten's music, and when they occur as part of a stratified texture, as in the *Sechs Hölderlin-Fragmente* (1958) or in the *Night-Piece* for piano solo (1963; see Ex. 8.1), he comes very close to the style of Debussy's Javanese borrowings. The parallel with Debussy is strengthened by Britten's use of low piano tones prolonged by the sustaining pedal as a form of 'gong' punctuation.

Ex. 8.1

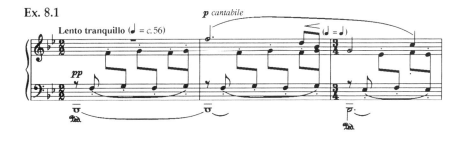

Ex. 8.2

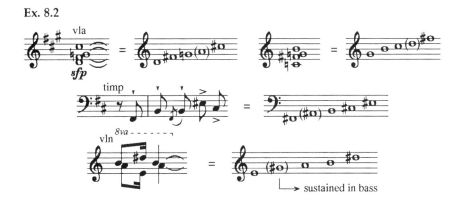

Other works from this period contain many passages reflecting Britten's continued interest in the Balinese tuning systems. The *Nocturne* includes several configurations recalling *selisir* (see Ex. 8.2). We have already seen how certain passages in the *Cantata academica* of 1959 reflect the renewed influence of *selisir* (Ex. 2.3), and it additionally appears in the recitative sections for tenor and piano. Britten's melodic style in this period frequently employs the characteristic cell of second-plus-third or third-plus-second which is reminiscent of both *selisir* and *saih gender wayang*. The 'Gloria' from the *Missa brevis* (1959) is constructed from such a motive, the cell being derived from the opening intonation. Britten deliberately exploited the pentatonic implications of Western plainsong in the Church Parables (see below), and we have already noted a similar preoccupation in the *Hymn to St Peter*. This is another example of a convenient parallel between Eastern and Western music which Britten clearly found satisfying, as his remarks on pentatonicism in Malaysian music testify (see above, p. 89). Melodic shapes based on the third-plus-second pattern continue to be found in the Cello Sonata (1961), *War Requiem* (1961) and *Cantata misericordium* (1963).

The interrelationship between melody and harmony pursued in the *Nocturne* is further explored in the *Missa brevis*, both in the 'Sanctus' with its dyadic partition of a twelve-note theme and in the 'Agnus Dei' where conflations of the melodic line provide the semitonal accompanying figure. The most thorough application of this technique in the period under discussion undoubtedly occurs in the scherzo of the Cello Symphony (1963), where virtually every harmony is a verticalized form of prevailing melodic notes, with both the horizontal and the vertical dimensions governed by a rigorous motivic technique. This extraordinarily intense movement may have provided Britten with a model for the economical musical techniques of *Curlew River* (composed in the following year), and suggests the close link between serial and heterophonic procedures in Britten's art pertinently identified by Hans Keller (see below, pp. 255–6).

Stratified textures of the kind employed towards the close of *Noye's Fludde* are epitomized in the masterly but unfortunately seldom-performed *Fanfare for St Edmundsbury* (1959), where three antiphonal trumpets each announce their own independent melodic strands and the contrasting themes are subsequently superimposed. This superimposition of horizontally conceived ideas is continued in the chatter-recitative at fig. 61 in Act III of *A Midsummer Night's Dream* (a direct descendant from *Albert Herring*) and throughout the *War Requiem*, a work which exploits the spatial contrast between the full orchestra/chorus, chamber orchestra/soloists and organ/boys' voices. When these forces are combined in free metrical alignment (as they are from fig. 77 in the 'Offertorium') we may clearly see the beginnings of the asynchronous style of the Church Parables. The experiment is further explored in the cadenza of the Cello Symphony, in which a timpani ostinato is rigidly prolonged in a tempo quite independent of the soloist's rubato material.

All the orchestral works discussed above employ gong or cymbal strokes as colotomic punctuation, often in association with a fixed pitch – as at the opening of the *War Requiem*, with its pedal note A heard throughout. Equally widespread is the new emphasis placed on sonorities directly recalling the instruments of the gamelan which may be detected in several works composed after the bold experiments with percussion scoring in *The Prince of the Pagodas*. The most significant is *A Midsummer Night's Dream*, since the prominent percussion allocated to the fairy characters fulfils a musico–dramatic function analogous to that of the 'gamelan' in *Pagodas* by depicting their supernatural allure in telling terms. This idea is part of a well-established tradition in Britten's orchestral style reaching at least as far back as *The Turn of the Screw* with its 'supernatural' celeste and gong. The first entry of the fairies in *A Midsummer Night's Dream* is coloured by triangle, glockenspiel, two harps and harpsichord, while Oberon's spell music at fig. 19 (and elsewhere) is accompanied by celeste and glockenspiel. In the second act, a vibraphone is added to the percussion ensemble. Many passages directly recall gamelan sonorities, particularly that which closes Act II (fig. 104) and the haunting music accompanying the fairies' entrance into Theseus' house in Act III (fig. 94). The latter example includes decelerating rhythms that look ahead to the rhythmic devices which Britten was frequently to employ in the 1960s under the direct influence of the Balinese *kebyar* style.

The opening of the 'Sanctus' from the *War Requiem* also betrays an obvious debt to the gamelan. Not only does the combination of vibraphone (without fans), glockenspiel, antique cymbals, bells (played with metal beaters) and piano strongly suggest the scoring used to represent the gamelan in *Pagodas*, but the distinctive *kebyar* accelerating tremolo is also virtually identical to that found on Britten's recording of a Balinese *legong* by the Peliatan troupe (Argo RG1). This unmeasured tremolo with gradual accelerando or rallentando is now indicated by the signs ⑂║ and ║⑂ which from here onwards appear frequently in the composer's works, especially in the Church Parables and in *Death in Venice*. In the *War Requiem* example, the unison attack (first on F♯ and then on C, thus encompassing the tritonal polarity of the entire work) is a further characteristic of the *kebyar* style. The choice of a gamelan sonority in this perhaps surprising context has two distinct explanations. First, the baritone solo which follows at fig. 93 begins with the line 'After the blast of lightning *from the East*' (my italics), and Britten would have delighted in such a musical pun.[3] Britten's decision to set the three acclamations of 'Sanctus' in such an overtly exotic manner suggests a desire to create a timeless, ritualistic atmosphere at this crucial point in the work. The use of a gamelan sonority to achieve this ideal looks both backwards to the closing pages of *Noye's Fludde* and forwards to the ritualized precision of the ballet music in *Death in Venice*.

In addition to its specific debt to Japan, certain features of the Church Parable trilogy continued to reflect Britten's strong interest in Bali. The sparse harmonic style marked the culmination of Britten's earlier explorations of heterophony and the interrelationship between melody and harmony, and led to stratified textures in which horizontal strands are superimposed and synchronized with the aid of the new 'curlew pause'. When these strands are all derived from the same restricted mode and presented in congruent metre the connection with the gamelan style becomes obvious. References to Balinese scales are still to be found in the music of the Parables, and some arise from the tonal characteristics of the chants which Britten employs as his principal motivic source. The second phrase of 'Te lucis ante terminum' (*Curlew River*) contains the prominent melodic cell (bracketed in Ex. 8.3a) we have noted as a hallmark of Britten's style and as a reminder of the intervallic contours of *selisir*. This cell colours much of the work's thematic material. In a similar way the chants 'Salus aeterna' and 'Iam lucis orto sidere', on which *The Burning Fiery Furnace* and *The Prodigal Son* respectively are based, contain notable pentatonic implications (see Exx. 8.3b–c) which are fully exploited throughout both works. In common with most Britten works from this period, the harmonic vocabulary of the Parables includes chords which reflect the influence of *selisir*.

The instrumentation of the Church Parables continues to suggest oriental

---

[3] Lest this interpretation appear fanciful, compare his reservation of Western triadic harmony for the Traveller's line 'I come from the Westland' in *Curlew River* (see p. 173).

Ex. 8.3

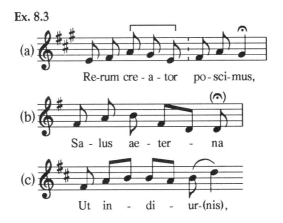

influences, not only in the specifically Japanese emphasis on flute and drums in *Curlew River* but also in more general terms. Colotomic punctuation occurs in all three works: the tolling of the bell in *Curlew River* at fig. 86 (here one remembers Prince Ludwig's description of the Balinese temple ceremony quoted on p. 65), the anvil strokes at fig. 11 in *The Burning Fiery Furnace* and the punctuation provided by the tuned gong after fig. 47 in *The Prodigal Son*. James Blades acted as 'engineer-in-chief' for Britten's specialized percussion requirements in the trilogy and designed instruments such as the multiple whip and lyra glockenspiel for use in *The Burning Fiery Furnace*.[4] The bell effect in *Curlew River* involved Blades in experimentation with bronze plates from the Mitcham Foundry, and the 'anvil' in *The Burning Fiery Furnace* was in reality a Rolls–Royce suspension spring. Blades advised Britten on the multiplicity of techniques available to the player of the five Chinese drums which provide much of the exotic atmosphere in the three scores. The free tremolo effect (𝄒) is now applied to the drums; Blades recalls that this derives from the taiko techniques of the Nō theatre (and it is also a feature of the kakko in Gagaku), but we have already seen how its origins may equally well be traced to the Balinese gamelan. The latter source is corroborated by the appearance of the tremolo on the cymbal in *The Prodigal Son* which creates an idiosyncratic Balinese sonority. The ritualistic use of a set of small bells towards the close of *Curlew River* unmistakably recalls the timeless ending of *Noye's Fludde* and once more reinforces the links between Britten's new musico-dramatic style and oriental sources.

Britten's continuing use of orientally inspired techniques was by no means restricted to the Church Parables. One of the most adventurous heterophonic

---

4 James Blades, *Percussion Instruments and their History* (London: Faber and Faber, 1970; 2nd edn, 1985), p. 130.

Ex. 8.4

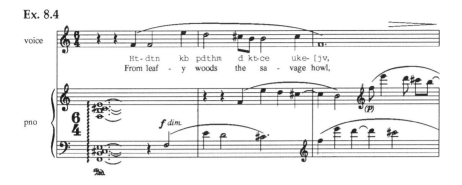

passages in his entire output occurs in the first song from the Pushkin cycle *The Poet's Echo* of 1965 (see Ex. 8.4). Heterophony is also prominent in the 1967 overture *The Building of the House*. Britten's preoccupation with percussion instruments was next displayed in *Children's Crusade* (1968) and the television opera *Owen Wingrave* (1970). In many respects, *Wingrave* marks a significant step towards the operatic language of *Death in Venice*, a work constituting the final fruition of all the oriental influences absorbed by the composer in the preceding 30 years. The liberation of the percussion section to depict Owen's martial heritage recalls the gamelan sonorities of many earlier works, but the new twelve-note context in which the 'gamelan' operates is entirely alien to the Balinese model. In the superimposed diatonic ostinati of the accompaniment to Owen's 'peace aria' in Act II the gamelan is suggested more directly (see Ex. 8.5). This passage constitutes another intricately conceived example of musico-dramatic symbolism. The colourful sonority not only illustrates the allure of peace to Owen, but also disturbingly reflects a parallel with the earlier martial music: Owen is therefore trapped by his heritage and there is a strong suggestion that his ideal is, in fact, unattainable. This interpretation is immediately confirmed by the appearance of the two ghosts who bring

Ex. 8.5

227

Owen's soliloquy to an abrupt conclusion on his ironic words 'And I am finished with you all.'

Other features of the opera may be related to Britten's earlier interests, including the use of side-drum and tenor drum as a paired unit recalling the tom-toms which served as kendang substitutes in *Pagodas*, and the regular five-beat colotomic punctuation provided by a tubular bell for the final stanza of the Ballad at the beginning of Act II. Heterophony is skilfully employed to depict the passage of time in the opera's final scene (fig. 280), where the motivic material is derived from the melodic contours of the Ballad's opening phrase. This is a further indication that Britten's interest in heterophony and the interrelationship of melody and harmony was, like his interest in serialism, connected with his perennial concern for motivic discipline and economy. Experience gained from the Parable trilogy is also in evidence here, the treatment of the Ballad as a thematic source for heterophonic elaboration reflecting the handling of the plainsong melodies in the three earlier works.

Britten's final opera, *Death in Venice* (1971–3), marks the culmination of all the Asian influences we have traced in the course of the preceding chapters. The work embodies a directly musical influence in its adoption of Balinese procedures for the 'gamelan' music which represents the Polish boy Tadzio and his associates, a clear development along the lines established by *The Prince of the Pagodas*.[5] It also illustrates Britten's appreciation of the aesthetic position of music and dance in Balinese society, and the strong attraction this can have for the Westerner. The treatment of Balinese elements in *Death in Venice* is far more adventurous than the gamelan reconstructions in *Pagodas*, and the opera constitutes an important attempt to achieve a workable synthesis between oriental and occidental musical and dramatic procedures.

There is an obvious emphasis on movement and gesture in Thomas Mann's novella *Der Tod in Venedig* (1911) which may be illustrated by the following quotation:

> [Tadzio] entered through the glass doors and walked diagonally across the room to his sisters at their table. He walked with extraordinary grace – the carriage of the body, the action of the knee, the way he set down his foot in its white shoe – it was all so light, it was at once dainty and proud, it wore an added charm in the childish shyness which made him twice turn his head as he crossed the room, made him give a quick glance and then drop his eyes.[6]

---

[5]   Britten's renewed interest in the gamelan shortly before embarking on the composition of *Death in Venice* is demonstrated by his invitation to David Attenborough to give a lecture entitled 'The Music of Bali' on 24 June 1971 at the Aldeburgh Festival. I am grateful to Jenny Wilson for drawing my attention to this event.

[6]   Thomas Mann, *Death in Venice*, trans. Mrs H. T. Lowe-Porter (London: Secker and Warburg, 1929; repr. Harmondsworth: Penguin, 1955), 30. This and all subsequent quotations from the Mann novella are taken from the same translation in its 1971 reprint. Both the Secker and Warburg and the Penguin editions were in Britten's possession

It was an idea both appropriate and inspired to represent Tadzio and his retinue with the non-vocal and graceful world of formalized dance, and the provision of music with a strong Balinese flavour to accompany their movements heightens the alluring effect which Mann conveys so vividly in his descriptions of Aschenbach's reactions to the group.

The concept of an attraction of the kind Tadzio exerts over Aschenbach (specifically an attraction which will ultimately lead to corruption and death) is a common theme in Britten's dramatic output. We have already seen how it had achieved an accomplished realization in *The Turn of the Screw*, where glittering music for the celeste and sombre gong strokes suggest the power of attraction the ghosts of Quint and Miss Jessel have over the imaginative children. We also saw how the fairies in *A Midsummer Night's Dream* inhabit a sound-world characterized by tuned percussion which is quite distinct from the other musical planes within the opera. A similar instance has been noted in *Owen Wingrave*, where the gamelan sonorities implied in the accompaniment to Owen's 'peace aria' illustrate both the attraction and the essential remoteness of the perfect state he seeks. The closest precursor to the procedures of *Death in Venice*, however, remains *The Prince of the Pagodas*, where the gamelan music accompanying the fantastic elements in Pagoda-land depicts the strong allure they hold for Belle Rose.

Britten clearly envisaged the possibility of using the medium of dance from a very early stage in the work's gestation since, in a red exercise book containing a preliminary outline scenario, he noted: 'T's + A's eyes meet. (Silent scene with Ballet music)'.[7] The choreographic idiom intended by the composer is revealed in an introductory note to the published score which reads:

> it is essential to avoid a completely naturalistic style of movement for the boy and his family. This could in no way realise the composer's basic intention, which was, through the use of appropriately stylised movement, to suggest the 'other' and different world of action inhabited by Tadzio, his family and friends, especially as seen through Aschenbach's eyes.

Although this concern for stylized gesture is partly related to Britten's interest in Japanese theatre as developed throughout the Church Parables, it may also be linked in the present context with the Balinese dancing Britten had witnessed at first hand in January 1956. In Balinese culture, music and dance are usually inseparable and very few pieces are composed independently from some element of choreography. The beauty and precision of the gestural

(*GB-ALb* 1-9700797 and 1-9700796 respectively), and Myfanwy Piper's libretto reflects the phraseology of this translation in many instances. Mrs Piper also consulted the eminent Mann scholar T. J. Reed, whose Oxford edition of the German text (Clarendon Press, 1971) was owned by Britten (*GB-ALb* 1-9700799).

7   *GB-ALb* 2-9702673.

language employed in Balinese dances have captivated many Western artists, and there can be no doubt that Britten visualized a similar unification of music and gesture when composing the 'gamelan' passages of *Death in Venice*. (The fact that the first major Balinese borrowings in Britten's oeuvre appeared in a full-length ballet is, of course, itself significant in this context.) The present instance is not the first example of the incorporation of balletic elements into one of Britten's dramatic works (cf. *Gloriana*, choreographed by Cranko), but it is the first real illustration of an approach which clearly parallels the Balinese aesthetic.

In their pioneering study of Balinese dance and theatre, Beryl de Zoete and Walter Spies discuss this cultural phenomenon with such relevance that their comments warrant quotation at some length:

> Watching dancing is not for the Balinese a matter of such concentrated attention as with us. It is almost a state of being, a feeling rather than an action. We gaze and gaze with an earnestness of purpose which fatigues us long before the dance is over. The Balinese, like other orientals, enters into the atmosphere of the dance and remains there as in a familiar landscape. Of course he expects the figures to appear which people his traditional landscape, just as we expect the landmarks on a familiar walk, or at least should be much surprised if they were not in their usual places. But like us on the familiar walk, he is not at a stretch of expectancy, what the Germans call *Spannung*, from the image of a stretched bow. His attitude towards the performance at which we gaze with such rapt and fatiguing attention must be a good deal like that of the fashionable world who had their boxes in the Italian opera; noticing now and then, criticizing technical points, enjoying the improvisations and topical jokes of the clowns, admiring pretty girls on the stage and off, flirting, talking to their friends, and then watching again.[8]

The parallel with *Death in Venice* is striking: Aschenbach watches the dancing Tadzio with a 'rapt and fatiguing attention' quite unique to him, whereas the dancing is only symbolic of a normal method of expression as far as the Poles are concerned. It is taken for granted by the other hotel guests because the movements of the Poles represent an externalization of Aschenbach's lyrical response to their beauty. This interpretation is corroborated by the stress Mann constantly places on the fact that Aschenbach's entire attitude towards the group was in reality nothing more than an illusion ('But the truth may have been that the ageing man did not want to be cured, that his illusion was far too dear to him')[9] and the many observations concerning his dream-like state.

One of Aschenbach's characteristic trances is interrupted by the following event:

[8] De Zoete and Spies, *Dance and Drama in Bali*, 16.
[9] Mann, *Death in Venice*, trans. Lowe-Porter, 50.

[Tadzio] looked towards the diagonal row of cabins; and the sight of the Russian family . . . distorted his features in a spasm of angry disgust. His brow darkened, his lips curled, one corner of the mouth was drawn down in a harsh line that marred the curve of the cheek, his frown was so heavy that the eyes seemed to sink in as they uttered beneath the black and vicious language of hate.[10]

It is intriguing to note the close correspondence between this incident, prominent in the opera as a mimed event on which Aschenbach subsequently comments, and McPhee's description of Nyoman Kalér's portrayal of a Balinese *keras* (i.e. evil) character: 'He drew himself up proudly. His gestures lost all suavity. His face was transformed; his eyes stared, his mouth was tense, drawn down at the corners. He advanced menacingly, and as he spoke his voice was loud and rasping.'[11]

During early discussions by the production team for the first performance of *Death in Venice*, it was suggested that the balletic sections should take place on a visual plane separated from the main action, a possibility which might have involved the use of raised staging or even the floor of the auditorium. Britten for a time contemplated isolating the percussion group from the remainder of the orchestra to emphasize the remoteness of the world inhabited by Tadzio: an early typed scenario includes marginal directions for ballets with off-stage orchestra and chorus.[12] This plan was soon abandoned, the musical characterization of Tadzio and his associates as perceived by Aschenbach being sufficiently strong to render any further means of isolation superfluous. As Myfanwy Piper has commented, 'the type of melancholy gaiety in the Balinese sound is in total contrast to the rather Germanic character of Aschenbach's self-absorption and underlines his feeling of alienation'.[13]

The choice of percussion as an accompanying medium is itself highly effective not only on account of the Balinese aesthetic outlined above but also because of the many associations between children and percussion instruments in general. Britten had already explored this connection in several of his works composed specifically for children, notably *Noye's Fludde* and *Children's Crusade*. During his visit to Bali in 1956, Britten was particularly struck by a gamelan composed entirely of adolescent boys which he described enthusiastically in a letter to Roger Duncan on 8 February of that year: 'Jolly good they were too, & enjoying it like fun!' If, as seems likely, this incident served as the initial stimulus for the adolescent 'gamelan' in *Death in Venice*,

---

[10] *Ibid.*, 32.
[11] McPhee, *A House in Bali*, 33.
[12] GB-ALb 2-9700619.
[13] Personal communication. This telling remark calls to mind Debussy's cultivation of a gamelan sound-world in open rejection of outmoded Austro-German musical procedures.

the idea was doubly apposite in view of Britten's earlier use of tuned percussion as a symbol of powerful attraction.

The 'gamelan' passages in *Death in Venice* differ significantly from those in *The Prince of the Pagodas*. In the ballet a percussion group had been given music which clearly attempted a direct reconstruction of specific Balinese prototypes. There appear to be no such obvious models for the corresponding passages in the opera. This is apparent on two levels: in the scoring, which departs significantly from that used in *Pagodas*, and in the treatment of Balinese scales, which are now employed with far greater flexibility. These observations suggest that the gamelan passages in *Death in Venice* were composed more in the spirit than to the letter of Balinese music – an impression confirmed by David Corkhill of the English Chamber Orchestra, with whom Britten worked on the percussion scoring. The other principal departure concerns the greater integration of Balinese elements into the main fabric of the opera, chiefly in the service of musico-dramatic symbolism.

In composing the music for the children's beach games Britten must nevertheless have been consciously aware of the scoring he had employed in *Pagodas*, since in his preliminary sketchbook for the opera he drew up the *aide-mémoire* reproduced in Figure 18.[14] A further reminder of musical procedures from the Balinese sections of the earlier work is found on a sheet of Red House notepaper which carries notes clearly referring to the reconstruction of 'Kapi radja' in the ballet score.[15] Both lists predate the composition sketch for *Death in Venice*,[16] which includes further indications of percussion scoring at relevant points. At a later stage, presumably prior to work on the opera's full score, Britten made use of four sheets of notes on percussion instruments, chiefly concerned with methods of notation (e.g. octave transpositions of marimba, etc.) and practicable ranges.[17] These were compiled with the aid of David Corkhill, one list being in his handwriting.

Britten's careful approach to the specialized nature of percussion writing has been noted earlier and it is evident that his ideas for the scoring of *Death in Venice* underwent several modifications. The final result is very different from the sonorities achieved in *Pagodas*, particularly in the new emphasis placed on wooden tuned percussion which contrasts with the predominantly metallic instrumentation of the earlier music inspired directly by the gamelan gong *kebyar*. This suggests the influence of the gamelan gambang[18] and

[14] *GB-ALb* 2-9202672.
[15] *GB-ALb* 2-9700622; reproduced in facsimile in Mervyn Cooke, 'Britten and the Gamelan: Balinese Influences in *Death in Venice*', in Mitchell (ed.), *Benjamin Britten: Death in Venice*, 118.
[16] *GB-ALb* 2-9202670.
[17] *GB-ALb* 2-9700622.
[18] An ensemble including at least four wooden xylophones (gambang) employed exclusively in cremation rites. Several sketches labelled 'cremation' were made by Britten in Bali.

Figure 18. *Death in Venice* sketchbook, p. 5

233

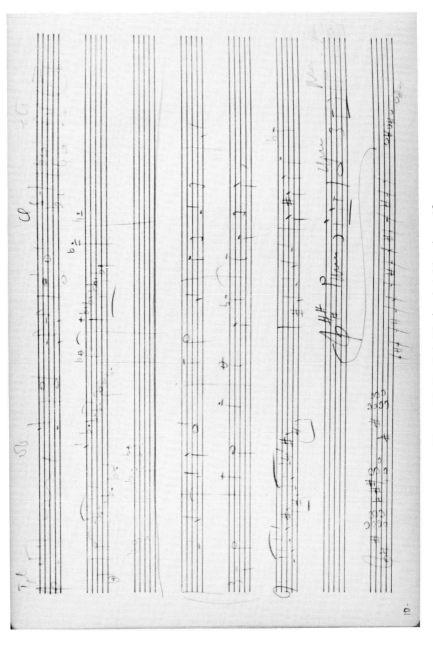

Figure 19. *Death in Venice* sketchbook, p. 10

gamelan *pejogedan*,[19] both of which Britten had witnessed in Bali. Another notable departure is the omission of the celeste, an instrument contributing much to the colouring of the ballet score. Indications for the use of a celeste are found in two places in the composition sketch of *Death in Venice* (at fig. 82 and before fig. 137), but Britten was clearly dissatisfied with the effect. On one sheet of the notes compiled prior to work on the full score, Rosamund Strode wrote an explanatory remark on an unusual instrument apparently contemplated as an alternative: 'Tuning-fork "celesta": Dulcitone (French Typophone) "rarely used orchestrally" (Scholes)'. This idea was not pursued, presumably for practical considerations, and the whole celeste idea was subsequently dropped.

Ex. 8.6

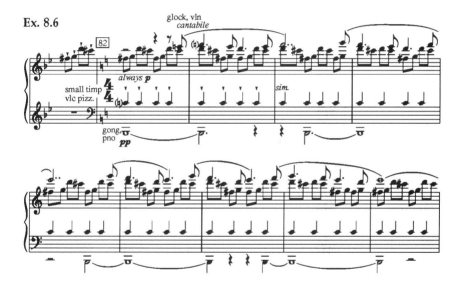

At fig. 82 (see Ex. 8.6) the accompaniment to the first presentation of the strawberry-seller's theme closely corresponds to fig. 72 in Act II of *Pagodas* (cf. Ex. 4.7): gong, piano and double-bass provide the colotomic punctuation while a piccolo timpano and secco cello pizzicato imitate the small pulse-keeping gong (kempli). The extraordinary scoring of the theme for glockenspiel and violin artificial harmonics may have been intended to imitate the sound of the Balinese suling, and there is a surprising precedent for this treatment in *Albert Herring* (Act I interlude, figs. 53–4). However, the overall effect is very different from anything in the earlier ballet because of the absence of any pentatonic scale inspired by *selisir*. In the other principal

---

[19] The group accompanying the *joged* dance and consisting of wooden xylophones known as rindik. Britten took part in a typical *joged* on 14 January 1956.

Ex. 8.7

'gamelan' passage (see Ex. 8.7) the function of the kempli is taken by the marimba (replacing the wood block indicated in the composition sketch at this point) and the colotomic punctuation is given to a small gong tuned to G.

In *Pagodas* Britten had employed two gongs of different pitches in an ostinato underlying the lengthy build-up to the revealing of the Palace in Act III: in *Death in Venice* the composer uses gongs of different pitches at fig. 95 to form a scheme of punctuation underlying the music for the children's playing in the waves. The two gongs correspond to the two large gongs of the gamelan (gong *ageng*), the *lanang* (male gong, high pitch) and the *wadon* (female gong, low pitch), but the overall effect is highly original because of the context in which this technique is employed.

Significantly, the first consciously exotic instrumentation in the opera occurs in the Traveller's aria 'Marvels unfold', in which Aschenbach is enticed to travel to Venice. The use of six drums (three tom-toms, side-drum, tenor drum and bass drum) strongly recalls the evocative use of the five drums in the Church Parables and, ultimately, the introduction of this sonority in Act II of *Pagodas* under the direct influence of Balinese kendang techniques. The tom-toms remain prominent in *Death in Venice* and once more function as kendang substitutes: *Pagodas* is strongly recalled when Aschenbach's 'Ah, here comes Eros' is accompanied by gentle drum strokes doubled by pizzicato cello solo (fig. 89). During the 'Games of Apollo' three Chinese drums are given a prominent solo in triplets which is reminiscent of the tom-tom cadenza at fig. 70 in the ballet. Shortly after this passage, cello pizzicati are again combined with tom-toms (see Ex. 8.8) and here the gamelan debt is much more obvious since each phrase is punctuated by a gong stroke. It will be noted, however, that the musical style of Ex. 8.8 is quite unlike Balinese music and this is one of many indications that in this score

Ex. 8.8

Ex. 8.9

Britten has achieved much more than the gamelan pastiche he essayed in *Pagodas*.

Tadzio is primarily characterized by a solo vibraphone which here acts as a trompong in much the same fashion as it had in *Pagodas*; Tadzio's theme itself (see Ex. 8.9) has the improvisatory quality of a Balinese trompong solo. The vibraphone is played without its motor in all but two short passages: this corresponds to the procedure in *Pagodas* which had been suggested by Blades (and reiterated by Corkhill) and must indicate that Britten still had the specific sound of the trompong in mind.

By far the most intriguing aspect of Britten's oriental appropriations in the opera, and one which constitutes a distinct and satisfying development from the procedures in *The Prince of the Pagodas*, is his more adventurous handling of Balinese scales and the manner in which these are deployed in the interests of dramatic symbolism. Tadzio's theme is constructed from a *selisir* scale (see p. 84, Ex. 3.2) corresponding to a sketch Britten had made in Bali in 1956 (Ex. 3.1h) at the pitch level with which Tadzio is always associated. The implication of A major is particularly important since this key almost always symbolizes innocence and purity in Britten's work[20] (as indeed does the Lydian mode, which he may also have perceived as a parallel to *selisir*). This

---

[20] Cf. *Young Apollo* (1939), the soprano solo 'Dear white children' in the *Hymn to St Cecilia* (1942), the Act I fisherfolk's chorus in *Peter Grimes* (1945; an ironic usage), the setting of 'Tom, Tom, the piper's son' in *The Turn of the Screw* (1954; also used ironically), the harp obbligato for 'a lovely boy, that beauteous boy' in the *Nocturne* (1958) and the closing pages of the *War Requiem* (1961). For a discussion of further symbolic uses of A major in Britten's operas, see Mervyn Cooke, 'Britten and Shakespeare: Dramatic and Musical Cohesion in *A Midsummer Night's Dream*', *Music & Letters*, 74 (1993), 266, and 'Britten's "Prophetic Song": Tonal Symbolism in *Billy Budd*', in Mervyn Cooke and Philip Reed, *Benjamin Britten: Billy Budd*, Cambridge Opera Handbooks (Cambridge: Cambridge: Cambridge University Press, 1993), 89–90 and 104–6.

variant of the *selisir* scale is also to be found on the checklist headed 'Balinese scales' which Britten compiled while composing *Pagodas*.

If the scale as employed in the opera is compared with the more familiar *selisir* pattern found elsewhere in Britten's work (cf. Ex. 3.1d) it will be seen that the note E is replaced by F♯. Throughout the opera E, both as a tonal centre and as an isolated pitch, is always associated with Aschenbach and its omission here may have been intentionally symbolic. Immediately the Tadzio music first appears, Aschenbach sings 'Poles, I should think' to a repeated E and this note remains insistent in his following phrase, although it is conspicuously avoided by the vibraphone in a subtle depiction of the essential incompatibility of the two characters (see Ex. 8.10). This contrapuntal idea is indicated by Britten on the first typed draft of the libretto for Act I, where the lines 'Surely the soul of Greece / Lies in that bright perfection' carry the handwritten annotation 'over T.'s music'.[21] The relationship between Aschenbach's E major and Tadzio's scale is exploited throughout the opera as a symbol for their incompatibility yet (at least as far as Aschenbach is concerned) unique intimacy, and occasionally Aschenbach's key adopts the characteristics of Tadzio's scale in a transposed form. This happens very obviously at his words 'I long to find rest in perfection' (fig. ³89).

Ex. 8.10

Two further motives are derived from Tadzio's scale: one is a complete vertical conflation often sounded by the full 'gamelan' in a chord inspired by *kebyar* techniques, and the other is the simpler dyadic conflation used for the calls of 'Adjiù'. In addition, the theme representing Tadzio's Mother is constructed from a chain of overlapping three-note cells clearly intended to display a generic similarity to Tadzio's music. As Aschenbach pursues the family in Act II, this theme is verticalized in the strings to produce a chord directly derived from Tadzio's scale: this melodic variant appears in Britten's preliminary sketchbook (see Ex. 8.11), thus demonstrating that he first conceived the Mother's theme in direct relation to the Tadzio scale.

---

[21] *GB-ALb* 2-9202674, fol. 25r.

Ex. 8.11

Ex. 8.12

Appropriately enough, the scale also makes conspicuous appearances in Apollo's vocal lines (see Ex. 8.12).

Several other Balinese-inspired scales are employed in the opera. The more familiar *selisir* configuration used in *Pagodas* is found at fig. 80 in a descending phrase on xylophone and marimba (see Ex. 8.13) characterized by heterophonic interplay. True to the composer's more flexible approach, a dissonant timpani ostinato is incorporated from the outset and Aschenbach's 'sirocco'

Ex. 8.13

motive (which owes nothing to Bali) is heard after only seven bars, accompanied by chords derived from a number of different *selisir* cells. The subsequent xylophone ostinato at fig. [8]82 is derived from *selisir* transposed to centre on D, and the tonality at the climax of this passage (before fig. 87) is entirely free. This is an excellent example of a tonal flexibility quite alien to the characteristically static use of Balinese scales in *Pagodas*. The percussion music for the long jump in the Games of Apollo is derived from *selisir* centring on B♭, the transposition used extensively in *Pagodas* under the direct influence of the Peliatan gamelan gong *kebyar*, and the passage at fig. 93 (Ex. 8.7 above) is constructed from a scale similar to another specimen Britten had collected in Bali (see Ex. 8.14).

Ex. 8.14

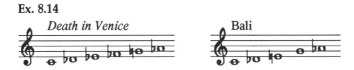

Britten's initial sketches for the opera reveal that before fig. 161, in the Games of Apollo, the composer originally planned a long vibraphone solo in the trompong style to accompany a stage direction which reads 'Tadzio wanders out of sight.' Two versions of this passage were deleted in the composition sketch. On a discarded sketch page there appears a striking passage for percussion which was presumably intended for the same context since it appears above an identical accompanying chord derived from Tadzio's scale.[22] Here Britten employs the non-alignment technique he had developed in the Church Parables. This entire section was ultimately abandoned, but it provides an intriguing glimpse of the possibilities with which Britten was experimenting during the process of composition.

Elsewhere in the sketches for the Games of Apollo (a scene which posed great difficulties for both composer and librettist and entailed extensive rewriting) Britten reveals his initial approach towards other Balinese elements in the opera. Several sketches predate the decision to include a choral commentary for the beach contests and are thus more fully conceived in instrumental terms. The section beginning at fig. 144 originally had its melodic profile outlined by tubular bells, giving much more emphasis to the *selisir* scale (see Ex. 8.15). This idea also appears in Britten's preliminary sketchbook in embryonic form, but it was eventually taken over by the chorus and the overtly Balinese sonorities were largely removed.

Britten's sketchbook for *Death in Venice* contains several other fragments of

[22] *GB-ALb* 2-97000623; reproduced in facsimile in Cooke, 'Britten and the Gamelan', 121.

Ex. 8.15

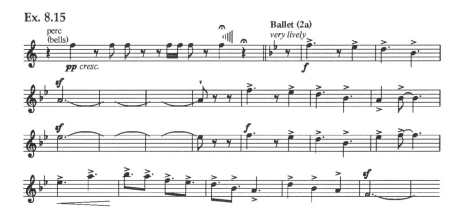

what was to become the opera's Balinese-inspired music. On p. 10, Tadzio's theme is sketched in a context which reveals its twelve-note derivation (see Figure 19)[23] and this idea is more fully explored on the following page, which includes several sketches for the beach games at fig. 93. The latter are interesting for their diatonic melodic profiles, which were subsequently transformed by the application of scales derived from Balinese music.

The first appearance of Tadzio has already been discussed at some length from a variety of viewpoints, including the symbolic use of Aschenbach's note E, which already constitutes a somewhat esoteric musical concept. If the harmonic support over which Tadzio's theme is presented is now examined, further subtleties will be seen to emerge. Aschenbach notices the Polish family when they enter and join the other guests for dinner in the hotel. Throughout the final great chatter-recitative a chord is sustained in the strings which consists of a verticalization of all the melodic fragments sung by the individual guests. Significantly, this chord is still sustained throughout the first vibraphone solo since Aschenbach first perceives Tadzio in the context of a large group of people (see Ex. 8.16a). Tadzio's theme is constructed from the five notes not present in this seven-note chord, a derivation typical of Britten's dodecaphonic interests. However, once Aschenbach has admitted to himself that the boy is a 'beautiful young creature', the vibraphone theme returns in a much more expansive form, now accompanied by a chord derived entirely from Tadzio's own pentatonic scale (see Ex. 8.16b). This is a telling reflection of the process by which Aschenbach focuses on the appearance of the boy and loses touch with his surroundings.

The discussion above illustrates several instances of a flexible approach to

---

[23] A popular anecdote relates that Britten hit upon this twelve-note derivation entirely subconsciously: see Mitchell (ed.), *Benjamin Britten: Death in Venice*, 3, 110–11, and Cooke, 'Britten and the Gamelan', 214, note 12.

Ex. 8.16

scale-forms derived from *selisir* which are evidence of Britten's more synthetic approach to the Balinese material employed in the score. This flexibility itself becomes a musico-dramatic symbol: when Aschenbach sees Tadzio's panto-mime of hatred for the Russians, he introduces the note F♮ into the boy's scale and this emendation subsequently comes to represent a human corruption which even threatens perfection of the kind embodied by the Polish boy. This alteration returns at significant dramatic moments: a notable example (using an enharmonically equivalent E♯) illustrates Aschenbach's panic when he fears that the family will hear of the plague and leave Venice (fig. 210). That this use of the note F♮ is also associated with the essential ordinariness of the family – the very fact which most threatens Aschenbach's idealized concep-tion of them – is demonstrated by the conversation between Aschenbach and the Hotel Manager in Scene 17 (cf. fig. ⁵318).

Sometimes *selisir* appears in surprising contexts for the sake of irony. For instance, it is introduced when Aschenbach pompously proclaims his own qualities at the very opening of the work ('self-discipline my strength, routine the order of my days', fig. 4²⁻⁷). This scale is subsequently used at the same pitch during the children's beach games and represents the very thing which will later make a mockery of the writer's self-discipline and orderly habits. Another brilliantly ironic touch occurs as Aschenbach stumbles from his gondola after his pitiful rejuvenation by the Hotel Barber and sings the song originally sung by the Elderly Fop's retinue in Scene 2 – significantly above a chord directly derived from Tadzio's scale. When he suddenly catches sight of Tadzio and panics, however, a modified form of the *kebyar*-inspired chord which represents the boy (and originally consisted of a vertical conflation of all the notes of his scale) frenetically explodes in a number of different transpositions (fig. 301). This is a stark symbol of both Aschenbach's dementia and the alienation between the two characters, and is all the more effective because of the rarity with which Tadzio's music appears outside its original pitch level.

One of the most startling examples of Britten's freely ranging tonality, in a passage where the sonorities are clearly inspired by the gamelan, is the final section of beach music which becomes increasingly chromatic and distorted as Jaschiù dominates Tadzio during the course of their fight. In the context of this highly claustrophobic second act (of which the fight between Jaschiù and Tadzio is the dramatic climax) the epilogue is truly cathartic. Following the recapitulation of Aschenbach's theme from his earlier Hymn to Apollo, which is now counterpointed with Tadzio's theme on vibraphone then glockenspiel, the strings adopt Tadzio's scale in its pure, original form. The opera's final cadence isolates the A which has already been established as a tonal symbol for innocence and perfection.

In *The Prince of the Pagodas*, gamelan sonorities were reserved exclusively for the Balinese-inspired sections, thus establishing them as a special effect. In *Death in Venice*, however, certain music associated with the gamelan appears on other instruments and in the vocal parts; the influence of Tadzio is therefore felt not merely as an isolated phenomenon but as a feature which infuses the entire musical fabric. Aschenbach's own adoption of the Tadzio theme and scale throughout the work is a very simple example of this, and the piano accompaniments to his soliloquies supply references to them at appropriate moments. The converse process is to be found at fig. 228 during Aschenbach's furtive pursuit of the Polish family by gondola: the percussion adopt the motive for 'Serenissima' (Venice), which is therefore transformed into the sound-world of the children and admirably depicts the writer's growing obsession. Venice can now mean only one thing for Aschenbach: Tadzio.

Two passages of effective synthesis may finally be cited. The first illustrates the children's playing in the waves by means of a remarkable combination of Western and Eastern elements: an expressive theme for lower strings and chromatic wind cadential figures presented simultaneously with a colotomic pattern on two gongs and revolving wind ostinati (fig. 95). The second is perhaps the most important of all and consists of the transformation of the Tadzio material in Aschenbach's nightmare. Here the chorus moan above an orchestral chord derived from the boy's *selisir* scale, and then burst in with his theme at fig. 284 to the accompaniment of a violent orchestral passage in which both the plague motive (tuba) and the Traveller's rhythm (drums) are included. As this hideously bloated music subsides, Aschenbach is heard wailing in his sleep to a distortion of the Tadzio theme, accompanied by an augmentation of the corruption motive in the tuba, the instrument associated with the plague throughout the opera.

There can be no doubt that *Death in Venice* constitutes Britten's most fruitful and original application of Balinese musical material. Gamelan procedures not only exist as a special effect of the kind employed in *The Prince of the Pagodas*, but are also integrated into a Western compositional idiom in a manner which allows Britten to execute an accomplished strategy of motivic and tonal symbolism. This is a notable development from the authentic reconstructions of gamelan music in *Pagodas* and the incidental application of Balinese techniques in Britten's other works, whether under the influence of McPhee before 1956 or as a direct result of the trip to Bali.

9

The Composer and his Critics

Critical reaction to Britten's various attempts to fuse oriental and occidental compositional procedures has been varied, ranging from total ignorance of the existence of any Asian influences to charges of plagiarism. Until recently, few commentators have discussed the possible motivation behind Britten's use of oriental material, an essential consideration in any attempt to establish whether a composer has achieved what he set out to accomplish. Since we have seen that Britten's oriental appropriations are subject to markedly different applications in a number of major works, it is clearly necessary to take each piece on its individual merits.

The motivation underlying the borrowing of specific oriental material is clearest by far in *The Prince of the Pagodas*, the earliest of Britten's large-scale attempts to unite East and West. We saw in Chapter 4 that the 'exotic' gamelan effects were conceived to depict the allure held over Belle Rose by the Pagodas and their mysterious Salamander-Prince. This is no more than a simple extension of the procedure in *The Turn of the Screw*, where Quint's glittering celeste and Miss Jessel's evocative gong hold the haunted children (and, indeed, the listener) in the grip of a powerful and evil attraction. The only difference between this process in the two works lies in the eventual dramatic outcome, which is fatal in the opera and festive in the ballet. In later works, including *Death in Venice*, Britten was to return to tuned percussion in the context of an attraction culminating in corruption and death.

The simple function of the 'gamelan' in *The Prince of the Pagodas* as an alien sound-world similar to that of the ghosts in *The Turn of the Screw* was entirely overlooked by every critic who reviewed the first performances of the ballet. This is surprising, not least because several attempted to dismiss Britten's gamelan reconstructions as stylistically inappropriate. The static effect caused by the relentless use of Balinese scales certainly seemed open to criticism, as Peter Heyworth implied in the *Observer* on 6 January 1957: 'Britten's ability to conjure up atmosphere is as evident as in any of his operas (although the difference between establishing atmosphere and giving a scene musical movement is all too apparent in the Balinese aura of the pagodas scene).' More surprisingly, Donald Mitchell was unimpressed by the work's Balinese sections in his review of the ballet for the *Musical Times*. Stressing the overall quality of the score as a 'brilliant amalgam of maximum dramatic effectiveness and maximum musical adventurousness', he too singled out the pagodas scene for criticism:

The work's remaining 'new' aspect – the incorporation into the second act of an Indonesian(?) percussion band (a consequence of Mr Britten's recent travels) – though dramatically justified, was a major musical error: once the ensemble's tinkling has been savoured, its motivic stagnation becomes painfully tedious, all the more so since it is surrounded by music so richly inventive. In any case, this oriental interlude is wildly out of stylistic place, though a transitional passage or two elsewhere proved that Mr Britten could, if he had insisted less on authenticity, have built his oriental inflections into his score without disrupting its consistency. It is a pity that the second act should be marred by an indiscretion not only inappropriate but boring.[1]

Although he has since become the work's staunchest advocate, Mitchell's earlier remarks raise two interesting points. First, he alone of all the early reviewers noted that the gamelan sections were 'dramatically justified'. Secondly, and more significantly, he questioned the effectiveness of 'authenticity' and pointed the reader's attention to certain passages which attempt to go beyond the restrictions of pastiche.

'Pastiche' is not an unduly pejorative term to apply to Britten's 'gamelan', since we have seen how he reconstructed the passages concerned from specific Balinese models with great attention to authentic details. It was a term Felix Aprahamian was quick to adopt in his review of *The Prince of the Pagodas* for the *Sunday Times* on 6 January: 'The quasi-Balinese sounds are contrived with Britten's usual skill, yet they remain pastiche, and there is little in the music more memorable than this colourful splash of oriental timbre.' We saw in Chapter 3 that Britten's gamelan pastiche arose almost accidentally from the circumstances in which the composer found himself at the time. He travelled to Bali in 1956 with work on the score suspended somewhere after the start of Act II, and on the very day he had the tape recordings of Balinese material made in Denpasar he telegraphed Ninette de Valois with renewed confidence to say that he could complete the work by the next deadline. There can be no doubt that, pastiche though they be, the gamelan passages are extremely skilfully executed. As Peter Evans observes: 'No gamelan orchestra ever drew on such [Western] resources, but Britten's re-creative act is one more testimony to a singularly acute ear.'[2] As shown in Chapter 4, Britten was even able to combine Balinese material of diverse origin without compromising the authenticity of his gamelan style.

Although Britten's achievement in reconstructing uncannily realistic

---

1 *Musical Times*, 98 (1957), 91. Dr Mitchell more recently explained his early response to the work in the following terms: 'The culture shock that the gamelan music in the *Pagodas* presented was altogether too much for me, which may explain, though not excuse, my inept response to it – an indication, however, of how novel the experience was that Britten's gamelan offered and how sharp was its impact.' Mitchell, *Benjamin Britten: Death in Venice*, 207, note 16.

2 Evans, *The Music of Benjamin Britten*, 226.

sonorities with Western instruments is clearly impressive *qua* pastiche, an attempt must also be made to assess the broader significance of his gamelan appropriations in *The Prince of the Pagodas* with reference to his overall stylistic development. In Chapter 2 we undertook an examination of Britten's music from the time of his earliest acquaintance with oriental techniques through the influence of Colin McPhee up to the time of composer's own visit to Bali and the composition of *Pagodas*. Britten's interest in heterophonic techniques, polyphonic stratification, sonorities reminiscent of the gamelan and Balinese scales (however coincidental) was considerable. Because most of these features were already inherent in Britten's style by 1956, the overtly gamelan-esque sections in *Pagodas* are in fact not as stylistically incongruous as some commentators were led to believe. Hindsight is, of course, indispensable in assessing the stylistic significance of these passages, as Mitchell has since pointed out:

> There is no doubt that the way we hear *Pagodas* in 1983 is very different from the way we heard it in 1957. Then, the Pagodas' music seemed to represent an enthralling, presumably one-off, dash of exotic colour, the result of Britten's visit to Bali in 1956. Now, we hear a whole future embodied within their glittering revolutions. But there is something else too: not just anticipations of something to come but methods of organization, ways of compositional thinking, that with hindsight we clearly perceive to have had their roots in the techniques Britten encountered and assimilated on his Far East trip.[3]

The most prophetic moments in *The Prince of the Pagodas* are those passages where Britten attempts to synthesize the specifically Balinese material into the musical fabric of the ballet as a whole: the sections where Belle Rose pursues the Prince at the end of Act II, the entry of the Salamander at the Emperor's court at the beginning of Act III and the long interlude before the revealing of the Pagoda Palace. (It is presumably to passages such as these that Mitchell alluded when he said in his 1957 review that 'a transitional passage or two elsewhere proved that Mr Britten could . . . have built his oriental inflections into his score without disrupting its consistency'.) In these brief sections Britten cultivates a greater tonal flexibility which permits him to incorporate configurations derived from Balinese scales in different transpositions, thus retaining a characteristically Western sense of harmonic progression. This looks ahead to the more fully synthesized style of *Death in Venice* and is a notable departure from the tonally static gamelan pastiche in Act II of the ballet.

Technical procedures reminiscent of gamelan music are found in Britten's works with increasing frequency in the years following the completion of *The Prince of the Pagodas*. Heterophonic techniques become an entirely natural

---

[3]   Mitchell, 'Catching on to the Technique', 201.

method of contrapuntal construction, and even form the principal technical premiss for the trilogy of Church Parables. The influence of Balinese scales is now to be felt in almost every composition. Britten's increasingly economical musical material throughout this period highlights the similarities between his own style and the characteristics of Far Eastern music. When he embarked on *Death in Venice*, the final project in which oriental features predominate, the preceding period of gradual assimilation enabled him to apply overt references to the gamelan with a musical and dramatic effectiveness immeasurably greater than that attempted in *The Prince of the Pagodas*.

Any doubt concerning the efficiency of Britten's absorption of oriental influences in *Death in Venice* is dispelled by the observation that no reviewer at the time of the first performance noticed that the distinctive percussion music was specifically Indonesian in origin. In the national daily newspapers, the only comment to mention possible Asian influences was Martin Cooper's description of the 'oriental-sounding gondolier-cries'![4] More recently, it has been acknowledged that the function of the percussion music characterizing Tadzio and the Polish children is directly analogous to that of the gamelan in *The Prince of the Pagodas*, this symbolic trait in Britten's orchestration having been further developed in the intervening years by the experiments in scoring embodied in *A Midsummer Night's Dream* and *Owen Wingrave*.

By the time of *Death in Venice*, these gamelan sonorities had evidently acquired a highly personal significance for the composer as a symbol of yearning towards an unattainable, perfect goal or ideal. Philip Brett has proposed that Britten's orientalism arose directly from his homosexuality, pointing out that McPhee and Poulenc were also homosexuals and that 'gamelan is a gay marker in American music'.[5] His starting-point is Edward Said's alleged 'failure of nerve' in not exploring the implications of the following remark in his influential study of cultural imperialism: 'Why the Orient seems still to suggest not only fecundity but sexual promise (and threat), untiring sensuality, unlimited desire, deep generation energies, is something on which one could speculate.'[6] The operative word here is, of course, 'speculate'. Any attempt to define the autobiographical significance of Britten's gamelan borrowings in the absence of concrete evidence must remain essentially speculative, and Prof. Brett's thought-provoking interpretations veer between the convincing and the fanciful.

Brett's suggestion that the homo-erotic dimension of *The Turn of the Screw*

---

[4] *Daily Telegraph*, 18 June 1973. In a broadcast talk given on the night before the second performance of the opera on 22 June 1973, however, Donald Mitchell drew attention to the gamelan dimension in the work for the first time.

[5] Philip Brett, 'Eros and Orientalism in Britten's Operas', in Philip Brett, Elizabeth Wood and Gary Thomas (eds.), *Queering the Pitch: The New Gay and Lesbian Musicology* (New York and London: Routledge and Kegan Paul, 1994), 235–56.

[6] Edward Said, *Orientalism* (New York: Routledge and Kegan Paul, 1978; repr. Harmondsworth: Penguin, 1991), 188.

is symbolized by pseudo-gamelan sonorities born of an orientalism which functions as a mechanism for projecting taboo desires on to 'the Other' self is the most compelling part of his argument, and it is regrettable that his essay ends without detailed examination of what he sees as a further development of this approach in *Death in Venice*. As we have seen, gamelan sonorities similar in some respects to those in *The Turn of the Screw* were used by Britten to portray the supernatural elements in *A Midsummer Night's Dream*, and Brett accordingly proposes a direct gay-gamelan lineage from Quint to Oberon. His proposal that the 'slightly phallic but nonthreatening' pagodas in *The Prince of the Pagodas* signify a 'nonspecific erotic sensualism' is much less plausible – especially since the composer had no apparent control over the scenario of the ballet, in contrast to his close involvement in every aspect of his operatic collaborations. In any case (and as Brett himself freely admits), it is difficult to conceptualize when the principal subject matter (i.e. the musico-dramatic language of Britten's operas) is designedly ambiguous, and audiences will doubtless retain their own views on the appropriateness of his arguments concerning the apparent 'demonizing of the homosexual through the orientalism'.

Even if the evidence of earlier works – especially *Owen Wingrave*, in which the tuned percussion represents peace (an ideal equally dear to the composer) – were insufficient, Britten's choice of percussion to represent a quest of great psychological magnitude and autobiographical significance in his final stage work eloquently demonstrates his personal attachment to the gamelan style. This attachment would have been furthered in Britten's later work, since *Death in Venice* was not intended to be the last composition to incorporate references to Balinese music. After the completion of the opera, Britten was asked to write a film score for Shakespeare's *The Tempest*, to be shot on location in Bali with John Gielgud as Prospero. The intention of the director, Richard Attenborough, was that Britten should provide music with an exotic, local colour. Britten's illness prevented him from undertaking the project, but he was apparently fascinated by the idea and would undoubtedly have continued to exploit his interest in gamelan music if he had been able to compose the score.[7]

The use of gamelan-derived material in *Death in Venice* progresses beyond the achievements of *The Prince of the Pagodas* in two fundamental respects, one musical and the other dramatic. The musical development, traced in detail in Chapter 8, constitutes a more ambitious application of specific Balinese elements as leitmotifs forming part of an impressive network of musico-dramatic symbolism. As mentioned above, Britten's more flexible handling of configurations derived from Balinese scales results in a greater sense of Western harmonic progression in the passages where the debt to the gamelan

---

[7] See Alan Blyth, *Remembering Britten* (London: Hutchinson, 1981), 135. A file containing correspondence relating to the project is preserved in the archives of Faber Music Ltd.

is most overt. In contrast, the musical material associated with Tadzio remains tonally static to symbolize the essential remoteness of the boy's perfection as perceived by Aschenbach – an idea carried over from Act II of *Pagodas* but now employed with much greater dramatic significance. Britten has here literally achieved the best of both musical worlds by applying a single Balinese scale and sonority (here simply the vibraphone acting as trompong) with an authentic strictness as a specific musico-dramatic symbol, but elsewhere integrating other Balinese elements more fully into his personal style. In both cases we may perceive a clear line of development from the earlier ballet.

The new dramatic approach in *Death in Venice* largely derives from the Church Parable trilogy, which had already exerted an influence on *Owen Wingrave* with its ritualistic Ballad and stylized tele-montages. It is significant that Colin Graham, whose vital contribution in shaping the dramatic style of the Parables was explored in Chapters 6 and 7, was chosen as producer for the first production of *Death in Venice*. Graham was praised by William Mann in *The Times* on 18 June 1973 for his 'pointed, highly theatrical production which conjures marvels from black drops and a few people'. In addition to the generally restrained dramatic style, the use of dance and mime (particularly in the 'Games of Apollo') is a clear development from the ritualistic methods of presentation evolved in the Church Parables, at the same time preserving the close link with the aesthetics of Balinese dancing.

The motivation behind the creation of the Parable convention itself was the strong desire to emulate the austerity and restraint of a single specific Nō play. The stimulus provided by the Japanese source was clearly much more intense than Britten's general fascination with the gamelan, and this is confirmed by the success with which Britten recaptured the atmosphere of Motomasa's *Sumidagawa* after an eight-year gestation. *Curlew River* was an appropriate context in which to find Britten's oriental musical interests surfacing with renewed conviction: the incorporation of material derived from Tōgaku and shamisen songs was a new departure presumably intended to replace the seemingly esoteric music of Nō with something more readily acceptable to the Western ear, while still retaining the connection with Japan.

Curlew River, as the *fons et origo* of the trilogy, is now usually considered to be the finest and most original of the three Church Parables. This is a defensible standpoint, although it offers the dangerous temptation to neglect the individuality of the two later works. Critical response to *Curlew River* at the time of its first performance in 1964 was generally positive, reviewers giving far greater attention to the presence of oriental influences in the score than they had done in the case of the Balinese elements in *The Prince of the Pagodas*. Colin Mason, writing in the *Guardian* on 15 June 1964, managed to combine both short-sighted and perceptive comments in one paragraph:

Musically . . . there is very little that is oriental in the work, except for a short prelude and postlude . . . and this sounds as much Balinese as specifically Japanese. On the other hand there is a carefully sought 'strangeness' in the music, which creates the effect of the exotic while rigorously refusing to imitate.

By far the most perceptive discussion of the music came from John Warrack, whose comments are well worth quotation at some length:

The interesting quality of the synthesis . . . does still lie in the way Britten has taken apparently Japanese procedures into his own language – which is thereby extended but not, of course, broken. The suspended tone-clusters on the chamber organ which are the work's first harmonic sound take their aural nature from an instrument used in Japanese *gagaku* court music, but their constitution from a more Western organizational method, derivations from the close intervals of the Gregorian chant 'Te lucis ante terminum' . . .

The robing music reverts to the chant in heterophony . . . The sounds of this strange, overlapping march over clopping percussion is neither Western nor Eastern – nor recognisably Brittenish . . .

What [*Curlew River*] presages, genius alone knows. But [Britten's] sure-footedness in making this foreign experience at once his own and supra-national allows no room for doubt about his still-increasing stature.[8]

The crucial observation here (and it has been too infrequently acknowledged) is that Britten's oriental borrowings – like Debussy's before him – constitute a direct extension of his compositional language, and not an alien feature uncomfortably grafted on to a fundamentally different style. Once more, this is a reminder of how well suited to the admixture of Asian techniques Britten's style was before 1956, largely due to the long-term influence of McPhee and to his own stylistic preoccupations from a very early stage.

Several reviewers openly criticized the Christian framework imposed on the *Sumidagawa* plot in *Curlew River*. Martin Cooper's review in the *Daily Telegraph* contained veiled dissatisfaction with this element, and Colin Mason singled it out for comment (without citing any specific evidence to support his view):

Although this Christian interpretation of the story is more closely integrated into the dramatic whole than in Britten's version of *The Rape of Lucretia*, it is not completely satisfactory or convincing . . . Moving, and indeed gripping, as the work is at its first impact, there is a slight uncertainty of aim and style about it.

Jeremy Noble found the work

flawed by what seems to me to be a confusion of its true aims . . . Britten

---

8   *Tempo*, 70 (1964), 19–22.

and his librettist . . . have contrived to Christianize what is fundamentally a story with no Christian implications at all. The boy assures
his mother that they will meet in Heaven, and the Abbot points the
moral at the end . . . But in spite of this . . . the dramatic emphasis
remains quite clearly where it obviously was in the Japanese original –
on the mother's anguish and the pathos of the boy's fate. Britten's music
too leaves us in no doubt that it is these facets of the play that attracted
him to it . . . It seems fairly clear to me that *Curlew River* is composed not
out of a generalized desire to make Nō available to the West, but out of
Britten's own most permanent obsession – innocence and its destruction. Nor is it any worse for that: in fact it is that which gives it its
hypnotic power. But it does set up a certain tension with the mediaeval/
Christian/liturgical framework that seems in the end to weaken its
impact.[9]

Noble is certainly correct in his explanation for Britten's original interest in
the *Sumidagawa* story and for his treatment of the theme of innocence and its
destruction. But in our discussion of the work's dramatic shape and its
relationship to the Nō model we saw that the Christian element is handled as
a gradual progression and revelation which imparts a thoroughly Western
cogency to the plot in an attempt to make the story more immediately
appealing to an audience unfamiliar with Zen-Buddhist philosophy. This
careful handling was probably the result of Britten's constructive response to
the widespread criticisms of *The Rape of Lucretia* in 1946, when it was widely
felt he had failed in a similar attempt to Christianize a pagan story. Clearly
any response to this religious element must remain highly subjective. It is,
however, significant that this potential dichotomy has scarcely been raised
since 1964, when the Christianization of the *Curlew River* plot was widely
publicized at the time of the first production. It seems unlikely that, had the
critics been ignorant of the original Japanese story, they would have taken the
composer to task so readily.

Britten's Christianized Parable opened up possibilities for the treatment of
further, now biblical, stories and thus created a convention which would have
been difficult to envisage if the original Buddhist apparatus of *Sumidagawa*
had been firmly retained. *The Burning Fiery Furnace* was the product of an
admirably sound choice of follow-up plot which retained all the simplicity
of *Curlew River* but introduced a new element of colourful vitality, thus
preventing the work from becoming a pointless imitation of its predecessor.
Opinions of the second Parable differed widely, and the controversy focused
on how wise Britten was in choosing to apply in another context an idiosyncratic idiom which had been specially designed to meet the needs of a
unique musico-dramatic venture. The creation of such an extrovert and
colourful work within the confines of the convention established by the

9   *Musical Times*, 105 (1964), 667.

introvert and consciously monochrome *Curlew River* is itself impressive and can easily be overlooked. The experiment is successful largely because Britten refuses to stick rigidly to the dramatic restrictions of Nō he had emulated in the earlier work. We saw in Chapter 7 how the increased activity given to the chorus in the second Parable was part of a progression away from Nō, and the inclusion of overtly theatrical passages such as the procession and adoration of Merodak are a welcome addition to the genre after the cultivated restraint of *Curlew River*.

Britten's range of musical gestures was also widened in the second Parable to parallel this greater dramatic freedom. This resulted in a less marked dependence on oriental models: we saw, for instance, how the shō chords are here less static and not constructed authentically – a change in emphasis forming a direct parallel to the different approaches to the gamelan represented by *The Prince of the Pagodas* and *Death in Venice*. The alto trombone adds an obvious dash of brazen colour to the score, as does the augmented percussion section. Certain musical devices introduced in *Curlew River* are re-adopted and newly applied in notably different contexts. The plainsong on which the work is based is more colourful than that in *Curlew River*, and its pentatonic flavour is found throughout the Parable. In addition, the haunting vocal portamento derived from Nō is transformed into the barbaric, spine-chilling invocation of Merodak – a climactic moment which impressed every commentator.

The new vitality in *The Burning Fiery Furnace* therefore compensates for any sense of repetitiveness caused by the presence of the musical formulae required by the Parable genre. A more viable criticism concerns the unfortunate dramatic effect created by the opulent musical treatment of the Babylonian court. Because the music for the Israelites is comparatively restrained, there is a danger that the resolution of the spiritual conflict in their favour may appear something of a musical anticlimax which detracts from the dramatic effectiveness of the dénouement. In the words of Robin Holloway: 'during the earnest chanting of the three goodies our ears stray guiltily to the musicians as they prepare one by one for their "unholy" procession'.[10] Or, as Jeremy Noble puts it, 'this is one more case where Babylon gets the best of it musically'.[11]

This is not a serious defect in a work which Holloway has himself described as 'clearly something of a fun piece', but a similar and more funda-mental flaw mars the overall dramatic effectiveness of the third and final Parable. In some respects *The Prodigal Son* marks a return to the introverted and humane issues with which *Curlew River* had been concerned. Since this partly necessitates a corresponding return to some of the more intimate musical procedures of the first Parable, a comparison with *Curlew River* is

[10] Holloway, 'The Church Parables II', 221.
[11] *Musical Times*, 107 (1966), 698.

more openly invited than it had been in *The Burning Fiery Furnace*. The difficulty lies principally in the contrast between the tonally static, largely restrained, music for the Father's estate and the colourful, vital music for the hedonistic pleasures of the city (the former recalling *Curlew River*, the latter *The Burning Fiery Furnace*). Holloway again:

> The deliberate blandness of the father's farm is all too effective; at the reconciliation our strongest reaction to the return of the seraphic unchanging B♭ chord from which the younger son fled is to remember the boredom that impelled him rather than be moved by his return.[12]

Stanley Sadie was of the same mind when reviewing the first performance, describing the B♭ chord as 'complacently anchored'.[13] The first section of the Parable's action is certainly static, with the notorious B♭ chord stated no fewer than nine times to create a tonal rigidity rare in Britten. The alto-flute melody derived from 'Raag Yaman' (although attractive in itself) is extended beyond comfortable limits, the Father mechanically delivers his truisms to every conceivable permutation of a diatonic four-note cell and the section is rounded off by three repetitions of a workers' chorus. The exquisite harp solo for the Tempter which follows rescues the music at a critical stage – and here the problems begin, because we can readily sympathize with the Younger Son's predicament. A final recapitulation of the bland chorus makes his mind up for him ('Why should I not, before it is too late?').

This is not to deny that there is much fine music in the central section of the work, although, as we have seen, this very fact tends to exacerbate the dramatic imbalance. It should also be stressed that Britten continues to put his convention to imaginative use in the third Parable, and that the dramatic inconsistency is nothing to do with the convention *per se*. Most striking is the Tempter's first appearance, which has been discussed for the influence of Kabuki which probably suggested it to Britten, and this divergence from the well-established format at such an early point in the work was found dramatically effective by every reviewer. We have also seen how the multi-role function of the chorus completes the gradual move away from the narrative orientation of the Nō *ji-utai*.

In general, Britten's decision to compose two further works in the convention established by *Curlew River* may readily be justified by the increasing use he makes of more realistic dramatic procedures derived from the composer's own, Western, operatic experience. For many, this may merely represent a severe weakening of the original Nō-inspired idiom; but this is certainly preferable to a trilogy in which no attempt is made to progress beyond the dramatic style of the first member. This development naturally involved a general decrease in importance of the original Japanese stimulus, but the

---

[12] Holloway, 'The Church Parables II', 221.
[13] *Musical Times*, 109 (1968), 744.

trilogy as a whole would scarcely have been possible without the initial Nō model, and the course of the three Parables demonstrates how Britten could make an external influence his own and progress beyond it by a process of gradual assimilation. Again, this is directly analogous to the more flexible and sophisticated use in *Death in Venice* of the Balinese procedures first encountered in *The Prince of the Pagodas*.

In a perceptive comment, William Mann observed of *Death in Venice*: 'Above all [Britten's] music has a unity of purpose, obtained by continual development of a few simple, yet subtle motives, which pulls the opera together not dogmatically but with the effortless blossoming of a masterly improvisation.'[14] These remarks might equally well be applied to a Balinese gamelan composition, which appears to have the spontaneity of improvisation but is always predetermined by set structural and motivic patterns. This parallel, conceived as it is on the broadest scale, might appear far-fetched at first glance. Yet it aptly summarizes the fundamental reasons underlying Britten's stylistic identification with oriental music. Motivic unity and economy of material constitute two of the most impressive features of *Death in Venice*, as William Mann suggests. They are the outcome of Britten's lifelong search for clarity of musical expression, a quest which had preoccupied him from the earliest stages of his stylistic development. His perennial desire to limit the materials at his disposal and to respond creatively to the challenge of self-imposed restrictions may partly be related to his increasing interest in gamelan techniques. His experiments with Balinese pentatonicism in *The Prince of the Pagodas* were an early manifestation of this interest in self-imposed limitations in a context inspired by Asian music. What Britten may have thought of as the 'restrictions' of the gamelan style are also important in two further respects. First, the *pokok* structural foundation of a gamelan composition might be seen to form a close parallel with Britten's lifelong fondness for passacaglia form. Secondly, the technique of polyphonic stratification within a deliberately limited tonal spectrum is a further reflection of the same ideal of musical economy.

Hans Keller viewed Britten's adoption of serial procedures in a number of important works as the ultimate product of this stylistic trend:

The 'sentimentalic' Schoenberg was another . . . anti-model, helping Britten to serialize, anti-serialize and trans-serialize – to discover and re-discover applications of the technique which Schoenberg might have dreamt of, but never realized. *The Turn of the Screw* is neither the first nor the most original product of this particular search, without which the heterophony in and beyond the Church Parables would, could never have come about – even though biographically and chronologically, Britten's visit to the Far East in 1956 seems 'the cause' of all later heterophonic ventures. *A* cause, yes, but *causa prima*? On the contrary, it was

14 *The Times*, 18 June 1973.

serial thought that was the *conditio sine qua non* of all later heterophonic developments.[15]

In this context, it is intriguing to recall Britten's remark in a letter written while on Bali that he considered the techniques of gamelan music to be 'about as complicated as Schönberg'. It is certainly true that the stark musical economy of the Parable idiom (in which heterophony plays a fundamental role) is the most extreme manifestation of the same trend: Britten does not resort to dodecaphonic serialism in the trilogy simply because a twelve-note theme would itself prove too complex in such a rarefied context. Here the heterophony is more directly linked to specific Japanese models, but the stylistic preoccupations which led to its widespread adoption are essentially similar.

In *Death in Venice* Britten combined the thematic economy of the Church Parables with colourful orchestration and a greater harmonic richness reminiscent of his pre-1964 style. The re-emergence of specific gamelan features and the inclusion of serial techniques creates an extraordinarily comprehensive synthesis which makes the opera a fitting culmination to the composer's stylistic development. *Death in Venice* must be regarded as the finest and most assured of those of Britten's works to incorporate Asian influences because the techniques borrowed from oriental music are inseparable from the technical processes of the work as a whole.

Whatever one's final opinion of Britten's treatment of oriental devices as an extension of his own compositional style, one can only marvel at the musical perception which enabled him to recreate elements of the Balinese gamelan and Japanese music with what was, in fact, a strictly limited knowledge of them. Although his research into Asian music appears extensive compared to the stereotyped orientalism of some of the earlier composers discussed in Chapter 1, it is easy to forget how little time Britten spent in direct contact with oriental music. The knowledge of Balinese music he gained from his friendship with McPhee must have remained largely subconscious, and he possessed no books on the gamelan. The majority of the Balinese material he incorporated into his own works was derived from a handful of gramophone records, one tape recording and the sketches he made during a mere thirteen days on Bali itself. Similarly, the entire Parable trilogy sprang from just two performances of a Nō play in Tokyo and a passing interest in shō techniques. Britten possessed a far larger collection of books on the traditional Japanese performing arts, but none deals with the music in any detail. He had spent only twelve days in Japan yet, as with the Balinese gamelan, his own subsequent works suggest a lifetime's involvement with the native culture.

The success with which Britten incorporated oriental material into his own

15 Hans Keller, 'Introduction: Operatic Music and Britten', in Herbert, *The Operas of Benjamin Britten*, xxix–xxx.

music, either reconstructing specific models or assimilating its general characteristics into his personal idiom, was ultimately made possible by three fundamental attributes: an astonishing aural facility which enabled him to emulate alien sonorities without a highly specialized knowledge of the traditions concerned; a musical instinct which permitted him to appropriate only those elements which might prove to be of seminal value; and, above all, a compositional style which had already displayed inherently similar technical properties for many years before.

Bibliography

Primary Sources

A. *Letters*

The tabular layout shows date, source and destination of letter and its current location in the Britten–Pears Library.

Ansermet, Ernest

17 April 1956	BB to Ernest Ansermet	4-9700711
27 April 1956	Ernest Ansermet to BB	4-9700307
11 May 1956	Ernest Ansermet to BB	4-9700308
18 May 1956	BB to Ernest Ansermet	4-9700712

Blades, James

[January 1956]	BB to James Blades [photocopy of postcard]	4-9700774

Coleman, Basil

25 September 1955	BB to Basil Coleman [photocopy]	4-9700718

Cranko, John

18 April 1955	John Cranko to BB	4-9700317
15 August 1955	BB to John Cranko [draft]	4-9700771
[August 1955]	BB to John Cranko [photocopy]	4-9700773

Duncan, Roger

19 December 1955	BB to Roger Duncan	4-9700698
23 December 1955	BB to Roger Duncan	4-9700697
18 January 1956	BB to Roger Duncan	4-9700699
8 February 1956	BB to Roger Duncan	4-9700700
21 February 1956	BB to Roger Duncan	4-9700701
11 March 1956	BB to Roger Duncan	4-9700702

Duncan, Ronald

27 March 1956	BB to Ronald Duncan	4-9700703
12 June 1956	BB to Ronald Duncan	4-9700704
14 August 1956	BB to Ronald Duncan	4-9700705

Gishford, Anthony

28 December 1954	BB to Anthony Gishford	4-9700706
2 December 1955	BB to Anthony Gishford	4-9700707
5 June 1956	BB to Anthony Gishford	4-9700708

18 August 1956	BB to Anthony Gishford	4-9700709
27 November 1956	BB to Anthony Gishford	4-9700710
25 July 1957	BB to Anthony Gishford	5-9700770

Graham, Colin
[1963]	Colin Graham to BB	4-9700326

Holst, Imogen
17 January 1956	BB to Imogen Holst	4-9700720
8 February 1956	BB to Imogen Holst	4-9700768

IJzerdraat, Bernard
7 June 1956	Bernard IJzerdraat to BB	4-9700304

Kurosawa, Kei-ichi
31 March 1956	Kei-ichi Kurosawa to BB	4-9700692

Mayer, Elizabeth
19 July 1944	BB to Elizabeth Mayer	4-9700723

McPhee, Colin
21 July 1942	Colin McPhee to BB	4-9700769
6 May 1943	Colin McPhee to BB	

Newton, John
9 February 1965	BB to John Newton (photocopy)	4-9700775

Pears, Peter
24 November 1943	BB to Peter Pears	4-9700693
30 July 1955	Peter Pears to BB	4-9700694
1 December 1955	Peter Pears to Janet Stone	*GB-Ob*, Stone, Box 20
26 July 1956	BB to Peter Pears	4-9700695
28 July 1956	BB to Peter Pears	4-9700696

Plomer, William
23 July 1953	William Plomer to BB	4-9400699
13 May 1956	BB to William Plomer	*GB-DRu*
14 May 1956	William Plomer to BB	4-9400725
5 July 1957	William Plomer to BB	4-9400729
10 July 1957	BB to William Plomer	*GB-DRu*
16 July 1957	William Plomer to BB	4-9400730
12 July 1958	BB to William Plomer	*GB-DRu*
2 October 1958	William Plomer to BB	4-9400734
8 October 1958	BB to William Plomer	*GB-DRu*
21 October 1958	William Plomer to BB	4-9400736
29 October 1958	BB to William Plomer	*GB-DRu*
4 November 1958	William Plomer to BB	4-9400737
7 November 1958	William Plomer to BB	4-9400738
16 November 1958	BB to William Plomer	*GB-DRu*
8 March 1959	BB to William Plomer	*GB-DRu*
15 April 1959	BB to William Plomer	*GB-DRu*

17 April 1959	William Plomer to BB	4-9400745
26 May 1959	William Plomer to BB	4-9400748
17 August 1959	BB to William Plomer	*GB-DRu*
23 November 1959	BB to William Plomer	*GB-DRu*
23 October 1963	BB to William Plomer	*GB-DRu*
4 January 1964	BB to William Plomer	*GB-DRu*
15 February 1964	BB to William Plomer	*GB-DRu*
4 August 1960	BB to William Plomer	*GB-DRu*
1 January 1961	BB to William Plomer	*GB-DRu*
8 November 1962	William Plomer to BB	4-9400784
17 July 1963	BB to William Plomer	*GB-DRu*
4 January 1964	BB to William Plomer	*GB-DRu*
15 February 1964	BB to William Plomer	*GB-DRu*
2 April 1964	BB to William Plomer	*GB-DRu*
9 July 1964	BB to William Plomer (postcard)	*GB-DRu*
8 September 1964	BB to William Plomer	*GB-DRu*
16 October 1964	William Plomer to BB	4-9400820
10 January 1965	William Plomer to BB	4-9400823
18 April 1965	William Plomer to BB	4-9400825
24 May 1965	William Plomer to BB	4-9400827
13 July 1965	William Plomer to BB	4-9400830
15 July 1965	BB to William Plomer	*GB-DRu*
16 July 1965	William Plomer to BB	4-9400831
17 July 1965	William Plomer to Taro Shiomi	*GB-DRu*
28 July 1965	BB to William Plomer	*GB-DRu*
30 July 1965	William Plomer to BB	4-9400832
27 October 1965	BB to William Plomer	*GB-DRu*
1 November 1965	William Plomer to BB	4-9400838
24 November 1965	BB to William Plomer	*GB-DRu*
6 December 1965	BB to William Plomer	*GB-DRu*
2 February 1966	BB to William Plomer	*GB-DRu*
14 February 1966	William Plomer to BB	4-9400846
26 March 1966	William Plomer to BB	4-9400852
6 January 1967	BB to William Plomer	*GB-DRu*
7 January 1967	William Plomer to BB	4-9400866
13 March 1967	BB to William Plomer	*GB-DRu*
20 March 1967	William Plomer to BB	4-9400867
27 July 1967	William Plomer to BB	4-9400875
29 July 1967	BB to William Plomer	*GB-DRu*
17 August 1967	BB to William Plomer	*GB-DRu*
22 November 1967	BB to William Plomer	*GB-DRu*
20 January 1968	BB to William Plomer	*GB-DRu*
29 April 1968	BB to William Plomer	*GB-DRu*

Potter, Mary
| 23 December 1955 | BB to Mary Potter | 4-9700722 |

Poulenc, Francis
| 14 July 1954 | BB to Francis Poulenc | 4-9700717 |

Searle, Humphrey
| 27 March 1956 | BB to Humphrey Searle | 4-9700719 |

Stein, Erwin
[18 January 1956]   BB to Erwin and Sophie Stein   4-9700721

Valois, Dame Ninette de
23 January 1956   Telegram from BB to Dame Ninette   Royal Opera
                                                              House Archive,
                                                              London

Webster, David

3 September 1954	BB to David Webster [photocopy]	4-9700713
[September 1954]	BB to David Webster [photocopy of postcard]	4-9700772
[August 1955]	BB to David Webster[photocopy]	4-9700773
1 October 1955	BB to David Webster [photocopy]	4-9700714
18 October 1955	David Webster to BB	4-9700325
1 May 1956	BB to David Webster [photocopy]	4-9700715
28 May 1956	BB to David Webster [photocopy]	4-9700716

B. *Other primary sources*

The final column of the tabular layout shows the location and/or catalogue number. Unless otherwise stated, all items are at *GB-ALb*; for the latter, the catalogue or shelf number only is supplied.

Recordings

	[Concert by Britten and Pears in Tokyo, 9 February 1956. Unpublished video recording]	VC0244
	Gagaku (Court Music), (Tokyo: Columbia, [1955]; BL 28, BL 29) [Britten's copies]	3-9401031–9401032 3-9401041–9401042
	[Gamelan music from Ubud: a tape recording made for Britten by B. IJzerdraat, 1956.]	3-9401043–9401050
	Music from Bali (Argo, [1953?]; RG1, RG2) [Britten's copies of LP recordings of Balinese *kebyar* music played by a gamelan from Peliatan]	3-9401051–9401060
	Music of Bali . . . transcribed by Colin McPhee (Schirmer, [1941?]; 513–514) [Britten's copy of the 78 r.p.m. recordings he made with McPhee]	3-9401034–9401038
	[Music from Java and Bali] (Parlophone, 1928) [Britten's copies of 78 r.p.m. recordings]	
	Singalese drumming (Kandy) [unpublishedtape recording, 1956]	3-9500154
	Sumi-kawa [unpublished tape recording of a Japanese performance of *Sumidagawa*, 1956]	3-9401064
Britten, Benjamin	*The Burning Fiery Furnace*, video of a Japanese production (March 1979)	3-9700528

262

Ghosh, Pannalal   *Raag Yaman* and *Raag Shri* (HMV, [n.d.];   3-9302387–9302388
                   EALP 1252) [Britten's copy]

Objets d'art
[Balinese pictures given to Britten by Peter Pears]
    [Balinese athletes by] Lempad   5-9700388
    [Balinese village scene by] W. J. Séntep   5-9700393
[Balinese Barong, presented to Britten by B. IJzerdraat]   5-9700554

Manuscripts, non-music
Britten, Benjamin   Diaries   Uncatalogued
                      The Burning Fiery Furnace, draft scenarios   2-9500557
                      (exercise book)
                      Death in Venice, draft scenario (exercise book)   2-9202673
                      Death in Venice, draft scenario (typescript,   2-9700619
                      (carbon copy))
Cranko, John   *The Green Serpent* [draft scenario for   2-9700608
                      The Prince of the Pagodas]
Pears, Peter   Engagement Diaries   Uncatalogued
Piper, Myfanwy   *Death in Venice*, libretto (first draft, typescript)   2-9202674
Plomer, William   *The Burning Fiery Furnace*, preliminary notes   GB-DRu
                      (exercise book)
                      The Burning Fiery Furnace, libretto (first   GB-DRu
                      draft, ms)
                      The Burning Fiery Furnace, libretto (second   2-9500545
                      draft, typescript)
                      The Burning Fiery Furnace, libretto (second   2-9500546
                      draft, typescript (carbon copy))
                      The Burning Fiery Furnace, libretto (third   2-9500547
                      draft, typescript (carbon copy))
                      The Burning Fiery Furnace, libretto (third   2-9500548
                      draft, typescript (carbon copy))
                      The Burning Fiery Furnace, libretto (third   2-9500549
                      draft, typescript (carbon copy))
                      The Burning Fiery Furnace, libretto (fourth   2-9500550
                      draft, typescript (carbon copy))
                      The Burning Fiery Furnace, libretto (fourth   GB-DRu
                      draft, typescript (carbon copy))
                      The Burning Fiery Furnace, libretto (fourth   2-9500555
                      draft, typescript (carbon copy))
                      The Burning Fiery Furnace, libretto (fifth   2-9500556
                      draft, typescript (carbon copy))   °
                      Curlew River, libretto (first draft, ms) [1958]   GB-DRu
                      Curlew River, libretto (first draft, typescript)   2-9100297
                      Curlew River, libretto (first draft, typescript   2-9100298
                      (carbon copy))
                      Curlew River, libretto (second draft,   2-9100299
                      typescripts)   GB-DRu
                      The Prodigal Son, scenario (notebook)   GB-DRu
                      The Prodigal Son, libretto (first draft, ms)   2-9700609
                      The Prodigal Son, libretto (second draft, ms)   2-9700610
                      The Prodigal Son, libretto (third draft,   2-9700611
                      typescript (carbon copy))

	The Prodigal Son, libretto (fourth draft, typescript (carbon copy))	2-9700612
	The Prodigal Son, libretto (fifth draft, typescript (carbon copy))	2-9700614
	The Prodigal Son, libretto (proofs)	2-9300038
Taynor, Leo	*A Young Britten's Guide to the Shō*	4-9700692

Manuscripts, music

Britten, Benjamin	*The Burning Fiery Furnace*, composition draft	2-9500543
	The Burning Fiery Furnace, full score (fair copy)	2-9500544
	The Burning Fiery Furnace, discarded sketch leaves, including 'Toda Welcome Song'	2-9700617
	Christmas Sequence, sketches for an unfinished work, 1976	2-9300010
	Death in Venice, sketchbook	2-9202672
	Death in Venice, composition draft	2-9202670
	Death in Venice, discarded sketch leaf	2-9700623
	Malayan National Anthem, composition draft	2–9300893
	The Prince of the Pagodas, composition draft	2-9300894
	The Prince of the Pagodas, discarded sketch leaves	2-9700607
	The Prince of the Pagodas, notes on percussion and 'Kapi radja'	2-9700622
	The Prodigal Son, composition draft	2-9104583
	[Transcriptions of Balinese music from gramophone recordings, [n.d.]]	2-9700605
	[Transcriptions of Balinese music made in Bali, [1956]]	2-9700606
	Variations on a Theme of Frank Bridge, arr. for two pianos by Colin McPhee	2-9700604

Printed books, Britten's copies

Daniélou, Alain	*The Râga-s of Northern Indian Music* (London: The Cresset Press, 1968)	1-9501237
Deimling, Hermann (ed.)	*The Chester Plays*, vol. 1 (London: The Cresset Press, 1958)	1-9400207
Mann, Thomas	*Death in Venice*, trans. Mrs H. T. Lowe-Porter (London: Martin Secker, 1929)	1-9700797
Mann, Thomas	*Death in Venice*, trans. Mrs H. T. Lowe-Porter (Harmondsworth: Penguin, 1971)	1-9700796
Mann, Thomas	*Der Tod in Venedig*, ed. T. J. Reed (Oxford, Clarendon Press, 1971)	1-9700799
Pollard, Alfred W. (ed.)	*English Miracle Plays, Moralities and Interludes: Specimens of the Pre-Elizabethan Drama* (Oxford: Clarendon Press, 1927)	1-9300358
Pound, Ezra	*The Translations of Ezra Pound* (London: Faber and Faber, 1953)	1-9500762
Young, Karl	*The Drama of the Medieval Church* (Oxford: Oxford University Press, 1933)	1-9400202
Waley, Arthur (trs.)	*Chinese Poems* (London: George Allen & Unwin, 1946)	1-9600214

Printed music, Britten's copies

| | *Gagaku: Japanese Classical Court Music*,
transcribed by Sukehiro Shiba, vol. 1
(Tokyo: Ryugin-Sha, 1955) | 2-9700615 |
| McPhee, Colin | *Balinese Ceremonial Music* (New York:
G. Schirmer Inc, [n.d.]) | 2-9202908–
9202910 |

Other

| [Posting certificate for Britten's recorder, sent to the Kurosawa family, 26 July 1956] | 4-9700692 |
| Shō [owned by Britten] | 5-9600001 |

Secondary Sources

The following pages provide a listing of secondary sources cited in the text, together with items of related or secondary interest.

Alexander, Peter, *William Plomer: A Biography* (Oxford: Oxford University Press, 1989)

Allen, Stephen Arthur, 'Britten and Christianity' (D.Phil. dissertation, University of Oxford, in progress)

Ambros, August Wilhelm, *Geschichte der Musik*, 4 vols. (Leipzig: F. E. C. Leuckart, 1862; 2nd edn, 1880)

Ansermet, Ernest, *Les fondements de la musique dans la conscience humaine* (Neuchâtel: La Baconnière, 1961)

Aprahamian, Felix, review of the first production of *The Prince of the Pagodas*, *Sunday Times*, 6 January 1957

Arndt, Jürgen, *Der Einfluss der javanischen Gamelan-Musik auf Kompositionen von Claude Debussy* (Frankfurt: Lang, 1993)

Ashbrook, William, and Harold Powers, *Puccini's Turandot: The End of the Great Tradition* (Princeton: Princeton University Press, 1991)

Balough, Teresa, *A Complete Catalogue of the Works of Percy Grainger* (Nedlands: Department of Music, University of Western Australia, 1975)

——, *A Musical Genius from Australia* (Nedlands: Department of Music, University of Western Australia,1982)

Banks, Paul (ed.), *Britten's Gloriana: Essays and Sources*, Aldeburgh Studies in Music, 1 (Woodbridge: The Boydell Press, 1993)

Beaumont, Antony, *Busoni the Composer* (London: Faber and Faber, 1985)

Bénédictus, Louis, *Les musiques bizarres à l'Exposition* (Paris, 1889)

Berger, Donald, 'The Nohkan: Its Construction and Music', *Ethnomusicology*, 9 (1965), 221–39

Bird, John, *Percy Grainger* (London: Faber and Faber, 1976)

Blacking, John, *'A Commonsense View of All Music': Reflections on Percy Grainger's Contribution to Ethnomusicology and Music Education* (Cambridge: Cambridge University Press, 1987)

Blades, James, *Percussion Instruments and their History* (London: Faber and Faber, 1970; 2nd edn, 1985)

Blyth, Alan (ed.), *Remembering Britten* (London: Hutchinson, 1981)

Blythe, Ronald (ed.), *Aldeburgh Anthology* (London: Faber Music/Snape Maltings Foundation, 1972)

Brett, Philip (ed.), *Benjamin Britten: Peter Grimes*, Cambridge Opera Handbooks (Cambridge: Cambridge University Press, 1983)

——, 'Eros and Orientalism in Britten's Operas', in Brett, Wood and Thomas (eds.), *Queering the Pitch*, 235–56

Brett, Philip, Elizabeth Wood and Gary Thomas (eds.), *Queering the Pitch: The New Gay and Lesbian Musicology* (New York and London: Routledge and Kegan Paul, 1994)

Britten, Benjamin, New Year's message to the people of Japan, 3 December 1957, transcript repr. in *Aldeburgh Festival Programme Book* (1991), 18–19

Britten, Benjamin, William Plomer and Colin Graham, 'Production Notes and Remarks on the Style of Performing *Curlew River*', in Britten, *Curlew River* (London: Faber Music, vocal score 1965; full score 1983)

Buckland, Sidney (ed.), *Francis Poulenc: Selected Correspondence, 1915–1963* (London: Gollancz, 1991)

Cage, John, 'The East in the West', *Modern Music*, 23 (1945–6), 111–15

Carner, Mosco, *Puccini: A Critical Biography* (London: Duckworth, 1958; 2nd edn, 1974)

Carpenter, Humphrey, *Benjamin Britten: A Biography* (London: Faber and Faber, 1992)

Coast, John, *Dancing out of Bali* (London: Faber and Faber, 1954)

Cooke, Mervyn, 'Britten and Bali: A Study in Stylistic Synthesis' (M.Phil. dissertation, University of Cambridge, 1985)

——, 'Britten and the Gamelan: Balinese Influences in *Death in Venice*', in Mitchell (ed.), *Benjamin Britten: Death in Venice*, 115–28

——, 'Britten and Bali', *Journal of Musicological Research*, 7 (1987), 307–39

——, 'Britten and the Shō', *Musical Times*, 129 (1988), 231–3

——, 'Oriental Influences in the Music of Benjamin Britten' (Ph.D. dissertation, University of Cambridge, 1989)

——, 'Britten's *The Prince of the Pagodas*', sleeve notes to recording by Oliver Knussen and the London Sinfonietta, Virgin Classics VCD 759578-2 (1990)

——, 'Britten in Japan', *Aldeburgh Festival Programme Book* (1991), 14–19

——, 'Britten's "Prophetic Song": Tonal Symbolism in *Billy Budd*', in Cooke and Reed, *Benjamin Britten: Billy Budd*, 85–110

——, 'Britten and Shakespeare: Dramatic and Musical Cohesion in *A Midsummer Night's Dream*', *Music & Letters*, 74 (1993), 246–68

——, 'From Nō to Nebuchadnezzar', in Reed (ed.), *On Mahler and Britten*, 135–45

——, *Benjamin Britten: War Requiem*, Cambridge Music Handbooks (Cambridge: Cambridge University Press, 1996)

——, 'Eastern Influences in Britten's *The Prodigal Son*', *Melos* 19/20 (Stockholm, 1997), 37–45

Cooke, Mervyn, and Philip Reed, *Benjamin Britten: Billy Budd*, Cambridge Opera Handbooks (Cambridge: Cambridge University Press, 1993)

Cooper, Martin, review of the first production of *Death in Venice*, *Daily Telegraph*, 18 June 1973

Covarrubias, Miguel, *Island of Bali* (New York: Alfred A. Knopf, 1942; repr. KPI Ltd, 1986)

Cowell, Henry, 'Towards Neo-Primitivism', *Modern Music*, 10 (1932–3), 150–51

——, 'Current Chronicle', *Musical Quarterly*, 34 (1948), 410–15

Cranko, John, 'Making a Ballet', *Sunday Times*, 13/20 January 1957

Daniélou, Alain, *The Rāga-s of Northern Indian Music* (London: Barrie and Cresset, 1968)

D'Aulnoy, Madame [Marie Catherine-Le Jumel-de Berneville], *Serpentin vert* (Milan, 1782)

Deimling, Hermann (ed.), *The Chester Plays*, 2 vols. (London: Kegan Paul, 1893–1916)

Dent, Edward J., 'The Pianoforte and its Influence on Modern Music', *Musical Quarterly*, 2 (1916), 271–94

Devriès, Anik, 'Les musiques de l'Extrême-Orient à l'Exposition Universelle de 1889', *Cahiers Debussy*, new series, 1 (1977), 25–37

Drew, David (ed.), *The Decca Book of Ballet* (London: Muller, 1958)

Duncan, Ronald, *Working with Britten* (Welcombe: The Rebel Press, 1981)

Ellis, A. J., 'On the Musical Scales of Various Nations', *Journal of the Society of Arts*, 33 (1885), 485–527

Enright, D. J., *Memoirs of a Mendicant Professor* (London: Chatto and Windus, 1969)

Evans, John, 'Britten's Venice Workshop: I. The Sketch Book', *Soundings*, 12 (1984), 7–24

Evans, John, Philip Reed and Paul Wilson, *A Britten Source Book* (Aldeburgh: Britten–Pears Library, 1987)

Evans, Peter, *The Music of Benjamin Britten* (London: Dent, 1979; 2nd edn, 1989)

Garfias, Robert, 'Gradual Modifications of the Gagaku Tradition', *Ethnomusicology*, 4 (1960), 16–19

——, *Music of a Thousand Autumns: The Tōgaku Style of Japanese Court Music* (Berkeley: University of California Press, 1975)

Gerstle, Andrew, and Anthony Milner (eds.), *Recovering the Orient: Artists, Scholars, Appropriations* (London: Harwood Academic Publishers, 1995)

Gillies, Malcolm (ed.), *Bartók Remembered* (London: Faber and Faber, 1990)

Gishford, Anthony (ed.), *A Tribute to Benjamin Britten on his Fiftieth Birthday* (London: Faber and Faber, 1963)

Graham, Colin, 'The Convention of *Curlew River*', Decca SET301 (1965)

——, 'Staging First Productions, 3' in Herbert (ed.), *The Operas of Benjamin Britten*, 44–58

Grainger, Percy, *A Commonsense View of All Music* (Melbourne: Australian Broadcasting Commission, 1934; repr. in Blacking, *'A Commonsense View of All Music'*, 151–80)

Greenfield, Edward, review of first performance of *The Burning Fiery Furnace*, *Guardian*, 10 June 1966

Happé, Peter (ed.), *English Mystery Plays* (Harmondsworth: Penguin, 1975)

Harewood, George [Earl of], *The Tongs and the Bones* (London: Weidenfeld and Nicholson, 1981)

Harich-Schneider, Eta, 'The Present Condition of Japanese Court Music', *Musical Quarterly*, 39 (1953), 49–74

——, *Rhythmical Patterns in Gagaku and Bugaku*, Ethno-musicologica, 3 (Leiden: E. J. Brill, 1954)

——, *A History of Japanese Music* (London: Oxford University Press, 1973)

Headington, Christopher, *Britten* (London: Eyre Methuen, 1981)

——, *Peter Pears: A Biography* (London: Faber and Faber, 1992)

Herbert, David (ed.), *The Operas of Benjamin Britten* (London: Hamish Hamilton, 1979)

Heyworth, Peter, review of the first production of *The Prince of the Pagodas*, *Observer*, 6 January 1957

Hodgins, Jean, 'Orientalism in Britten's *Curlew River*' (M.A. dissertation, University of British Columbia, 1981)

Holloway, Robin, 'The Church Parables II: Limits and Renewals', in Palmer (ed.) *The Britten Companion*, 215–26

Hood, Mantle, and others, 'Indonesia', in Sadie (ed.), *The New Grove Dictionary of Music and Musicians*, IX, 167–220

Howard, Patricia (ed.), *Benjamin Britten: The Turn of the Screw*, Cambridge Opera Handbooks (Cambridge: Cambridge University Press, 1985)

Howat, Roy, 'Debussy and the Orient', in Gerstle and Milner (eds.), *Recovering the Orient*, 45–81

Immoos, Thomas, *Japanese Theatre* (London: Studio Vista, 1977)

Japanese Classics Translation Committee, *Japanese Noh Drama* (Tokyo: Nippon Gakujutsu Shinkokai, 1955)

Jō, Kondō, and Joaquim Bernítez (eds.), *Contemporary Music Review*, 8/2: *Flute and Shakuhachi* (Yverdon: Harwood Academic Publishers, 1994)

Keene, Donald, *Anthology of Japanese Literature: From the Earliest Era to the Mid-Nineteenth Century* (Rutland, Vermont: Charles E. Tuttle, 1955)

——, *Nō: The Classical Theatre of Japan* (Tokyo: Kodansha, 1973)

——, *Twenty Plays of the Nō Theatre* (New York and London: Columbia University Press, 1970)

Keller, Hans, 'Introduction: Operatic Music and Britten', in Herbert (ed.), *The Operas of Benjamin Britten*, xiii–xxxi

Kennedy, Michael, *Britten*, Master Musicians (London: Dent, 1981; 2nd edn, 1993)

Ketukaenchan, Somsak, 'The Oriental Influence on Benjamin Britten' (M.A. essay, University of York, 1984)

——, 'A (Far Eastern) Note on *Paul Bunyan*', in Reed (ed.), *On Mahler and Britten*, 275–9

Kishibe, Shigeo, and others, 'Japan', in Sadie (ed.), *The New Grove Dictionary of Music and Musicians*, IX, 504–52

——, *The Traditional Music of Japan* (Tokyo: Japan Foundation, 1984)

Komparu, Kunio, *The Noh Theater: Principles and Perspectives* (New York and Tokyo: Weatherhill/Tankosha, 1983)

Kunst, Jaap, *Music in Java*, 2 vols., trans. Emile van Loo (The Hague: Martinus Nijhoff, 1949; 3rd edn, 1973)

Kurosawa, Hiroshi [Peter], 'Benjamin Britten and *Sumidagawa*', in programme book to the Tokyo Chamber Opera Theatre production of *Curlew River* (July 1982)

Laade, W., 'Benjamin Brittens Mysterienspiel *Curlew River* und die japanischen Vorbilder', *Musik und Bildung* 1/12 (1969), 562–65

Lentz, Donald, *The Gamelan Music of Java and Bali* (Lincoln, Nebraska: University of Nebraska Press, 1965)

Locke, Ralph P., 'Constructing the Oriental "Other": Saint-Saëns's *Samson et Dalila*', *Cambridge Opera Journal*, 3 (1991), 261–302

Lockspeiser, Edward, *Debussy: His Life and Mind*, 2 vols. (Cambridge: Cambridge University Press, 1962; 2nd edn, 1966; repr. with corrections, 1978)

Ludwig, Prince of Hesse and the Rhine, *Ausflug Ost* (Darmstadt: privately printed, 1956)

——, '*Ausflug Ost*, 1956', in Gishford (ed.), *A Tribute to Benjamin Britten*, 56–66

McNaught, William, 'String Orchestras', *Musical Times*, 78 (1937), 990–91

——, 'The Promenade Concerts', *Musical Times*, 79 (1938), 702–3

McPhee, Colin, 'The "Absolute" Music of Bali', *Modern Music*, 12 (1934–5), 163–9

——, 'Scores and Records', *Modern Music*, 21 (1943–4), 48–9

——, *A House in Bali* (New York: The John Day Company, 1946; repr. New York: Oxford University Press, 1987)

——, 'Dance in Bali', *Dance Index*, 7–8 (1948), 156–207

——, 'The Five-Tone Gamelan Music of Bali', *Musical Quarterly*, 35 (1949), 250–81

——, *Music in Bali: A Study in Form and Instrumental Organization in Balinese Orchestral Music* (New Haven: Yale University Press, 1966; repr. New York: The Da Capo Press, 1976)

Malm, William, 'The Rhythmic Orientation of the Two Drums in the Japanese Nō Drama', *Ethnomusicology*, 2 (1958), 89–95
——, *Japanese Music and Musical Instruments* (Rutland, Vermont: Charles E. Tuttle, 1959)
——, 'An Introduction to Taiko Drum Music in the Japanese Nō Drama', *Ethnomusicology*, 4 (1960), 75–8
——, *Six Hidden Views of Japanese Music* (Berkeley: University of California Press, 1986)
Malm, William, and James Irving Crump (eds.), *Chinese and Japanese Music Dramas* (Ann Arbor: Center for Chinese Studies, University of Michigan, 1975)
Mann, Thomas, *Death in Venice*, trans. Mrs H. T. Lowe-Porter (London: Secker and Warburg, 1929; repr. Harmondsworth: Penguin, 1955)
Mann, William, review of the first production of *Death in Venice*, *The Times*, 18 June 1973
Maruoka, Daiji, and Tatsuo Yoshikoshi, *Noh* (Tokyo: Hoikusha, 1969)
Mason, Colin, review of the first production of *Curlew River*, *Guardian*, 15 June 1964
Matthews, David, 'Act II Scene 1: An Examination of the Music', in Brett (ed.), *Benjamin Britten: Peter Grimes*, 121–47
Mellers, Wilfrid, *Percy Grainger* (Oxford: Oxford University Press, 1992)
Minagawa, Tatsuo, 'Japanese Noh Music', *Journal of the American Musicological Society*, 10 (1957), 181–200
Mitchell, Donald, review of the first production of *The Prince of the Pagodas*, *Musical Times*, 98 (1957), 91
——, sleeve notes to *The Prince of the Pagodas*, Decca GOM 558-9 (1957)
——, 'Jinx', in Drew (ed.), *The Decca Book of Ballet*, 414–16
——, 'The Background to *Curlew River*', Decca SET301 (1965)
——, 'Britten's Church Parables', Decca SET356 (1967)
——, 'Double Portrait: Some Personal Recollections', in Blythe (ed.), *Aldeburgh Anthology*, 431–7; repr. in Mitchell, *Cradles of the New*, 481–9
——, 'An Introduction to *Death in Venice*', Decca SET 581-3 (1974)
——, *Britten and Auden in the Thirties: The Year 1936* (London: Faber and Faber, 1981)
——, 'Catching on to the Technique in Pagoda-land', *Tempo*, 146 (1983), 13–24; repr. in Palmer (ed.), *The Britten Companion*, 192–210
——, 'What Do We Know about Britten Now?', in Palmer (ed.), *The Britten Companion*, 21–45
——, *Gustav Mahler*, III: *Songs and Symphonies of Life and Death* (London: Faber and Faber, 1985)
——, 'An Afterword on Britten's *Pagodas*: The Balinese Sources', *Tempo*, 152 (1985), 7–11
—— (ed.), *Benjamin Britten: Death in Venice*, Cambridge Opera Handbooks (Cambridge: Cambridge University Press, 1987)
——, *Cradles of the New: Writings on Music, 1951–91*, selected by Christopher Palmer, ed. Mervyn Cooke (London: Faber and Faber, 1995)
Mitchell, Donald, and John Evans, *Benjamin Britten: Pictures from a Life, 1913–76* (London: Faber and Faber, 1978)
Mitchell, Donald, and Philip Reed (eds.), *Letters from a Life: The Selected Letters and Diaries of Benjamin Britten*, vol. 1 1923–39, vol. 2 1939–45 (London: Faber and Faber, 1991)
——, 'The French Connection: Britten–Milhaud–Poulenc', programme book to the Aldeburgh October Britten Festival (1994), 8–17
Morton, David, 'Colin McPhee: *Music in Bali*', *Ethnomusicology*, 11 (1967), 412–15

Mueller, Richard, 'Javanese Influence on Debussy's *Fantaisie* and Beyond', *19th-Century Music*, 10 (1986–7), 157–86

Nakanishi, Toru, and Kiyonori Komma, *Noh Masks* (Tokyo: Hoikusha, 1983)

Nichols, Roger, *Debussy* (Oxford: Oxford University Press, 1972)

—— (ed.), *Debussy Remembered* (London: Faber and Faber, 1992)

Noble, Jeremy, 'Britten's *Songs from the Chinese*', *Tempo*, 52 (1959), 25–9

——, review of the first production of *Curlew River*, *Musical Times*, 105 (1964), 667–8

——, review of the first production of *The Burning Fiery Furnace*, *Musical Times*, 107 (1966), 698–9

Oja, Carol, 'Colin McPhee: A Composer Turned Explorer', *Tempo*, 148 (1984), 2–7

——, *Colin McPhee: Composer in Two Worlds* (Washington and London: Smithsonian Institution Press, 1990)

Orledge, Robert, *Debussy in the Theatre* (Cambridge: Cambridge University Press, 1982)

Ornstein, Ruby, 'Gamelan Gong Kebjar: The Development of a Balinese Tradition' (Ph.D. dissertation, University of California at Los Angeles, 1971)

——, 'Indonesia (III): Bali', in Sadie (ed.), *The New Grove Dictionary of Music and Musicians*, IX, 179–89

Palmer, Christopher, 'Britten's Venice Orchestra', in Mitchell (ed.), *Benjamin Britten: Death in Venice*, 129–53

—— (ed.), *The Britten Companion* (London: Faber and Faber, 1984)

Parmenter, Ross, 'Records: From Bali/An Album of Works Prepared by Colin McPhee', *New York Times*, 15 June 1941

Pears, Peter, *Armenian Holiday* (Colchester: Benham and Co., 1965); repr. in Reed (ed.), *The Travel Diaries of Peter Pears*, 98–134

——, *Moscow Christmas* (Colchester: Benham and Co., 1967); repr. in Reed (ed.), *The Travel Diaries of Peter Pears*, 135–52

Percival, John, *Theatre in my Blood: A Biography of John Cranko* (London: Franklin Watts, 1983)

Piguet, Jean-Claude, and Jacques Burdet (eds.), *Ernest Ansermet–Frank Martin: Correspondance, 1934–68* (Neuchâtel: La Baconnière, 1976)

Pillaut, Léon, 'Le gamelan javanais', *Le ménestrel*, 3 July 1887

Plomer, William, *Double Lives: An Autobiography* (London: Jonathan Cape, 1942; repr. as *The Autobiography of William Plomer*, 1975)

——, programme note on Britten's Church Parables, *Edinburgh Festival Programme Book* (1968)

Pollard, Alfred W., *English Miracle Plays, Moralities and Interludes: Specimens of the Pre-Elizabethan Drama* (Oxford: Clarendon Press, 8th edn, 1927)

Potter, Robert, *The English Morality Play: Origins, History and Influence of a Dramatic Tradition* (London: Routledge and Kegan Paul, 1975)

Poulenc, Francis, 'Hommage à Benjamin Britten', in Gishford (ed.), *A Tribute to Benjamin Britten*, 13

Pound, Ezra, *Certain Noble Plays of Japan* (Dublin: Dundrum Cuala Press, 1916)

——, *The Translations of Ezra Pound* (London: Faber and Faber, 1953)

Pound, Ezra, and Ernest Fenellosa, *'Noh' or Accomplishment: A Study of the Classical Stage of Japan* (London: Macmillan, 1916)

Powers, Harold, 'Mode', in Sadie (ed.), *The New Grove Dictionary of Music and Musicians*, XII, 436–47

Ravel, Maurice, 'Esquisse autobiographique', *Revue musicale* (December 1938), 21

Reed, Philip (ed.), *The Travel Diaries of Peter Pears, 1936–1978*, Aldeburgh Studies in Music, 2 (Woodbridge: The Boydell Press, 1995)

—— (ed.), *On Mahler and Britten: Essays in Honour of Donald Mitchell on his 70th*

Birthday, Aldeburgh Studies in Music, 3 (Woodbridge: The Boydell Press, 1995)

Reich, Steve, 'Postscript to a Brief Study of Balinese and African Music, 1973', in *Writings about Music* (New York: New York University Press, 1974), 38–40

Ritchie, Lady Anne Isabella, *The Fairy Tales of Madame D'Aulnoy, Newly Done into English* (London, 1892)

Sadie, Stanley, review of the first production of *The Prodigal Son*, *Musical Times*, 109 (1968), 744

—— (ed.), *The New Grove Dictionary of Music and Musicians*, 20 vols. (London: Macmillan, 1980)

Said, Edward, *Orientalism* (New York: Routledge and Kegan Paul, 1978; repr. Harmondsworth: Penguin, 1991)

Schafer, Murray, *British Composers in Interview* (London: Faber and Faber, 1963)

Shiba, Sukehiro, *Gagaku: Japanese Classical Court Music*, I (Tokyo: Ryugin-Sha, 1955)

——, *Gosen-fu ni yoru Gagaku sō-fu*, 4 vols. (Tokyo, 1968–72)

Sorrell, Neil, *A Guide to the Gamelan* (London: Faber and Faber, 1990)

Stock, Noel, *The Life of Ezra Pound* (London: Routledge and Kegan Paul, 1970)

Sunaga, Katsumi, *Japanese Music* (Tokyo, 1936)

Tamba, Akira, *The Musical Structure of Nō* (Tokyo and Paris: Tokai University Press, 1974; repr., 1981)

Tanabe, Hisao, *Japanese Music* (Tokyo: Kokusai Bunka Shinkokai, 1959; 3rd edn, 1960)

Tiersot, Julien, *Musique pittoresques: Promenades musicales à l'Exposition de 1889* (Paris: Fischbacher, 1889)

Tippett, Michael, *Those Twentieth-Century Blues: An Autobiography* (London: Hutchinson, 1991)

Toita, Yasuji, and Chiaki Yoshida, *Kabuki* (Tokyo: Hoikisha, 1967)

Togi, Masataro, *Gagaku: Court Music and Dance* (New York: Walker/Weatherhill, 1971)

Waley, Arthur, *The Nō Plays of Japan* (London: George Allen and Unwin, 1921)

——, *Chinese Poems* (London: George Allen and Unwin, 1946)

Warrack, John, review of *Curlew River*, *Tempo*, 70 (1964), 19

Yoshikoshi, Tatsuo, Hisashi Hata and Don Kenny, *Kyōgen* (Tokyo: Hoikusha, 1982)

Young, Douglas, 'Colin McPhee's Music (I): From West to East', *Tempo*, 150 (1984), 11–17

——, 'Colin McPhee (II): "Tabuh-tabuhan"', *Tempo*, 159 (1986), 16–19

Young, Karl, *The Drama of the Medieval Church*, 2 vols. (Oxford: Oxford University Press, 1933)

de Zoete, Beryl, and Walter Spies, *Dance and Drama in Bali* (London: Faber and Faber, 1938; repr. Kuala Lumpur: Oxford University Press, 1973)

Index

Bold numbers refer to illustrations and music examples.